SHAKESPEARE
A *Playgoer's and Reader's Guide*

Michael Dobson is Professor of Shakespeare Studies and Director of the Shakespeare Institute, University of Birmingham, a member of the Council of the Shakespeare Birthplace Trust, and an honorary governor of the Royal Shakespeare Company: his previous appointments include posts at Oxford, Harvard, the University of Illinois at Chicago and the University of London, and he has held fellowships and visiting appointments in California, Sweden and China. His publications include *The Making of the National Poet* (1992), *England's Elizabeth* (with Nicola Watson, 2002), *Performing Shakespeare's Tragedies Today* (2006), and *Shakespeare and Amateur Performance* (2011).

Sir Stanley Wells, CBE, FRSL, is Honorary President, Life Trustee, and former Chairman of the Shakespeare Birthplace Trust. He was Professor of Shakespeare Studies and Director of the Shakespeare Institute, University of Birmingham, from 1988–1997, and is now Emeritus Professor. He is an Honorary Emeritus Governor of the Royal Shakespeare Company. He has been General Editor of the Oxford Shakespeare since 1978 and is General Editor of the Penguin Shakespeare. One of the most distinguished Shakespearian scholars currently working, his publications include *The Oxford Dictionary of Shakespeare* (1998), *Shakespeare: The Poet and his Plays* (2001), *The Oxford Shakespeare: King Lear* (2001), *Shakespeare For All Time* (2002), *Shakespeare & Co* (2006), *Shakespeare, Sex, and Love* (2010), *Great Shakespeare Actors* (2015), and *William Shakespeare: A Very Short Introduction* (2015).

SHAKESPEARE

A Playgoer's and Reader's Guide

Edited by
MICHAEL DOBSON and **STANLEY WELLS**

Revising Editorial Assistant
GEORGINA LUCAS

OXFORD
UNIVERSITY PRESS

Great Clarendon Street, Oxford, ox2 6DP,
United Kingdom

Oxford University Press is a department of the University of Oxford.
It furthers the University's objective of excellence in research, scholarship,
and education by publishing worldwide. Oxford is a registered trade mark of
Oxford University Press in the UK and in certain other countries

Database right Oxford University Press (maker)
First published 2020
Articles previously published as part of *The Oxford Companion to Shakespeare*:
Published in hardback 2001
Published online 2003
First issued as an OUP paperback 2005
Reprinted with corrections 2008
Updated online 2012
Second edition published 2015

Impression: 1

Published in the United States of America by Oxford University Press
198 Madison Avenue, New York, NY 10016, United States of America

British Library Cataloguing in Publication Data
Data available

Library of Congress Control Number: 2020943921

ISBN 978-0-19-885523-1

Printed and bound in Great Britain by
Clays Ltd, Elcograf S.p.A.

PREFACE

This book is intended as an aid to the enjoyment of the plays and poems of William Shakespeare (1564–1616), long regarded as the most important writer in English, as the most versatile and accomplished playwright of the European Renaissance, and as a cornerstone of modern world drama. After a short biography of Shakespeare, the book's contents are organized alphabetically. Entries consist of descriptions of the plays and poems of Shakespeare, supplying information about when each was written and what sort of information we can deduce from its early texts. For the plays, we also supply a character list, a summary of what happens in each scene, a short account of the continuing discussion the play has occasioned among critics and admirers over the last four centuries, a short account of major trends in its performance history (mainly limited, for reasons of space, to its performance history in Britain), and a short list of extant film and television versions. We have appended a family tree of characters in the English history plays; a very short list of further accessible reading on different aspects of Shakespeare and his works; and a chronology listing events in Shakespeare's life and career and some milestones in the dissemination, performance, and interpretation of his work down to the early twenty-first century.

The entries in this book have been adapted and updated from entries in our *Oxford Companion to Shakespeare*, to which readers wanting a large and more comprehensive encyclopedia of Shakespearean knowledge should immediately turn. Like that book, this one takes its line and scene references from the second (2005) edition of the *Complete Oxford Shakespeare* (edited by Stanley Wells, Gary Taylor, William Montgomery, and John Jowett), and its account of the canon and chronology of Shakespeare's works is essentially that explained in depth in Gary Taylor and Stanley Wells's *William Shakespeare: A Textual Companion* (1987). It may be useful here to explain a few terms used about the early printing of the plays in several of our play entries, terms which aren't elsewhere defined in this *Guide*:

Folio—a large book made of sheets of paper which have been folded only once. The 'First Folio'—abbreviated by specialists to 'F1'—is the collected edition of Shakespeare's plays assembled by his fellow actors John Heminge and Henry Condell after Shakespeare's death and published— as *Mr William Shakespeare's Comedies, Histories, and Tragedies*—in 1623.

This volume provides the only authoritative texts for about half of Shakespeare's plays, on which all subsequent reprintings are based.

Foul papers—an Elizabethan term for a playwright's rough draft manuscript. The theatre company would transcribe this manuscript to produce an official 'book', from which individual actors would then have their own lines transcribed by a scribe and which would be used to monitor and supervise performances in the playhouse. It is thought by many scholars (though not all) that some of Shakespeare's foul papers were released to printers after they had been transcribed. This hypothesis would explain several features of some early texts of the plays, among them open-ended, provisional-looking stage directions which are vague about how many characters should enter or leave, idiosyncratic spellings (Shakespeare appears to have liked 'scilence' for 'silence', for instance), false starts, and an inconsistency with speech headings (those for Lady Capulet include Capulet's Wife, Wife, Old Lady, Lady, and Mother, suggesting that Shakespeare sometimes conceived of characters primarily by their relation to others onstage).

Quarto—a smaller book than the folio, made of sheets which have been folded twice. Specialists will sometimes refer to the first quarto version of any given play as Q1, the second as Q2, and so on. About half of Shakespeare's plays were printed individually in this format before the appearance of the First Folio. In some cases—as with *Hamlet* and *King Lear*—there are differences between the quarto and folio versions which may provide evidence about how Shakespeare composed and revised his plays.

Stationers' Register—Copyright legislation was in its infancy in Shakespeare's time, but the printing business was regulated by its own guild, the Stationers' Company, chartered in 1557. According to the company's articles, a printer could secure his right to print a particular work by recording its title alongside his name in a register book. What stationers (in effect, publishers) called 'copy' belonged to the member concerned once he or she had 'entered' it in this volume, which as a result often provides valuable evidence towards the dating of many sixteenth- and seventeenth-century publications.

The individual entries in this book, now much revised, were originally composed by Michael Dobson and Stanley Wells, with the exception of those describing the first tetralogy of history plays (which were written by Randall Martin) and those describing *Measure for Measure*, *Pericles*, and *Titus Andronicus* (which were written by Sonia Massai). The short accounts of the plays' screen incarnations were written by Anthony Davies.

This material was updated when *The Oxford Companion to Shakespeare* was reissued in 2015, with considerable help from Will Sharpe and Erin Sullivan on the critical and performance histories of the plays, and those sections have now been revised again, this time with the assistance of Dr Georgina Lucas.

MICHAEL DOBSON and **STANLEY WELLS**

Stratford-upon-Avon, January 2020

CONTENTS

A SHORT LIFE OF WILLIAM SHAKESPEARE (1564–1616)

Actor, playwright, poet, theatre administrator, and landowner; baptized, probably by John Bretchgirdle, in Holy Trinity church, Stratford-upon-Avon, on Wednesday, 26 April 1564, the third child and first son of John Shakespeare and his wife Mary (Arden). His date of birth, traditionally celebrated on 23 April—St George's Day—is not known, but no more than a few days are likely to have elapsed between birth and baptism. The statement on his monument that he was 53 when he died on 23 April 1616 can only be understood to mean that he had started his 53rd year, i.e. had been born on or before 23 April 1564. Thomas De Quincey suggested that his granddaughter Elizabeth Hall chose to be married on 22 April 1626 because this was his birthday, but this may reflect an anachronistic enthusiasm for anniversaries.

Shakespeare probably grew up in the Henley Street house now known as the Birthplace, with his younger sisters Anne (d. 1579) and Joan, and his younger brothers Gilbert, Richard, and the late-born Edmund, who like him became an actor. Two sisters, Joan and Margaret, had died in infancy, and William was lucky to escape the plague, which hit the town a few months after he was born; in the second six months of 1564, at least 237 burials are recorded—something like one-eighth of the town's population.

Stratford had a splendid church, fine houses, a well-established grammar school, and townsmen who were both educated and wealthy. It had regular links with London through carriers such as William Greenway (d. 1601), and throughout Shakespeare's boyhood and youth it was frequently visited by leading companies of actors. His father's position as bailiff in 1568, presiding over the burgesses and aldermen at meetings of the corporation, and undertaking other official duties such as presiding at fairs and markets and licensing travelling groups of actors to perform, would have carried privileges for his family. His sons are likely to have acquired the rudiments of their education at a petty school, proceeding at the age of 6 or 7 to the King's New School, an established grammar school with a succession of well-qualified teachers, each assisted by an usher to help with the younger pupils. We have no lists of the school's pupils in Shakespeare's time, but his father's position would have qualified him to attend, and the school offered the kind of education in classical literature, grammar, logic, and rhetoric that lies behind the plays and poems. A scene (4.1) in *The Merry Wives of Windsor* showing a master taking a pupil named William through his Latin grammar no doubt draws on memories of Shakespeare's own schooldays. Fellow pupils probably included Richard Field, who as a London printer was responsible for *Venus and Adonis* (1593), *The Rape of Lucrece* (1594), and *Love's Martyr* (the volume to which Shakespeare contributed his poem 'The Phoenix and Turtle', 1601). Shakespeare's education would have been furthered too by compulsory attendance with his family at church, where he would have become familiar with the Bible, the Book of Common Prayer, and the Homilies. And though school hours were long and arduous, he would have found time for sports and pastimes in the surrounding countryside.

He is likely to have left school when he was about 15. What he did then has been the subject of much speculation. The seventeenth-century antiquary John Aubrey, in his miscellaneous jottings about Shakespeare, stated that 'he had been in his younger years a schoolmaster in the country'. If true, this might seem more likely to have been after rather than before his marriage, but some scholars have linked it with the hypothesis that he is the William Shakeshaft mentioned in the will of Alexander Houghton in Lancashire. If so, he was soon back home. He married Anne Hathaway, approximately eight years his senior, towards the end of 1582, when he was still technically a minor; a daughter, Susanna, was baptized on 26 May of the following year (which meant that, not unusually for the time, Anne was already pregnant when the couple married), and twins, Hamnet and Judith, were christened on 2 February 1585. Shakespeare must have been gainfully occupied during this time, but no one knows how. He may simply have helped his father with the family business. Presumably he started to write before joining a theatre company, but only a sonnet (No. 145) that seems to pun on the name 'Hathaway' has been confidently assigned to his early years. (It is also possible that sonnets 153 and 154, which are versions of a classical epigram, were written at school). The sole record of him during these so-called 'lost years' is a bare mention in a lawsuit involving his uncle by marriage, Edmund Lambert, in 1587. It has been guessed that he joined the Queen's Men when they visited Stratford in this year, but this distinguished company would have been unlikely to hire a novice. Still, Shakespeare's familiarity with plays in their later repertoire gives cause to suppose that he may at some point have been a member.

The first printed allusion, in Robert Greene's *Groatsworth of Wit*, which accuses Shakespeare of imitating the literary style of his betters ('an upstart crow, beautified with our feathers') suggests that by 1592 he was well known on the theatrical scene. He had probably already written his earliest comedies and history plays. During the plague years of 1593 and 1594 he seems to have thought of establishing himself as a non-dramatic poet; the Ovidian narrative poems, *Venus and Adonis* and *The Rape of Lucrece*, were published successively in 1593 and 1594, each with Shakespeare's dedication to the young Henry Wriothesley, 3rd Earl of Southampton (1573–1624), who on this evidence, as well as that of later legend, may be regarded as Shakespeare's patron—though for how long and to what effect we cannot know. He has often been supposed to be the 'Fair Youth' of Shakespeare's Sonnets, most of which may well have been written round about 1593–6, though they may have been revised and reordered around 1602.

The earliest positive evidence of Shakespeare's affiliation with a particular theatre company comes on 15 March 1595, when he is named as joint payee of the Lord Chamberlain's Men, formed a few months earlier for performances at court during the previous Christmas season. He was to remain with them for the rest of his working life, the only playwright of his time to enjoy so stable a relationship with a single company. We do not know the exact terms of his agreement with his colleagues, but he seems to have been expected to produce an average of around two plays a year, and to ring the changes among the dramatic kinds. Having demonstrated his versatility early in his career with the neo-Senecan tragedy of *Titus Andronicus*, the Plautine *Comedy of Errors*, and the tragical histories on the reigns of Henry VI and Richard III, he veered away from tragedy for a while during the late years of the century with more romantic comedies and with the comical histories of *Henry IV* and *Henry V*.

Inevitably Shakespeare had to base his professional life on London, and a number of legal records bear witness to his presence there (though, as the name was not particularly uncommon, we cannot be sure that all references are to the dramatist). In 1596, for example, one William Wayte petitioned for sureties of the peace against 'Willm Shakspere' and others; in November 1597 a William Shakespeare of Bishopsgate ward was listed as not having paid taxes due in February; on 1 October 1598 a man of the same name was named as a tax defaulter in the same ward, and in 1600 brought an action against one John Clayton of Bedfordshire for a debt of £7. (This last record, usually ignored or dismissed, is as likely to refer to the dramatist as any of the others.) In a manuscript document of 16 May 1599 the newly built Globe theatre is mentioned as being in the possession of William Shakespeare and others. The deposition made by William Shakespeare of Stratford-upon-Avon in the Belott–Mountjoy case of 1612 clearly shows that he was lodging with the Mountjoy family (expatriate French jewellers and wigmakers) in Silver Street (part of the present-day Barbican site) in 1604.

Shakespeare's growing reputation as both poet and dramatist during the 1590s is witnessed by a variety of documentary evidence. He is mentioned as the author of *The Rape of Lucrece* in Henry Willobie's *Willobie his Avisa* in 1594 and, as 'Sweet Shakespeare', in William Covell's *Polimanteia* in 1595. In 1598 his name appears for the first time on the title pages of any of his plays—the second quartos of *Richard II* and *Richard III* and the first (surviving) quarto of *Love's Labour's Lost*—and his narrative poems are praised by Richard Barnfield in his *Poems in Divers Humours*. On 13 May 1602 an Inns of Court man, John Manningham, confided to his journal a mildly scurrilous anecdote about Shakespeare and Richard Burbage, the leading actor of his company. In 1603 Shakespeare, along with other poets, is called upon— apparently in vain—to lament the death of Queen Elizabeth in Henry Chettle's 'A Mournful Ditty, entitled Elizabeth's Loss', and is named among 'The principal tragedians' in Ben Jonson's *Sejanus*, just as in 1598 he had been named as one of the 'principal comedians' who had acted in Jonson's *Every Man in his Humour*. Apart from the list of actors in the First Folio, these are the only contemporary references to Shakespeare as actor, and it is usually assumed that he gave up acting around 1603. There is no contemporary record of which roles he played except a cryptic epigram by John Davies referring to his playing 'some kingly parts in sport'; later gossip assigns to him Adam in *As You Like It* and the Ghost in *Hamlet*.

Shakespeare's succession of romantic comedies comes to an end probably around the close of the 16th century with *As You Like It* and, early in the 17th century, *Twelfth Night*. Subsequent essays in comic form are darker in tone. And in 1599, whether by personal inclination, professional necessity, or both, he had turned again to tragedy with *Julius Caesar*, followed before the death of Queen Elizabeth by *Hamlet* and *Othello*. Soon after the accession of James I, in 1603, his company of players came under James's patronage as the King's Men. He remained with them for the rest of his career, which saw the composition of the sequence of tragedies from *King Lear* to *Coriolanus*, the late romances, and, in collaboration with John Fletcher, *All Is True (Henry VIII)*, *The Two Noble Kinsmen*, and the lost *Cardenio*.

Along with references to Shakespeare in London go others relating to his family and to his home town. In August 1596 his only son died and was buried there. Shakespeare may have been in Stratford for the burial, but communications were slow; if the death was sudden and he was in London or on tour, he may have been unable to arrive in time. Two months later John Shakespeare was granted a coat of arms, which gave him (and subsequently his son) the status of gentleman, though it was not until 1599 that John was permitted to impale his arms with those of the Arden family. In 1597 Shakespeare bought a substantial property, New Place, said to have been the second-largest house in Stratford. He was already very prosperous. There can be no doubt that he regarded New Place as home for him and his family. He is generally assumed to have spent almost all his working life away from Stratford, but he never seems to have established a real home in London, and it would not be surprising if he retreated to New Place as often as he could to work in peace as well as to see his family. His wife was to give birth to no more children, but since—to look no further—his elder daughter Susanna had only one child and his younger three, it seems gratuitous to use this fact to support the theory of a marital breakdown.

Though London was the centre of the theatrical profession, a succession of legal and other records indicates Shakespeare's continuing involvement with Stratford and its people. On 15 October 1598, for instance, Richard Quiney, visiting London, wrote to him asking for a loan of the very considerable sum of £30. In 1602 Shakespeare consolidated his Stratford estates with the purchase, for £320, of land in Old Stratford as well as buying a cottage in Chapel Lane. In 1605 he paid £440 for an interest in a lease of the Stratford tithes, which brought him £60 a year; in June 1607 Susanna married John Hall there; and there his first grandchild (and the only one he can have known), Elizabeth Hall, was born in 1608. His mother died there later that year.

From about 1609 Shakespeare's increasing involvement with Stratford, along with the decrease in his output of plays, suggests that he was withdrawing from his London responsibilities and spending more time at New Place. It is often said that he 'retired' to Stratford around this time, but he was only 45 years old in 1609, an age at which a healthy man was no more likely to 'retire' then than now. On the other hand, the increasingly introverted poetic style of his late work, especially in the plays written with John Fletcher, suggests a growing distaste for the demands of the popular theatre. He may have deliberately devoted himself to his family's business interests. If he was ill, he was not totally incapacitated; he was in London for the Belott–Mountjoy suit in 1612, and in March 1613 he bought a property conveniently near his company's indoor theatre, the Blackfriars Gatehouse. His younger brothers Gilbert and Richard died in Stratford in 1612 and 1613. In 1614 and 1615 he was involved in disputes relating to enclosures of the land whose tithes he owned in the area. In February 1616 his second daughter Judith married Thomas Quiney, causing her father to make alterations to the draft of his will, which he signed on 25 March. He died on 23 April, and was buried in a prominent position in Holy Trinity Church.

No printed tributes marked the occasion, but memorial verses by William Basse proposing that he be buried in Westminster Abbey circulated widely in manuscript, and other verses printed in the First Folio may have been written years before they were published. Thomas Pavier embarked on an abortive collection of his plays in 1619, and the First Folio of 1623, compiled by John Heminges and Henry Condell, both of whom, along with Richard Burbage, who died in 1619, are mentioned in his will, is his greatest memorial. A monument which was commissioned presumably by members of his family, and was in position in Holy Trinity Church by 1623, likens the Stratford landowner to Socrates and Virgil; in the Folio, the memorial elegy by Jonson links this 'Star of Poets' with his home town as the 'Sweet Swan of Avon', and lines by Leonard Digges speak of his 'Stratford monument'. The only two likenesses of Shakespeare with a strong claim to authenticity are the bust (by Geerhart Janssen) incorporated in the monument and the Martin Droeshout engraving which adorns the title page of the Folio. His widow died in 1623, the year in which the Folio collection of his plays appeared, and his last surviving descendant, Elizabeth Hall, who became Lady Bernard, in 1670.

Though we know more mundane facts about Shakespeare's life than about any other dramatist of his time except Ben Jonson, they reveal little of his personality. That lies buried deep beneath the surface of his writings. A dramatist's success is measured by the extent to which he removes himself from his plays, his 'nature | Subdued to what it works in, like the dyer's hand' (Sonnet 111). This makes it peculiarly difficult to arrive at an assured conception of Shakespeare as a person. Ben Jonson wrote that he 'loved the man', and did 'honour his memory (on this side idolatry) as much as any'. Other contemporaries—Henry Chettle, John Heminges and Henry Condell, Augustine Phillips—seem to have liked him; 'sweet' was a favourite epithet (though it may refer rather to his poetic style than to his personality); friends and colleagues left him money. But there is not much by way of personal testimony to go on.

Study of the records of his life creates the impression of an educated, well-read, and ambitious man who knew how to manage his business affairs and could pursue his financial interests astutely, who, while caring deeply for his family and his roots in Stratford, cared too for his career and was willing to make domestic sacrifices in order to pursue it, who took pleasure in his prosperity and the status it gave him, and who hoped to pass on something of what he had earned to his descendants. Absence of private utterances, with the possible but important exception of the Sonnets, suggests that, unlike the assertive and aggressive Ben Jonson, he kept himself to himself, a listener rather than a talker. That impression is supported by what John Keats was to call his 'negative capability'—the extraordinary capacity for empathy with a vast range of human beings revealed by the plays.

If we read the Sonnets as evidence of the inner man, we see beneath the controlled exterior a turbulent inner life, passions not easily mastered, self-knowledge wrested with difficulty and pain from the crucible of experience, an intense need to love and to be loved, a desire to idealize the beloved and to abase himself in the process, immense susceptibility to emotional pain, a demanding sexuality that led to adulterous relationships with one or more women, and possibly to male sexual relationships (in spite of the Sonnets' idealization of the 'fair friend'); a volatility of response that can veer rapidly from one extreme of emotion to its opposite; a belief in the power of the imagination along with an awareness of the fragility of illusion. We see this because of the shaping, expressive powers of art, because the man who has suffered this extremity of passion has also summoned up the self-control, the discipline to shape and contain it within the demanding verse structures of the sonnet form.

We might receive similar impressions from the plays alone. The ambition is there in the range and scope of the work, the determination to master all the dramatic kinds, the restless experimentation, the exploitation of the conventions of poetic drama in a manner that never quite loses sight of the need to entertain while constantly stretching the imaginative and intellectual responses of its audiences. The emotional turbulence is there in the frequent depiction of extreme states of mind, both comic and tragic. The sexuality, which can be both despicable and glorious, is omnipresent. So is the idealizing imagination that can transform man from (in Hamlet's words) a 'quintessence of dust' to 'the beauty of the world, the paragon of animals'. And all is projected by the deployment of a verbal and structural artistry that reflects the self-control and determination evident in the more practical aspects of the career.

All Is True (*Henry VIII*)

During a performance of this play on 29 June 1613 the cannon fired to salute the King's entry in 1.4 set alight the Globe theatre's thatch, and the whole building was destroyed. According to one letter about the disaster, this was at most the play's fourth performance, and stylistic examination confirms that this must have been a new play in 1613.

 TEXT

Three out of five surviving accounts of the fire refer to the play by what was clearly its original title, *All Is True* (a ballad on the subject even has the allusive refrain 'All this is true'), while the other two cite only its subject matter, calling it 'the play of Henry 8'. A decade later the compilers of the First Folio adopted the latter procedure (as they did with the other English histories), publishing the play's only authoritative text as *The Famous History of the Life of King Henry the Eight* (abbreviated to *The Life of King Henry the Eight* for the running title: the Oxford edition, 1986, was the first to restore the title by which Shakespeare knew the play). The text (to judge, in part, from its unusual number of brackets) was probably set from a scribal transcript of authorial papers, possibly annotated for theatrical use.

Although there is no external evidence to confirm what many students of the play's versification have believed since the mid-19th century, *All Is True* was probably written in collaboration with John Fletcher, as were two other plays from this final phase of Shakespeare's career, *The Two Noble Kinsmen* (1613–14) and the lost *Cardenio* (1613). Based on a variety of linguistic and stylistic criteria (particularly the frequency and nature of rare vocabulary, usage of colloquialisms in verse passages, and the use of certain grammatical constructions), the Prologue, 1.3–4, 3.1, 5.2–4, and the Epilogue are most commonly attributed to Fletcher, who may also have revised Shakespeare's 2.1–2, much of 3.2, and all of 4.1–2.

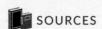 **SOURCES**

The playwrights' principal sources for their account of the middle years of Henry's reign—from the Field of the Cloth of Gold (1520) to the christening of Princess Elizabeth (1533)—were the chronicles of Raphael Holinshed and Edward Halle. Foxe's *Book of Martyrs* (1563) supplied material for Cranmer's scenes in Act 5, and Samuel Rowley's earlier play on Henry's reign, *When You See Me, You Know Me* (c. 1603–5), may have influenced the depiction of Wolsey's fall. The dramatists' principal alterations to their material consist in the compression of events, and the sometimes cosmetic alteration of their sequence. Despite the impression given by the play, Queen Katherine was still alive when Princess Elizabeth was born (hence the Catholic view that she was illegitimate), and despite the impression of an achieved harmony at the play's close, Cranmer's troubles with the Council, dramatized in 5.1–2, still lay seven years ahead when she was christened.

 CHARACTER LIST

Prologue
King Henry the Eighth
Duke of **Buckingham**
Lord **Abergavenny** ⎤ *his sons-*
Earl of **Surrey** ⎦ *in-law*

Duke of **Norfolk**
Duke of **Suffolk**
Lord Chamberlain
Lord Chancellor
Lord **Sands** (also called
  Sir William *Sands*)
Sir Thomas **Lovell**
Sir Anthony **Denny**
Sir Henry **Guildford**
Cardinal Wolsey
Two **Secretaries**
Buckingham's **Surveyor**
Cardinal Campeius
Gardiner *the King's*
  new secretary, later
  Bishop of Winchester

His **Page**
Thomas **Cromwell**
Cranmer *Archbishop of Canterbury*
Queen **Katherine,** later **Katherine**,
  Princess Dowager
Griffith *her gentleman usher*
Patience *her waiting woman*
Other women
Six spirits who dance before
  Katherine in a vision
A **Messenger**
Lord **Caputius**
Anne Boleyn
An **Old Lady**
Brandon ⎤ *who arrest*
Sergeant- ⎬ *Buckingham and*
  at-Arms ⎦ *Abergavenny*

Sir Nicholas **Vaux**

Tipstaves ⎤ *after*
Halberdiers ⎬ *Buckingham's*
Common people ⎦ *arraignment*

Two vergers ⎤
Two **Scribes**
Archbishop of
    Canterbury
Bishop of **Lincoln**   *appearing*
Bishop of Ely   *at the*
Bishop of Rochester   *Legantine*
Bishop of St. Asaph   *Court*
Two priests
Serjeant-at-arms
Two noblemen
A **Crier** ⎦

Three **Gentleman** ⎤
Two judges
Choristers
Lord Mayor of London
Garter King-at-Arms   *appearing*
Marquess of Dorset   *in the*
Four Barons of the   *Coro-*
    Cinque Ports   *nation*
Stokesley *Bishop of*
    London
Old Duchess of Norfolk
Countesses ⎦

A Door-Keeper ⎤
Doctor **Butts** *the*   *at*
    King's physician   *Cranmer's*
Pursuivants, pages,   *trial*
    footboys, grooms ⎦

A **Porter** ⎤
His **Man**
Two aldermen
Lord Mayor of London
Garter King of Arms
Six noblemen   *at the*
Old Duchess of   *Christening*
    Norfolk *godmother*
The child, Princess
    Elizabeth
Marchioness Dorset
    godmother ⎦

Epilogue
Ladies, gentlemen, a **Servant**,
    guards, attendants, trumpeters

:≡ SYNOPSIS

A prologue promises a serious play which will depict the abrupt falls of great men.

1.1 The Duke of Norfolk tells the Duke of Buckingham about the spectacular recent meeting in France between King Henry VIII, his French counterpart, and their respective courts, arranged by Cardinal Wolsey. As Buckingham marvels at Wolsey's influence, Lord Abergavenny joins the conversation, and the three lament the Cardinal's power, noting that the spurious peace he negotiated with France has already been broken. When Wolsey enters he and Buckingham exchange disdainful stares before the Cardinal, questioning his secretary about a pending interview with Buckingham's Surveyor, leaves, confident the Duke will soon be humbled.

As Buckingham informs Norfolk of his intention to denounce Wolsey, officials arrest him for high treason.

1.2 Queen Katherine, seconded by Norfolk, speaks against Wolsey's special taxations: surprised by what he hears, the King orders them to be repealed and their defaulters pardoned, a decision Wolsey quietly instructs his secretary to credit to his own intercession. Despite the Queen's scepticism, the allegations made at Wolsey's instigation by the surveyor are sufficient to persuade the King of Buckingham's treason.

1.3 The Lord Chamberlain, Lord Sands, and Sir Thomas Lovell deplore the influence of French fashions before leaving for a lavish supper at Wolsey's palace.

1.4 During Wolsey's feast, the King and his party arrive disguised as shepherds and choose dancing partners: the King takes Anne Boleyn, in whose company he withdraws after his identity is revealed.

2.1 Two gentlemen discuss Buckingham, just condemned to death: under guard, Buckingham speaks to his sympathizers, forgiving his enemies and comparing his downfall to that of his father, also unjustly condemned on a corrupted servant's evidence. The gentlemen lament his fate and speak of a rumour that Wolsey has incited the King to initiate divorce proceedings against Katherine, to be heard before the newly arrived Cardinal Campeius.

2.2 The Lord Chamberlain, Norfolk, and the Duke of Suffolk deplore Wolsey's machinations against the Queen. The pensive King dismisses Norfolk and Suffolk but welcomes Campeius and Wolsey, and confers with Wolsey's secretary Gardiner: meanwhile Wolsey assures Campeius of Gardiner's complete obedience. The King sends Gardiner to Katherine: their case will be heard at Blackfriars.

2.3 In conversation with an old lady, Anne Boleyn pities Katherine the sorrows of queenship, and is ribaldly accused of hypocrisy, especially when the Lord Chamberlain arrives to tell Anne that the King has made her Marchioness of Pembroke.

2.4 After ceremonious preliminaries, the divorce hearing begins with Katherine pleading eloquently for the validity of her marriage and her own status as a loyal wife: she denies the authority and impartiality of the court, which has her enemy Wolsey as one judge, appeals to the Pope, and walks out. The King explains his grounds for seeking the divorce: since Katherine was formerly married to his elder brother, his conscience tells him their marriage is incestuous, although if the court decrees otherwise he will accept its decision. Prevaricating, Campeius adjourns the case, and the King places his hopes instead in his adviser Thomas Cranmer.

3.1 Katherine, among her women, listens to a song before Wolsey and Campeius arrive to urge her to accept the divorce: angrily insisting that they speak English rather than Latin, she defends her position with spirit before subsiding into a more biddable despair.

3.2 Norfolk, Suffolk, Lord Surrey, and the Lord Chamberlain muster their opposition to the now vulnerable Wolsey: the King has intercepted letters to Rome in which the Cardinal, opposing the King's wish to marry Anne Boleyn, advised the Pope to refuse the divorce, and with Cranmer's support he has secretly married Anne already. They watch as a discontented Wolsey is called to the King, who has been reading an inventory of the Cardinal's personal wealth accidentally enclosed with some state papers. Sarcastically praising Wolsey's selfless devotion to duty, the King leaves with his nobles, giving Wolsey two papers to read as he goes—the inventory and the letter to the Pope. The nobles return in triumph to announce the Cardinal's arrest for high treason and the confiscation of his property. Left alone, Wolsey bids farewell to his glory, before a commiserating Thomas Cromwell confirms his utter defeat: Sir Thomas More will replace Wolsey as Chancellor, Cranmer is Archbishop of Canterbury, and Anne Boleyn will shortly be crowned. The humbled Wolsey, weeping at Cromwell's loyalty, urges him to forsake him and serve the King faithfully.

4.1 The two gentlemen watch Anne Boleyn's coronation procession, after which a third describes the ceremony itself, and reports the enmity between Cranmer and Gardiner, now Bishop of Winchester.

4.2 The ailing Katherine hears of Wolsey's death from her usher Griffith, who speaks of Wolsey's virtues and assures her that he died a penitent. Falling asleep, Katherine has a vision of six white-robed figures who hold a garland over her head: both Griffith and her woman Patience are sure she is near death. Caputius, ambassador from her nephew the Holy Roman Emperor, arrives, and Katherine gives him a letter to the King asking him to look after their daughter and her attendants, before she is carried away to bed.

5.1 Gardiner, in response to Lovell's news that Anne is in labour, says he would be glad if she, Cranmer, and Cromwell were dead: he has moved the Council against Cranmer, whom they will interrogate next morning. The King speaks privately with Cranmer, whom he warns against his enemies' malice and to whom he gives a ring as a sign of his protection. The Old Lady announces the birth of a daughter.

5.2 Cranmer is kept waiting outside the council chamber: seeing this, Doctor Butts places the King where he can secretly watch the Council's proceedings. The Lord Chancellor, seconded by Gardiner, accuses Cranmer of spreading heresies, and though defended by Cromwell the Archbishop is sentenced to the Tower. Cranmer's enemies are discomfited when he produces the King's ring, and more so when the King enters, reprimanding

Gardiner, whom he forces to embrace Cranmer, and further showing his support for the Archbishop by inviting him to be his daughter's godfather.

5.3 A porter and his man are unable to control the mob trying to see the state christening, and are rebuked by the Lord Chamberlain.

5.4 At the grandly ceremonial baptism of Princess Elizabeth, Cranmer is inspired to prophesy that both her reign and that of her successor will be golden ages. An epilogue hopes the play may at least have pleased female spectators by its depiction of a good woman.

ARTISTIC FEATURES

As its title suggests, *All Is True* is unusually interested in historical verisimilitude, although the history it narrates between its elaborate recreations of Tudor royal pageantry (described in the longest and most detailed stage directions in the canon) is one which counsels against putting any faith in specious appearances. Compared to the earlier histories it is episodic, resembling an anthology of morality plays in its successive depictions of the falls of Buckingham, Wolsey, and Katherine (each given memorable rhetorical set pieces rather than sustained characterization), and its version of history has a strong tinge of the non-realistic late romances. The wronged Katherine's self-defence at her trial is reminiscent of Hermione's in *The Winter's Tale*, and her husband too will perhaps ultimately be redeemed, according to Cranmer's concluding prophecy, by his infant daughter.

CRITICAL HISTORY

Despite the perennial presence of its great speeches in anthologies of Shakespeare's beauties (most famously Wolsey's farewell to his greatness), the play was long dismissed by literary critics as a mere theatrical showpiece, notable for what Dr Johnson called its 'pomp', interesting primarily as a specimen of how far Shakespeare was prepared to depart from his historical sources in the interests of flattering King James's views of kingship and of the dynasty which had preceded his own accession. The German critic Georg Gervinus, writing from outside the British engagement with this crucial passage of royal history, was one of the few 19th-century commentators to praise Shakespeare's portrayal of Henry. Much commentary on *All Is True* remains inextricably bound up with the interpretation of the history it depicts, its significance to Shakespeare's Jacobean audience, and, to a lesser degree, how far the authors intended that responses to the play should be coloured by a knowledge of the events it chooses not to dramatize (such as the imminent judicial murder of Anne Boleyn). To E. M. W. Tillyard and others, the play upheld the 'Tudor Myth', showing the King's gradual accession to maturity (and, by extension, that of his kingdom), which is signalled by his break from Wolsey and Rome and ultimately rewarded by the birth of the destined Protestant national heroine Elizabeth. More recent critics, when not sidetracked by the issue of the play's authorship, have found the play at best sceptical about Tudor politics, if not nostalgically Catholic in its sympathies, preferring to focus on the unusually sympathetic depiction of Queen Katherine (the only Catholic character granted a heavenly vision in all of English Renaissance drama), and the downplaying, compared to other contemporary plays about the Tudors, of Reformation doctrine. New directions on the play have sought to theorize its lateness in the Shakespearean canon, Katherine's foreign and gendered status, and the play's musicality.

 STAGE HISTORY

The play enjoys the unusual distinction in the canon of being less popular on stage now than at any time in its history. Sir Henry Wotton, reporting the Globe fire, admittedly, feared that its detailed representation of state ceremonies might be 'sufficient in truth within a while to make greatness very familiar, if not ridiculous', but it was still in the King's Company's repertoire in 1628 (when Charles I's favourite George Villiers, Duke of Buckingham, commissioned a private performance at the rebuilt Globe), and after the Restoration it established itself as a regularly revived 'stock' play from 1664 onwards. Thomas Betterton played the King, coached (according to a memoir of 1708) by Sir William Davenant, who had his view of the role from John Lowin, said to have been instructed in it by Shakespeare himself. During the 18th century the play was performed often, especially whenever public interest in royal pageantry was piqued by a real-life coronation, at ever-increasing expense: David Garrick's production (much revived between 1742 and 1768, with Garrick as Henry) employed 140 actors for the coronation procession in 4.1. These spectacular interludes necessitated ever-greater cuts to the text as later generations of actor-managers, more usually casting themselves as Wolsey, sought to outdo their predecessors. John Philip Kemble played the Cardinal in his own redaction, with his sister Sarah Siddons as a much admired Queen, from 1788 to 1816: he was succeeded by William Charles Macready from 1823, and by the time Samuel Phelps first played Wolsey at Sadler's Wells in 1845 the play was finishing at his final exit, though Phelps later restored Act 4. The vogue for spectacle reached a climax with Charles Kean's production, which achieved a record 100 performances at the Princess's Theatre in 1855 and was repeated three years later (with the young Ellen Terry as one of Katherine's visionary angels): this featured numbers of grandly robed aldermen heading for Elizabeth's christening in state barges, in front of a moving diorama of all London. Henry Irving's popular 1892 production at the Lyceum, with himself as Wolsey, also cut most of Acts 4 and 5, and Beerbohm Tree's in 1910 (which subsequently toured the United States) ended with Anne's coronation.

In the 20th-century theatre the play, apparently inseparable from pictorial traditions of staging which now seemed quaintly or offensively Victorian, fell into some disfavour, though still revived at intervals for major actors to measure themselves against the starring roles: Sybil Thorndike played Katherine (Old Vic, 1918, Empire theatre, 1925), Charles Laughton played Henry (Sadler's Wells, 1933, directed by Tyrone Guthrie, with Flora Robson as Katherine), and John Gielgud played Wolsey (Old Vic, 1958). Guthrie revived the play twice more, the last time in 1953, when the onlookers at Anne's coronation held anachronistic newspapers above their heads against rain in an allusion to the recent coronation of Elizabeth II. There were two notable attempts to rebel against the dominant, Holbein-based way of designing the play, one at the Cambridge Festival Theatre in 1931, when Terence Gray caused an uproar by using a modernist aluminium set and Lewis Carroll-influenced costumes based on playing cards (further defying expectations by having the baby doll Elizabeth thrown into the audience in 5.4), and one at Stratford in 1984, when Howard Davies offered a professedly Brechtian production full of deliberate anachronisms associating Henry's regime with Stalin's. The play's last major 20th-century revival, though, directed by Greg Doran for the RSC at the Swan in 1996, returned opulently to Tudor dress, with Jane Lapotaire as a traditionally poignant Katherine, and Gregory Thompson helmed a hauntingly spare and intimate—though, again, lavishly costumed—production in the space of Holy Trinity church in Stratford, as part of the RSC's Complete Works Festival in 2006. The play staged a kind of home-coming in 2010 when Mark Rosenblatt directed it at the replica Globe in London: fortunately the thatch there is elaborately fireproofed.

ON THE SCREEN

Two silent versions were made, a British film featuring Sir Herbert Beerbohm Tree (1911) and an American one from Vitagraph (1912). The only sound film to date is BBC TV's *Henry the Eighth* (1979). The play's original title was adopted by Kenneth Branagh for his film about Shakespeare's retirement, *All is True*. While the film starts with the Globe inferno of 1613, it has little to say about the play during which it happened.

All's Well That Ends Well

Ambivalent and autumnal in mood, *All's Well That Ends Well* clearly belongs to the early Jacobean period of the so-called 'problem comedies' (of which it is perhaps the most accomplished and the most elusive), although its precise date, in the absence of any external evidence or clear topical references, is harder to fix. In vocabulary it is closely linked to *Measure for Measure*, *Troilus and Cressida*, and *Othello*, and it is most likely to have been written just after them, probably around 1604–5.

 TEXT

The play's only substantive text is that printed in the First Folio, apparently (to judge from its inconsistent speech prefixes, idiosyncratic punctuation, and mute characters) from Shakespeare's own foul papers. This was probably the first play the Folio's compositors set from such copy, which may help to explain its high percentage of misprints, errors, and cruces. Some details—such as the play's division into five acts, its specification of cornets in stage directions, and its use of the initials 'G' and 'E' in speech prefixes for the respective Dumaine brothers (possibly indications that these roles once belonged to King's Company actors Gough and Ecclestone)—suggest that this authorial manuscript may have been used as a promptbook for a conjectural revival around 1610–11. Recent scholarship has suggested that the script may on this occasion have undergone partial adaptation and updating by Thomas Middleton.

SOURCE

The main plot of the play is from Boccaccio, the novella of Beltramo de Rossiglione and Giglietta de Narbone recounted on the third day of the *Decameron*, which Shakespeare probably read in English in William Painter's *Palace of Pleasure* (1566–7). Shakespeare's additions are, principally, the comic roles of Paroles and Lavatch.

CHARACTER LIST

The Dowager **Countess** of Roussillon

Bertram, Count of Roussillon *her son*

Helen *an orphan, attending the Countess*

Lavache, a **Clown** *the Countess's servant*

Reynaldo *the Countess's steward*

Paroles *Bertram's companion*

The **King** of France

Lafeu *an old lord*

First Lord Dumaine ⎤
                                    ⎟ *brothers*
Second Lord Dumaine ⎦

Interpreter *a French soldier*

An **Austringer**

The **Duke** of Florence

Widow Capilet

Diana *her daughter*

Mariana *a friend of the Widow*

Lords, attendants, soldiers, citizens

SYNOPSIS

1.1 The widowed Countess of Roussillon takes leave of her son Bertram, who has been summoned to court by the terminally ill King of France, of whom he is a ward: with him goes the Countess's old friend Lord Lafeu. The Countess's own ward, Helen, weeping orphaned daughter of the physician Gérard de Narbonne, confesses in soliloquy that her tears are inspired not by her father's death but by Bertram's departure, lamenting that the difference between their ranks renders her secret desire for him hopeless. She is interrupted by the self-styled captain Paroles, Bertram's companion, who engages in a bantering dialogue about virginity before following the Count: alone again, Helen hints that she may use the King's illness as a means towards furthering her pursuit of Bertram.

1.2 The King, declining to aid Florence in its campaign against Siena, nevertheless agrees that French noblemen may volunteer on either side.

Presented with Bertram by Lafeu, he waxes nostalgic about the Count's late father, laments his own sickness, and asks wistfully after the dead Gérard de Narbonne.

1.3 The Countess is asked for permission to marry by her misogynistic servant Lavatch, whom she sends to fetch Helen, reported to have been overheard sighing for Bertram. Alone with Helen, the Countess exacts a confession of love from her, and gives her approval for Helen's plan to visit Paris in the hopes of curing the King by means of one of her late father's prescriptions.

2.1 The King bids farewell to the two Lords Dumaine, off to the Italian wars, as does Bertram, who longs to follow them despite the King's commands to the contrary. Lafeu introduces Helen to the King, and she succeeds in persuading him to try her father's remedy: he agrees that if it succeeds he will grant her any husband in his power.

2.2 The Countess sends Lavatch to court with a letter for Helen.

2.3 The fully restored King calls together all his lords for Helen to make her choice of bridegroom: she picks Bertram, who indignantly resists the idea of marrying a poor physician's daughter. The King compels him, however, to go through an immediate wedding ceremony: meanwhile Lafeu scoffs at Paroles's pretensions to courage and social status. Returning from his enforced wedding, Bertram tells Paroles he means to send Helen back to Roussillon without consummating the marriage and run away to the wars.

2.4 Paroles tells a grieved but compliant Helen that Bertram must depart at once on unspecified business and wishes her to return home.

2.5 Lafeu warns Bertram, in vain, against placing any faith in Paroles. Bertram takes a cold farewell from Helen, before he and Paroles leave for Italy.

3.1 The Lords Dumaine are welcomed to the battlefront by the Duke of Florence.

3.2 The Countess, delighted by the news of Bertram's marriage to Helen, is shocked to learn that he has run off, never intending to consummate it. Helen arrives with the Lords Dumaine, who confirm that Bertram has joined the Duke of Florence's army: in a letter he vows that he will never be Helen's husband until she can show him the ring from his finger (which he never means to take off) and a child of hers to which he is father (which he never means to beget). Alone, Helen resolves to steal away, so that Bertram may be willing to return home from the perils of combat.

3.3 The Duke of Florence makes Bertram general of his cavalry.

3.4 The Countess receives a letter from Helen explaining that she has gone away on a pilgrimage so that Bertram may come home: she dispatches this news towards Bertram, hoping that both he and Helen may return to Roussillon.

3.5 A Florentine widow, her daughter Diana, and their neighbour Mariana are looking out for the army: Mariana warns Diana against Paroles, who has been soliciting on Bertram's behalf, before an incognito Helen arrives as a pilgrim, and, accepting a lodging at the Widow's guesthouse, learns of Bertram's pursuit of Diana. They watch the troops pass—and see Paroles's affected vexation about the capture of a drum—and agree, at Helen's insistence, to speak further.

3.6 The Lords Dumaine persuade Bertram to expose Paroles's cowardice by encouraging his boasted solo attempt to recapture the drum, offering to capture Paroles disguised as enemy soldiers and allow Bertram to overhear his interrogation.

3.7 Helen, her identity revealed, persuades the Widow to allow Diana to pretend to accept Bertram's advances so that she can be replaced at a clandestine rendezvous by Helen.

4.1 The Lords Dumaine and others lie in wait for a frightened Paroles: simulating an absurd foreign language, they ambush him and lead him off to be questioned.

4.2 Bertram ardently woos Diana, who, following Helen's instructions, persuades him to give her his ring before inviting him to her darkened chamber, for an hour only, at midnight.

4.3 The Lords Dumaine reflect on Bertram's vices and virtues, on his reported seduction of Diana, and on the reported death of Helen: an exhilarated and unrepentant Bertram arrives to witness Paroles's interrogation before setting off for France, the wars being over. The blindfolded Paroles, questioned through a supposed interpreter, invents scandalous gossip about the Lords Dumaine as well as revealing military secrets, and denounces Bertram as an immature seducer. Finally unmuffled and confronted by his comrades, who leave in contempt, Paroles resolves henceforth to make a shameless living as a laughing stock.

4.4 Helen, the Widow, and Diana set off for Marseille to see the King on their way to Roussillon.

4.5 Awaiting Bertram's arrival, Lafeu and the Countess plan that the forgiven Bertram should marry Lafeu's daughter, a scheme the King has already approved.

5.1 Hearing that the King has left Marseille for Roussillon, Helen and her two companions proceed thither.

5.2 Paroles begs to be received by Lafeu, who has already heard of his exposure and agrees to employ him as a fool.

5.3 The Countess, Lafeu, and the King, though lamenting the supposedly dead Helen, receive a pardoned Bertram, who claims that he disdained Helen only because already in love with Lafeu's daughter, for whom, with the King's approval, he produces an engagement ring. The ring, however, is one given him in the dark by Helen in Florence, and is recognized by the King as one he himself gave her. Bertram's denials that he took it from Helen are in vain, and he is arrested under suspicion of having killed her. A letter arrives from Diana, revealing that Bertram promised to marry her on Helen's death: she and the Widow are admitted and confront Bertram, confounding his insistence that Diana was a common prostitute by producing the ancestral ring he gave her. Diana's claim that it was she who gave Bertram Helen's ring, though, brings her evidence into question, and Paroles's comically equivocal testimony clarifies nothing. Finally, a riddling Diana sends the Widow to fetch the pregnant Helen, whom Bertram, the conditions of his earlier letter now conclusively fulfilled, has to accept as his wife. The King, after promising to reward Diana with any husband she chooses, speaks an epilogue.

 ARTISTIC FEATURES

The play highlights the folk-tale origins of its story by casting dialogue in rhyme at crucial points of the narrative: these include Helen's last soliloquy in 1.1, her interview with the King in 2.1, her choice of husband in 2.3, and the epistolary sonnet in 3.4 by which she announces her departure as a pilgrim, as well as Diana's riddles and Bertram's final capitulation in 5.3. Since this folk tale, however, is depicted as taking place in a realistic world (in which even the clown Lavatch is a bitter and unhappy cynic), the play is most remarkable for its irony, holding us at a reflective distance from its driven and unconfiding heroine and its caddish hero alike. Shakespeare multiplies the story's ironies and parallelisms by his pointed juxtaposition of the gulling of Paroles (who believes himself to be committing treason when he is merely destroying his credit with his comrades) with the bed-trick used against Bertram (who believes himself to be committing adultery when he is really condemning himself to his arranged marriage).

 CRITICAL HISTORY

Before the mid-20th century, *All's Well That Ends Well* characteristically received only qualified or grudging praise from literary critics, when it enjoyed their attention at all. Throughout its critical history the play's inversions of the normal patterns of romantic comedy—its sympathy with an older generation who are usually right to circumscribe the freedom of the younger, the relentless pursuit by the play's heroine of a love she knows to be unrequited, and the general atmosphere of disenchantment, loss, and mourning within which the plot unfolds—have made readers happier with Shakespeare's more festive comedies uncomfortable. The play's closeness to a single narrative source has allowed some to dismiss it as a hasty piece of professional scriptwriting, some of whose faults (such as the indelicacy or improbability of the bed-trick) can be blamed on Boccaccio. Charlotte Lennox was among the first to make the comparison between play and source, in 1753, generally to the play's disadvantage, and her dislike of Bertram in particular was memorably seconded by Samuel Johnson (1765): 'a man noble without generosity, and young without truth; who marries *Helen* as a coward, and leaves her as a profligate: when she is dead by his unkindness, sneaks home to a second marriage, is accused by a woman whom he has wronged, defends himself by falsehood, and is dimissed to happiness.' Samuel Taylor Coleridge, more sympathetic to Bertram's plight, defended him by attacking Helen instead ('it must be confessed that her character is not very delicate, and it required all Shakespeare's consummate skill to interest us for her', *Table Talk*, 1835, although elsewhere he describes her as 'Shakespeare's loveliest character'), and for most of the next century discussions of the play continued to centre on whether its hero (hapless victim or bounder) or its heroine (virtuous exemplar of self-help or rapist upstart) was less objectionable. George Bernard Shaw, for example, who praised the play as a prefiguration of Ibsen, sided with Helen, Frank Harris with Bertram. Only since the 1930s have what once seemed the play's moral failures or equivocations been revalued as successful dramatizations of an ethically complex world, its interest in expiation, pilgrimage, and forgiveness (particularly its plays on the word 'grace') often linked with the (similarly revalued) late romances. Enthusiastic supporters have included George Wilson Knight and E. M. W. Tillyard, although it is notable that the first monograph devoted solely to this play (by J. G. Price) only appeared in 1968, and is called *The Unfortunate Comedy*. Criticism often remains centred on the play's genre, cataloguing its problems both textual and narrative. Nonetheless, recent reappraisals have sought instead to understand *All's Well* according to the 'comedies of rule' tradition, attending to the play's interest in law and sovereign power. Recent performance criticism, on the other hand, has emphasized the emotional realism and feminist potential of the play.

 STAGE HISTORY

Price's book is largely concerned with the fortunes of the play on the English stage down to the 1960s, which had amply earned it this title. No performances are recorded before a revival at Goodman's Fields in 1741: over the next 60 years it had only 51 London performances and for the whole of the 19th century only seventeen. Early comment on the play is largely confined to the much loved role of Paroles, played successively by Theophilus Cibber, Charles Macklin, and, especially, Henry Woodward: the nature of the play's 18th-century appeal is suggested by Frederick Pilon's unpublished adaptation of 1785, which concentrated almost entirely on Paroles's gulling, cutting most of the first three acts. In 1794 John Philip Kemble became the first major actor to bother with the role of Bertram, in an adaptation of his own which offered an idealized Helen, played by Dorothea Jordan, as its sentimental focus: this achieved only one performance, and when revived by Samuel Phelps in 1852 (in a cut form which politely eliminated the bed-trick) it proved equally unpopular. Meanwhile a musical version by Frederick Reynolds (1832) had equally failed to reconcile play-goers to what now seemed an unacceptably indecent plot line, and the play was not performed professionally again until Frank Benson cast himself as Paroles in a Stratford revival in 1916.

The play's unfamiliarity and unpopularity freed 20th-century directors to take unusual liberties with its text, and even purists sought to justify their revivals by highlighting topical parallels. William Poel's production in 1920, taking a hint from Shaw, presented Helen as a proto-suffragette, while Barry Jackson's Birmingham Repertory Theatre production seven years later was in modern dress, with Laurence Olivier as a would-be sophisti-cated jazz-age Paroles. Robert Atkins produced the play three times (1921, 1932, 1940), to little avail, and it was only when Tyrone Guthrie turned his attentions to it during the opening season of the Stratford, Ontario, festival in 1953 that *All's Well That Ends Well* began to receive good notices again. Guthrie's production (of a heavily cut and altered text which omitted Lavatch altogether), repeated in Stratford in 1959 (with Edith Evans as the Countess), was given an Edwardian setting, except for the comically elaborated war scenes, which were set as if among General Montgomery's Desert Rats. Michael Benthall's 1953 production for the Old Vic was if anything even more drastically cut and pasted, adding music and comic business in the interests of light-heartedness, so that Paroles, played by Michael Hordern, once more became the centre of the play.

A return to Shakespeare's text was marked in John Houseman's pro-duction at Stratford, Connecticut, in 1959, and emulated in John Barton's successful 1967 production for the Royal Shakespeare Company (with Ian Richardson as a redeemable Bertram). The play was at last fully vindicated by two widely praised revivals a decade later, David Jones's at Stratford, Ontario, in 1977 (with Margaret Tyzack as the Countess), and, especially, Trevor Nunn's for the RSC in 1981 (with Peggy Ashcroft as the Countess, Harriet Walter as Helen, and Robert Eddison as Lafeu), a production which followed Guthrie in setting the play in Edwardian dress but which played it more consistently as a moving Chekhovian tragicomedy. Gregory Doran's successful RSC production of 2003, with Judi Dench as the Countess, achieved a similarly autumnal tone but returned the play to Jacobean dress. In 2009 Marianne Elliott directed an equally sumptuous but more stylized production at the National Theatre, praised by critics as 'a fairytale for adults', and Nancy Meckler pursued a similarly storybook style in her 2013 production for the RSC. More Gothic productions were seen in 2016 at Bristol's Tobacco Factory (dir., Andrew Hilton) and in 2018 at Shakespeare's Globe. The latter, directed by Caroline Byrne and performed in the indoor Sam Wanamaker auditorium, prioritized metaphorical and literal darkness: the playhouse's main chandeliers were barely fired up, the cast using handheld candles and torches to light themselves instead. Issues of consent, particularly in relation to the play's bed-trick, read differently and disconcertingly in a post-#MeToo era.

 **ON THE SCREEN**

Four television films were based on the play between 1968 and 1985, three adapted from stage productions. Only Elijah Moshinsky's BBC TV version (1980) was initially designed for television. The play has yet to tempt Hollywood.

Antony and Cleopatra

Extravagantly fluid in language and structure alike, *Antony and Cleopatra* marks a major stylistic departure from its immediate predecessors *King Lear* and *Macbeth*, although external evidence suggests that it cannot have

been written much later. Echoes of its phraseology have been detected in Samuel Daniel's revision of his play on the same subject, *Cleopatra*, published in 1607, and in Barnabe Barnes's play *The Devil's Charter*, acted by the King's Men in February 1607, so in all probability *Antony and Cleopatra* enjoyed its first performances late in 1606. It was entered in the Stationers' Register on 20 May 1608.

 TEXT

Despite this entry, the play was not printed until the publication of the First Folio in 1623, which provides the only authoritative text. It seems to have been printed from a good transcript of Shakespeare's own foul papers, though not a promptbook: although the spelling suggests the work of a scribe, some of the text's minor errors (such as mistaken speech prefixes) are characteristically authorial, and others (such as entry directions for characters who play no part in the subsequent action) would have been eliminated if the manuscript had been used in the theatre.

 SOURCE

Although possibly influenced in minor respects by the earlier version of Daniel's *Cleopatra* (1594), and drawing some historical details from Appian's *Civil Wars*, the play is primarily a dramatization of the latter part of Plutarch's life of Marcus Antonius, as it appeared in Sir Thomas North's translation of *Lives of the Noble Grecians and Romans* (1579). (This was also a source for *Julius Caesar*, to which *Antony and Cleopatra* can be regarded as a sequel.) Shakespeare, though, greatly compresses Plutarch's narrative: the events dramatized here took place over an entire decade, and began only two years after the battle of Philippi with which *Julius Caesar* concludes (though this play makes that remembered victory seem a comparatively remote event in Antony's youth). Most crucially, Shakespeare has Antony's involvement with Cleopatra pre-date the death of his wife Fulvia, although historically it began after Antony had already married her successor Octavia. (This makes the relationship between the lovers at once more adulterous and, after a fashion, more faithful.) Shakespeare seems to have had a similar eye for telling details of human behaviour to Plutarch's, from whom he takes many minor incidents almost verbatim. He develops, though, the roles of Cleopatra's women Charmian and Iras and, especially, the almost choric figure of Antony's lieutenant Enobarbus, who is at times allowed to speak words taken directly from Plutarch's third-person narration—most famously, the set-piece description of Cleopatra on her barge in 2.2, a stunningly effective but very faithful versification of North's prose.

👥 CHARACTER LIST

Mark **Antony** (Marcus Antonius) *triumvir of Rome*

Demetrius ⎤
Philo |
Domitius **Enobarbus** | *friends*
Ventidius | *and*
Silius | *followers*
Eros | *of*
Camidius | *Antony*
Scarus |
Dercetus ⎦

Octavius Caesar *triumvir of Rome*

Octavia *his sister* ⎤
Maecenas |
Agrippa | *friends*
Taurus | *and*
Dolabella | *followers*
Thidias | *of*
Gallus | *Caesar*
Proculeius ⎦

Lepidus *triumvir of Rome*

Sextus **Pompey** (Pompeius)
Menecrates ⎤
Menas | *friends of Pompey*
Varrius ⎦

Cleopatra *Queen of Egypt*

Charmian ⎤
Iras |
Alexas | *attending*
Mardian *a eunuch* | *on*
Egyptian | *Cleopatra*
Diomed |
Seleucus ⎦

A **Soothsayer**
An **Ambassador**
A **Boy** who sings
A **Sentry** and men of his **Watch**
Men of the **Guard**
An **Egyptian**
A **Clown**
Servants
Eunuchs, attendants, captains, soldiers, servants

📑 SYNOPSIS

1.1 In Alexandria Antony, teased by Cleopatra, declines to hear a messenger sent from his fellow triumvir Octavius Caesar.

1.2 While Antony's second-in-command Enobarbus makes arrangements for yet another feast, Cleopatra's attendants Charmian, Iras, and Alexas talk with a soothsayer, who prophesies that Charmian will outlive Cleopatra but that the most fortunate part of their lives is already over. From the messenger, Antony learns of his wife Fulvia's reverses in the civil war she and his brother have been waging against Caesar, and of Parthian advances in the Middle East; from another he learns of Fulvia's subsequent death. Aware that he has been neglecting his political and military interests,

Antony passes on this news to Enobarbus, announcing that they must leave for Rome.

1.3 Antony breaks the news of Fulvia's death and his immediate departure to a contrary but ultimately compliant Cleopatra.

1.4 In Rome Caesar tells Lepidus, the third triumvir, of Antony's idleness in Egypt, the more regrettable since they are now threatened by seaborne rebels Pompey (son of Julius Caesar's old adversary Pompey the Great), Menecrates, and Menas.

1.5 In Alexandria Cleopatra, daydreaming of the absent Antony, receives a letter from him; Charmian taunts her with her former passion for Julius Caesar.

2.1 Menas tells Pompey and Menecrates that Caesar and Lepidus have assembled an army; Varrius brings the unwelcome news that Antony is on his way to Rome to join them.

2.2 In Rome, at a formal meeting between the triumvirs, Antony denies responsibility for Fulvia's conduct, and defends himself against charges of denying Caesar military aid: Enobarbus impertinently suggests that the triumvirs should simply postpone this feud until they have defeated Pompey together. Agrippa, one of Caesar's subordinates, proposes that the alliance between Antony and Caesar should be reaffirmed by a marriage between Antony and Caesar's sister Octavia, to which Antony and Caesar agree. Left among Caesar's staff, Enobarbus boasts of Antony's Alexandrian hedonism, describes Cleopatra's appearance when she sailed down the River Cydnus on a barge to meet Antony for the first time, and declares that marriage to Octavia will not be sufficient to keep Antony away from the Egyptian Queen.

2.3 Antony bids a formal goodnight to Caesar and Octavia, promising that he will behave honourably, but after the Soothsayer urges him to stay away from Caesar—in whose presence, he observes, Antony's luck fails—he resolves to return to the pleasures of Egypt. He sends Ventidius to Parthia.

2.4 Lepidus parts from two of Caesar's subordinates, all of them on their way to confront Pompey.

2.5 Cleopatra's nostalgic reveries about her past games with Antony are interrupted by a messenger who brings the news of his marriage; enraged, she strikes him repeatedly, but finally subsides into lovelorn grief.

2.6 Parleying before their armies, Pompey accepts the triumvirs' terms for peace, and the leaders repair to a feast on Pompey's barge. Menas and Enobarbus reflect on Pompey's unwise submission, and Enobarbus, reporting Antony's marriage, again predicts that Antony will return to Cleopatra.

2.7 At the feast, Menas urges Pompey to cut the barge's cable and assassinate the triumvirs; wishing that Menas had done this first on his own initiative, Pompey nonetheless refuses his suggestion. Lepidus is carried off drunk before the party disperses.

3.1 Victorious Roman forces, led by Ventidius, parade the corpse of the Parthian Prince Pacorus: Ventidius, however, declines to pursue his advantage against the Parthians, aware that too much success on his part would make his superior Antony dangerously envious.

3.2 Agrippa and Enobarbus ridicule the absent Lepidus, before Antony and Octavia, leaving for Athens, bid Caesar farewell.

3.3 Cleopatra interrogates the still-frightened messenger, who humours her by dispraising Octavia.

3.4 Antony, angry with Caesar for launching new hostilities against Pompey, allows Octavia to leave for Rome as a mediator, though continuing to gather his forces against her brother.

3.5 Enobarbus and his comrade Eros have heard that Caesar has defeated and killed Pompey and deposed Lepidus, taking over his third of the empire.

3.6 In Rome Caesar reports that Antony, now back in Alexandria with Cleopatra, has held a public ceremony granting the kingdoms of the eastern empire to her and to their children: when Octavia arrives he tells her bluntly of Antony's return to Cleopatra and of their preparations for war.

3.7 Near Actium, Enobarbus urges Cleopatra in vain to absent herself from Antony's military campaign, since her presence affects his judgement: despite repeated advice to the contrary from their soldiers, Antony and Cleopatra resolve to fight Caesar by sea.

3.8 Caesar orders his army to avoid battle until after the naval engagement.

3.9 Antony disposes his land forces.

3.10 The armies cross the stage and the noise of a sea-fight is heard. A horrified Enobarbus has seen the Egyptian flagship flee, taking the rest of Cleopatra's navy with it: Scarus, another soldier, reports that this happened just as Antony might have achieved victory, but that when Cleopatra fled he followed; Camidius, another of Antony's disgusted commanders, deserts.

3.11 In shame and despair Antony urges his attendants to leave his service; when Cleopatra arrives he rages at her, but when she cries he asserts that one of her tears is worth more than all they have lost.

3.12 Caesar receives Antony's schoolmaster, sent with terms for peace: continuing queenship for Cleopatra, and a private life in either Alexandria or Athens for Antony. Caesar offers to grant Cleopatra's request only on condition that she expel or kill Antony, and sends Thidias further to woo Cleopatra from Antony.

3.13 Antony, receiving Caesar's answer, challenges him to single combat. Cleopatra receives Thidias and his proposals kindly; when Antony finds him kissing Cleopatra's hand he has him whipped, railing at Cleopatra until, reassured of her fidelity, he rallies and decides to feast all his captains once more. Enobarbus, convinced of his folly, resolves to defect.

4.1 Caesar scoffs at Antony's challenge and prepares for one last battle.

4.2 Antony takes leave of each of his tearful followers, belatedly telling them he still hopes for victory.

4.3 His sentries hear supernatural music, which they are convinced is the sound of the god Hercules abandoning Antony.

4.4 Cleopatra helps Antony to arm, and he departs for battle in high spirits.

4.5 A soldier tells Antony Enobarbus has joined Caesar: magnanimously, Antony sends Enobarbus' treasure after him.

4.6 Caesar orders that defectors should be placed in the front rank against their former commander. Enobarbus, learning of Antony's generosity, feels he will die of shame.

4.7–9 Antony, Scarus, and others pursue Caesar's retreating forces before returning in triumph to Cleopatra at the end of the day's fighting.

4.10 Caesar's sentries overhear Enobarbus lamenting his disloyalty and dying of grief.

4.11–13 The second day's battle takes place mainly by sea: watching from the shore, Antony sees the Egyptian fleet surrender and, despairing, orders his army to disperse. When Cleopatra appears he drives her away with threats, claiming she has betrayed him to Caesar, and he resolves to kill both her and himself.

4.14 As Cleopatra and her attendants retreat to her monument, she instructs the eunuch Mardian to tell Antony she has committed suicide and to report his reaction.

4.15 Antony is telling Eros all is lost when Mardian brings his message. Antony instructs Eros to help him unarm and, reconciled to Cleopatra, whom he longs to join in death, orders Eros to kill him with his own sword. Eros, however, kills himself instead, and the wound Antony then inflicts upon himself is not immediately fatal. The guards who arrive also refuse to kill him: when news comes that Cleopatra is not really dead, the dying Antony is carried off towards her monument.

4.16 Cleopatra, Charmian, and Iras hoist Antony up into the monument: dying, after a final kiss, he urges her to seek safety with Caesar and to trust none of Caesar's followers except Proculeius. Cleopatra's response, though, suggests that she too intends suicide, and she confirms this in the passionate lament that follows his death.

5.1 Among his followers Caesar learns of Antony's death: pointing out that the news makes him weep, he insists that only necessity, not ambition, prompted this war against his old ally. A messenger from Cleopatra asks his intentions: Caesar replies that he means her only kindness, but he tells Proculeius to flatter Cleopatra only to dissuade her from suicide, so that she may be carried in triumph to Rome.

5.2 At the monument, while Proculeius gives Cleopatra promises of gentle treatment from Caesar, his soldiers ambush and disarm her, narrowly preventing her from stabbing herself. She speaks elegiacally of Antony to another of Caesar's followers, Dolabella, who just has time to warn her that Caesar really means to lead her captive through Rome before Caesar himself arrives. Submitting an inventory of her possessions to her conqueror, Cleopatra is apparently embarrassed when her treasurer Seleucus informs Caesar that she has declared less than half of her wealth, but Caesar leaves still professing friendship. Dolabella hurries back to tell her she and her children will be sent away within three days: horrified at the idea of being exhibited in Rome, Cleopatra and her attendants prepare to die. A rustic, who engages the Queen in quibbling banter, brings asps concealed in a basket of figs. Iras and Charmian dress Cleopatra in the same royal robes she wore on the Cydnus: she kisses them farewell, Iras dying before the Queen, who applies an asp to her breast and arm, and herself dies, anticipating a reunion in the afterlife with Antony. Charmian adjusts Cleopatra's crown and puts an asp to her own arm as Caesar's guards enter, too late. Caesar himself arrives with his train and deduces the cause of their deaths, conceding that Cleopatra shall be buried with Antony.

🎭 ARTISTIC FEATURES

One of Shakespeare's longest plays (at over 3,000 lines), *Antony and Cleopatra* has an unusually large number of scenes, some very short. Its action flows rapidly all around a Mediterranean world which in its concluding movement inexorably contracts to the monument, where most of the last act after Antony's death is given over to Cleopatra's self-transfiguring suicide. Despite its profusion of character and incident, the play is remarkable for the degree to which its poetry—dense in metaphor, unprecedentedly free in versification—defies its onstage drama, with key events (including most of Antony and Cleopatra's time together, and the decisive battle of Actium) evoked in language rather than shown on stage. The lovers' glamorous past seems as significant as the coldly rational present (personified by the efficient Octavius Caesar) in which they are being defeated: during the last act Cleopatra's poetic invocation of a heroic Antony seeks to upstage and eclipse the flawed failure whom the action of the play has in fact shown. In so far as she succeeds, *Antony and Cleopatra* anticipates the late romances by moving from tragedy back into something closer to Shakespearian comedy, its final death coming at the hands of a rural clown and serving as the means to a transcendent (albeit posthumous) marriage ('Husband, I come', 5.2.282).

⭐ CRITICAL HISTORY

Although its influence on Daniel and Rich shows that it impressed contemporaries, *Antony and Cleopatra* was long neglected after its author's death. John Dryden's much tidier, domesticated, neoclassical play on the same subject, *All for Love; or, The World Well Lost* (1676, professedly 'written in imitation of Shakespeare's style'), with its mild, would-be virtuous Cleopatra and simpler conflict between love and honour, made more sense to later 17th-century sensibilities. To Charles Gildon (1710) Shakespeare's play was 'full of scenes strangely broken', and Samuel Johnson (1765) felt that its events were 'produced without any art of connection or care to disposition' (a fault Henry Brooke attempted to mend in his unacted adaptation, printed in 1778). It was not until the Romantic age that the play's exoticism and excess, and what then seemed its disdain for theatrical practicality, came to be valued, with S. T. Coleridge declaring it Shakespeare's 'most wonderful' play. Subsequent 19th-century critics largely concentrated on the character of Cleopatra, to whom even those who regarded the play as a simple moral warning against dissipation responded vigorously. Anna Brownell Jameson called Cleopatra 'one brilliant impersonation of classical elegance, Oriental voluptuousness, and gipsy sorcery' (1832), and the serpent of old Nile predictably fascinated the self-consciously decadent writers (and painters, such as John Collier) of a later generation, A. C. Swinburne enthusing that 'here only once and for all [Shakespeare] has given us the perfect and the everlasting woman' (1880). A. C. Bradley, though an admirer of the play, excluded it from his category of Shakespeare's 'great' tragedies, sensing that it belonged to some less affective genre ('It is better for the world's sake, not less for [Antony and Cleopatra's] own, that they should fail and die...the fact that we mourn so little saddens us,' 1909), but over the following century it was this very avoidance of heroic, operatic emotion, and the play's apparent preference for language over character, which endeared it to modern criticism, and its highly patterned poetry lent it perfectly to the studies in Shakespeare's imagery pioneered by Caroline Spurgeon. Since the later 20th century the play has been of particular importance to feminist critics interested in Shakespeare's representations of sexual difference, and to postcolonial commentators concerned with its images of empire and of race. Cleopatra's self-definition as black has been central to these studies, which have pushed back against prevailing assumptions about the play's lack of interest in ethnicity. Such thriving conversations have recently been connected to considerations of other stage Cleopatras from the early modern period.

STAGE HISTORY

Although early allusions allow us to infer that the play was performed in 1606–7, no records exist of any further performances before 1759, when David Garrick and Edward Capell prepared it for the proscenium stage by a great deal of transposition and cutting. Despite Garrick's efforts as Antony, and heavy expenditure on sets and costumes, this achieved only four performances: contemporaries preferred Dryden's *All for Love*. The next two attempts to revive the play (by J. P. Kemble in 1813, and W. C. Macready in 1833) attempted, as the preface to Kemble's adaptation put it, 'to blend the regular play of Dryden with the wild tragedy of Shakespeare', but this hybrid failed to please. Samuel Phelps returned to a cut version of Shakespeare only at Sadler's Wells in 1849, and although this was not a commercial success the spectacular potential of the play's subject matter attracted further 19th-century producers, in both London and New York, despite the difficulties presented by its profusion of scenes. These included Charles Calvert in 1867, F. B. Chatterton in 1873, Rose Eytinge (who played Cleopatra) on Broadway in 1877, and even Lily Langtry, who cast herself as Cleopatra at the Princess's in 1890. Although Beerbohm Tree staged a predictably lavish version in 1907, this approach to the play had already been superseded in Frank Benson's much sparer production (with himself as Antony) at Stratford, seconded by Robert Atkins's revolutionary, almost bare-stage production at the Old Vic in 1922, in which Edith Evans played her first Cleopatra.

Throughout the play's stage history, productions in which both central performances have been equally praised have been rare: for many Vivien Leigh's Cleopatra (1951) outshone Laurence Olivier's Antony, and Michael Redgrave's Antony (1953) overpowered Peggy Ashcroft's Cleopatra, felt by some to be 'too English' (a complaint still often raised against British actresses by critics with a more exotic, Orientalist view of the role). In the later 20th century, many directors tried to solve this problem by scaling down both performances and the entire play: Trevor Nunn's much-praised RSC production of 1972, with Janet Suzman as Cleopatra, used a comparatively simple set, and Peter Brook's of 1978 (his last work for the company), with Glenda Jackson as Cleopatra, a stylized setting framed by glass panels. (Peter Hall, however, successfully bucked this trend at the National Theatre in 1987, casting Judi Dench and Anthony Hopkins in a satisfactorily lavish production in the Olivier auditorium). It is interesting in this respect that one of the most admired productions of the period was Adrian Noble's (1981), in the tiny Other Place in Stratford (with Michael Gambon as Antony), where Helen Mirren was a concentrated, intelligent Cleopatra, while when Mirren repeated the role in 1998 at the National, in a production by Sean Mathias which aimed at spectacle, the effort was a critical disaster. Gregory Doran's RSC production of 2006, with Patrick Stewart and Harriet Walter, achieved the brilliant compromise of a simple set, traditionally opulent and mimetic costumes, and a small auditorium, the Swan. When Jonathan Munby mounted his 2014 production for Shakespeare's Globe, he made a virtue of the play's whopping forty-two scenes, allowing one to dissolve cinematically into the next, foregrounding Cleopatra's (Eve Best) sensuality and a ruffian Antony (Clive Wood). The year 2017 represented an important moment for the play's performance history, with Josette Simon becoming the first actor of colour to play Cleopatra on the RSC's main stage. Produced as part of the company's wider 'Rome' season and directed by Iqbal Khan, the production's opulent design set the scene for Simon's politically astute and notably physical Cleopatra and Antony Byrne's soldierly Antony. Simon Godwin's 2018 all-star production for the National Theatre began with Cleopatra's (Sophie Okonedo) death; the queen was revived by an embrace from Antony (played as a reflective soldier gone slightly to seed by Ralph Fiennes) before the production returned to the play's beginning, encouraging a retrospective view of what followed and positioning the ensuing action as an extended flashback. But it will be remembered, first and foremost, for the cries of its audiences when the production's very live, very big snake darted towards Okonedo's neck.

 ## ON THE SCREEN

A five-minute version (now lost) was made by George Méliès in 1899, the same year as Beerbohm Tree's *King John*. Between 1951 and 1980 five versions were made, including a British film with Robert Speaight as Antony, a TV adaptation as part of the *The Spread of the Eagle* series (1963), a low-budget-looking film by Charlton Heston (1972), Trevor Nunn's much-acclaimed TV film of his RSC production (1972), and a BBC production by Jonathan Miller, with Jane Lapotaire as Cleopatra (1980).

As You Like It

One of the best loved of Shakespeare's mature comedies, *As You Like It* was entered in the Stationers' Register in 1600: the fact that it is not mentioned in Francis Meres's list of Shakespeare's works in September 1598, coupled with its high proportion of prose and the precise frequency with which its verse uses colloquial contractions, has inclined most scholars to date the play in 1599–1600, just after *Henry V* (with which it shares some unusual vocabulary) and *Julius Caesar*. Although it may pre-date the play, the publication of 'It was a lover and his lass' (sung in 5.3) in Thomas Morley's *First Book of Airs* in 1600 would appear to support this dating.

 TEXT

Despite the Stationers' Register entry of 1600 the play was not printed until the First Folio appeared in 1623. The Folio supplies a generally reliable text which, lacking distinctively authorial spellings and errors, was probably set from a promptbook, or perhaps a literary transcript of foul papers.

 CHARACTER LIST

Duke Senior *living in banishment*
Rosalind *his daughter, later disguised as Ganymede*
Amiens ⎤
Jaques ⎦ *Lords attending on him*
Two Pages
Duke Frederick
Celia *his daughter, later disguised as Aliena*
Le Beau *a courtier attending on him*

Charles *Duke Frederick's wrestler*
Touchstone *a jester*
Oliver *eldest son to Sir Roland de Bois*
Jacques ⎤
Orlando ⎦ *his younger brothers*
Adam *a former servant to Sir Roland*
Dennis *Oliver's servant*
Sir Oliver Martext *a country clergyman*

Corin *an old shepherd*
Silvius *a young shepherd, in*
   love with Phoebe
Phoebe *a shepherdess*
William *a countryman, in*
   love with Audrey

Audrey *a goatherd, betrothed*
   to Touchstone
Hymen *god of marriage*
Lords, pages, and other
   attendants

 SOURCES

The main plot of *As You Like It* derives from Thomas Lodge's *Rosalynde* (1590), a prose tale interspersed with poems which had already reached its fourth edition in 1598, although Shakespeare makes some telling alterations to this well-known pastoral romance. The play, for example, makes Lodge's rival dukes into brothers (so that their antagonism parallels that between the hero and his eldest brother), and has the usurper spontaneously repent so as to permit the concluding restoration of the exiled court (enabled in *Rosalynde* only by a bloody battle in which the usurper dies). Shakespeare, moreover, changes all the characters' names except those of Phoebe and the (respelled) Rosalind, sometimes allusively: Lodge's Rosader becomes Orlando—named after the hero of Ariosto's *Orlando furioso*, dramatized by Robert Greene in around 1591, who runs mad after learning from inscriptions on trees that his beloved has married another—and his brother becomes Oliver, after Orlando's legendary comrade. Shakespeare adds the characters of Touchstone, Le Beau, Amiens, Jaques, William, Sir Oliver Martext, and the old shepherd Corin, whose name may derive from the anonymous play *Sir Clyomon and Clamydes* (pub. 1599).

:≡ SYNOPSIS

1.1 Orlando laments to the old servant Adam that since the death of his father Sir Roland de Bois his elder brother Oliver has denied him the education and treatment due to his rank, and on Oliver's arrival Orlando confronts him to demand his patrimony. Dismissing him, Oliver summons Charles the wrestler, and after Charles has recounted the (stale) news that the Duke has been driven into exile in the forest of Ardenne (spelt 'Arden' in the Folio text) by his younger brother Frederick, who retains the Duke's daughter Rosalind at court to keep his own daughter company, Oliver maligns Orlando, instructing Charles to be sure to kill him in the following day's wrestling tournament. Alone, Oliver reflects briefly on his rancorous envy of his deservedly admired younger brother, before leaving to encourage Orlando to enter the wrestling.

1.2 At court, Celia, the usurping Duke's daughter, attempts to cheer up Rosalind; they are joined first by the jester Touchstone and then by the courtier Le Beau, who brings news of the wrestling. Frederick and his court arrive to watch Charles wrestle against Orlando, whom the two princesses endeavour in vain to dissuade from the contest: cheered on by Rosalind and Celia, Orlando defeats Charles, but when Frederick learns who his father was he leaves in an ill temper without rewarding him. Instead the cousins congratulate him, and Rosalind gives him her necklace, Orlando finding himself comically tongue-tied with love. Le Beau warns him to flee from Frederick's displeasure.

1.3 Rosalind has just confided her own love for Orlando to Celia when the angry Frederick banishes her from his court. After his departure Celia proposes they both flee to Ardenne together in peasant disguise, and Rosalind, agreeing, decides to dress as a man and call herself Ganymede, while Celia will become Aliena. They leave to enlist Touchstone and make plans for their flight.

2.1 In the forest of Ardenne the exiled Duke Senior speaks to his followers about the moral lessons which console him for the discomforts of their bucolic existence: they leave in search of their melancholy comrade Jaques, last seen pronouncing a sententious lament over a wounded deer.

2.2 Duke Frederick interrogates his courtiers about the disappearance of Celia, feared to have fled with Rosalind in pursuit of Orlando, and has Oliver summoned to court to assist in the manhunt.

2.3 The returning Orlando is warned to flee his murderous brother by Adam, who offers to accompany him as his servant.

2.4 Rosalind and Celia, in their respective disguises, arrive wearily in Ardenne with Touchstone, and overhear the young shepherd Silvius bemoaning his love for Phoebe to his older colleague Corin: questioned, Corin tells Rosalind that his master's cottage, pastures, and flocks are now for sale, and Rosalind and Celia resolve to buy them.

2.5 Amiens sings 'Under the greenwood tree' to some of Duke Senior's lords: they are joined by Jaques, who contributes a satirical verse of his own.

2.6 Adam is fainting with hunger: Orlando promises to fetch him food.

2.7 Duke Senior and his lords, about to eat, are joined by Jaques, who describes meeting Touchstone and speaks of his own ambition to be a satirical jester: they are interrupted when Orlando arrives, sword drawn, to demand food, a demand which is graciously met. Apologizing for his rudeness, Orlando goes to fetch Adam, while Jaques reflects that all the world's a stage. Feeding Adam while Amiens sings 'Blow, blow, thou winter wind', Orlando is warmly welcomed by the Duke, who loved his father.

3.1 An angry Frederick sends Oliver to fetch the missing Orlando, confiscating his lands until his brother is delivered.

3.2 Orlando pins a love poem about Rosalind on a tree before leaving to pin up many more. Corin and Touchstone engage in a comic debate about the relative merits of country and court life before Rosalind arrives, reading another unsigned poem in her own praise, which is mocked by Touchstone. Celia arrives reading yet another such verse: alone with Rosalind, she teases her cousin before finally letting her know that the poet is Orlando, who is also in the forest. They watch as Orlando arrives engaged in a prickly conversation with Jaques: when these two part by mutual consent, Rosalind accosts Orlando in her guise as Ganymede, questions him about his love poems, and proposes to cure him of his love by posing as a realistically contrary Rosalind during daily counselling sessions.

3.3 Touchstone is persuaded to postpone his marriage to Audrey, the ignorant goatherd he lusts after, by Jaques, who feels Touchstone deserves a better priest than Sir Oliver Martext.

3.4 Rosalind is distressed that Orlando is late for his appointment with Ganymede: Celia says he is not to be trusted. Corin arrives, promising to take them to see Silvius trying to woo the disdainful shepherdess Phoebe.

3.5 Seeing Phoebe's scorn for Silvius, Rosalind steps forward and accuses her of ingratitude before she, Celia, and Corin leave. Phoebe, falling in love at first sight with Ganymede, says she will give Silvius an angry letter to deliver to him.

4.1 Rosalind scoffs at Jaques, who leaves on the arrival of Orlando: Rosalind rebukes Orlando for his tardiness, and parries his clichéd declarations of love for Rosalind with a more realistic account of the relations between husbands and wives. Nonetheless, she has Celia act as priest for a mock-betrothal ceremony, and allows Orlando to leave only after exacting solemn promises of a punctual return: alone with Celia she confesses the depth of her love.

4.2 Jaques has some of the Duke's lords, who have been hunting, sing a jovial song about cuckoldry, 'What shall he have that killed the deer?'

4.3 Once more waiting for Orlando, Rosalind and Celia receive Phoebe's letter, delivered by Silvius: instead of a challenge, as Silvius believes, it is a love poem to Ganymede, and Rosalind sends Silvius away with a scornful reply. Oliver now enters, bearing a bloody cloth for Ganymede, whom he recognizes by his description. He relates how Orlando, finding him asleep and at the mercy of a waiting lioness, overcame his righteous indignation against his treacherous brother and killed the lioness, incurring a wound to his arm in the process. Waking in the midst of this, Oliver explains, he has been entirely converted from his former wickedness, and has been sent by his reconciled brother Orlando—who back among the exiled court briefly fainted from loss of blood—to carry the bloody cloth to Ganymede as an apology for his absence. Receiving it, Rosalind faints, nearly betraying her male disguise.

5.1 Audrey and Touchstone meet her rustic suitor William, whom Touchstone, flaunting his superior vocabulary, dismisses.

5.2 Oliver tells Orlando that he and Aliena have fallen instantaneously in love and that he means to marry her immediately, leaving the family estate to Orlando while he remains in Ardenne as a shepherd: Orlando consents to this and urges Oliver to prepare to marry her before Duke Senior and his lords the following day. Rosalind arrives, and after Oliver's departure she promises Orlando that he will be able to marry Rosalind at the same time that his envied brother marries Celia, claiming she will be able to effect this by magic. Phoebe and Silvius arrive, and Rosalind promises that if she ever marries a woman it will be Phoebe: she assures Silvius that he too will be married, and instructs him, Orlando, and Phoebe to meet her the following day in their best clothes, ready for marriage.

5.3 Touchstone and Audrey, too, will be married the next day: in the meantime two pages sing them 'It was a lover and his lass'.

5.4 Before Duke Senior, his followers, Oliver, and Celia, Rosalind, still disguised as Ganymede, has the participants in the multiple wedding ceremony she purports to have devised recap what they have promised: Duke Senior to give Rosalind in marriage to Orlando if she can be produced, Orlando to marry Rosalind, Phoebe to marry Ganymede or, if she chooses not to, to accept Silvius as her husband, Silvius to marry Phoebe. Rosalind and Celia then leave: meanwhile Touchstone and Audrey arrive, and with Jaques' encouragement Touchstone recounts the comically elaborate rules by which courtiers challenge one another but avoid fighting. To the accompaniment of music, Rosalind and Celia enter dressed in their own clothes, conducted by Hymen, god of marriage: Rosalind presents herself to her father and to Orlando, Phoebe renounces her claim to Ganymede, and Hymen blesses the four couples with the song 'Wedding is great Juno's crown'. The festivities are interrupted by the arrival of Jaques de Bois, Sir Rowland's second son, who brings the news that Frederick, leading an expeditionary force against Duke Senior, has undergone a religious conversion and become a hermit, returning all the banished lords' sequestered lands and restoring the dukedom to Duke Senior. Only Jaques declines to return home with them, leaving to join Frederick. After a rustic dance, Rosalind is left to speak a flirtatious epilogue, conjuring women to like as much of the play as pleases them for the sake of the love they bear to men, and vice versa.

 ## ARTISTIC FEATURES

As You Like It casts some of its most important passages in prose (including the wonderfully inconclusive set-piece debate between court and country in 3.2, Rosalind's dialogues on love with Orlando in 3.2, 4.1, and 5.2, and her epilogue), and, in keeping with its engagement with the pastoral tradition, is correspondingly relaxed about its own (or Lodge's) plot: once most of the cast have got into the forest Shakespeare seems simply to let them pass the time meeting one another and talking until Rosalind feels that the time has come to relinquish her disguise.

CRITICAL HISTORY

The earliest critical responses to this play are two adaptations, Charles Johnson's *Love in a Forest* (1723) and John Carrington's unacted *The Modern Receipt; or, The Cure for Love* (1735), both of which share with later 18th-century commentators a sense that the play could use some tidying up. However, although Dr Johnson (in sympathy with Jaques) felt that Shakespeare had rushed his happy ending and should have shown the sketchily reported dialogue between Frederick and the hermit, most were prepared to forgive its looseness of construction, accepting that it was in keeping with the play's pastoral nature that it should concentrate on character and sentiment at the expense of plot. What the 18th century had forgiven, the Romantics worshipped, finding in Duke Senior's celebration of the moral lessons of Nature a statement of Shakespeare's own imputed views on the wisdom to be found outside a corrupted urban society, and finding the play's preference for reflection over action equally sympathetic. The German critic August Wilhelm Schlegel influentially, saw the play as a manifesto for the view that 'nothing is wanted to call forth the poetry which has its dwelling in nature and the human mind but to throw off all artificial constraint, and restore both to their native liberty' (1811).

Nineteenth-century criticism in general concentrated on the play's characters, with Rosalind often idealized as the perfect, morally superior heroine. A well-established tradition of valuing Shakespeare's depiction of the relationship between Rosalind and Celia as literature's prime celebration of female bonding found its fullest expression in Mary Cowden Clarke's 'Rosalind and Celia: The Friends' in *Girlhood of Shakespeare's Heroines* (1850–2). Victorian and Edwardian comments on the play's pastoralism stressed the forest's kinship with the Arden of Warwickshire rather than the French Ardenne, seeing Shakespeare's woodland as a place where native common sense triumphed over the foreign affectations represented by Phoebe: according to Frederick Boas, for example, the play replaced 'the artificial atmosphere of the Renaissance pastoral' with 'the open-air freshness, the breeze and blue of the old English ballad-poetry' (1896).

The 20th century saw a renewed and usually more complicated interest in the play's dealings with the literary conventions of its time, with scholars reading it not only against Lodge's *Rosalynde* (dismissed as 'worthless' by George Steevens in 1770, but studied with increasing respect thereafter) but alongside the versions of pastoral offered by Philip Sidney, Edmund Spenser, Robert Greene, and others. Such critics, unusually, tended to concur in seeing the play as simultaneously a celebration and a debunking of the pastoral convention as Shakespeare had found it (although attempts to find topical references in the play, whether to Sir John Harington or to riots against enclosure, commanded less agreement). Two further influential lines of enquiry combined with this one later in the century: one, following Northrop Frye and C. L. Barber, pursued the play's interest in patterns of seasonal renewal and fertility, while another remains more interested in its sexual politics, particularly the issues raised by Rosalind's successful disguise as Ganymede. New directions on the play have highlighted its representation of queer identities and performativities.

STAGE HISTORY

The play's early history is haunted by two ill-substantiated rumours: one, not recorded before 1865, that the play was acted for James I at Wilton House in Wiltshire in 1603, and the other, reported by Edward Capell in 1779, that Shakespeare himself played the role of Adam. Whether or not there is any truth in these, there are no records of any performances of the play before Johnson's *Love in a Forest* appeared at Drury Lane in 1723 (though most have assumed that the play was first acted at the Globe soon after its opening in 1599). It did not appear in unadapted form until 1740, when it was revived at Covent Garden with Hannah Pritchard as Rosalind, Kitty Clive as Celia, and the songs set by Thomas Arne: this sparkling production immediately established *As You Like It* as one of the most popular plays of the century, and since then few major actresses have not attempted the role of Rosalind. Peg Woffington was the first to compete with Pritchard, at Drury Lane (for six nights in 1741 both Theatres Royal competed with their rival productions), and indeed she made her final stage appearance in the role, collapsing with a stroke in the middle of the epilogue in 1757. Even Sarah Siddons played Rosalind in 1785 and 1786, but her gravity of demeanour suited her badly to the part (generally played at the time with tomboyish extroversion): far more successful was Dorothea Jordan, whose roguish performance helped to assure that from 1787 to her departure in 1814 the play was acted at Drury Lane more frequently than any other in the Shakespeare canon. Nineteenth-century Rosalinds, increasingly performing on lavishly decorated sets and in carefully specified period costumes (a trend initiated by W. C. Macready's 1842 production, with its French 15th-century designs), tended to be more ladylike, even in disguise: Helen Faucit, who shed tears of joy in her love scenes with Orlando, was especially praised for always being 'the Duke's daughter' even at her most playful moments. The decorously cut and decorative productions in which a succession of such Rosalinds predominated—from Faucit to Ada Rehan, Mary Anderson, and Lily Brayton—perhaps reached their apogee in 1908, when Richard Flanagan's Manchester production filled the forest with real deer, which unfortunately terrified the Orlando, Harcourt Williams.

In the 20th century this Merrie English tradition was gradually supplanted—most notably by Nigel Playfair's controversially stylized production at Stratford in 1919—and a less jolly side to the play has sometimes been found by directors embarrassed by deer except as potential archetypal symbols. Despite a continuing succession of joyously sunny Rosalinds—from Peggy Ashcroft (Old Vic, 1932) through Edith Evans (Old Vic, 1936, in Watteau-style costumes, with Michael Redgrave as Orlando) to Vanessa Redgrave (RSC, 1961), Pippa Nixon (RSC, 2013), and Michelle Terry (Globe, 2015)—the play has often belonged more to Jaques than to Touchstone on the modern stage, with Duke Senior's remarks on the joys of exile rendered ironic by uncomfortably snowbound Ardens. Notably tense readings of the play include Adrian Noble's (RSC, 1985, with Fiona Shaw as a memorably cut-glass Celia) and Michael Grandage's (Sheffield and on tour, 2000, with Nicholas le Prevost a commanding Jaques). In 2015, Polly Findlay's production for the National Theatre seemed, to some critics, to banish merriment altogether. Lizzie Clachan's set figured Duke Frederick's court as part soulless City-like corporation, part Butlins: the transition to the forest saw the set explode upwards so that the office tables and chairs were suspended above the stage. This was an angular, subdued Arden.

This continuing disagreement as to whether the play works best as 'hard' or 'soft' pastoral has been compounded by discussions as to whether it is best played by mixed or same-sex companies: Ben Greet directed an all-male production in 1920 (appropriately, at the Central YMCA in London), Clifford Williams another for the National Theatre in 1967, and Cheek by Jowl's exuberant all-male version of 1991–2, which toured extensively around the world, was the most successful and talked-about Shakespeare production of its time. More recently, both the Globe (2018) and the RSC (2019) have sought to employ casting more statistically representative of contemporary Britain, with, for instance, the deaf Nadia Nadarajah cast as Celia (at the Globe), and a lesbian Silvia replacing Silvius (at the RSC).

ON THE SCREEN

The Paul Czinner film (1936) with Laurence Olivier as Orlando was the first sound cinema adaptation of the play. An acclaimed BBC TV production in 1953 included Margaret Leighton and Michael Hordern; Cedric Messina directed another small-screen version for the BBC in 1978, with Helen Mirren. Christine Edzard's independent film As You Like It (1992), while refreshing and daring in its approach, sets the play amidst urban dereliction which runs against the grain of the play's language. Kenneth Branagh's 2006 film, even more incongruously, sets the play among Europeans in nineteenth-century Japan.

Cardenio

The King's Men were paid for performing a play referred to as *Cardenno* or *Cardenna* at court on 20 May and 9 July 1613, presumably based on the story of Cardenio told in Cervantes' *Don Quixote*, which had first appeared in English translation in 1612. In September 1653 Humphrey Moseley entered 'The History of Cardenio, by Mr Fletcher and Shakespeare' in the Stationers' Register, but there is no evidence that he ever published it. (Some, however, suspect that the words 'and Shakespeare' are a later addition.) While he might have known that Fletcher had dramatized material from *Don Quixote* elsewhere, and that he had collaborated with Shakespeare on *The Two Noble Kinsmen* (though not when), Moseley is very unlikely to have known that Shakespeare's company had given performances of a play called *Cardenno* at court—at exactly the same time, moreover, that Shakespeare and Fletcher were also collaborating on *All Is True* (*Henry VIII*) and *The Two Noble Kinsmen*. Although Shakespeare's colleagues John Heminges and Henry Condell, for whatever reason, omitted this play when they compiled the First Folio (just as they excluded *Pericles*, *The Two Noble Kinsmen*, and the mysterious *Love's Labour's Won*), it seems likely that Shakespeare co-wrote *Cardenio* with Fletcher in 1612–13, and that a manuscript of the play was still extant in the 1650s.

Tantalizing glimpses of this otherwise lost play were provided in 1728 by the publication of *Double Falsehood; or, The Distressed Lovers*, 'Written Originally by W. SHAKESPEARE, and now Revised and Adapted to the Stage by Mr. THEOBALD'. Lewis Theobald's preface to this play, which was acted with considerable success at Drury Lane, states that it is an adaptation of an otherwise unknown work by Shakespeare, of which he claims to possess three copies in manuscript. (One of these was said to be in the library of Covent Garden theatre as late as 1770, but the playhouse burned down in 1808). Theobald's preface, though arguing strenuously for the play's authenticity, betrays no knowledge of either Moseley's entry in the Stationers' Register or the traces of *Cardenio*'s performances at court, so the otherwise extraordinary coincidence that *Double Falsehood* is in fact a version of the Cardenio story suggests that whatever Theobald possessed in manuscript must at least have derived from the missing Fletcher–Shakespeare *Cardenio*.

If this is the case, however, *Double Falsehood* represents *Cardenio* only at one or more removes, its language heavily rewritten for a post-Restoration stage which found Fletcher's style much more congenial than that of Shakespeare's late romances (as is demonstrated by William Davenant's version of *The Two Noble Kinsmen*, *The Rivals*, which cuts most of the lines now attributed to Shakespeare). Nonetheless, some commentators have found lingering traces of Shakespearian imagery, and others have been impressed by the way in which *Double Falsehood* assimilates the Cardenio story to the characteristic patterns of Shakespearian romance. The play was even included in the Arden 3 edition of Shakespeare's works in 2010.

Various attempts have been made to 'reconstruct' *Cardenio* for perform-ance, principally with student drama groups: the most notable of these has been Gregory Doran's 'reimagining' of *Cardenio*, performed by the Royal Shakespeare Company in 2011.

The Comedy of Errors

According to an eyewitness account, 'a comedy of errors (like to Plautus his *Menaechmus*) was played by the players' during the Christmas revels at Gray's Inn on 28 December 1594: this can only have been Shakespeare's play, which is indeed based on Plautus' comedy *Menaechmi*, and it is unlikely that the lawyers and students would have hired actors to appear at a grand festive occasion with anything but a new, or at least current, play. Although this debt to classical farce has inclined some scholars to see the play as apprentice work from the very start of Shakespeare's career, stylistic tests confirm a dating around 1594, with rare vocabulary placing it between *The Taming of the Shrew* and *Romeo and Juliet* and its heavy use of rhyme placing it early in the lyrical period initiated by *Venus and Adonis*.

 TEXT

The play was first printed in the Folio in 1623: inconsistencies in speech prefixes and theatrically superfluous information in some stage directions suggest that it was set from Shakespeare's foul papers. Certain stage directions, which state which of three 'houses' (the Phoenix, the Porcupine, or the Priory) characters are to enter from, indicate that the play may have been written with indoor performance (such as at Gray's Inn) in mind: academic and court performances sometimes employed a conventional 'arcade' setting with three doors at the rear of the stage, labelled by signs. The play's careful and logical division into five acts (which would have been marked by intervals in indoor performance) would support this view.

SOURCES

The play's chief plot, in which a man searching for his long-lost twin brother is repeatedly mistaken for him (with discomfiting consequences for the sought-for twin), derives, as recognized above, from Plautus' *Menaechmi*. (This play was published in an English translation by William Warner in 1595, entered in the Stationers' Register in summer 1594, but the hypothesis that Shakespeare may have had access to this version in manuscript is hardly necessary, since Plautus' plays were already familiar to most Elizabethan grammar-school boys). Shakespeare complicates this plot by adding long-separated twin servants (the Dromios) for the twin masters (the Antipholi), drawing on another Plautus play, *Amphitruo*, which also provided the scene in which a wife shuts out her husband while unwittingly entertaining another in his place. Shakespeare, however, adds the un-Plautine frame narrative of Egeon and Emilia, derived from the Greek romance of Apollonius of Tyre (which also lies behind Shakespeare's other play about twins, *Twelfth Night*, and *Pericles*). He also changes the setting from Plautus' Epidamnus to Ephesus, and the play abounds with allusions to St Paul's Epistle to the Ephesians, especially its strictures on marriage.

 CHARACTER LIST

Solinus, Duke of Ephesus
Egeon *a merchant of Syracuse, father of the Antipholus twins*

Antipholus of Ephesus ⎤
Antipholus of Syracuse ⎦ *twin brothers, sons of Egeon*

Dromio of Ephesus ⎤
Dromio of Syracuse ⎦ *twin brothers, and bondmen of the Antipholus twins*

Adriana *wife of Antipholus of Ephesus*
Luciana *her sister*
Nell *Adriana's kitchen maid*
Angelo *a goldsmith*
Balthasar *a merchant*
A **Courtesan**
Doctor **Pinch** *a schoolmaster and exorcist*
Merchant of Ephesus *a friend of Antipholus of Syracuse*

Second Merchant
  Angelo's creditor
Emilia *an abbess at Ephesus*

Jailer, messenger, headsman,
officers, and other
attendants

SYNOPSIS

1.1 Egeon, an old merchant, is under sentence of death for entering Ephesus, currently at war with his native Syracuse, unless he can raise a 1,000-mark ransom. Questioned by the Duke of Ephesus as to why he has entered this hostile territory, he recounts how years earlier his wife bore him identical twin sons, for whom they bought identical twin slaves born at the same time, but that in a shipwreck he and the younger son and servant were separated from his wife and the other two twins. At 18 his younger son, given the same name as his missing twin, set off with his servant in quest of their brothers: Egeon subsequently set off after them, and has arrived in Ephesus on his way home after five years' fruitless search. Moved, the Duke allows Egeon the remainder of the day to raise the ransom.

1.2 Antipholus of Syracuse and his servant Dromio of Syracuse have arrived in Ephesus: Antipholus sends his servant to their lodging to lock up his money. Shortly afterwards Dromio of Ephesus arrives and, mistaking this Antipholus for his own master, calls him home to dinner. Antipholus of Syracuse, thinking this is his own Dromio having a joke, grows angry, asking anxiously after his money, and drives Dromio away with blows before setting off to check on his belongings.

2.1 Adriana laments the continuing absence of her husband Antipholus of Ephesus to her unmarried sister Luciana, and after Dromio of Ephesus brings the story of his beating and dismissal (and is sent back to make another attempt to bring Antipholus home) she says she would be willing to forgo the gold chain her husband has promised if only he would be faithful.

2.2 Antipholus of Syracuse, having found his money safe, meets his own Dromio and berates him for the incomprehensible invitation to dinner he in fact received from Dromio of Ephesus: after a squabble their comic banter is interrupted by the arrival of Adriana and Luciana. Adriana preaches Antipholus a sermon on marital fidelity, and she and Luciana take his and Dromio's denials of their acquaintance as mere jests. Softening, she invites him home to dinner, instructing Dromio to deny all visitors: Antipholus, though he and Dromio begin to suspect that their names are known to these strangers by magic, accepts.

3.1 Antipholus of Ephesus, together with Dromio of Ephesus and his guests Balthasar the merchant and Angelo, the goldsmith who has just completed the chain for Adriana, are locked out of his house. The enraged

Antipholus decides they will all dine instead with the Courtesan, and he sends Angelo to fetch the chain so that he can give it in spite to the Courtesan.

3.2 Luciana urges Antipholus of Syracuse to maintain at least a show of marital concord with Adriana: when he responds by wooing her instead she leaves to find her sister. A horrified Dromio of Syracuse reports to his master that a fat kitchen-wench claims she is engaged to him, and after a spate of comic puns likening the wench's body to the globe the two Syracusans resolve to flee from Ephesus. While Dromio seeks a ship, Antipholus is met by Angelo, who to his amazement gives him the chain.

4.1 Angelo has met another merchant, just arrested for debt, to whom he owes exactly the sum of money now owed to him by Antipholus for the chain. Antipholus of Ephesus now arrives, sending Dromio of Ephesus to buy a rope with which to chastise his household for locking them out, and berates Angelo for failing to deliver the chain. Convinced that he has already delivered it, Angelo has Antipholus arrested for debt. Dromio of Syracuse now arrives and tells Antipholus of Ephesus he has found a ship for their escape: infuriated, Antipholus sends Dromio back to Adriana to fetch money to redeem him from imprisonment.

4.2 Adriana is enraged to hear that her husband has apparently been wooing her sister: Dromio of Syracuse reports Antipholus' arrest, and they give him the purse of money he requests.

4.3 Antipholus of Syracuse is musing on how many people he meets treat him with kindness and respect when Dromio of Syracuse, amazed to find him at liberty, gives him the money. About to leave for the harbour, they are accosted by the Courtesan, who, seeing the promised chain around Antipholus' neck, asks for it, or, failing that, for the return of the diamond ring she gave him during dinner. Convinced she is a witch, Antipholus and Dromio flee: the Courtesan, convinced they are mad, decides that the only way to secure the return of her diamond is to tell Adriana her husband has lost his wits.

4.4 Antipholus of Ephesus, still under arrest, is beside himself with violent rage when Dromio of Ephesus brings not the money to redeem him but only a rope: this behaviour helps convince Adriana, arriving with the Courtesan, Luciana, and a schoolmaster-cum-exorcist called Dr Pinch, that Antipholus is insane. Pinch tries to exorcize him and is beaten for his pains: Antipholus asserts his sanity and rebukes Adriana for locking him out, to which she insists that he dined with her: as the dispute grows louder Antipholus attacks Adriana, and both he and Dromio have to be restrained with ropes. The two are carried off homewards, bound, with Pinch, while Adriana attempts to ascertain what has been happening from the arresting officer and the Courtesan: just then Antipholus of Syracuse and Dromio of Syracuse arrive, with swords, and the others flee, convinced that the two lunatics have escaped their captors.

5.1 Angelo and his creditor the merchant are just discussing Antipholus' apparent treachery when Antipholus of Syracuse, still wearing the chain, arrives with Dromio of Syracuse: insisting that he has never denied having received the chain, Antipholus is about to duel with the vexed merchant when Adriana, Luciana, the Courtesan, and their party arrive to attempt to capture him. Antipholus and Dromio flee into a nearby priory for sanctuary, from which the Abbess appears, and asks Adriana about her husband's apparent madness. The Abbess diagnoses that he has been driven mad by Adriana's continual reproaches about his infidelity, and insists that she will nurse him back to health in the abbey: a furious Adriana demands the return of her husband to her own custody and, refused, threatens to appeal to the Duke. The Duke now arrives, bringing Egeon to the nearby place of execution. Adriana kneels before him, recounting her husband's madness and escape to the Abbey, and implores the Duke to exert his authority over the Abbess so that her husband may be returned to her. When a messenger interrupts, reporting in horror that Antipholus and Dromio have got loose and are avenging themselves on Dr Pinch, he is disbelieved until Antipholus of Ephesus and Dromio of Ephesus arrive in person. Antipholus appeals to the Duke for justice against his wife, who he claims has locked him out of his house and conspired to have him falsely imprisoned as a madman, and against Angelo, who he claims has falsely demanded payment from him for an undelivered chain. The Duke, Angelo, the merchant, the Courtesan, Antipholus, and Dromio are trying in vain to make sense of all this contradictory testimony, and the Duke has just sent for the Abbess, when Egeon steps forward, saying he has seen someone he thinks will ransom him. When he speaks to Antipholus and Dromio of Ephesus, however, both deny him, Antipholus assuring him, as the Duke confirms, that he has never seen either his father or Syracuse in his life. At this point, though, the Abbess arrives, bringing with her Antipholus of Syracuse and Dromio of Syracuse, to the astonishment of all beholders. Adriana and the Duke are trying to ascertain which is the real Antipholus, and the Syracusan Antipholus and Dromio are wondering why Egeon is here and in bonds, when the Abbess recognizes Egeon and declares that she is his long-lost wife Emilia. As the Duke at last understands that the two Antipholi and Dromios are the long-separated twins Egeon had spoken of, Emilia explains that soon after the shipwreck she was separated from the baby Antipholus of Ephesus and Dromio of Ephesus by Corinthian fishermen, who took them away from her, and subsequently became a nun in Ephesus: Antipholus of Ephesus confirms the

Duke's recollection that he only came to Ephesus from Corinth later on, in military service with the Duke's uncle. The Antipholi and their various debtors and creditors untangle the events of the day, Antipholus of Syracuse assuring Luciana that he will resume his suit, now she knows he is not her brother-in-law. Antipholus of Ephesus, finally obtaining the ransom money he sent for, offers to pay it to redeem Egeon, but the Duke reprieves the old man without payment. The Courtesan gets her ring back from Antipholus of Ephesus, before the Abbess invites the entire cast to what she describes as a long-delayed christening party for her twin sons. The Dromios are the last to leave the stage: not knowing which is the elder, they go hand in hand rather than in order of precedence.

 ARTISTIC FEATURES

The play's opening scene centres on the longest passage of sheer exposition in the canon, the hundred lines of narrative spoken by Egeon before he disappears from the play until the final reunions. Despite the tight, fast-moving structure of the intervening scenes, the play is notable for other solo performances too, which similarly go beyond the normal emotional range of farce: these include Adriana's complaint, in couplets, of her husband's neglect (2.1.86–114), Antipholus of Syracuse's wooing speech, in quatrains, to Luciana (3.2.29–52), and Dromio of Ephesus' lament, in prose, about the lifetime of beatings he has suffered from his master (4.4.30–40).

CRITICAL HISTORY

The play has often been dismissed as a formulaic exercise in Plautine farce (even by William Hazlitt), although later writers, from Charles Knight onwards, have been more willing to be moved by the romance materials with which Shakespeare frames his borrowings from *Menaechmi*, and by the extra depth they confer on the plot of mistaken identity. Harold Brooks drew attention to the play's interest in authority, relating its discussion of marriage to *The Taming of the Shrew*, while his successors have pursued the play's allusions to St Paul on the same topic, often reflecting at the same time on the play's canny thematic juxtaposition of three phenomena which confound the notion of the single, self-determining individual, namely birth, marriage, and twinship. Reappraisals of *Errors* have emphasized the play's more disturbing elements: the gaslighting, psychologically confounding effects of its 'dark-working' magic; the violent, racialized ideologies imposed upon the Dromios; and the sobering context of its composition, the Elizabethan refugee crisis.

▛▜ STAGE HISTORY

Apart from the 1594 performance at Gray's Inn, only one other performance of *The Comedy of Errors* is recorded during Shakespeare's lifetime, albeit a prestigious one, when the play was revived before James I's court during the Christmas season of 1604. Since then a high proportion of the play's stage history has been one of adaptation: it first reappeared, in 1723, in an unpublished version called *Every Body Mistaken*, succeeded in 1734 by a two-act abbreviation, similarly unpublished, called *See If You Like It*. During the 1741–2 season the original enjoyed five performances at Drury Lane, with Charles Macklin as Dromio of Syracuse, and it was in this unlikely role that J. P. Kemble chose to appear from 1808 onwards in his own elaboration of the cut version by Thomas Hull, *The Twins; or, Which is Which?*, which had been in the repertory since 1762. Frederick Reynolds produced a character-istic musical version in 1819, adorned with songs from other plays, and since then the play has continued to be shortened to a farce or extended to a musical at regular intervals. In the United States, where their style perfectly suited the emergence of vaudeville, the Dromios served as vehicles for the Placide brothers (until 1877) and then the Robson brothers, and the play later became the basis for a long-running Broadway hit by Richard Rodgers and Lorenz Hart, *The Boys from Syracuse* (1938). In Britain notable produc-tions featuring added music have included Theodore Komisarjevsky's eclectic romp of the same year, Julian Slade's opera (televised in 1954, staged in 1956), and Trevor Nunn's café-cum-circus version for the RSC (1974), although others have found the play's dramatization of a broken and uneasily restored family sufficiently compelling (and sufficiently funny) without such assistance, notably Tim Supple's small-scale, modern-dress production for the RSC (1996). Lynne Parker's lavish main-house production for the RSC in 2000 placed emphasis on large-scale pantomimic fun, directing a then-unknown David Tennant as Antipholus of Syracuse in an audience-friendly production, while Nancy Meckler's 2005 realization for the same company aimed to unsettle through the *Alice in Wonderland*-esque expressionism of its design and costuming, and through a menacing array of Ephesian low-life stalking the public spaces of the stage. Dominic Cooke's 2012 production for the National also had its darker sides. Set in the (often sleazier) parts of modern-day London, the production was less interested in the farce-like comedy often expected of *Errors* than it was in the foreigner status of Antipholus and Dromio of Syracuse (Lucian Msamati and Lenny Henry). Differentiated from their Ephesian counterparts by West African accents, the Syracusans' welcome, or lack thereof, spoke vol-umes about the production's London and our own.

 ON THE SCREEN

Apart from a ten-minute silent film (1908) and the heavily transposed *The Boys from Syracuse* (1940), adaptations for television include a British film (1954) with Joan Plowright as Adriana, a West German production (1964), two British TV films of RSC stage productions (1964 and 1974), and the BBC TV production (1983). The 1974 musical version directed by Trevor Nunn, and with Dame Judi Dench as Adriana, has achieved wide circulation on video.

Coriolanus

The last and most uniformly political tragedy in the canon can be dated by a number of topical allusions. Shakespeare's interest in the story of the legendary Caius Martius and his antipathy towards the hungry mob may have been stimulated by the food riots which took place in the Midlands during 1607 and 1608, while two minor details point to other recent events: the great frost of December 1607–January 1608 (alluded to at 1.1.171) and Hugh Middleton's project to bring water to the City of London via the artificial 'New River', only completed in early 1609, though under preparation some time beforehand (alluded to at 3.1.99–100). The play cannot have been written before 1605, since its first scene draws on William Camden's *Remains of a Greater Work Concerning Britain*, published in that year, nor after 1609, when it was itself echoed in two separate works by authors associated with Shakespeare's company, Robert Armin's *The Italian Tailor and his Boy* (entered in the Stationers' Register that February), and Ben Jonson's *Epicoene* (completed later in the year). All stylistic tests place the play later than *The History of King Lear*, *Macbeth*, and *Antony and Cleopatra*, and it probably appeared shortly after *Pericles*, in spring or summer 1608.

 TEXT

The dating of the play in 1608 is further confirmed by two details of its sole authoritative text, published in the Folio in 1623, namely the specification of cornets in some of the musical stage directions and the division of the play into acts. Both of these features are associated with indoor theatres (which could use smaller brass instruments than the public amphitheatres, and needed pauses in the action for the changing of footlights), and suggest that *Coriolanus* may have been the first of Shakespeare's plays to have been written with the Blackfriars theatre, acquired by the King's Men in 1608, in mind. The text printed in the Folio preserves a few idiosyncrasies of Shakespeare's foul papers (such as the occasional spelling of 'Scicinius' for 'Sicinius', which matches other examples of Shakespeare's preference for 'sc' spellings elsewhere), although other accidentals appear to be scribal. It also gives unusually full stage directions, some of them apparently the result of authorial directions being clarified and duplicated for theatrical use. It probably derives either from a promptbook transcribed from foul papers, or from a transcript of such a promptbook.

 SOURCES

The play's depiction of the semi-legendary Caius Martius (banished from the early Roman republic in 491 BC, not so long after the events Shakespeare had narrated in *The Rape of Lucrece*) closely follows Plutarch's 'Life of Caius Martius Coriolanus' in his *Lives of the Noble Greeks and Romans*: several major passages, notably Volumnia's appeal in 5.1 (95–183), are taken almost verbatim from Sir Thomas North's translation. Shakespeare, however, greatly expands Volumnia's role (inventing all the other episodes in which she appears), as he does that of Menenius, while Menenius' fable of the belly (1.1.85–152) shows a familiarity with other versions of this parable than Plutarch's: from Camden's *Remains*, from Livy's version of the story in his *Annales*, and from William Averell's *Meruailous Combat of Contrarieties* (1584).

 CHARACTER LIST

Caius **Martius**, later
    surnamed **Coriolanus** ⎤
                      patricians
Menenius Agrippa   *of Rome*
Titus **Lartius** ⎤
         generals
Cominius ⎦

Volumnia *Coriolanus' mother*
Virgilia *his wife*
Young Martius *his son*

Valeria *a chaste lady of Rome*
Sicinius ⎤
          tribunes of Rome
Junius **Brutus** ⎦

Citizens of Rome
Soldiers in the Roman army
Tullus **Aufidius** *general of*
    the Volscian army
His **Lieutenant**

His **Servingmen**
Conspirators with Aufidius
Volscian **Lords**
Volscian **Citizens**
Soldiers in the Volscian army
Adrian *a Volscian*
Nicanor *a Roman*

A Roman **Herald**
Messengers
Aediles
A gentleman, an usher, Roman
and Volscian senators and
nobles, captains in the Roman
army, officers, lictors

☰ SYNOPSIS

1.1 Mutinous Roman citizens have banded together to avenge their hunger on the aristocrat Caius Martius, but are intercepted by Menenius, a more sympathetic patrician, who attempts to dissuade them from rebellion by telling a fable of how the parts of the body once mistakenly rose against the belly, accusing it unjustly of selfish greed. Martius himself arrives and harangues the citizens, wishing the Senate would let him kill them, and regretting that they have instead conceded the people two tribunes as representatives, Sicinius and Brutus. News arrives that a Volscian army is approaching Rome, and the senators, arriving with the tribunes, appoint an eager Martius as second-in-command under Cominius to lead a Roman force against the Volsces and their leader, Martius' arch-enemy Tullus Aufidius. Left alone, Sicinius and Brutus resolve to watch Martius, sworn enemy of their political interests, carefully.

1.2 The senators of the Volscian city Corioles, aware that the Romans have sent an army to meet their attack, send Aufidius and his troops to meet it.

1.3 Volumnia, Martius' mother, is sewing with his wife Virgilia. Delighting in Martius' military record, Volumnia has no sympathy with Virgilia's anxieties about his safety, nor, when her friend Valeria arrives to invite them out, with her refusal to leave the house while her husband is away. Valeria congratulates Virgilia on the resemblance between Martius and his young son (whom she has recently watched chasing and dismembering a butterfly), and has heard that Martius, along with his fellow commander Titus Lartius, is now besieging Corioles while Cominius leads the other half of the Roman army against the Volscian expeditionary force.

1.4–8 At the battlefront Martius reverses a Roman retreat, haranguing his soldiers and leading them into the Volscian city: the gates close behind him alone, but he survives to lead the successful taking of Corioles. Though wounded, he then joins Cominius' temporarily withdrawing force, leading a fresh and decisive assault on Aufidius' army.

1.9 Martius duels with Aufidius, driving back both him and the unwelcome fellow Volscians who take his part.

1.10 Before the victorious Roman army Cominius, despite Martius' complaints that he hates to be praised, gives Martius the title of Coriolanus for his deeds.

1.11 Aufidius, disgusted by the peace terms the Volscians have had to accept, determines to destroy his vanquisher Martius by any means, honourable or not.

2.1 Menenius is bickering with the tribunes about Martius' vices when Volumnia brings the news of his victory: to Virgilia's horror they gleefully count up how many scars he now bears. Martius, garlanded with oak and ceremonially renamed Coriolanus, is triumphantly welcomed into the city with Cominius, Lartius, and the army, and they set off for the Capitol: the tribunes, anxious that their enemy will be made consul, resolve to prevent this by provoking Coriolanus into alienating the people.

2.2 In the Capitol, Cominius gives an oration about Coriolanus' heroic deeds, which Coriolanus himself refuses to hear: the Senate name him as a consul, but this, to Coriolanus' distaste, will oblige him to appeal to the people for their acceptance by showing them the wounds he has received in their defence.

2.3 Wearing the gown of humility, Coriolanus is brought to the market place by Menenius, where he unwillingly and disdainfully requests the people's voices, which they give. After his departure, however, the tribunes persuade them to change their minds.

3.1 On their way to his investiture, Coriolanus and the senators are stopped by the tribunes, who tell him the people have withdrawn their consent: infuriated, Coriolanus rages at them, asserting that the people do not deserve political representation, and the tribunes, supported by a crowd of citizens, attempt to arrest him for treason. After a scuffle Coriolanus is persuaded to withdraw, while Menenius promises the tribunes that Coriolanus will soon answer the people's accusations in the market place.

3.2 At a patrician's house Volumnia rebukes her son for prematurely exposing his political objectives: she and the senators persuade him to speak mildly to the assembled people in order to regain the consulship he has nearly lost.

3.3 In the market place, however, the tribunes' accusations of treason goad Coriolanus into ranting against the people once more, and he is sentenced to banishment.

4.1 A stoical Coriolanus bids farewell to Volumnia, Virgilia, Menenius, Cominius, and the patricians.

4.2 Volumnia rails against the gloating tribunes.

4.3 A Roman informer tells a Volscian of Coriolanus' banishment, certain the news will encourage the regrouping Volscian army to launch a fresh attack on Rome.

4.4 Disguised, Coriolanus arrives in the Volscian city of Antium, and seeks out Tullus Aufidius.

4.5 Refusing to be denied entry by servants, Coriolanus reveals himself to Aufidius and announces that he wishes to defect to the Volscians and avenge himself on Rome. Aufidius welcomes him eagerly, to the amazement of the servants, who fear that Coriolanus will displace their master.

4.6 The mutual congratulations of Roman tribunes and people are interrupted by the news that a Volscian army, led by Coriolanus, is approaching: Menenius tells them they have deserved their impending destruction.

4.7 Aufidius, warned by his lieutenant that he appears to be Coriolanus' subordinate in their campaign, confides that he is only waiting for Coriolanus either to defeat or to refuse to attack Rome before moving against him.

5.1 Cominius returns from a wholly unsuccessful attempt to persuade Coriolanus to spare Rome, and Menenius sets off on another such embassy.

5.2 Menenius, though scorned by the Volscian watchmen, gains access to Coriolanus and Aufidius, but Coriolanus refuses to yield to his plea for mercy.

5.3 Watched by Aufidius, Coriolanus receives one last embassy from Rome before the next day's attack: Virgilia, Volumnia, Valeria, and his son Young Martius. Though he greets them with duty and love, he resolves not to accede to their request. Volumnia pleads eloquently for mercy, and at the conclusion of her speech she, Virgilia, Valeria, and Young Martius kneel before him: finally Coriolanus holds Volumnia silently by the hand before conceding, crying, that he will make peace, however dangerously to himself.

5.4 Menenius is assuring Sicinius that Coriolanus will not yield to his mother when the news arrives that he has done so.

5.5 Volumnia, Virgilia, and Valeria are welcomed back into Rome in triumph.

5.6 In Corioles, Aufidius rallies his supporters before Coriolanus arrives to report to the Volscian lords his success in obtaining a submissive peace from the Romans. Aufidius accuses him of treachery for calling off the Volscian attack at his mother's entreaty, and further provokes him by calling him 'boy': the enraged Coriolanus reminds Aufidius how often he has scarred him, and of his many victories against the Volscians. Despite the lords' attempts to keep the peace, the Volscian people cry out for Coriolanus' death: two of Aufidius' party fatally stab him and the rest, along with Aufidius, trample his corpse. Aufidius seeks to justify the killing, but, subsiding, grants that despite the casualties he inflicted on Corioles, Coriolanus should be buried with full military honours.

 ARTISTIC FEATURES

The play is unusual for the single-mindedness with which its action builds up to a single, decisive, wordless moment, Coriolanus' yielding to Volumnia (5.3.183), while its virtuoso crowd scenes almost make the Roman people into its hero's single collective antagonist. The play has a distinctively harsh and gritty vocabulary and poetic tone throughout, thriving on rough monosyllables.

CRITICAL HISTORY

William Hazlitt's essay on the play, in *Characters of Shakespear's Plays* (1817), continues to set the agenda of much discussion of the play's political concerns. Hazlitt praises the thoroughness with which Shakespeare articulates the rival claims of aristocracy and democracy ('anyone who studies [*Coriolanus*] may save himself the trouble of reading Burke's *Reflections*, or Paine's *Rights of Man*, or the debates in both Houses of Parliament since the French Revolution or our own'), though he fears that *Coriolanus* demonstrates that poetry is innately liable to prefer dictators to the abstract claims of social justice. Before Hazlitt, commentators had tended to complain—as in their different ways did adaptors—of what Dr Johnson called the excessive 'bustle' of the early scenes and the inadequate business of the last, which John Dennis and other neoclassical critics had also accused of violating poetic justice. During the 19th century and the first part of the 20th much criticism of the play was similarly dedicated to showing how and why it was inferior to the earlier tragedies, with A. C. Bradley commenting on the critical distance Shakespeare maintains between audience and characters by ironic humour and Harley Granville-Barker praising the play's supreme, focused craftsmanship at the expense of its vitality. Frank Harris pioneered one recurrent strain in 20th-century criticism in *The Women in Shakespeare* (1911) when he claimed that the intense mother–son bond between Coriolanus and Volumnia must have had a basis in Shakespeare's own experience, and since the advent of Freud many commentators have applied a psycho-analytic vocabulary, with greater and lesser degrees of sophistication, to the exploration of the relationship between the play's protagonist and the most fully developed older woman in the canon: the most influential example would be Janet Adelman. Since then, the play has been of interest to a great variety of approaches from the medical humanities, the history of emotions, and conflict studies.

STAGE HISTORY

Apart from the early allusions by Armin and Jonson, there are no records of specific performances of the play before the 1680s, and its stage history thereafter is largely one of more and less propagandist adaptations until the early 19th century: Nahum Tate's anti-Whig *The Ingratitude of a Commonwealth* (1681), John Dennis's anti-Jacobite *The Invader of his Country* (1719), in which Coriolanus becomes a figure for the banished Stuarts, and, later, Thomas Sheridan's version, *Coriolanus; or, The Roman Matron* (1754). This hybrid of Shakespeare's play and James Thomson's 1748 work on the same subject was still being used, in successively rewritten forms, by J. P. Kemble for his highly successful productions (with himself in the title role and Sarah Siddons as Volumnia) between 1789 and 1817. It became Kemble's favourite role, his own perceived arrogance and singularity in the face of his mass audience's expectations finding its perfect counterpart in Martius' imperious defiance of the Roman mob. Occasional attempts at reviving the original—in 1719, 1754, and, with Edmund Kean as Coriolanus, in 1820—were unsuccessful, but it returned to the repertory when William Charles Macready took the title role at Covent Garden in 1838, a part in which he was succeeded by Samuel Phelps in 1848. Frank Benson played Coriolanus with some success between 1893 and 1910, but the role was a disaster for Henry Irving, who chose it as his final Shakespearian role at the Lyceum (with an equally miscast Ellen Terry as Volumnia) in 1901. Over the 19th century as a whole the play was more successful in the republican United States, where the original had supplanted the Sheridan version (staged in Philadelphia in 1767) as early as 1796. It was the highly physical and aggressive Edwin Forrest's greatest role, from 1831 to 1863, and he was even sculpted in the part, though some commentators preferred his successor John E. McCullough, who played Coriolanus in a more intellectually superior style in 1878.

Despite some notable revivals at the Old Vic in the 1920s, the play did not enjoy particular prominence in the 20th century until the rise of fascist movements across Europe brought it a renewed topicality. In France in 1934 the Action Française party induced the Comédie-Française to stage a version of the play which treated it as an all-out attack on democracy (stimulating violent demonstrations outside the theatre, though these failed to provoke the hoped-for military coup), and in Moscow the following year a version approved by Stalin's propagandists instead treated Coriolanus as a wholly contemptible, aristocratic, Western-style enemy of the people. The Nazis' enthusiasm for the play, which they regarded as a hymn to strong leadership, led to its banning in occupied Germany until 1953: Bertolt Brecht's anti-Coriolanus adaptation was not acted until 1963, seven years after his death. Back in England, where attitudes to the play's protagonist have been more ambivalent, Laurence Olivier achieved one of his greatest successes as Coriolanus, with Sybil Thorndike as Volumnia, at the Old Vic in 1938, a role he repeated in Peter Hall's production at Stratford in 1959, with Edith Evans as his mother. With characteristic physical bravado Olivier made Coriolanus' death resemble the throwing from the Tarpeian rock threatened earlier by the tribunes, falling precipitately from an upper stage to dangle upside down by his ankles. His notable successors in the role have included Richard Burton (at the Old Vic in 1954), Alan Howard (at Stratford and on an acclaimed international tour in 1977), Ian McKellen (in Peter Hall's uneasy modern-dress production in the National Theatre's Olivier auditorium, with a powerful Irene Worth as Volumnia, 1984), Kenneth Branagh (outclassed by Judi Dench's Volumnia at Chichester in 1992) and Toby Stephens, who played Coriolanus as a sneering Regency public-school prefect in David Thacker's RSC production, with Caroline Blakiston as Volumnia, in 1994. This intelligent production was one of very few to produce the play in neither modern nor Roman dress, taking up an idea of Hazlitt's by setting the production in the era of the French Revolution. In homage to Peter Hall's 1959 production at the same venue, Gregory Doran's 2007 Coriolanus, with William Houston in the title role and Janet Suzman as Volumnia, was the last RSC production staged in the proscenium-arch Royal Shakespeare Theatre before its remodelling. In 2013 the fan frenzy around Tom Hiddleston ensured that Josie Rourke's Donmar Warehouse production was packed to the rafters each night, though it was broadcast to cinemas around the world to relieve some of the pressure on the building's aching joints and the bereft souls out in the cold.

 ON THE SCREEN

The play was serialized in three parts of The Spread of the Eagle series (1963) for BBC TV. The BBC TV production (1983) featured Alan Howard and Irene Worth. Ralph Fiennes directed himself in the title role of a stirring modern-dress version in 2011, filmed in the Balkans, with Vanessa Redgrave as Volumnia.

Cymbeline, King of Britain

Intricately and eclectically plotted, and producing in its last scene the most elaborate series of revelations and surprises in the canon as it snatches its multiple happy endings from the jaws of several disasters, *Cymbeline* belongs to the Jacobean vogue for tragicomedy which began with the success of Francis Beaumont and John Fletcher's *Philaster* in 1609. *Cymbeline* and *Philaster* are in fact closely related, and it seems most likely that Shakespeare's play was influenced by the work of his two younger colleagues—with one of whom he would later collaborate on *All Is True* (*Henry VIII*), *The Two Noble Kinsmen*, and possibly the lost *Cardenio*. Simon Forman records seeing *Cymbeline* performed in April 1611, when it was probably relatively new: unlike *Pericles* and *The Winter's Tale* it nowhere echoes the writings of Plutarch which Shakespeare had consulted so heavily when composing *Timon of Athens*, *Antony and Cleopatra*, and *Coriolanus*, so it was probably composed later than both of these previous experiments with the romance genre, in 1610.

 TEXT

The play first appeared in print in the Folio in 1623, where its text provides the first recorded instance of the name 'Imogen': one of Shakespeare's sources for the play, however, the ancient British section of Holinshed's *Chronicles*, tells of an Innogen (wife of the legendary Brute), a name Shakespeare had earlier given to Leonato's non-speaking wife in the opening stage direction of *Much Ado About Nothing*. Since Forman's eyewitness account of seeing *Cymbeline* performed refers to its female protagonist as 'Innogen' throughout, it is almost certain that Shakespeare actually called his heroine Innogen, and that the spelling 'Imogen' only appears in the Folio through scribal or compositorial error. Otherwise the Folio text is a good one: variations in spelling, and a high incidence of parentheses (even in stage directions), suggest that it was set from a scribal copy, probably by Ralph Crane, of an earlier transcript (whether of foul papers or a prompt-book) prepared by more than one scribe.

 SOURCES

Cymbeline combines three distinct plot lines, concerning, respectively, Cymbeline's dealings with the Romans, the wager on Innogen's chastity, and the exile of Belarius. Shakespeare's information about the semi-legendary king, supposed to have ascended the British throne in 33 BC, came from Holinshed's *Chronicles*, as did the account of the heroic defence of a narrow pass attributed in the play to Belarius, Guiderius, and Arviragus but deriving from an incident at the battle of Loncart (976: this is described in the Scottish section of the work which Shakespeare had consulted when writing *Macbeth*). Other minor details show that Shakespeare had also read the account of Guiderius in the second part of *A Mirror for Magistrates* (1578) and Robert Fabyan's *New Chronicle of England and of France* (1516). More centrally, the wager plot comes from Boccaccio's *Decameron* (where it provides the ninth story on the second day), though Shakespeare draws some of its details from a version called *Frederyke of Jennen* (first printed in Dutch in 1518, translated into English in 1520, and reprinted in 1560). Much of the other material dramatized in the play—including the banishment of the hero, the jealousy of his foolish rival, and the flight of the heroine to an unjustly banished courtier's cave—derives from an anonymous Elizabethan play, *Rare Triumphs of Love and Fortune*, performed in 1582 and published in 1589.

 CHARACTER LIST

Cymbeline, King of Britain
Princess **Innogen** *his daughter, later disguised as a man named Fidele*
Guiderius, known as Polydore ⎤
Arviragus, known as Cadwal ⎦ *Cymbeline's sons, stolen by Belarius*
Queen *Cymbeline's wife, Innogen's stepmother*
Lord **Cloten** *her son*

Belarius *a banished lord, calling himself Morgan*
Cornelius *a physician*
Helen *a lady attending on Innogen*
Two **Lords** attending on Cloten
Two **Gentlemen**
Two British **Captains**
Two **Jailers**
Posthumus Leonatus *a poor gentleman, husband to Innogen*

Pisanio *his servant*
Filario *a friend of Posthumus*
Giacomo *an Italian* ⌉
A Frenchman   *Filario's*
A Dutchman   *friends*
A Spaniard ⌋
Caius **Lucius** *ambassador from Rome, later General of the Roman forces*
Two Roman **Senators**
Roman **Tribunes**

Roman **Captain**
Philharmonus, a **Soothsayer**
Jupiter
Ghost of **Sicilius** Leonatus *father of Posthumus*
Ghost of the **Mother** of Posthumus
Ghosts of the **Brothers** of Posthumus
Lords attending on Cymbeline, ladies attending on the Queen, musicians attending on Cloten, messengers, soldiers

⠿ SYNOPSIS

1.1 Innogen, sole remaining child of King Cymbeline (her two elder brothers having been abducted in infancy), has married the commoner Leonatus Posthumus, preferring him to her stepmother's foolish son Cloten. Her parting from the banished Posthumus—during which she gives him a diamond ring and he her a bracelet—is interrupted, thanks to the Queen's machinations, by the angry Cymbeline. At Posthumus' insistence his servant Pisanio remains with Innogen while he embarks for Rome.

1.2 Cloten, loser of a sword-skirmish with the departing Posthumus, is flattered by two lords who confide their actual contempt for him to the audience.

1.3 Pisanio describes Posthumus' departure to the yearning Innogen.

1.4 In Rome, Posthumus speaks with a Frenchman and an Italian, Giacomo, about the relative chastity of their countrywomen: despite the objections of his host Filario, Posthumus bets the mocking Italian the diamond ring and 10,000 ducats that Giacomo will be unable to seduce Innogen.

1.5 The Queen obtains what she thinks is lethal poison from the doctor Cornelius, though he, not trusting her, supplies a drug which induces only a deathlike trance: she gives it to Pisanio, saying It is a powerful medicine.

1.6 Giacomo arrives at the British court and almost convinces Innogen that Posthumus is unfaithful before his offer of himself as a replacement alerts her to his ulterior motives. Giacomo claims he was only attempting her virtue to test her, mollifies her by praising Posthumus, and persuades her to look after his trunk in her private chamber.

2.1 Cloten, angry after losing at bowls, is again mocked behind his back by two flattering lords.

2.2 After Innogen retires to bed and falls asleep, Giacomo emerges from the trunk and takes notes about the room's decor before stealing the bracelet from her arm: in doing so he further notices a distinctive mole on Innogen's left breast, before returning undetected to the trunk.

2.3 The following morning Cloten employs musicians to serenade Innogen (with the song 'Hark, hark, the lark'): antagonized by his insults to Posthumus and anxious about the loss of her bracelet, she tells him he is less valuable than Posthumus' meanest garment.

2.4 Back in Rome Giacomo, showing the bracelet and describing Innogen's mole, persuades Posthumus she has betrayed him, and is given the ring.

2.5 The enraged Posthumus rails against all women.

3.1 The Roman ambassador Caius Lucius demands payment of the annual tribute Cymbeline owes to Augustus Caesar: at the Queen's instigation he refuses, and Lucius regretfully declares war.

3.2 To his horror, Pisanio has received a letter from Posthumus instructing him to kill Innogen for her alleged infidelity, using the opportunity his letter to her will provide. This letter, which Pisanio gives Innogen, claims Posthumus is waiting for her at Milford Haven in Wales, towards which she is impatient to flee.

3.3 Outside their Welsh cave, Belarius warns his untravelled sons Polydore and Cadwal against the vices of court life: when they have gone hunting, he confides to the audience that though brought up to think he is their father they are really Guiderius and Arviragus, Cymbeline's sons, whom he stole 20 years earlier to avenge his unjust banishment.

3.4 Near Milford, Pisanio is unable to carry out Posthumus' orders, which he shows to Innogen: outraged, she renounces Posthumus and implores Pisanio to kill her as instructed. Pisanio tells her he is sure Posthumus has been deceived, but means to placate him for the time being by sending a bloodstained piece of clothing, as requested, as evidence that Innogen is dead: meanwhile he advises her to get to Rome by disguising herself as a boy and taking service as a page with Caius Lucius, who will shortly be at Milford. Leaving, he gives her the so-called medicine he had from the Queen.

3.5 Cymbeline, the Queen, and Cloten part from Caius Lucius: the King's preparations for war are distracted by the news that Innogen has vanished. Pisanio, interrogated by Cloten, shows him the letter inviting Innogen to Milford. Cloten resolves to avenge Innogen's earlier remark by dressing in some of Posthumus' clothes, going to Milford, and there killing Posthumus and raping Innogen.

3.6 Dressed as a man a hungry Innogen, now calling herself Fidele, finds Belarius' cave, where Belarius, Guiderius, and Arviragus make her welcome.

3.7 In Rome recruitment is afoot for Lucius' campaign against Britain.

4.1 Cloten, dressed as Posthumus, is near Milford.

4.2 Innogen remains at the cave while the men go hunting: she feels unwell, and takes the Queen's drug. The men see Cloten, and while Belarius and Arviragus check he is not part of a whole party seeking them, Guiderius, provoked, fights with him and decapitates him. Belarius is horrified, though Guiderius unrepentantly throws the head into a river. Arviragus finds Fidele apparently dead in the cave: sorrowfully he and Guiderius lay out the corpse and recite a dirge, 'Fear no more the heat of the sun'. Belarius lays Cloten's headless body alongside before the three depart. Innogen regains consciousness to find what she thinks is her husband's headless corpse, concluding that Pisanio and Cloten must have conspired against her. Lucius, passing by to Milford (where he expects troops from Rome led by Giacomo), is touched by what seems to be the sorrow of a page over his dead master, and takes Fidele into his service.

4.3 At court the Queen is sick with anxiety at Cloten's absence. Cymbeline learns that Roman troops have landed, but Pisanio has heard nothing from either Posthumus or Innogen.

4.4 Belarius, Guiderius, and Arviragus, despite Belarius' fear of being recognized, resolve to join the British army.

5.1 Posthumus, carrying the bloody cloth Pisanio sent, has come to Britain with the Roman army: repenting of Innogen's death, he takes off his Italian clothes and resolves to fight on the British side.

5.2 In battle, Posthumus, dressed like a peasant, defeats but spares a guilt-stricken Giacomo, who does not recognize him.

5.3–4 Cymbeline is captured but rescued by Belarius, Guiderius, Arviragus, and Posthumus: the Romans retreat.

5.5 Posthumus narrates to a British lord how Belarius, Guiderius, and Arviragus reversed a British retreat down a narrow lane into a victorious renewed assault. He decides to dress as a Roman again in the hopes of dying at British hands, and is taken prisoner. Jailed, he prays for death, imploring Innogen's forgiveness before falling asleep. In a vision the ghosts of his father, mother, and two brothers appear and call to Jupiter on his behalf. Jupiter descends in thunder, promises that he has not forsaken Posthumus, and gives the ghosts a tablet which they lay on Posthumus' breast before disappearing. Waking, Posthumus reads the riddling tablet, which he is unable to interpret, before, after bantering with his miserable jailer, he is called before Cymbeline.

5.6 Cymbeline is rewarding Belarius, Guiderius, and Arviragus for their deeds in battle, unable to find their unknown comrade Posthumus, when Cornelius brings the news both of the Queen's death and of her dying confession that she had planned to kill both Innogen and Cymbeline in her bid to make Cloten king. Lucius, Giacomo, a soothsayer, Posthumus, and Innogen, still dressed as Fidele, are brought in as captives, expecting to be killed: Lucius successfully pleads that Fidele should be spared. Instead of begging for Lucius' life in return, however, Innogen has recognized Giacomo, and with Cymbeline's support demands to know how he obtained the ring he is wearing. Giacomo confesses how he cheated in his wager with Posthumus, at which the enraged Posthumus steps forward, striking Innogen down when she tries to interrupt him: Pisanio, however, has recognized her and makes her known, though, reviving, she accuses him of giving her poison. Cornelius explains the nature of the drug he gave the Queen, which on her deathbed she had mentioned giving to Pisanio. Posthumus, Innogen, and Cymbeline embrace. Pisanio now explains where Cloten went, and Guiderius completes his narrative by boasting of having killed him. Cymbeline sentences him to death, but Belarius intervenes by revealing the true identities of himself, Guiderius, and Arviragus, to the delight of Cymbeline and Innogen, whom Belarius and the princes have already recognized as Fidele. Cymbeline spares all the remaining prisoners: Posthumus is recognized as the unknown soldier who spared Giacomo in battle, and now spares him again despite his penitent willingness to die for his crimes: and Lucius' soothsayer interprets the tablet as a prediction of the reunion of Cymbeline's family. Cymbeline embraces peace by deciding to resume paying tribute to Rome.

ARTISTIC FEATURES

The difficulty and complexity of the play's plotting is matched by an unusual density and knottiness of syntax, from which some of *Cymbeline*'s most famously simple and affecting passages (notably the dirge, 'Fear no more the heat of the sun') can seem a relief. It is at once one of the most puzzlingly uncertain in tone, and one of the most weirdly affecting, of Shakespeare's later plays.

CRITICAL HISTORY

Eighteenth-century comments on the play, like 18th-century adaptations (see below), predictably object to the unclassical irregularities of its plotting: Dr Johnson famously observed that 'to remark the folly of the fiction, the absurdity of the conduct, the confusion of the names and manners of different times, and the impossibility of the events in any system of life, were to waste criticism upon unresisting imbecility, upon faults too evident for detection, and too gross for aggravation' (1765). (This did not, however, prevent contemporary engravers from choosing Giacomo's voyeurism in Innogen's chamber as one of the most frequently illustrated scenes from the late plays.) The Victorians were willing to forgive many of the play's perceived faults for the sake of Innogen ('undoubtedly one of the most exquisite of all Shakespeare's female creations', wrote Thomas Kenny in 1864), while the 20th century was more interested in explaining them by reference to the play's contexts both in the politics of the Jacobean court and in the last phase of Shakespeare's career. In terms of content, the play's interests in British unification, in imperial peace, in the masque, and even in Milford Haven—where James I's dynastic ancestor Henry VII came ashore to claim the throne—have all been explored in relation to James's cultural and political agendas: in style, its tragicomic experimentations with shocking incongruity, and its self-conscious reuse of motifs from earlier works in the Shakespeare canon (whether Juliet's potion, Othello's jealousy or Lear's loved and lost youngest daughter), have been related to similar techniques deployed less conspicuously in the other late romances. New directions have theorized *Cymbeline* as an indoor play, thinking through its spectacles and the technologies used to represent them. Feminist criticism has explored issues of agency, sexual violence, and consent, and queer approaches to the text have stressed the play's focus on ideas of representation. The play was strangely reanimated by the UK's drawn-out debate over its withdrawal from the European Union. Brexiteers found a fondness for the immovable affirmation that 'Britain is / A world by itself; and we will nothing pay / For wearing our own noses'—apparently forgetting that these lines are spoken by Cloten, a boorish, would-be rapist.

 STAGE HISTORY

Simon Forman's account of the play does not indicate where he saw it, though the masque-like special effects of 5.5 suggest it may have been written with the indoor Blackfriars theatre in mind. It was revived at court for Charles I and Henrietta Maria in 1634, but was displaced later in the century by Thomas Durfey's adaptation *The Injured Princess, or, The Fatal Wager* (1682), in which Giacomo becomes a splendidly louche Restoration rake. In 1746 the original returned to the stage (despite William Hawkins's adaptation of 1759), and in a moderately cut and transposed text David Garrick made Posthumus one of his best-loved Shakespearian roles from 1761 until his retirement: Kemble was equally successful in the part, with Sarah Siddons as his slandered bride. In the 19th century Imogen (as she was then known), both innocent and married, was one of Shakespeare's favourite heroines, attracting actresses such as Helen Faucit (who played the part for nearly 30 years, from 1837 to 1865) and Ellen Terry (with Irving as Iachimo [Giacomo], 1896). Over the next 50 years, though, the play's combination of artifice and enchantment fell from favour, and despite Peggy Ashcroft's two triumphs as Imogen (at the Old Vic in 1932, and at Stratford, in a fairy tale-style production by Peter Hall, in 1957) few 20th-century productions were conspicuous successes: modern dress, then novel, did not help the play in Barry Jackson's Birmingham production of 1923 (derisively called 'Shakespeare in plus-fours'), and B. Iden-Payne's critically acclaimed attempt to direct the play on sets derived from Jacobean masques (Stratford, 1937) did not dissuade George Bernard Shaw from producing his own critical rewriting of the last act, *Cymbeline Refinished*, in which Imogen is much less willing to forgive Posthumus for trying to kill her. John Barton tried without success to make *Cymbeline* into a 'state of England' play in the oil crisis year of 1974, alluding in his production's designs to the vast refinery that now dominates Milford, and it is an index to directors' continuing lack of confidence in the play that a subsequent RSC revival, directed by Adrian Noble in 1997, modified the script to supply a narrator. Kneehigh's superbly inventive 2006 production, as part of the RSC's Complete Works Festival, similarly crowbarred in a narrator, a pantomime dame called Joan, just returning after 30 years in the Costa del Sol to find the country precariously poised as it is at the play's opening. In 2012, Yukio Ninagawa brought his lavish, fairy-tale-like production to the Barbican, where the play was presented with the grand, almost filmic visual beauty characteristic of his company. During the run-up to, and aftermath of, the UK's Brexit vote, both the Globe (2015, dir., Sam Yates) and the RSC mounted productions of *Cymbeline* (2016, dir., Melly Still). Revived in the indoor Sam Wanamaker theatre as part of a wider season of late plays, Yates's production emphasized *Cymbeline*'s comedic elements. Still's post-Brexit dystopia, on the other hand, opted for a very different register. Recasting Cymbeline as a queen, Gillian Bevan's gender added a new dimension to the rule of this graffitied, dismal land and cast new light on the play's wishful tale of family reunion.

 ## ON THE SCREEN

A 45-minute TV version (1937) was one of the earliest British TV Shakespeare transmissions. Other TV productions include one from the USA (1981), one from Belgium (1981), and Elijah Moshinsky's BBC TV production (1982) with Helen Mirren as Imogen, generally regarded as one of the best of the BBC series. Michael Almereyda directed the first major Hollywood studio version (2014), alternatively titled *Anarchy*, with Ed Harris as Cymbeline, Ethan Hawke as Iachimo, and Dakota Johnson as Imogen in a modern-day setting of the play (the tagline on the poster read 'Kings, Queens, Soldiers, Bikers, War').

The First Part of the Contention of the Two Famous Houses of York and Lancaster (*2 Henry VI*)

This play was originally known and performed as *The First Part of the Contention of the Two Famous Houses of Lancaster and York, with the Death of the Good Duke Humphrey*, a title supplied by its first published version, printed in 1594. The second title is probably editorial and comes from the more familiar text of the play, longer by about a third, published in the 1623 First Folio. Like the titles of the other plays about Henry's reign, the title *2 Henry VI* was given when the Folio presented all of the English histories in chronological order of their kings, even though Shakespeare did not compose the plays in this sequence. *The Contention* was written in 1590–1 as the first of two parts. Its final scenes directly anticipate the opening of *Richard Duke of York* (*3 Henry VI*), written in 1591 and published In 1595. It was composed after the second edition of Raphael Holinshed's *Chronicles* (1587, see below), and probably after publication of Edmund Spenser's *The Faerie Queene* (1590). In September 1592 the playwright Robert Greene parodied a line from *Richard Duke of York* (1.4.138) when deriding Shakespeare as someone 'with a tiger's heart wrapped in a player's hide'. His allusion indicates that *The Contention* had also been written prior to this date and before the theatres were closed because of the plague on 23 June. On 3 March the manager-owner of the Rose theatre, Philip Henslowe, records a 'new' performance of 'Harry the VI' in his diary. Conceivably, this entry may refer to any of the three *Henry VI* plays. But contextual evidence suggests it refers only to *Part 1*, which must have been written by August 1592, when Thomas Nashe admired its inspiring heroism in *Piers Penniless his Supplication to the Devil*. If that is the case, *The Contention* and *Richard Duke of York* would have to have been written and performed between March and June. But this period has struck some, but not all, scholars as unrealistically brief, thus leading to the alternative theory that Shakespeare wrote *The Contention* before *1 Henry VI*. This explains several historical inconsistencies between the plays that one would not expect to find if the latter had come first, in particular the fact that *The Contention* makes no mention of *Part 1*'s ostensible hero, Talbot.

 TEXT

The play was attributed to Shakespeare prior to the 1623 Folio by the title page of the unauthorized Pavier quarto of 1619 (Q3), which presented both *The Contention* and *Richard Duke of York* as *The Whole Contention between the Two Famous Houses, Lancaster and York*. From the late 18th century, however, Shakespeare's whole or part authorship began to be contested, and many recent editors continue to accept the possibility that Shakespeare may have collaborated with Greene, Nashe, George Peele, and even Christopher Marlowe. Multiple authorship might explain Francis Meres's failure to mention *Henry VI* in *Palladis Tamia* (1598), which lists other—but not all—known Shakespeare plays. Other modern editors believe Shakespeare was the sole author of *The Contention* and that the *Henry VI* plays were written in chronological order. Certain passages may sound like Greene, etc., because as a young playwright Shakespeare followed the normal early modern practice of imitating fashionable verbal styles as he was developing his own. However, recent stylometric studies suggest plausibly that Christopher Marlowe himself is present as a co-author in the Jack Cade scenes (4.2–10).

Q1 of *The Contention* was entered in the Stationers' Register on 12 March 1594 and printed that year. A second edition published in 1600 (Q2) was based on Q1, as was the Pavier edition (Q3) in 1619. The provenance of Q1 has been questioned since the 18th century. One theory proposed by Edmond Malone in 1790, was that Shakespeare revised and expanded Q1, which he believed was written by Greene and/or others. Alternatively, Dr Johnson and Edward Capell speculated that Q1 was some kind of report of the Folio text made from memory or shorthand. A. W. Pollard supported this view in 1909 by dividing Shakespeare quarto editions into 'Good' legitimate texts, and 'Bad' unauthorized and corrupt ones. In 1928 Madeleine Doran argued that Q1 was deliberately revised and shortened for touring performances outside London, and (independently) in 1929 Peter Alexander demonstrated that it was constructed from memory by actors who had performed the Folio version (probably Pembroke's Men after their collapse in August 1593, when they lost possession of the original playbooks). Alexander's thesis remains the accepted explanation of Q1's origins, notwithstanding valuable corrective challenges to the universal applicability of memorial reporting and to Pollard's morally inflected terminology. While Doran's arguments have also been accepted, with modifications, the derivation and purpose of Q1's often detailed stage directions continue to be disputed (namely they may be intended for readers), as do the reductions in playing personnel achieved by Q1.

Most modern scholars believe the Folio text is based on Shakespeare's manuscript, since several missing, imprecise, or discretionary stage directions suggest a draft, still open to revision, rather than a finished state or fair copy. Shakespeare also possibly revised several passages in the Folio manuscript at a later stage in his career (e.g. Clifford's speech at 5.3.31–49). Minor adjustments in the Folio, such as its elimination of Q1's Buckingham, may reflect topical political sensitivities. At several points the Folio typesetters consulted Q3 because the manuscript copy was unclear.

SOURCES

The Contention is the first of Shakespeare's English history plays to make use of Edward Halle's *Union of the Two Noble and Illustrious Families of Lancaster and York* (1548), and the compilation edited by Raphael Holinshed, *Chronicles of England, Scotland, and Ireland* (2nd edn. 1587). The established view is that Halle—traditionally regarded as more ideologically conservative—was Shakespeare's chief source, but recent scholarship has shifted the balance towards Holinshed. Shakespeare's presentation of Cade's rebellion in Act 4 draws on their accounts of the Peasants' Revolt of 1381. The story of Simpcox's false miracle in 2.1 is from John Foxe's *Acts and Monuments* (the *Book of Martyrs*). Details of Eleanor Cobham's penance in 2.4 derive from a possible range of Elizabethan accounts, including *The Mirror for Magistrates*. Robert Fabyan's *New Chronicles of England and France* (1516) is another minor source.

CHARACTER LIST

Of the King's Party
King Henry VI
Queen Margaret
William de la Pole, Marquis,
   later Duke, of **Suffolk**
   the Queen's lover
Duke Humphrey, Duke of
   Gloucester, the Lord Protector
   the King's uncle

Dame Eleanor Cobham, **Duchess**
   of Gloucester
Cardinal Beaufort, Bishop of
   Winchester *Gloucester's*
   uncle and the King's
   great-uncle
Duke of **Buckingham**
Duke of **Somerset**
Old Lord **Clifford**

Young Clifford his son

Of the Duke of York's Party
Duke of **York**
Edward, Earl of March ⎤
Richard, Duke of ⎥ his sons
   Gloucester ⎦
Earl of **Salisbury**
Earl of **Warwick** his son

The petitions and the combat
Two or three **Petitioners**
Thomas **Horner** an armourer
Peter Thump his man
Three **Neighbours** who drink
   to Horner
Three **Prentices** who drink
   to Peter

The conjuration
Sir John **Hume** ⎤
John **Southwell** ⎦ priests

Margery Jordan, a **Witch**
Roger **Bolingbroke** a conjurer
Asnath a spirit

The false miracle
Simon **Simpcox**
Simpcox's Wife
The **Mayor** of St Albans
Aldermen of Saint Albans
A **Beadle** of Saint Albans
Townsmen of Saint Albans

Eleanor's penance
Gloucester's **Servants**
Two **Sherrifs** of London
Sir John **Stanley**
Herald

The murder of Gloucester
Two **Murderers**
Commons

The murder of Suffolk
Captain of a ship
Master of that ship
The Master's **Mate**
Walter **Whitmore**
Two **Gentlemen**

The Cade Rebellion
Jack **Cade** a Kentishman suborned by
   the Duke of York

Dick, **the Butcher** ⎤
Smith, the **Weaver** ⎥ Cade's
A **Sawyer** ⎥ followers
John ⎥
Rebels ⎦

Emmanuel, the **Clerk** of Chatham
Sir Humphrey **Stafford** ⎤ those
Safford's Brother ⎥ who
Lord **Saye** ⎥ die at
Lord **Scales** ⎥ the
Matthew Gough ⎥ rebels'
A **Sergeant** ⎦ hands

Three or four **Citizens** of London
Alexander **Iden** an esquire of Kent,
   who kills Cade

Others
Vaux
A **Post**
Messengers
A **Soldier**
Attendants, guards, servants,
   soldiers, falconers

⦂☰ SYNOPSIS

1.1 Suffolk presents Margaret of Anjou to the English court, having wooed her by proxy for King Henry. Her lack of a dowry and the negotiated repatriation of Anjou and Maine to the French appal Gloucester.

Winchester and Buckingham demand his removal as protector, but Salisbury is sceptical of their motives. York, alone on stage, expresses his frustrated ambitions for the crown but decides to allow factionalism to deepen before challenging the Lancastrians.

1.2 Gloucester's wife Eleanor reveals her dream of supplanting Henry and Margaret. Gloucester chides her ambitions. She hires Hume to invite witches to determine her fortunes, but he is in the pay of Winchester and Suffolk.

1.3 Seeking redress for feudal grievances, commoners mistakenly petition Suffolk and Margaret, who dismiss them disdainfully. Gloucester suppresses his rage against accusations of corruption, while Margaret tangles with Eleanor. Gloucester appoints a trial by combat between Peter, one of the petitioners, and Horner, who accuses him of saying York was true heir to the crown. York loses his bid to become regent in France to Somerset.

1.4 During Eleanor's conjuring, a spirit prophesies ominous fortunes for Henry, York, Suffolk, and Somerset. York and Buckingham interrupt the meeting and arrest the participants.

2.1 Gloucester and Winchester bicker while falconing. Gloucester exposes Simpcox's false claims of a miraculous cure of sight.

2.2 York convinces Salisbury and Warwick to support his future claim to the throne.

2.3 Eleanor is sentenced to banishment and Gloucester surrenders the protectorship. Peter defeats a drunken Horner in their trial by combat.

2.4 Eleanor does public penance and bids her sorrowful husband farewell.

3.1 Before a Parliament, Margaret leads allegations against Gloucester. Somerset reports the loss of England's remaining French territories, Gloucester is blamed and arrested, but Henry defends his innocence. Margaret, Suffolk, and York conspire with Winchester to kill Gloucester. York is dispatched to suppress an Irish rebellion. Alone on stage, York tells how he has persuaded a physically powerful Kentishman, Jack Cade, to be his stalking horse by impersonating his dead ancestor John Mortimer and inciting a civil insurrection against Lancastrian rule.

3.2 Suffolk reports Gloucester's death to Henry, who accuses him of complicity and repudiates Margaret. Gloucester's dead body is examined in his bed. Warwick concludes he was murdered and accuses Suffolk, who is exiled by Henry. Margaret and Suffolk part sadly.

3.3 Winchester, deranged and conscience-stricken, dies in his bed.

4.1 Suffolk is murdered on his way into exile by a sea captain and his crew, who express popular outrage at his and other lords' murder of Gloucester and abuse of the country's interests.

4.2–3 Cade's rebellion breaks out in Kent. The Staffords confront the rebels but are killed in battle.

4.4–7 Henry learns of Cade's advances towards London. Margaret grieves over the head of Suffolk, vowing revenge. Cade crosses London Bridge and sacks the Savoy and Inns of Court. He arrests Lord Say, charging him with corrupting the country through education, literacy, and print. Say defends himself eloquently and his words touch even Cade, but he and his son-in-law are beheaded and their heads made to kiss on poles.

4.8 The rioters are confronted by Old Clifford and Buckingham, who offer Henry's pardon to those who will disperse, invoking the patriotic memory of Henry V's French conquests. Cade flees.

4.9 Henry pardons the rebels. York is reported to have returned from Ireland with his army, demanding the arrest of Somerset.

4.10 Cade, utterly famished, takes refuge in the Kentish garden of Alexander Iden, who fights and kills him.

5.1 Iden presents Cade's head to Henry and is knighted. York and his sons Edward and Richard, backed by Salisbury and Warwick, openly challenge Henry and his supporters.

5.2 The first battle of St Albans. York kills Clifford, whose son vows revenge, and Richard kills Somerset. Henry and Margaret are defeated and flee to London.

5.3 The victorious Yorkists pursue them there.

★★★ CRITICAL HISTORY

The Contention has frequently been better appreciated on the stage than in academic criticism, which has frequently been preoccupied with issues of text and authorship (and notwithstanding Ben Jonson's snipe: 'three rusty swords…Fight over York and Lancaster's long jars'). Nineteenth-century German Romantic critics such as A. W. Schlegel situated the play in the wider context of Shakespeare's histories as a whole, viewed as an epic national drama of political evolution. In 1944 E. M. W. Tillyard's *Shakespeare's History Plays* adopted this interpretation but emphasized the divinely-destined triumph of the Tudor dynasty: the history plays trace a pattern of national transgression, which begins with the deposition of Richard II, a descent into civil chaos, and the restoration of order in the political marriage of Henry VII and Elizabeth of York. Since then, critics have gradually dismantled Tillyard's idealizing and totalizing premises by studying the multiple perspectives and non-elite voices in this and other history plays that resist the notion of a monolithic ideology. The commoners' petitions and Cade's rebellion, although simultaneously comical and brutal, vividly express 16th-century traditions of popular radicalism and political protest against real social inequality and economic hardships. The play also focuses attention on the political vacuum created by Henry's personal weakness, the failures of public law and systematic justice (which collapse entirely after Duke Humphrey's death), and the destructive selfishness of the country's feudal rulers. Above all, the unceasing verbal and physical violence of the play and its macabre spectacles of severed heads and suffering bodies reflect the social disorder and material culture of Elizabethan society as well as of late medieval England. They continue also to be read in the light of modern experiences of class conflict and political power struggles.

STAGE HISTORY

The Contention was probably written for and performed by Lord Strange's Men, a large company able to accommodate the play's numerous roles. Q1's title page does not identify an acting company, but *Richard Duke of York*'s does: Pembroke's Men, who must also have performed *The Contention* after they came into being in May 1591. There is no further evidence of performance until John Crowne's *The Misery of Civil-War* (1680, staged 1681), a Royalist propaganda piece which adapted material from Cade's rebellion. Crowne then reworked Acts 1–3 as *Henry the Sixth* (1681), focusing popular anti-Catholic sentiment on Cardinal Winchester's murder of Duke Humphrey. From this point until the end of the 19th century, *The Contention* was performed in England only in distant adaptations, including a tercentenary revival by the Surrey Theatre in April 1864. In Germany and Austria, however, strong interest in Shakespeare's histories by Romantic critics stimulated many innovative productions. F. R. Benson mounted *The Contention* on 21 April 1899 in Stratford-upon-Avon, and again in 1906 and 1909. On the second occasion all three *Henry VI* plays were performed as a historical cycle (another idea borrowed from Germany). Benson satisfied Victorian tastes for sumptuous pageantry, but paced the action between scenes more continuously. Sir Barry Jackson and Douglas Seale's Birmingham Repertory Theatre production in 1951 launched the play's modern stage life. Seale successfully alternated between still and lucid passages of formal verse, and explosions of factional violence. Barbara Jefford drew serious attention to Queen Margaret's tragic role for the first time. Her powerful performance was surpassed only by Dame Peggy Ashcroft in Peter Hall and John Barton's legendary *Wars of the Roses* for the RSC in 1963–4, later broadcast internationally in a 1965 television adaptation. Barton condensed *Part 1* and *The Contention* up to Margaret's grief for Suffolk's death into one play, *Henry VI*. He also added hundreds of lines of Shakespearian pastiche to clarify personal motives and story-lines. *The Contention* was performed unadapted in Terry Hands's well-received 1977 RSC production of the whole trilogy, a precedent followed by Michael Boyd in 2000. In 1986 Michael Bogdanov and Michael Pennington reverted to Barton's condensed format—minus his invented lines—for their spiky 'post-Falklands' production, *The Wars of the Roses*, for the English Shakespeare Company, which toured internationally in 1986–9 and is preserved on videotape. Adrian Noble followed their format but not their production's 'radical' ideology for his two-play version *The Plantagenets* for the RSC in 1988. In America, Pat Patton based his stirring 1991 Oregon Shakespeare Festival production on Noble's *House of Lancaster*. Previous productions of *The Contention* at Ashland in 1954, 1965, and 1976 had employed strong ensemble acting and Shakespeare's full script. Michael Boyd's haunting, semi-abstract realization of the three plays for the RSC (2000), part of the 'This England' history cycle, won enormous critical acclaim. Boyd's trilogy was revived in 2006 for the company's Complete Works Festival in which he also directed the other five parts of the First and Second Tetralogies, staging the entire sequence together in 2007–8 as 'The Histories'. Edward Hall's gory, all male, abattoir-set *Rose Rage* (2001) was, like the *Henry VI* chapter in his father Peter's *Wars of the Roses* (RSC 1963–4), a two-part adaptation of the three plays. Ninagawa continued the trend of presenting a wider cycle when he directed the three parts of *Henry VI* for the Sai-no-Kuni Shakespeare Series in 2010. In 2012, the National Theatre of Albania produced a notably pantomimic *Part 2* for the 'Globe to Globe' festival in London. The Globe followed up a touring production of the three parts, directed by Nick Bagnall in 2013, with a 2019 production in the Sam Wanamaker Playhouse. Directed by Sean Holmes and Illinca Radulian, this *Henry VI* conflated *Parts 2* and *3* and presented the young king as a hoodie-wearing, well-meaning teenager, starkly contrasted against Sophie Russell's psychotic, chainsaw-wielding Richard, Duke of York.

ON THE SCREEN

The play featured as one episode of the BBC's *An Age of Kings* in 1960, and in Barton's rewritten form as part of the televised *The Wars of the Roses* in 1965. Jane Howell's full-text version for BBC TV in 1983, with its Brechtian asides-to-camera and visible use of the TV studio space, had Cade (Trevor Peacock, returning as anti-hero after playing Talbot in *1 Henry VI*) leading his followers in a book-burning reminiscent of Nazi Germany. In 2016, the BBC aired the concluding cycle of their *Hollow Crown* series. Directed by Dominic Cooke, the films presented the three parts of *Henry VI* in two films before finishing with *Richard III*. An all-star cast included Sophie Okonedo as Queen Margaret, Sally Hawkins as the Duchess of Gloucester, Hugh Bonneville as Humphrey, and Samuel West as the Bishop of Winchester.

Hamlet, Prince of Denmark

The one Shakespearian tragedy from which almost every speaker of English can quote at least one or two phrases, *Hamlet* is also one of the most difficult to date. *The Revenge of Hamlet Prince [of] Denmark*, 'lately acted by the Lord Chamberlain his servants', was entered in the Stationers' Register in July 1602, and printed in quarto in 1603 as *The Tragical History of Hamlet, Prince of Denmark*: this edition attributes the play to Shakespeare but is drastically shorter than either a subsequent quarto (1604/5, 1611, 1622, 1637) or the play as printed in the Folio (1623). Contemporary allusions to *Hamlet* are complicated by the existence of an earlier play on the same story, cited by Thomas Nashe in 1589, documented in the repertory of the Admiral's Men in 1594 and mentioned by several other writers, but this lost 'ur-*Hamlet*', already in existence before Shakespeare is known to have written anything, is very unlikely to have been a first draft of Shakespeare's own. It is not listed among his works by Francis Meres in 1598, for example, and a possible pun in Nashe would attribute it plausibly to Thomas Kyd. External and internal evidence between them suggest that Shakespeare wrote his own *Hamlet* around the turn of the 17th century: Gabriel Harvey refers approvingly to Shakespeare's play in a manuscript note written between 1598 and early 1601, while stylistic evidence, although in some respects contradictory, places it just before *Troilus and Cressida*, around 1600.

 TEXT

The discrepancies between the three substantially different texts of the play have vexed its editors ever since the publishers of the 'good' quarto of 1604–5, distinguishing this new version from the 'bad' quarto they had printed the previous year, advertised it as 'newly imprinted and enlarged to almost as much again as it was, according to the true and perfect copy'. It seems likeliest that Shakespeare wrote *Hamlet* in about 1600 (producing the version printed as the 'good' quarto), but had revised it by 1602 to produce the acted version which was printed in the Folio and which also lies behind the first, 'bad' quarto of 1603 (a reported text, possibly assembled by the hired actor who played Marcellus, Valtemand, and Lucianus, whose scenes are more fully and accurately rendered than the rest of the play). There is no complete assent on the relations between the three texts, however: some editors have favoured the 'good' quarto, insisting that the Folio text, though in places puzzlingly superior, mainly reflects unauthorized cuts by actors, while others, including those of the Oxford edition, see the Folio as Shakespeare's own mature revision of his earlier draft. The 'bad' quarto, further disputed over by editors, is also valuable despite its obvious errors and inconsistencies (and eminently actable, as sporadic modern revivals have demonstrated): its vivid stage directions may supply genuine details of the play's early performances omitted by the other printed versions, and its variations in character names—Polonius, for example, is here called Corambis, and Reynaldo is Montano—may result from an accidental conflation with the lost ur-*Hamlet*, in which the reporter had perhaps also acted.

 SOURCES

Shakespeare's chief source was the Norse folk tale of Amleth, written down in Latin by the Danish historian Saxo Grammaticus (fl. *c.* 1200) and expanded by the French writer François de Belleforest in his *Histoires tragiques* (7 vols., 1559–80), though it is possible that Shakespeare knew the story only at second hand via the lost earlier play. Belleforest's version was translated into English in 1608 in a version, *The Historie of Hamblet*, which itself incorporates phrases from Shakespeare's play, but the savage old Scandinavian legend is worlds away from the Renaissance tragedy Shakespeare made of it. Although Saxo provides the originals for most of Shakespeare's main characters and much of his plot (while Belleforest further supplies the adultery of Amleth's mother and uncle before the murder of his father), in the old story no ghost has to return to demand vengeance. The identity of the King's killer is not a secret, and Amleth, feigning near-idiocy as a ruse, needs no prompting to undertake his revenge against the usurper. Deported to England, he kills his companions, as in the play, by tampering with their commission, but he reaches England himself (where he marries the King's daughter) before returning in disguise to get the entire court drunk while they celebrate his supposed death, upon which he burns down their hall, kills his uncle, and proclaims himself king. It is impossible to imagine Belleforest's Amleth commissioning the performance of

'The Murder of Gonzago', musing in the graveyard, or making fun of Osric, and Shakespeare's additions to this material (if they do not derive from the ur-*Hamlet*, as we know from Nashe the Ghost does) also include Ophelia's madness, Laertes' revenge and the character of Fortinbras.

 CHARACTER LIST

Ghost of Hamlet *the late King
   of Denmark*
King Claudius *his brother*
Queen Gertrude of Denmark,
   *widow of King Hamlet, now
   wife of Claudius*
Prince **Hamlet** *son of King Hamlet
   and Queen Gertrude*
Polonius *a lord*
Laertes *son of Polonius*
Ophelia *daughter of Polonius*
Reynaldo *servant of Polonius*
Horatio
Rosencrantz ⎤ *friends of*
Guildenstern ⎦ *Prince Hamlet*
Francisco ⎤
Barnardo | *soldiers*
Marcellus ⎦

Valtemand ⎤
Cornelius |
Osric | *courtiers*
Gentlemen ⎦
A **Sailor**
Two **Clowns** *a gravedigger and his
   companion*
A **Priest**
Fortinbras *Prince of Norway*
A **Captain** *in his army*
Ambassadors *from England*
Players, who play the parts of
   the Prologue, Player King,
   Player Queen, and Lucianus
   in 'The Mousetrap'
Lords, messengers, attendants,
   guards, soldiers, followers of
   Laertes, sailors

SYNOPSIS

1.1 Sentries at the Danish royal castle of Elsinore are insisting to the student Horatio that they have seen a ghost resembling the late King Hamlet when the Ghost appears again: they resolve to tell the old King's son, Hamlet.

1.2 The new King Claudius, old Hamlet's brother, recounts to his court that he has married his brother's widow Gertrude, and sends ambassadors to Norway to protest against young Fortinbras' plans to repossess by force the lands won from his royal father by old Hamlet. With the consent of Laertes' father, the counsellor Polonius, Claudius permits Laertes to return to his studies in France, before turning to his silent, black-clad nephew Prince Hamlet, urging him, with Gertrude's backing, to abandon his excessive grief over his father's death, and denying him permission to return to university at Wittenberg. Left alone, Hamlet reflects in horror over his mother's hasty remarriage before his fellow student Horatio and the sentry Marcellus arrive to narrate the apparition of the silent ghost: Hamlet agrees to meet them on the battlements that night.

1.3 Laertes, taking leave of his sister Ophelia, warns her against trusting Hamlet as a suitor: after Polonius has seen Laertes off, with many proverbs, he too urges her to break off her relationship with the Prince.

1.4–5 On the battlements, the ghost of Hamlet's father beckons the Prince away from his companions, and relates how, so far from having died of a snake bite as was announced, he was murdered in his sleep by Claudius, who had already seduced Gertrude: he urges Hamlet to spare Gertrude but to avenge him on Claudius, before departing, asking to be remembered. Hamlet vows to remember nothing else, and when his companions return, though he does not recount what the Ghost has told him, he swears them to secrecy, hinting that he may feign madness later on.

2.1 Polonius sends a servant, Reynaldo, to spy on Laertes' conduct in Paris, before a shocked Ophelia recounts how she has been visited by Hamlet, apparently mad: Polonius decides Ophelia's rejection of Hamlet has driven him insane, and resolves to inform Claudius.

2.2 Claudius and Gertrude welcome Rosencrantz and Guildenstern, student companions of Hamlet summoned from Wittenberg, whom they send to the Prince to attempt to discover the cause of his mental disorder. Claudius receives the ambassadors he earlier sent to Norway, who recount how a rebuked Fortinbras has now redirected his efforts against Poland, before Polonius expounds his theory that Hamlet's madness has been caused by frustrated love. They plan to spy on Hamlet at a future, engineered meeting with Ophelia, but meanwhile Polonius alone meets Hamlet, who insults him repeatedly under a guise of insanity and speaks darkly of Ophelia. Polonius is replaced as his interlocutor by Rosencrantz and Guildenstern, from whom Hamlet exacts an admission that they have been sent by Claudius and Gertrude, and to whom he expresses his profound disenchantment with life before reviving when they tell him an acting company is on its way. They discuss theatrical affairs before the players arrive, when Hamlet has their chief tragedian recite a speech about the destruction of Troy. He confidentially requests them to act 'The Murder of Gonzago' before Claudius and the court, with a new additional speech by himself. Left alone, Hamlet berates himself for seeming so much less impassioned about his father's murder than the player does about the legendary Queen Hecuba, but concludes that by watching Claudius' response to the play, which resembles his father's death, he can satisfy himself as to his uncle's guilt.

3.1 Disappointed by Rosencrantz and Guildenstern's report, Claudius hides with Polonius to watch Hamlet encounter Ophelia. Hamlet arrives, and reflects on suicide, action, and the fear of death before seeing Ophelia, whom he hysterically instructs to retreat to a nunnery: after he leaves, Ophelia laments that he has lost his reason. Claudius, distrusting his nephew, resolves to send him to England, while Polonius undertakes to overhear, unseen, a conversation between Hamlet and Gertrude.

3.2 Hamlet instructs the players on the art of acting before briefing Horatio about the secret purpose of the performance he has commissioned, urging him to watch Claudius. The court arrives and settles to watch the play. A player queen makes promises of eternal fidelity to a player king, vowing never to remarry should he die: while the player king sleeps, his nephew Lucianus pours poison into his ear, just as the Ghost had described the means of his own murder. At this point Claudius rises and demands lights, and the court disperses in disarray, Hamlet and Horatio agreeing that Claudius is guilty. Rosencrantz and Guildenstern, and then Polonius, summon Hamlet to speak privately with his mother.

3.3 Claudius, alarmed, tells Rosencrantz and Guildenstern they must take Hamlet to England at once. Alone, he prays that he may be forgiven for murdering his brother despite his inability to renounce Gertrude and the crown. Hamlet, unseen, finds him at prayer, and is about to kill him, but postpones his vengeance until another occasion for fear of sending his uncle's soul to Heaven rather than to Hell.

3.4 Polonius hides behind the arras in Gertrude's closet: Hamlet arrives and retorts so violently to her rebukes that she fears he may kill her. Polonius cries out and Hamlet, thinking it is Claudius, stabs him fatally through the arras. Hamlet, hinting at his father's murder, and comparing pictures of his father and his uncle, reproaches his mother for her remarriage: as he rants, the Ghost, unseen by Gertrude, reappears and urges him not to be distracted from his revenge. Hamlet assures Gertrude he is not insane and makes her promise secrecy before dragging off Polonius' body.

4.1–3 Claudius, learning of Polonius' death from Gertrude, sends Rosencrantz and Guildenstern to seek Hamlet: with great difficulty they bring the morbidly joking prince before Claudius, who tells Hamlet he is to be sent at once to England for his own protection but who discloses in soliloquy that he is sending letters along with the Prince instructing the English authorities to kill him.

4.4 Fortinbras leads his army, by permission, across Danish territory. (In the 'good' quarto of the play, Hamlet, on his way to England, sees this and reflects self-critically on the contrast between Fortinbras' vigorous ambition and his own slow revenge.)

4.5 Ophelia, mad since her father's death, comes to Gertrude and to Claudius, singing distractedly: Laertes, at the head of a mob, arrives to demand vengeance for Polonius' death, for which he blames Claudius, but his anger dissipates when he sees his sister, who distributes herbs. Claudius promises to explain the circumstances of Polonius' death and to assist Laertes' revenge against the real criminal.

4.6 Horatio receives a letter from Hamlet explaining that he alone has returned to Denmark on board a pirate ship which intercepted his.

4.7 Claudius, conspiring with Laertes, also receives word from Hamlet: the two resolve that Laertes shall kill Hamlet as if by accident in a fencing match, Laertes' unblunted point made the more lethal by venom, with a poisoned drink ready for the Prince should this fail. Gertrude arrives and narrates how the mad Ophelia has drowned.

5.1 Two gravediggers are jesting at their work. Hamlet, arriving with Horatio, banters with one of them, before learning that one of the skulls they have just uncovered is that of the jester Yorick he knew as a child. His reflections on mortality are interrupted by Ophelia's funeral procession, and when Laertes leaps into her grave in extravagant grief Hamlet steps forward, declares himself to the assembled court, and leaps in too. The struggling Laertes and Hamlet are parted, and Claudius promises Laertes that their planned revenge will be immediately put into motion.

5.2 Hamlet tells Horatio how, on board ship, he secretly unsealed Rosencrantz and Guildenstern's letter to the English King and, discovering its contents, substituted a forgery telling the King to have Rosencrantz and Guildenstern killed instead. The affected courtier Osric brings Laertes' challenge to a fencing bout, which a fatalistic Hamlet, despite his forebodings, accepts. Claudius, Gertrude, and their court arrive and, after ceremonial apologies, Hamlet and Laertes duel. Hamlet is winning at first, and declines the poisoned cup, from which Gertrude unwittingly drinks. Laertes wounds Hamlet, but in a scuffle they exchange rapiers and he too is wounded with the envenomed point. Gertrude collapses, knowing she has been poisoned, and dies, and the dying Laertes tells Hamlet of the plot to kill him, blaming Claudius. Hamlet stabs Claudius and forces him to drink some of the remaining poison: he dies, and Hamlet and Laertes exchange forgiveness before Laertes' own death. Hamlet prevents Horatio from drinking poison, begging him to live on in order to tell his story, and, after hearing the approach of Fortinbras' army and prophesying that Fortinbras will be the next king, the Prince dies. Fortinbras, accompanied by the English ambassadors who have come to report the deaths of Rosencrantz and Guildenstern, takes control and makes arrangements for Hamlet's military funeral.

 ARTISTIC FEATURES

Hamlet is characterized by an unprecedented range of dramatic techniques and styles, but the most central is that of the soliloquy: Hamlet's 'O that this too too solid flesh would melt...' (1.2.129–58), 'O, what a rogue and peasant slave am I...' (2.2.553–607), and 'To be, or not to be...' (3.1.58–90) are among the most famous opportunities in the world's theatrical repertoire for an actor to exhibit consciousness in action. The play combines a powerful impression of design (with, for example, its careful parallels between the families of Hamlet, Laertes, and Fortinbras) with an equally strong effect of casual improvisation, its inset stories (and, indeed, its play-within-a-play) perpetually cut short by new circumstances. The Prince himself seems to step outside the conventions of the revenge tragedy to reflect on his own predicament and comment on his own volatile impromptu performances in the successive episodes which overtake him, to such an extent that, despite being the most familiar play in the world, *Hamlet* still seems one of the most excitingly unpredictable, its ending as abrupt and tragic an interruption as ever.

CRITICAL HISTORY

It would be impossible, even in a book-length study, to do full justice to any more than the bare outlines of this play's impact, not just in literary criticism and on the stage, but on Western culture at large: its characters have entered the realm of myth, and its motifs have been endlessly reworked, in fiction (Gothic and otherwise), painting, opera, and film no less than in subsequent drama (from Middleton's *Revenger's Tragedy* through 19th-century burlesque to Chekhov and Stoppard and beyond). It has, indeed, had a profound effect on conceptions of Shakespeare himself, the rumour that Shakespeare originally played the Ghost (recorded by Nicholas Rowe in 1709) shaping many subsequent views of Shakespeare's relations to his texts and their latter-day interpreters.

The play has held such an important place in the literary canon that the history of writing about *Hamlet* is practically the history of literary criticism itself, successive interpreters and schools of thought inevitably having to try out their ideas, sooner or later, on this most celebrated and enigmatic of texts. In the 18th century strict Neoclassical critics such as Voltaire objected to the indecorous gravediggers and to the concluding proliferation of onstage deaths, but its English popularity never wavered, Dr Johnson defending its range and variety. The Romantics found Hamlet's interview with the Ghost particularly sublime, and were above all preoccupied with the Prince's apparent paralysis of will, Coleridge and Hazlitt reflecting on the relations between thought and action in ways heavily influenced by Goethe and Schlegel. From then until the late 20th century much writing about the play was dominated by the question of Hamlet's character, his sanity or otherwise, and why he delays. A. C. Bradley influentially found the core of the play's power in its juxtaposition of the scope of human thought with the limitations of mortality: other scholars continued to worry at a number of more local questions which the play deliberately leaves unresolved, such as the extent of Gertrude's guilt, the nature of the Danish succession, and the precise status of the Ghost (who, apparently on temporary release from Purgatory, seems to belong to a Catholic theology rather than a Protestant one). The emergence of Marxist criticism saw the Prince variously lauded as a revolutionary ahead of his feudal time and reviled as a vacillatingly uncommitted bourgeois intellectual, but the play has been more central to the development of psychoanalytic criticism, and indeed of psychoanalysis itself. Since the time of Edmond Malone *Hamlet* had been regarded as especially revealing of Shakespeare's own emotional nature (its plot occasionally related both to the death of Shakespeare's father John in 1601 and to the death of his son Hamnet in 1596), and in 1919 T. S. Eliot famously declared the play an artistic failure on the grounds that Shakespeare's depiction of Gertrude did not supply an adequate 'objective correlative' for the private sense of disgust with which he felt the play was nonetheless overburdened. Eliot's concerns substantially overlap with those of Sigmund Freud, who refers to the play in outlining his theory of infantile repression in *The Interpretation of Dreams* (1900), and whose idea that Hamlet is immobilized in part because he too desires Gertrude and has entertained murderous wishes against his father was influentially developed by Ernest Jones in *Hamlet and Oedipus* (1949). Since then Hamlet's dealings with Gertrude and Ophelia have continued to preoccupy psychoanalytic criticism and the feminist and deconstructive strains which have derived from it, while historically inclined commentators of different shades have related the play to the fall of the Earl of Essex, the Elizabethan succession crisis, Renaissance attitudes to death, the Reformation, and the philosophy of Montaigne, among much else.

STAGE HISTORY

The play seems to have been an immediate success, performed in London, the universities, the provinces, and on the Continent, as title pages, annotated copies, contemporary allusions, and the existence of a seventeenth-century German adaptation (*Der Bestrafte Bruder-mord*, 'Fratricide Punished') testify. The role of the Prince was almost certainly created by Richard Burbage, and was assumed after his death by Joseph Taylor. Popular enough to survive in performance during the Puritan Interregnum, albeit only as the one-scene sketch *The Grave-Makers*, the play was assigned to Sir William Davenant's company at the Restoration, since which time an unbroken line of leading actors have measured themselves against its title role, starting with Thomas Betterton (from 1661 until his retirement more than 40 years later) and extending through David Garrick, John Philip Kemble, Edmund Kean, William Charles Macready, Edwin Forrest, Edwin Booth, and Henry Irving to John Barrymore, John Gielgud, Laurence Olivier, Richard Burton, Michael Pennington, Kenneth Branagh, and Benedict Cumberbatch, among many others. It would in fact be hard to list any major anglophone actors who have not played Hamlet. The play has been equally important, since the early 19th century, in the theatres of (in particular) France, Germany, Russia, and Scandinavia: furthermore the title role's sensitive qualities have attracted not only actors but actresses, including Sarah Siddons, Asta Nielsen, Sarah Bernhardt and, more recently, Maxine Peake and Michelle Terry. Long even without editorial conflation of the quarto and Folio versions, the play has usually been shortened in performance, the Fortinbras plot often disappearing entirely: over the course of his career Garrick gradually restored many formerly cut lines, but at the expense of the gravediggers, whom he excised, along with Ophelia's funeral and Laertes' death, in 1772. Broadly speaking, the 18th-century Hamlet was less indecisive than the Romantic one exemplified by Kemble, Kean, and their Victorian successors, who was an idealized figure too complex and imaginative for the corrupt world in which he found himself. In the 20th century, this tradition was notably sustained by Gielgud, who played the role at different times between 1930 and 1944, while his contemporary, Olivier, experimented with a Freudian approach to the Prince's psychology in 1937. Since then the Prince has often been played less sympathetically (David Warner's sullen student in Peter Hall's production of 1965, and Ben Kingsley's determinedly ungraceful Prince in Buzz Goodbody's of 1970, stand out), while the play's interest in an isolated, anxious, and possibly disordered consciousness has lent it ideally to the methods and concerns of modernism and postmodernism. Notable avant-garde readings of the play include those of Charles Marowitz, Peter Brook, Heine Müller, and Robert Lepage. Into the 21st century the role has continued both to attract star actors and to make reputations, most notably Simon Russell Beale (2000) and Rory Kinnear (2010) at the National Theatre, Ben Whishaw (2004) at the Old Vic, and Samuel West (2001), David Tennant (2008), Jonathan Slinger (2013), and Paapa Essiedu for the RSC. From 2014 to 2016 Shakespeare's Globe asserted *Hamlet*'s status as the most global of plays in an extraordinary logistical undertaking, touring an English-language production of the play to every country on the planet.

ON THE SCREEN

A five-minute French version (1900) is the earliest on record, but the significant achievements on silent film are the 1913 *Hamlet* with Sir Johnstone Forbes-Robertson in the title role, and Svend Gade's film with Asta Nielsen as the Prince (1920). Ernst Lubitsch's 99-minute *To be or not to be* (1942) might be seen as opening the way for the sound films that were to follow, but the best-known *Hamlet* remains Laurence Olivier's 1948 film, in which the 40-year-old Olivier played the title role and was director. There is about the camera's elegiac journey into and through the loneliness of the Prince a nostalgia which arguably reflects the mood of post-war Europe. Sixteen years later the Russian director Grigori Kozintsev made his *Hamlet* (1964). Like Olivier's, it was filmed in monochrome, but Kozintsev dramatized his images in a more arresting way. There is a starkly elemental basis to his cinematography and his is a more vigorously political view of the play than Olivier's. Less cinematic was Tony Richardson's adaptation (1969) of his Round House theatre production, with Nicol Williamson as a Hamlet who was more student than Prince. Franco Zeffirelli's *Hamlet* (1990) with Mel Gibson in the title role is a move away from psychological complexity, and is more consciously an attempt to present the drama in a fragmented cinematic style. Using little more than 30% of the full text, Zeffirelli's priority was clearly to target a young audience with a racy film made up of short-duration shots. Kenneth Branagh's *Hamlet* (1996) incorporates the First Folio text uncut with some additions from the second quarto. The complete version lasting over four hours is filmed on a lavish scale and the cast lists an array of famous names even in the small parts. The inclusion of a number of American film actors moves the film away from the British tradition of casting established stage actors for Shakespeare film roles. A shortened two-hour version has been edited from the original. Branagh's choice of late 19th-century costuming contrasts with Michael Almereyda's modern-dress version, released in 2000, with Ethan Hawke as a New York businessman Prince and Sam Shephard as the Ghost. The play has also inspired films well outside the Anglophone world, including Akira Kurosawa's *The Bad Sleep Well* in Japan (1960) and, in India, Vishal Bhardwaj's *Haider* (2014).

Henry IV Part 1

Immediately and enduringly popular, this rich and assured sequel to the events dramatized in *Richard II* (1595) was probably composed and first acted in 1596: the changes to certain characters' names, discussed below, were probably connected with court performances at the end of that year.

 TEXT

The play was entered in the Stationers' Register in February 1598 (as 'The history of Henry the IIIIth with his battle of Shrewsbury against Henry Hotspur of the North with the conceited mirth of Sir John Falstaff'), and was published in at least two quarto editions in the same year (the earliest known of which survives only in an eight-page fragment). Five more appeared before the publication of the Folio (in 1599, 1604, 1608, 1613, and 1622), and its early texts also include the manuscript compiled for an amateur performance by Sir Edward Dering in the early 1620s, though this derives from the 1613 quarto rather than from an independent source. The Folio, which retitles the play *The First Part of Henry the Fourth*, also draws its text from the 1613 quarto, but removes all oaths in scrupulous compliance with the Act to Restrain the Abuses of Players of 1606. This was not the first time the play had undergone censorship: when first composed its greatest comic character was called Sir John Oldcastle, but a descendant of this real-life historical figure (who was regarded as a Protestant hero, and features in Foxe's *Book of Martyrs*), insisted on its being changed. (This was either William Brooke, 7th Lord Cobham—Elizabeth's Lord Chamberlain from August 1596 until his death the following March—or his son Henry, 8th Lord Cobham.) Even the play's altered text, though, retains traces of the original name (Sir John is called 'my old lad of the castle' by the Prince, 1.2.41–2), as well as the original names of two of his tavern companions (Harvey and Russell, changed to Bardolph and Peto, probably for fear of offending the earls of Bedford, whose surname was Russell, and Sir William Harvey, who was about to marry the dowager Countess of Southampton). There is some evidence that the substitution of 'Falstaff' (a name based on that of the cowardly Fastolf who appears in *1 Henry VI*) was not always made in performance even after 1596. The Oxford edition, consequently, restores not only the fat knight's blasphemies but his original surname, but maintains the continuity of the sequence by calling him only Sir John in speech prefixes throughout this play and the subsequent *Merry Wives of Windsor* and *2 Henry IV*.

 ## SOURCES

Shakespeare drew both the name and the reprobate character of Oldcastle from an anonymous play about Prince Harry's wild youth, sudden reformation, and glorious kingship, *The Famous Victories of Henry V*, entered in the Stationers' Register in 1594 and printed in 1598: this work undoubtedly influenced not only *1 Henry IV* but the rest of the Second Tetralogy, but the surviving text offered by the 1598 edition is so evidently garbled and truncated that it is hard to tell how much. For his historical material Shakespeare also consulted Raphael Holinshed's *Chronicles* and Samuel Daniel's *The First Four Books of the Civil Wars* (1595), while his comic scenes draw broadly on the traditions of medieval mystery and morality plays.

 ## CHARACTER LIST

King Henry the Fourth,
   also called King Harry
   and Bolingbroke
Prince Henry, Prince of Wales, also
   called Hal and Harry *King
   Henry's eldest son and heir*

Lord John of Lancaster,
   also called Prince John of
   Lancaster *a younger son
   of the King*
Earl of West-Morland ⎤ *loyal to*
Sir Walter Blunt   ⎦ *the King*

Earl of Northumberland, Henry Percy

Earl of Worcester, Thomas Percy *North-umberland's younger brother*

Sir Henry (or Harry) Percy, known as **Hotspur** *Northumberland's son and heir*

Lord Mortimer, Edmund Mortimer *Hotspur's brother-in- law, also referred to as the Earl of March*

Owain Glyndŵr, *a Welsh lord, Morti-mer's father-in-law*

Earl of Douglas, Archibald Douglas *a Scottish lord*

Sir Richard Vernon *an English knight*

Archbishop of York, Richard le Scrope

Sir Michael *a priest or knight in the Arch-bishop's household*

rebels against King Henry

Lady Percy, also called Kate *Hotspur's wife and Mortimer's sister*

Lady Mortimer *Glyndŵr's daughter and Mortimer's wife*

Sir John Falstaff

Edward **Poins,** also called Ned and Yedward

Bardolph
Peto
followers of Falstaff

Gadshill *setter for the highway robbery*

Hostess of the tavern (Mistress Quickly)

Francis *a drawer, or tapster*
Vintner *or tavern-keeper*
at the tavern

First Carrier, or transporter of produce
Second Carrier
Ostler, or stable groom
Chamberlain, or room servant
at an inn near Gad's Hill

First Traveller
Sheriff
Servant to Hotspur
Messenger
Second Messenger
Soldiers, travellers at Gad's Hill, others attending

⋮≡ SYNOPSIS

1.1 King Henry IV speaks of his long-standing desire to mount a crusade, but this scheme has to be postponed once more when news arrives that after a fierce battle Edmund Mortimer has been taken prisoner by the Welsh rebel Glyndŵr. In the north, however, Harry Percy, known as Hotspur, has won a great victory against the Scots—causing the King to envy Northumberland for having such a valiant son, unlike the dissipated

Prince Harry—but at the instigation of his uncle Worcester Hotspur has refused to deliver more than one of his prisoners to the King, who has summoned them to Windsor to explain themselves.

1.2 In London the King's eldest son Prince Harry is bantering with the fat old knight Sir John when Poins invites them to take part, along with three other confederates, in a highway robbery planned for the following morning at Gads Hill: Poins privately suggests that he and Harry should allow Sir John and the others to commit the robbery alone and should subsequently rob them of the spoils, in disguise, meeting them in the evening in Eastcheap to hear how they explain their loss. Alone, Harry confides that he is only pursuing this career of idleness for the time being, the better to amaze the world when he finally stages his reformation.

1.3 The King confronts Worcester, Northumberland, and Hotspur with their refusal to deliver their prisoners. After Worcester is dismissed for insolence, Hotspur claims he only failed to do so because tactlessly asked for them by an effeminate courtier in the immediate aftermath of the battle, and he has now made it clear that he will hand them over as soon as the King pays Mortimer's ransom. The King, however, insists that Mortimer, who has married Glyndŵr's daughter, is a traitor, and, refusing to believe Hotspur's account of Mortimer's combat with the Welshman, reiterates his demand for the prisoners. Left alone, Northumberland and the angrily voluble Hotspur, soon rejoined by Worcester, reflect on the ingratitude of the man they helped to make king in Richard II's place and on Richard's alleged choice of Mortimer as his heir, and Worcester, when Hotspur has finally calmed down sufficiently to listen, outlines an eagerly seconded plot to combine their forces with those of the Scots, the Welsh, and the Archbishop of York against the King.

2.1 Before dawn at an inn, two carriers and a chamberlain meet Gadshill, on his way to take part in the planned highway robbery.

2.2 The robbers, including Prince Harry, Poins, Gadshill, and an already exhausted Sir John, meet, and after the Prince and Poins slip away to disguise themselves the travellers arrive and are robbed.

2.3 In disguise the Prince and Poins easily rob their confederates, who run away.

2.4 Hotspur, having angrily read a letter from someone declining to join the rebellion, is asked by his wife Lady Percy why he has been so sleepless and agitated: declining to tell her of the conspiracy, he only promises that though he must set off shortly she will follow the next day.

2.5 At the Boar's Head Tavern in Eastcheap, Prince Harry has been fraternizing with the bar staff, and he and Poins perplex the drawer Francis.

Sir John and the other robbers arrive, Sir John railing against the Prince's absence from the robbery and its sequel, and in reply to Harry's promptings he gives an increasingly exaggerated account of how they were robbed of their booty, claiming to have fought eleven of over 50 attackers in single combat, killing at least seven. When Harry finally confronts him with the truth he claims to have known his identity all along and to have instinctively declined to fight against a true Prince. News arrives of the rebellion, and in a mock-play an undaunted Harry rehearses for the upbraiding he expects to receive from his father for his absence from court, Sir John playing the King and urging the Prince to banish all his idle companions except Sir John. When they swap roles the Prince as King urges Sir John as Harry to banish Sir John, and hints that in time he himself will indeed do so. Nonetheless when officers come seeking to arrest Sir John and his associates for the robbery Harry protects them, concealing the fat knight behind an arras, where he falls asleep. Having sent the officers away on a false trail Harry picks the sleeping Sir John's pocket and finds a bill for little food and much drink. He promises to repay the robbed travellers, and undertakes to obtain Sir John a place in the King's army during the impending civil war.

3.1 In Wales Mortimer, Hotspur, and Glyndŵr divide a map of England and Wales into the three parts each hopes to receive after the defeat of King Henry, supervised by Worcester, who does what he can to moderate Hotspur's impatience with Glyndŵr's grandiloquent claims to possess magic powers. Along with Lady Percy comes Mortimer's wife, who can speak only Welsh to her monoglot anglophone husband: interpreted by her father Glyndŵr, she laments his impending departure, and sings a Welsh song.

3.2 King Henry reproaches Harry at length for his cheapening of himself among the taverns, comparing him unfavourably to Hotspur and to his own younger self, but is appeased by Harry's promise to win back his honour in combat against Hotspur: the royal forces set off to confront the rebels at Shrewsbury.

3.3 Sir John accuses the Hostess of allowing his pocket to be picked of valuables: Harry arrives, busy with military preparations, and having confronted the bluffing Sir John with the truth about what was taken from his pocket assigns him an infantry command.

4.1 Worcester, Hotspur, and the Scots commander Douglas receive news that Northumberland is sick and will not be present with his forces at the impending battle: Sir Richard Vernon brings further news, that the royal army is gathering, including both the King himself and the unexpected Prince Harry, and that Glyndŵr's army will not be ready in time for the battle.

4.2 In Warwickshire Sir John has accepted bribes to exempt able-bodied men from conscription and has instead mustered a regiment with which he is ashamed to be seen: Prince Harry, passing with Westmorland, comments on their poverty, and urges an unenthusiastic Sir John to hurry their march lest he miss the battle.

4.3 The rebels, disputing whether their outnumbered forces should give battle at once, are visited by Sir Walter Blunt, sent by the King to learn of their grievances: Hotspur outlines their cause and questions the King's right to the crown, promising to send Worcester to parley with him the next morning.

4.4 The Archbishop of York, anxious about the outcome of the battle, musters forces to defend himself should the rebels lose at Shrewsbury.

5.1 Worcester outlines the rebels' grievances to the royal party, including Harry, who offers to fight Hotspur in single combat: the King promises to pardon them if they will abandon their rebellion, but Harry has little hope the offer will be accepted, and the royal army makes ready for battle. Sir John, left alone, reflects on the frail vanity of honour, preferring survival.

5.2 Worcester does not tell his fellow rebels of the King's offer of clemency, convinced that even if the young impetuous Hotspur is forgiven he and the older rebels never will be, and they prepare for immediate battle.

5.3 In the fighting Douglas kills Blunt, who is one of many royal troops disguised as the King, and is disappointed to learn from Hotspur of his real identity. Sir John, whose own soldiers have been decimated, is met by Harry, who is furious to find that Sir John's pistol case contains only a bottle of sack.

5.4 Harry, though wounded, declines to leave the field. He rescues his father from the assault of Douglas, then duels with Hotspur, while Sir John, spectating, is apparently killed by the Scot. The Prince kills Hotspur and speaks regretfully of his courage, then, seeing Sir John lying beside him, laments his disreputable friend. When Harry has left, though, Sir John gets up, and, resolving to claim to have killed Hotspur himself, wounds his corpse and lifts it onto his back. Harry arrives with his younger brother John of Lancaster and is astonished to find Sir John alive and willing to make such boasts, but undertakes not to hinder Sir John from receiving an unearned reward.

5.5 The battle won, the King sentences Worcester and Vernon to death. Harry reports that Douglas has been captured, and is allowed to have him set free as a tribute to his valour. The King divides his forces so that they may follow up this victory against the remaining rebels throughout the kingdom.

🎭 ARTISTIC FEATURES

The play is the first of Shakespeare's histories to weave together tragedy and comedy (into the 'double plot' influentially analysed by William Empson): its mainly prose scenes in which Prince Harry seems disloyally to prefer the company of his surrogate parent Sir John to that of his real father provide a comic counterpoint to the political rebellion with which King Henry is confronted in the main plot. The play is remarkable for the range of distinctive voices and vocabularies with which it supplies its characters, from the realistic common speech of the carriers to the chivalric idealism of Hotspur, with Prince Harry's centrality to its design underlined by his protean ability to operate across all of them.

✯✯✯ CRITICAL HISTORY

The play's initial popularity is attested by the proliferation not only of early editions but of allusions, principally to Sir John, who has dominated much writing about the entire Second Tetralogy. Largest in conception as well as in bulk of all Shakespeare's comic characters—the funnier and the apparently freer for his running combat with the realities of chronicle history— Sir John captivated the imagination of the (equally corpulent) Dr Johnson ('*Falstaff*, unimitated, unimitable *Falstaff*, how shall I extol thee? Thou compound of sense and vice; of sense which may be admired but not esteemed, of vice which may be despised, but hardly detested'), inspired a pioneering essay on Shakespearian characterization by Maurice Morgann (1777), and has been preferred to the calculating Prince who will eventually reject him by commentators from William Hazlitt through A. C. Bradley to W. H. Auden and beyond. Outside the long-running discussion of Sir John's career— which has variously depicted him as a representative of Vice, a ritual sacrificial substitute for the King, and an image of national fertility, an ancient but undying personification of the English people—the play has usually been discussed in relation to Shakespeare's view of history, and to 16th-century views of national destiny more generally. The Second Tetralogy has often been seen, from the early 20th century onwards, as showing England's fall from Richard II's lost Eden and its providential reunification and redemption under Henry V, a view associated particularly with E. M. W. Tillyard. He and subsequent commentators have pointed out that the England of *1 Henry IV* seems far less remote from Shakespeare's own times than the more recent events dramatized in the First Tetralogy (with Hotspur embodying a nostalgic idea of feudal valour doomed to defeat at the hands of modern politicians like King Henry and his son), and have related the play plausibly to the interests of the Tudor nation-state, an institution for which critics have in general expressed progressively less enthusiasm since Tillyard's own time. In an influential essay the American New Historicist Stephen Greenblatt compared Harry's strategies among the common people of Eastcheap with those of 16th-century English colonists in the New World, while King Henry's attempts to subdue the Welsh have been repeatedly compared to Queen Elizabeth's efforts to put down rebellions in Ireland. Grounding these enquiries is a critical interest in the play's writing of history and alternative histories. Recent studies have built upon Phyliss Rackin's magisterial work by investigating the play's construction of gender. Ever fascinated by Falstaff, scholars have also explored this character's uncomfortable proximity to festivity, exploitation, and war crimes.

STAGE HISTORY

Early records of performances, especially at court, are complicated by the different titles under which both *1 Henry IV* and its immediate sequel seem to have gone: it was certainly acted before the Flemish ambassador in 1600, and the plays referred to as *The Hotspur* and *Sir John Falstaff* at the wedding of Princess Elizabeth in 1612–13 were probably the two *Henry IV* plays. The two were combined by Sir Edward Dering for a private, amateur performance in Kent around 1623, and *Part 1* was performed at court in 1625 (as *The First Part of Sir John Falstaff*) and in 1638 (as *Oldcastle*, unless this was the collaborative *Sir John Oldcastle* written in 1600 to counter Shakespeare's depiction of the knight, though this seems less likely). In the public theatres, it is generally assumed that Richard Burbage created the role of the Prince, but the identity of the original Sir John is uncertain: Edmond Malone claimed to have seen a document which assigned the part to John Heminges. The role, however, was certainly one of the best loved of the entire pre-war repertory: in 1699 James Wright could still remember the applause John Lowin received in it before the Civil War. Sir John was popular enough to be acted even under Oliver Cromwell in the droll *The Bouncing Knight* (and to become one of the first Shakespearian characters depicted pictorially, on the title page to the anthology in which the droll was later printed, *The Wits*). At the Restoration in 1660 this play about the successful defeat of a rebellion was one of the first Shakespeare plays to be revived: in the hands of Thomas Killigrew's King's Company it became a firm favourite with Samuel Pepys. The subsequent stage history of the play has often been shaped by which of its major roles leading actor-managers have preferred. Thomas Betterton played Hotspur in 1682 but graduated to Sir John in 1700 (reviving both *2 Henry IV* and *The Merry Wives of Windsor* to give himself even more scope), and this trajectory was repeated by James Quin, who excelled as the fat knight from the early 1720s until his retirement in 1753. John Philip Kemble, however, was too thin and too dignified to move beyond Hotspur (whom he first played in 1791), leaving the role of Sir John to his brothers, first Stephen and then Charles, who in 1824 became one of the first 19th-century producers to well-nigh bury the play under historically researched costumes and sets (which necessitated extensive cuts and transpositions of scenes). The Victorians found the tavern scenes coarse, and the play fell from favour, though Samuel Phelps was a notable Sir John in 1847 and, at Drury Lane, in 1864, in a production otherwise best remembered for its spectacular pictorial recreation of the battle of Shrewsbury.

In the 20th century the play gradually regained some measure of its earlier popularity, though unlike *Richard III* it has never attracted very much interest outside the nation whose history it dramatizes, Sir John seeming as inexplicably English a joke as Mr Punch. Barry Jackson staged a full text of *1 Henry IV* in 1913, and revived both it and *2 Henry IV* for Shakespeare's birthday in 1921, anticipating subsequent directors who have sought to stage the Second Tetralogy as a grand, Wagnerian sequence. At the Old Vic in 1930 John Gielgud played Hotspur to Ralph Richardson's Prince Harry, and another conspicuous production of that decade found the music-hall comedian George Robey playing a widely praised Sir John, in 1935. The legendary production of the century, though, of both *1 Henry IV* and *2 Henry IV*, took place at the Old Vic in 1945, when Ralph Richardson returned to the play as an alert, mercurial Sir John, Laurence Olivier played a fiery, stammering Hotspur, and Sybil Thorndike played the Hostess. Another impressive cast was assembled six years later in Stratford, where Anthony Quayle played Sir John, Michael Redgrave Hotspur, Harry Andrews the King, and Richard Burton Prince Harry. Peter Hall mounted an impressive production for the RSC in 1964, with Ian Holm as Harry, part of an ambitious presentation of the Second Tetralogy which staged it as a prelude to the First (which was famously condensed into the three-part *The Wars of the Roses*). This immense undertaking was repeated, in a very different manner, by Michael Bogdanov's English Shakespeare Company in 1985–6, with Michael Pennington as a cold Harry and John Woodvine as a memorably cynical Sir John. Other notable Hal-Falstaff pairings in more recent times include William Houston and Desmond Barrit (RSC, 2000); Matthew Macfadyen and Michael Gambon (National, 2005); Geoffrey Streatfeild and David Warner (RSC, 2007); Jamie Parker and Roger Allam (Globe, 2010); and Alex Hassell and Antony Sher (RSC, 2014). In 2014, Phyllida Lloyd directed a path-breaking, all-female production of *Parts 1* and *2* at the Donmar Warehouse. Starring Harriet Walter as a quietly authoritative Henry, and set in a women's prison, this production asked important questions about who and what Shakespeare is for. In 2019, Sarah Bedi and Federary Holmes produced both parts of *Henry IV* at the replica Globe as part of a wider season on the Second Tetralogy. Performed by a compact ensemble under the subtitles *Hotspur* and *Falstaff*, the productions were notable for Michelle Terry's impetuous, restive, and remarkably witty Hotspur, Helen Schlesinger's joyfully padded Falstaff, and the remarkable progression of Sarah Amankwah's Hal from rascal to regnant.

 ON THE SCREEN

The earliest version for BBC TV (1959), an abbreviation in the tradition of *The Bouncing Knight* entitled *The Gadshill Job*, aimed to attract younger viewers. More memorable was the BBC TV series *An Age of Kings* (1960), allotting four out of its fifteen parts to the *Henry IV* plays. A two-hour adaptation of *1 Henry IV* on American television was transmitted in the same year. BBC TV screened full versions of both parts of *Henry IV* in 1979, and in 1995 John Caird adapted them for BBC television. In 2012 the BBC produced them again as part of *The Hollow Crown*, a grand retelling of the Second Tetralogy.

On film, Orson Welles's *Chimes at Midnight* (1965), which draws on both *Henry IV* plays, stands as a classic. Welles makes Falstaff the dramatic centre of his adaptation, and it is clearly Welles's affinity with Falstaff's condition which gives the film its poignancy. In 2019, Netflix released *The King*, directed by David Michôd and starring Timothée Chalomet. A loose adaptation of the whole Henriad, the film dispenses entirely with Shakespeare's language and offers a revisionist version of the story, in which Falstaff is killed fighting heroically on the front lines of Agincourt (a battle to which he never makes it in Shakespeare's text, and which one feels he would have done all in his power to avoid).

Henry IV Part 2

A darker, more worldly play than its exuberant predecessor, *2 Henry IV* was probably begun soon after *1 Henry IV*, in 1597, but it may have been laid aside while Shakespeare composed *The Merry Wives of Windsor*: the fact that the February 1598 entry in the Stationers' Register for *1 Henry IV* does not refer to it as 'Part 1' probably indicates that *Part 2* had not then been performed. It must pre-date *Henry V*, however, which could have been completed by late 1598, and so was probably finished and first performed during the spring or summer of 1598.

TEXT

The play was entered in the Stationers' Register in August 1600, and appeared in quarto in the same year, as *The Second Part of Henry the Fourth* ('Continuing to his death, and coronation of Henry the Fifth. With the humours of Sir John Falstaff, and swaggering Pistol. As it hath been sundry times publically acted by the right honourable the Lord Chamberlain his servants. Written by William Shakespeare.'). This text—set from Shakespeare's own foul papers—was reissued, probably in the same year, with the addition of Act 3 Scene 1, omitted from the original printing. The play reappeared in the Folio in 1623 in a text derived from a promptbook but 'corrected' by a compositor who, wishing to make the text more literary, also consulted a transcript of the play derived from the quarto version. The Folio text restores material apparently cut from the earlier editions at the insistence of the censors, as well as showing some evidence of independent authorial revision. Much of the censored material (such as Lord Bardolph's advice on planning a rebellion in 1.3 and the Archbishop's recapitulation of the rebels' grievances in 4.1) refers to the fate of the deposed Richard II, and it has usually been assumed that the stirrings of what would become the Earl of Essex's rebellion had by 1600 made these speeches look uncomfortably topical. The Folio text has been purged of oaths in compliance with the Act to Restrain the Abuses of Players, but seems otherwise complete, though in one respect the play does respond to earlier censorship. Although Shakespeare had by now adopted the surname Falstaff for Sir John (though in the quarto one speech prefix still calls him Oldcastle), the play's Epilogue carefully points out that he is not Oldcastle—thereby, however, drawing attention to the fact that in *1 Henry IV* he was.

SOURCES

As with *1 Henry IV*, Shakespeare drew on the anonymous *The Famous Victories of Henry V*, Raphael Holinshed's *Chronicles* and Samuel Daniel's *Civil Wars*, here supplemented by Sir Thomas Elyot's *The Governor* (1531), which supplied the story of Prince Harry's dealings with the Lord Chief Justice. In this play, though, more space is given to the invented adventures of Sir John compared to the historical events of Henry IV's reign.

👪 CHARACTER LIST

Rumour *the Presenter*
King Henry IV
Prince Henry, later
King Henry V ⎤
Prince John of
Lancaster ⎜ *sons of*
Humphrey, Duke of ⎜ *King*
Gloucester ⎜ *Henry IV*
Thomas, Duke of ⎜
Clarence ⎦

Earl of **Warwick** ⎤
Earl of **Surrey** ⎜ *of*
Earl of **Westmorland** ⎜ *King*
Harcourt ⎜ *Henry IV's*
Sir John Blunt ⎦ *party*

Scrope, **Archbishop of York** ⎤
Lord Bardolph
Thomas, Lord **Mowbray**
the Earl Marshal
Lord **Hastings**
Sir John **Coleville**
Percy, Earl of
Northumberland *rebels*
Lady **Northumberland**
his wife
Kate, **Lady Percy**
Hotspur's widow
Travers *Northumberland's*
servant
Morton *messenger*
from Shrewsbury ⎦

Northumberland's **Porter**
Lord Chief Justice

Servant of the Lord Chief Justice
Gower *a messenger*

Sir John **Falstaff** ⎤
Page *Falstaff's*
servant
Bardolph *'irregular*
Pistol *humorists'*
Poins
Peto ⎦

Mistress Quickly
Doll Tearsheet
Robert **Shallow** ⎤ *country*
Silence ⎦ *justices*
Davy *Shallow's servant*

Ralph **Mouldy** ⎤
Simon **Shadow**
Thomas **Wart** *country*
Francis **Feeble** *recruits*
Peter **Bullcalf** ⎦

Fang ⎤ *two sergeants*
Snare ⎦

Francis ⎤
William *drawers at the*
Second Drawer *Boar's Head* ⎦

Musicians
First Beadle
First Groom
Second Groom
Page to the King
Messenger
Soldiers, Attendants, Beadles
Epilogue

≔ SYNOPSIS

In an Induction, Rumour, wearing a robe decorated with images of tongues, explains that the play is about to show false reports about King Henry's victory at Shrewsbury reaching the malingering Northumberland.

1.1 Lord Bardolph brings Northumberland the supposed news that their fellow rebels have defeated the royal army at Shrewsbury, where the King has been mortally wounded and Northumberland's son Hotspur has killed Prince Harry: the servant Travers, however, has heard that the rebels have been defeated and Hotspur killed. The truth of Travers's version of events is confirmed in full by an eyewitness, Morton, who adds that an army led by Prince John and the Earl of Westmorland is on its way northwards. Northumberland, throwing away his pretended sickness, rages, but is calmed by Morton and Lord Bardolph, who reassure him that their rebellion is not fully defeated yet, especially since the Archbishop of York is mustering large numbers to their cause.

1.2 Sir John, accompanied by a small page given him by Prince Harry for the sake of the comic contrast between their sizes, is accosted by the Lord Chief Justice, who we learn has earlier been struck by Prince Harry: though Sir John at first attempts continually to change the subject, he makes it clear that Sir John's part in the highway robbery (depicted in *1 Henry IV*) is well known, rebukes him for misleading Prince Harry, and tells him he has only escaped punishment because of his reputedly good service at the battle of Shrewsbury. He also points out that Sir John has now been sent northwards with Prince John's forces specifically to separate him from Prince Harry, upon which Sir John, posing as an indispensable war hero, requests the loan of £1,000 towards his expenses. After the Justice leaves, refusing, Sir John sends begging letters to several other figures, reflecting that the limp he has acquired through either venereal disease or gout will at least make him look more eligible for a military pension.

1.3 The Archbishop of York, Mowbray, Hastings, and Lord Bardolph discuss the prospects of their rebellion, comforted to reflect that only a third of the King's forces can march against them, the rest divided between opposing Glyndŵr in Wales and fighting the French: the Archbishop comments on the fickleness of public opinion, as Henry Bolingbroke's former supporters are now rallying to them, nostalgic for the dead Richard II.

2.1 Mistress Quickly has Sir John arrested for breach of promise, explaining, before the Lord Chief Justice, who happens to pass, that he has lived at her expense for many years, owes her money, and has promised her marriage. Sir John attempts to convince the Justice that she is mad, but finally takes her aside, renews his promises to her, and convinces her to pawn her silver in order to lend him yet more money: Mistress Quickly even invites him to supper, asking whether he would like the prostitute Doll Tearsheet to be there too. The Justice receives discouraging news of the King's illness.

2.2 Prince Harry, in self-disgusted conversation with Poins, confides that he is sad about his father's sickness though he knows Poins will think him a hypocrite to say so. Sir John's companions Bardolph and the Page bring the Prince a letter in which Sir John warns him that Poins has been boasting that the Prince will marry his sister, though Poins denies this. Harry and Poins learn that Sir John is to dine at the tavern in Eastcheap with Doll Tearsheet and resolve to spy on him there disguised as bar staff.

2.3 Northumberland, about to set off to join the Archbishop's forces, is dissuaded by his daughter-in-law Lady Percy, Hotspur's widow, who argues that since Northumberland betrayed her lamented husband he should not keep his word to others. She is seconded by Northumberland's wife, and Northumberland decides to fly to Scotland until the success or otherwise of the rebellion is more evident.

2.4 In a private room at the tavern Sir John, dining with Mistress Quickly and Doll Tearsheet, is interrupted by the swaggering Pistol, who, after ranting in garbled fragments of Marlovian verse, is finally expelled, after a scuffle, by Bardolph. To the strains of music Sir John takes Doll on his knee, watched and overheard by the disguised Prince and Poins, and speaks disparagingly of the Prince before kissing her, lamenting his age. The Prince and Poins confront him, and he claims to have been deliberately dissuading sinners like Doll from loving the Prince, for his own good. Prince Harry is called away to his father, reproaching himself for wasting his time at the tavern during a crisis, and Sir John too is summoned to join the army, sending back, however, to summon Doll to him before he does so.

3.1 King Henry, in his nightgown, envies his subjects the freedom from anxiety that comes with sleep, before reflecting with Warwick and Surrey on his betrayal, prophesied by Richard II, by the nobles who helped him to power. Warwick, comforting him with the news that Glyndŵr is dead, persuades him to go to bed for fear of worsening his sickness.

3.2 In Warwickshire Sir John is welcomed by his old acquaintances Justice Shallow and Justice Silence, where he chooses recruits from among a number of villagers: the fittest of them, Mouldy and Bullcalf, offer bribes, through Bardolph, to be exempted from military service, and Sir John does not select them despite Shallow's protests, picking the unimpressive Feeble, Wart, and Shadow instead. Alone, Sir John reflects with amusement at the discrepancy between the insignificant Shallow he remembers and the tales he now tells of his wild youth, planning to fleece him on his return from the impending campaign.

4.1 In the forest of Gaultres, the Archbishop of York, Thomas Mowbray, and Lord Hastings have just heard that Northumberland will not be joining them when Westmorland arrives from the approaching royal army: they outline their grievances to him, and give him a written text of their demands, which he undertakes to give to the royal army's commander, Prince John.

The Archbishop and Hastings try to reassure Mowbray that the King will be willing to make peace with them and will keep to any terms agreed. This is confirmed at a parley between the two armies by Prince John, who promises that all their demands will be met, and drinks with them to this seeming peace: as soon as the rebels have dismissed their army, however, he arrests them for capital treason, promising that though they will be executed the grievances to which they have drawn his attention will be redressed.

4.2 Sir John meets a rebel commander, Coleville, who, hearing of his adversary's identity, surrenders in terror: Sir John hands him over to Prince John, who arrives with Westmorland and soldiers pursuing fleeing rebels, and Coleville is sent to York to be executed. The nobles set off for London, where the King's sickness has worsened. Sir John reflects that Prince John's cold nature is the result of insufficient drinking, a fault from which Harry is free, and speaks eloquently of the beneficial effects of consuming sherry-sack.

4.3 On his sickbed, the King speaks of Prince Harry and his anxiety about the chaos that may befall his kingdom when he inherits the throne: Warwick tries in vain to reassure him that the Prince is only studying his present companions, and will renounce them in due course. Westmorland brings news of the defeat of the Archbishop's forces, and Harcourt news that Northumberland and his Scottish and English confederates have been defeated by the Sheriff of Yorkshire, but this good news brings on a seizure, and the King sleeps, the crown beside him on the pillow, while his nobles speak of omens prophesying his death. Prince Harry arrives, and watches over his father while the others depart: alone with the sleeping King he reflects on the cares that come with the crown and then, sorrowfully convinced that his father has died, takes it and puts it on. After he has left, however, the King awakens, and becomes convinced that his son has taken the crown, wishing him dead: alone with Harry he upbraids him at length, lamenting the riotous reign he is convinced the Prince longs for. A weeping Harry convinces him of the truth, however, and they are reconciled, the King advising Harry that although his inheritance of the crown will be less controversial than his own snatching of it from Richard he should be sure to distract his people with military campaigns abroad to prevent further domestic rebellions. Convinced he is dying, he learns that the room in which he collapsed is called the Jerusalem Chamber, and reflects that it was once prophesied that he would die in Jerusalem but he had always hoped this would be on the crusade he has never been able to lead.

5.1 On his way back from the campaign, Sir John has arrived at Shallow's house, where he sees the overbearing servant Davy effectively running the entire household: Sir John plans to keep Prince Harry amused with stories and jests involving Shallow.

5.2 The Lord Chief Justice learns to his sorrow from Warwick that the old King has died, and much of the court assembles, including Prince John and his brothers Clarence and Gloucester, all deeply apprehensive about how they will be treated now that the wild Prince Harry has inherited the throne. When Harry arrives, however, he speaks with dignity, promising a well-governed reign, and in response to the Lord Chief Justice's defence of his earlier decision to send him to prison the new King warmly ratifies his position at the head of the judicial system.

5.3 Sir John, his page, and Bardolph are dining, along with Silence, at Justice Shallow's house, the meal punctuated by Silence's unexpected bursts of song, when Pistol arrives in a state of incomprehensible excitement. He brings the news that Prince Harry has inherited the crown, upon which Sir John, convinced that thanks to the new King's friendship he will have unlimited power and scope, sets eagerly off for London.

5.4 Mistress Quickly and Doll Tearsheet are arrested by beadles, accused of taking part, with Pistol, in a fatal beating.

5.5 Sir John, Shallow, Pistol, Bardolph, and the Page eagerly await King Henry V's coronation procession, the more so since Sir John has borrowed £1,000 from Shallow on his expectations from the new King: Sir John confidently expects, too, to be able shortly to procure Doll Tearsheet's release from prison. When the King and his attendants arrive, however, he refuses to recognize Sir John, publicly renouncing his former ways, and declares that if Sir John comes within 10 miles (16 km) of him again he will be put to death. After his departure, Sir John insists that the King will send for him privately later on, but the Lord Chief Justice returns to commit him and his followers to the Fleet prison. Prince John approves, and has heard a rumour that the King means shortly to launch a military campaign in France. An epilogue promises a sequel which will include comic scenes involving Princess Catherine of France, and in which Sir John—who is not Oldcastle, we are reminded—may go to France and die of a sweat.

ARTISTIC FEATURES

The play in many respects recapitulates that of 1 *Henry IV* in a minor key, the Machiavellian defeat of the rebellion a far cry from Hotspur's heroic death at Shrewsbury, while the sub-plot, though exquisitely funny, is tinged throughout with a melancholy which is only underlined by the potential pathos of Sir John's final rejection at the hands of Henry V. The scene of the evening at Shallow's house in Gloucestershire, punctuated by the memories of old men and culminating in the news of a king's death, has no equal as a simultaneously comic, lyrical, and rueful dramatization of the passage of time.

 CRITICAL HISTORY

The critical history of this play is in practice impossible to disentangle from that of *Part 1*, and to a lesser extent the remainder of the Second Tetralogy: see the entry on *1 Henry IV*.

STAGE HISTORY

2 Henry IV has only rarely been acted wholly independently of *Part 1*: since at least the time of the Dering manuscript, which condenses *Part 1* into the first three-quarters of its length and *Part 2* into the last, the plays have been largely inseparable in the theatre no less than in criticism. The earliest post-Restoration revival came when Thomas Betterton produced a cut version in which he extended his depiction of Falstaff, but the play was better known in the 18th century for the role of Pistol, memorably played by Theophilus Cibber (who was nicknamed Pistol thereafter). In the 19th century it was revived by William Charles Macready in 1821 to mark the coronation of George IV (a production which later visited New York), and from then onwards more attention seems to have been paid to the role of Justice Shallow, which Samuel Phelps doubled with the King in 1853 and at intervals thereafter. In the 20th century Laurence Olivier's performance as Shallow alongside Ralph Richardson's poignant but impish Falstaff, at the New Theatre in 1945, entered the realms of legend.

ON THE SCREEN

See HENRY IV PART 1.

Henry V

The culmination of Shakespeare's mature sequence of English histories, *Henry V*, the last play of the Second Tetralogy, is comparatively easy to date thanks to an uncharacteristic topical reference. At the start of Act 5 the Chorus explicitly compares Henry V's welcome back to London after his campaign in France to the anticipated welcome the Earl of Essex would receive should he return victoriously from his current expedition against Tyrone's rebellion in Ireland (5.0.30–5). Essex's planned campaign was common knowledge as early as November 1598, but this passage, and probably the rest of the play too, is more likely to have been written between the Earl's departure in March 1599 and his return in disgrace that September.

 TEXT

The play was first printed in quarto in 1600, said to have been 'sundry times played by the Right Honourable the Lord Chamberlain his servants', and reappeared in the Folio of 1623 in a version derived from Shakespeare's own foul papers. The quarto is in many respects corrupt, apparently a memorial reconstruction assembled by actors who had appeared in a version of the play shortened for performance by a small cast (perhaps on a provincial tour), but it seems to derive from a later authorial text of the play than does the Folio. In particular, the quarto chooses to follow Shakespeare's historical sources in not representing the Dauphin as a combatant at Agincourt, giving the lines he speaks there in the Folio to the Duke of Bourbon.

 SOURCES

Shakespeare again worked from the materials he had used in the *Henry IV* plays, namely the chronicles of Raphael Holinshed and Edward Halle and the anonymous play *The Famous Victories of Henry V*. It is possible that he was also influenced by other contemporary plays on this subject, now lost.

 CHARACTER LIST

Chorus

Henry the Fifth, King of England
claimant to the French throne

Duke of **Gloucester** ⎤ *his*
Duke of **Clarence** ⎦ *brothers*
Duke of **Exeter** *his uncle*

Duke of **York** *his cousin*
Earl of **Salisbury**
Earl of **Westmorland**
Earl of **Warwick**
Archbishop of **Canterbury**
Bishop of **Ely**

Richard, Earl of
Cambridge
Henry, Lord **Scrope** | *traitors*
of Masham
Sir Thomas **Grey**

Pistol | *formerly*
Nim | *Falstaff's*
Bardolph | *companions*

Boy *formerly Falstaff's page*
Hostess *formerly Mistress Quickly,*
now Pistol's wife
Sir Thomas **Erpingham**
Captain **Gower** *an Englishman*
Captain **Fluellen** *a Welshman*
Captain **Macmorris** *an Irishman*
Captain **Jamy** *a Scot*
John **Bates** | *English*
Alexander **Court** | *soldiers*
Michael **Williams**

Herald
Charles the Sixth *King of France*
Isabel *his wife and queen*
Louis the Dauphin *their son*
and heir
Catherine *their daughter*
Alice *Catherine's lady-in-waiting*
The **Constable**
of France
Duke of **Bourbon** | *French*
Duke of **Orléans** | *noblemen at*
Duke of **Berri** | *Agincourt*
Lord **Rambures**
Lord **Grandpré**
Duke of **Burgundy**

Montjoy *the French Herald*
Governor of Harfleur
French **Ambassadors**
to England

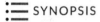 SYNOPSIS

The Chorus speaks a prologue, lamenting the inadequacy of the theatre to so great a subject and imploring the audience to use their imaginations.

1.1 The Archbishop of Canterbury and the Bishop of Ely are anxious that the new King, whose transformation from reveller to statesman they applaud, may support a measure heavily taxing the Church: the Archbishop has attempted to dissuade him from this by offering a large grant towards a military expedition urging his title to the French crown.

1.2 Before receiving a French embassy, King Harry calls upon the Archbishop to explain his right to the French throne, which he does at some length, urging Harry to attack France. The Archbishop is seconded by Ely and a number of English nobles including the King's uncle the Duke of Exeter, who convince Harry that he can mount a campaign in France while satisfactorily garrisoning England against potential Scottish invasion. The French ambassador is admitted with a message from the Dauphin, who has heard of Harry's plans to claim French territory and, as a comment on his youth and alleged frivolity, has sent a barrel of tennis balls as a present. The King dismisses the ambassadors after promising that he will soon avenge this mockery in full, and sets the preparations for his campaign in motion.

2.0 The Chorus describes the country's eager preparations for the war, but also outlines a French-funded conspiracy to assassinate the King at Southampton.

2.1 Corporal Nim and Ensign Pistol quarrel about Nim's former fiancée the Hostess, Mistress Quickly, whom Pistol has married: they are prevented from duelling by Bardolph, and by a summons home to the bedside of their sick master Sir John Falstaff, broken-hearted over his rejection by Harry (dramatized at the end of *2 Henry IV*).

2.2 At Southampton the King, about to embark with his forces for France, is advised by the traitors Scrope, Cambridge, and Grey against showing mercy to a drunk who has shouted abusively at him, but has the man released. He then presents the three traitors with what he says are their commissions but are in fact their indictments for capital treason, decrying their treachery and refusing them mercy by their own earlier advice. They confess and apologize before being led away to execution, and the King embarks.

2.3 Pistol, Nim, Bardolph, and the Boy are also leaving for France, sorrowful over the death of Sir John, which is poignantly narrated by the Hostess, from whom they part.

2.4 King Charles of France is making arrangements to defend his realm against King Harry, whom the Dauphin scorns to take seriously despite the misgivings of King Charles and the Constable: Exeter arrives as Harry's ambassador, delivering his claim to France, demanding an immediate response, and passing on Harry's personal defiance to the Dauphin. King Charles insists on a night in which to consider his reply.

3.0 The Chorus asks the audience to imagine Harry's army crossing the Channel and laying siege to Harfleur.

3.1 Harry urges his troops to make one more assault on the breach in Harfleur's walls.

3.2 Bardolph is eager enough to join the attack but Nim, Pistol, and the Boy would rather stay alive: they have to be driven towards the breach with blows by the Welsh captain Fluellen. The Boy remains behind and comments on the cowardice and petty thieving of his associates, whom he plans to leave.

3.3 Fluellen laments to his English comrade Captain Gower that the operation to lay mines under Harfleur's walls is not being carried out according to proper military precedent, for which he blames the Irishman, Captain MacMorris, who arrives in the company of the Scots captain Jamy.

MacMorris, furious himself at the mismanagement of the mines, is in no mood to enter into a discussion about military discipline with Fluellen, and is especially touchy about Fluellen's reference to his nationality, but they postpone their quarrel to another occasion when they hear a parley sounded. King Harry urges the Governor of Harfleur to surrender, threatening that his soldiers will otherwise commit rape, infanticide, and other atrocities when they finally gain entrance, and the Governor capitulates, having received word that the Dauphin will not be able to send reinforcements. Harry plans to retire to Calais with his increasingly sickly army.

3.4 At the French court the Princess Catherine is learning English from her gentlewoman Alice, naming parts of the body and finding the English words 'foot' and 'gown' shockingly immodest.

3.5 King Charles's nobles are astonished that the English have hitherto been so successful, lamenting that their women are taunting them for being less virile. Detaining the Dauphin with him, King Charles sends an immense force against Harry led by the Constable of France, first sending the herald Montjoy to ask what ransom Harry will pay to be spared.

3.6 Fluellen has been impressed by Pistol's valiant language, but is disillusioned when Pistol asks him to intercede with Exeter to have Bardolph spared from hanging after being caught looting: Gower confirms that Pistol is a fraud. The King arrives and receives a progress report from Fluellen, including the news of Bardolph's execution, which the King endorses. Montjoy arrives with King Charles's request that Harry name his ransom: Harry, however, though admitting that his army is enfeebled by sickness and few in number, says he will not decline a battle, ordering his soldiers to encamp for the night and be ready to fight the next morning.

3.7 The French nobles, eager for battle, scoff at the supposedly doomed English: Bourbon [in the Folio, the Dauphin] brags absurdly about his horse.

4.0 The Chorus describes the two armies the night before the battle—the over-confident French dicing for English prisoners, the demoralized English being cheered by the King in person—and apologizes that the stage is so inadequate to the task of representing the battle of Agincourt.

4.1 During the night King Harry borrows a cloak from Sir Thomas Erpingham and wanders incognito among his soldiers: he is defied by Pistol for calling himself a friend of Fluellen, and approvingly overhears Fluellen reproaching Gower for speaking too loudly so close to the enemy army. He then joins a discussion among three common soldiers, Bates, Court, and Williams, about the justice of the King's war and his responsibility for its casualties: Williams insists that the King's declaration that he will not be ransomed is so much cynical propaganda, and he and Harry exchange gloves, by which they will recognize one another again, so that they may take up this quarrel after the battle. Alone, Harry laments the responsibilities laid on him by his subjects, ill compensated by the idle ceremonies of royalty, and prays that God will make his soldiers brave, imploring pardon for his father's crime in usurping the crown from the murdered Richard II.

4.2 In the morning the French nobles eagerly prepare for battle.

4.3 The English nobles, their army outnumbered by five to one, bid farewell to one another, Warwick wishing their numbers were swelled by 10,000 of those at home who will do no work on this day: arriving from reviewing his troops the King overhears and rebukes him, saying the fewer they are the more honour they will share. In a stirring oration Harry claims that on this day, the feast of St Crispin, the heroic deeds of this small band of brothers will forever be remembered. Montjoy comes with one final appeal that Harry should negotiate a ransom instead of fighting, but Harry defies him, allowing the Duke of York to lead the English vanguard into battle.

4.4 In the fighting Pistol takes a French prisoner, with whom, using the Boy as interpreter, he negotiates a ransom. The Boy is anxious that the English camp is currently guarded only by boys.

4.5 Some of the French nobles are appalled that their army is losing, all order confounded: Bourbon leads them back into the battle, preferring death to the shame of defeat.

4.6 Exeter tells the King how York and Suffolk have died together in chivalric brotherhood: seeing the French regrouping, Harry orders the English to kill their prisoners.

4.7 Fluellen and Gower are horrified that the French have killed the English boys who were guarding the camp. Fluellen praises Harry, proud that the King was born in Monmouth, and makes a far-fetched comparison between Harry and Alexander the Great, likening Alexander's killing of his friend Cleitus to Harry's rejection of Falstaff. The King, angry to have heard of the slaughter of the boys, receives Montjoy, who concedes defeat. Fluellen congratulates the King for living up to the example of his ancestors and for being proud to be Welsh: heralds go to count the dead. Harry speaks with Williams, who does not recognize him; he then gives Fluellen the glove he had from Williams the previous night, telling him whoever challenges it is a traitor and should be arrested, but he sends Warwick and Gloucester to follow and prevent any mischief.

4.8 Williams challenges Fluellen's glove and Fluellen tries to have him arrested: the King arrives with Warwick, Gloucester, and Exeter, however, explains his trick, reveals the identity of the man Williams challenged the previous night, and rewards Williams by returning his glove filled with gold coins. A herald brings the lists of the dead from both sides: the French have lost 10,000, including the Constable and many nobles, while the English have lost only 25 men all told. The King attributes the victory to God and decrees a mass.

5.0 The Chorus describes the King's triumphant return to London, but says the play will not show this, cutting ahead to his return to France for the peace negotiations.

5.1 Fluellen has been affronted by Pistol on St David's Day and mocked for wearing a Welsh leek in his cap: he now seeks out Pistol, cudgels him and makes him eat the leek, with Gower's approval. Pistol, alone, laments that the Hostess has died of venereal disease, but looks forward to returning to England, resuming his career as a bawd and pickpocket, and passing off the marks of his beating as heroic war wounds.

5.2 At a grand summit between Harry and his delegation and the French court, Burgundy laments the damage the war has done to French agriculture, urging the swift conclusion of a peace: while his nobles discuss their proposed settlement with King Charles and his Queen, Harry remains with Alice and the Princess Catherine, whose marriage to Harry is one of the English demands under discussion. In a mixture of English and French Harry woos Catherine, assuring her that he loves France so well that he means to keep it, and on her concession that she will marry him if her father agrees he kisses her, much to her shock. Burgundy, finding them kissing on his return with the negotiators, jests elaborately. King Charles has agreed to all the English terms, including his daughter's marriage to Harry, except the requirement that he should officially call Harry the heir to France. At Harry's insistence, however, he cedes this point, and peace is concluded, the nobles looking forward to Harry and Catherine's wedding. The Chorus speaks an epilogue, in the form of a sonnet, reminding the audience that despite Harry's triumphs his son Henry VI lost France and allowed England to fall into renewed civil wars.

🎭 ARTISTIC FEATURES

The Chorus's speeches contain some of Shakespeare's most exciting and ambitious poetry, reaching towards the territory of epic, and the King's two great orations, 'Once more unto the breach' (3.1) and 'This day is called the Feast of Crispian' (4.3.18–67), are classics of English patriotic rhetoric. The play is more double-edged, however, than these frequently quoted passages may suggest: its depiction of warfare never precisely matches the glamorous and heroic pictures conjured by the Chorus, while its protagonist, aptly parodied by his comic counterpart Pistol, is both more insecure and more Machiavellian than the 'warlike Harry' promised in the Prologue.

✯✯ CRITICAL HISTORY

The success with which the play has monopolized the representation of the historical Henry V has often led commentators to conflate Shakespeare's Henry with the real one, and this in turn has exacerbated a tendency to identify the play solely with its titular hero. Romantic critics, from William Hazlitt to W. B. Yeats and beyond, tended to disparage Henry as somehow mechanical, convinced that as a true poet Shakespeare must have preferred his more contemplative protagonists, such as Hamlet and Richard II, to anyone so decisive and successful. Much 20th-century commentary, particularly before 1950, was interested in relating this play to the design of the Second Tetralogy as a whole, often presenting Henry as Shakespeare's culminating ideal of English kingship (a view particularly associated with E. M. W. Tillyard): since then critics have more often been divided between those who accuse the play of jingoism, or at best of complicity with Tudor policy in Ireland and elsewhere, and those more interested in highlighting Shakespeare's awareness of the contradictions and moral problems implicit in Harry's attack on France. Recent work has explored further these questions, debating in detail the legality and criminality of Henry's warcraft and the play's representations of nation and national difference.

▮ STAGE HISTORY

The play was revived at court in 1605, but the extant evidence suggests that it did not achieve the same popularity in its own time as the *Henry IV* plays or *Richard III*, something for which it would wait until the 18th century. When it was first revived, however, it appeared only in pieces, the Fluellen–Pistol scene appearing in Charles Molloy's farce *The Half-Pay Officers* in 1720 and some of the rest of the play the following year in Aaron Hill's adaptation *King Henry the Fifth; or, The Conquest of France by the English*. The original was first revived in 1735, during the wave of patriotism that preceded the War of Jenkins's Ear, and from then on a succession of wars with France kept it in the repertory for most of the rest of the century: it was revived at Covent Garden, for example, in every single season during the Seven Years War (1756–63). David Garrick cast himself as the Chorus in 1747, but the role was more usually cut, and the increasingly spectacular style in which the play was mounted mandated further cuts over the ensuing years. Major actors taking the role of Henry included John Philip Kemble, W. C. Macready, Samuel Phelps, and, in New York, George Rignold, whose 1875 production lost even more of Shakespeare's text to make way for a grand recreation of Harry and Catherine's betrothal ceremony. In England the role became a favourite of Frank Benson from 1899 onwards: his athletic ascent of the proscenium arch in full armour during 'Once more unto the breach' and his subsequent vaulting over the walls of Harfleur remain legendary, although he had strong competition during the Boer War years from Lewis Waller. The play was much revived during the First World War (Sybil Thorndike played the Chorus at the Old Vic) and remained a favourite during the inter-war years, with Laurence Olivier playing his first Henry in 1937. Since the Second World War interpretations of the title role have been largely shaped by their response to his portrayal, filmed in 1944, with some actors closely following his approach (such as Alan Howard in Terry Hands's important Stratford production of 1975), some reacting strongly against it (such as Michael Pennington, playing Henry as a cold cynic in Michael Bogdanov's production of 1985–6), and some attempting to do both, notably Kenneth Branagh, who first played the role in Adrian Noble's ambivalently post-Falklands War production for the RSC in 1984. Wilford Leach's production in Central Park (1984) did its best to further undermine the identification of Henry as a hero, having the King participate in the bloodily staged slaughter of the French POWs. Matthew Warchus's 1994 production for the RSC made clear the parallels between early modern and modern conflict: Tony Britton's overcoat-wearing, poppy-sporting Chorus recalled the trenches of the First World War, contrasting with Henry's (Iain Glen) decidedly medieval religious zeal. The replica Shakespeare's Globe officially opened with *Henry V* in 1997. Directed by Richard Olivier with Mark Rylance in the title role, this production demonstrated the company's early fidelity to 'original practices': the all-male cast were costumed according to early modern conventions and Rylance vented his mercurial King on a rush-strewn stage. The audience at Edward Hall's 1997 production at the Watermill theatre did not have to imagine horses: they saw them. Taken outside for Henry's (Jamie Glover) speech to Harfleur, the audience watched the King deliver his threats mounted on a bay mare. Later that year, Ron Daniels' khaki production for the RSC foregrounded the grim realities of war and the play's contemporary resonances. In a visual echo of the USA's Vietnam Veterans Memorial, over 2,000 names of the fallen covered the walls of the stage, while Michael Sheen's Henry was first sighted watching footage of the muddy carnage of the First World War's trenches. Nicholas Hytner's *Henry V* for the National Theatre was rehearsed during the 2003 invasion of Iraq, with the military vehicles, desert fatigues, and manipulated press briefings signalling this production's intense topicality. In this war-world, Adrian Lester's coldly rigid Henry was confronted by his recalcitrant troops along with the French: Henry shot his old buddy Bardolph himself, while the English mutinously refused orders to slay their prisoners of war. Michael Boyd's 2007 production for the RSC demonstrated his trademark interest in verticality. The English emerged from under the stage, while the French were frequently presented on trapezes in the theatre's upper spaces; Katherine was flown in from the roof in a smoke-filled production of explosions and spectacle. Jamie Parker's Henry for Dominic Dromgoole's 2012 Globe production was played as a valiant soldier, his heroism standing in stark contrast to Jude Law's ruthless King in Michael Grandage's production at the Noel Coward Theatre in 2013. Once committed to war, Alex Hassell's Henry (RSC, 2015) likewise embraced the King's potential for brutality, bellowing orders to slaughter. Unlike most other contemporary productions, the Open Air Theatre at Regent's Park drew parallels with domestic rather than international conflict. Robert Hastie's *Henry V* (2016) was mounted in the weeks during and after the UK's vote to leave the European Union. In this version, when Michelle Terry's nuanced and thoughtful Henry offered her troops the chance to depart during the St Crispin's Day speech, for once one soldier did break away from the rest.

ON THE SCREEN

The two outstanding *Henry V* films were made by Laurence Olivier (1944) and Kenneth Branagh (1989) who, like Olivier before, was director and played the title role. Olivier's film, despite its vigorous wartime patriotism, remains a classic, exploiting with imaginative brilliance cinema's ability to embrace a range of visual styles and to effect transitions in time and place, and between theatre and cinema. With William Walton's rousing orchestral score punctuating the soundtrack with sparkle and wistfulness, it is the first sound film to establish both artistic stature and public appeal for filmed Shakespeare. Branagh's *Henry V*, made for an audience far more suspicious of the glamorization of war, has been seen as a reaction to Olivier's film. Yet Branagh incorporates and modifies some of Olivier's devices. His is a profoundly searching Henry, with none of the easy

RAF-style nonchalance so evident in Olivier's portrayal: he finds the body of the slain Boy at Agincourt, for example, and carries it, grieving, across the battlefield. On the small screen, the play was filmed as part of the BBC Shakespeare series in 1979, with David Gwillim as Henry, and it formed the final chapter of the BBC's grand retelling of the Second Tetralogy, *The Hollow Crown* (2012), with Tom Hiddleston as Henry. In 2019, the streaming service Netflix released *The King* (dir., David Michôd), a modern speech/medieval dress mash-up of Shakespeare's Second Tetralogy starring Timothée Chalamet as Hal/Henry. Chalamet's Henry is a pacifist with a monastic aesthetic, spurred to *Game of Thrones*–style war by the machinations of his Machiavellian advisers.

Henry VI Part 1

On 3 March 1592 the manager-owner of the Rose theatre, Philip Henslowe, recorded a 'new' performance of 'Harry the VI' in his diary. While this may conceivably allude to any of the three *Henry VI* plays, contextual evidence suggests it refers only to *Part 1*. (There is no early edition to help with the question of dating, since *1 Henry VI* did not appear in print until the appearance of the First Folio in 1623.) The box-office receipts of £3 16s. 8d. set a record that season, and the play was performed another fifteen times by Lord Strange's Men over the next ten months. Thomas Nashe attested to its popularity in August that year in his pamphlet *Piers Penniless his Supplication to the Devil*. He invokes the inspiring deeds of *Part 1*'s warrior hero, Lord Talbot, to defend the theatre against moralistic attacks and as a 'reproof to these degenerate effeminate days of ours': 'How would it have joyed brave Talbot, the terror of the French, to think that after he had lien two hundred years in his tomb he should triumph again on the stage, and have his bones new-embalmed with the tears of ten thousand spectators at least, at several

times, who in the tragedian that represents his person imagine they behold him fresh bleeding!' Many scholars now believe that *Part 1* was written before these dates but after *The First Part of the Contention* (*2 Henry VI*) in 1590–1, and also *Richard Duke of York* (*3 Henry VI*) in 1591, in effect as what would now be called a 'prequel'. Although *Part 1* presents events early in Henry's reign that are continued by those plays, there are historical anomalies between *The Contention* and *Part 1* that one would not expect to find if the latter had come first, in particular the fact that *The Contention* makes no mention of Talbot. The Stationers' Register entry for 8 November 1623 covering the play's Folio publication also misleadingly records 'The Third Part of Henry the Sixth', even though *Richard Duke of York* had long been in print. The numbering thus refers to *Part 1*'s first publication after the other *Henry VI* plays had been issued, and perhaps to its sequence of composition. It must have been written after the second edition of Holinshed's *Chronicles* (1587, see below), as well as the publication of Edmund Spenser's *The Faerie Queene* (1590). The play's action may allude to English military expeditions to France between 1590 and 1591, particularly the Earl of Essex's (ultimately unsuccessful) siege of Rouen, October 1591–January 1592.

AUTHORSHIP

Although it first appeared in the authoritative 1623 Folio, *Part 1* is perhaps the least likely of the *Henry VI* plays to be wholly by Shakespeare, whose authorship has been questioned since the 18th century. Collaborative writing might explain Francis Meres's failure to mention *Henry VI* in *Palladis Tamia* (1598), which lists other—but not all—known Shakespeare plays. Modern scholars and editors have argued that Thomas Nashe wrote Act 1 and perhaps other scenes, which may partly explain his enthusiastic notice of the play, while the 2016 New Oxford attributes some passages to Christopher Marlowe. Other possible collaborators are Robert Greene and George Peele. Other recent editors, however, such as Michael Hattaway (Cambridge, 1990), argue that Shakespeare was the sole author, and that the play's episodic design, monochromatic characterization, and stylistic unevenness indicate that the play was composed at an earlier stage in his career, before the superior achievements of *The First Part of the Contention* and *Richard Duke of York*. The parts of the play most frequently and confidently attributed to Shakespeare are the Temple Garden or 'rose-plucking' scene (2.4), and the portion of Act 4 covering 4.2 to the death of Talbot in 4.7.

 SOURCES

1 Henry VI skilfully telescopes wide-ranging and often diffuse accounts in Edward Halle's *Union of the Two Noble and Illustrious Families of Lancaster and York* (1548), and the compilation edited by Raphael Holinshed, *Chronicles of England, Scotland, and Ireland* (2nd edn. 1587). The established view is that Halle—traditionally regarded as more ideologically conservative—was Shakespeare's chief source, but some scholars have questioned this priority. Robert Fabyan's *New Chronicles of England and France* (1516) probably supplied information for 1.3 and 3.1, while Geoffrey of Monmouth's medieval *Historia Regum Britanniae*, Froissart's *Chronicles* (trans. 1523–5), and John Stow's *Chronicles of England* (1580) are sources for individual minor details.

 CHARACTER LIST

The English
King Henry VI
Duke of **Gloucester**,
    Lord Protector *uncle of*
    King Henry
Duke of **Bedford**, Regent
    of France
Duke of **Exeter**
Bishop of **Winchester** (later
    Cardinal) *uncle of King Henry*
Duke of **Somerset**
Richard Plantagenet, later
    Duke of York, and Regent
    of France
Earl of **Warwick**
Earl of **Salisbury**
Earl of **Suffolk**
Lord **Talbot**
John Talbot
Edmund **Mortimer**
Sir William **Glasdale**
Sir Thomas **Gargrave**
Sir John **Fastolf**
Sir William **Lucy**

Woodville, Lieutenant of
    the Tower of London
Mayor of London
Vernon
Basset
A **Lawyer**
A **Legate**
Messengers, warders and
    keepers of the Tower of
    London, servingmen,
    officers, captains, soldiers,
    herald, watch
The French
Charles, Dauphin of France
René, Duke of Anjou,
    King of Naples
Margaret *his daughter*
Duke of **Alençon**
Bastard of Orléans
Duke of **Burgundy** *uncle of*
    King Henry
General of the French garrison
    at Bordeaux
Countess of Auvergne

Master Gunner of Orléans
A **Boy** *his son*
Joan la Pucelle
A **Shepherd** *father of Joan*

Porter, French sergeant, French
sentinels, French scout, French
herald, the Governor of Paris,
fiends, and soldiers

≔ SYNOPSIS

1.1 Henry V's state funeral is disrupted by news of the loss of conquests in France and the nobles' quarrelling, especially between Humphrey, Duke of Gloucester, and Henry Beaufort, Bishop of Winchester.

1.2 The French are beaten back after trying to disperse the English siege of Orléans. Joan la Pucelle presents herself as a holy peasant maid divinely destined to liberate France; she recognizes Charles the Dauphin without ever having seen him, and defeats him in a test of combat.

1.3 A violent brawl between Gloucester, Winchester, and their men is dispersed by the Mayor of London.

1.4 The Master Gunner of Orléans fires upon a tower from where Talbot and the English have surveyed the French defences. Salisbury is mortally wounded.

1.5–6 Joan disarms Talbot and captures Orléans. The victorious French celebrate her victory on the city walls.

2.1 Using scaling-ladders, Talbot, Bedford, and Burgundy assault Orléans and drive out the French.

2.2–3 Salisbury's funeral. The Countess of Auvergne invites Talbot to visit her castle, where she tries to take him prisoner, but he secretly forearms himself with a troop of soldiers.

2.4 In the Temple Garden, Richard Plantagenet, Somerset, and their supporters display their rival loyalties by plucking white and red roses, symbolizing the beginning of the Wars of the Roses.

2.5 York visits the dying Edmund Mortimer, heir to Richard II but long imprisoned by the Lancastrians. He describes Plantagenet's dynastic claim to the throne deriving from Edward III.

3.1 Gloucester and Winchester quarrel before the young Henry, who creates Plantagenet Duke of York. Henry leaves to be crowned in France.

3.2 Joan la Pucelle leads the French in disguise to take Rouen. The English are first defeated in battle but then recover the city.

3.3 Joan persuades Burgundy to switch sides to support the French.

3.4 Henry creates Talbot Earl of Shrewsbury. Vernon and Basset, respective supporters of York and Somerset, challenge each other.

4.1 Henry's coronation is interrupted by the banishment of John Fastolf, disgraced for cowardice. Henry tries to mediate Vernon and Basset's quarrel, unwittingly favouring the latter and infuriating York.

4.2 Talbot challenges the French before the walls of Bordeaux.

4.3 York blames Somerset's lack of cooperation for his inability to rescue Talbot, as the French recapture more towns.

4.4 Somerset blames York for his delay in sending aid and Talbot's imminent defeat.

4.5 Talbot's son John vows to accompany his father in battle.

4.6 Talbot rescues him when he is endangered.

4.7 Talbot dies after his dead son is brought before him. Lucy solemnly claims their bodies from the victorious and scoffing French.

5.1 The French offer Henry the Earl of Armagnac's daughter in peace negotiations. Winchester is made a cardinal.

5.2 The Parisians revolt against Charles and Joan.

5.3 Joan is captured by York while raising demonic spirits. Suffolk captures Margaret of Anjou and woos her for Henry's queen so that she may secretly become his paramour. Margaret's father René consents to give her to Henry, but without any dowry and on condition that Anjou and Maine are returned to French rule.

5.4 Joan denies knowing her old father and is condemned to the stake by York. He and Winchester negotiate a peace with the French, who agree in the hope of gaining future advantage.

5.5 Suffolk persuades Henry to accept Margaret as his queen over the English nobles' objections.

✯✯ CRITICAL HISTORY

Until recently, *1 Henry VI* attracted little critical attention. The play's arguably collaborative origins have suppressed interest on the grounds that it is not fully or genuinely Shakespearian. Its stylistic hybridity and loose structure have also been taken as a sign of apprentice work, especially if *Part 1* is positioned as the first play of the *Henry VI* trilogy, near the beginning of Shakespeare's professional career, while literary critics have missed the dramatic unity and aesthetic refinement they value in Shakespeare's later histories. An exception to these negative assessments was made by 19th-century German critics such as A. W. Schlegel, who situated the play in the wider context of Shakespeare's histories as an epic national drama of political evolution from feudalism. In 1944 E. M. W. Tillyard's *Shakespeare's History Plays* adopted this interpretation but emphasized a pattern of national transgression and redemption. The retributive consequences of originally deposing Richard II continue in *Part 1* with the premature death of the heroic Henry V. The subsequent plunge into domestic factionalism and humiliation in France is ultimately corrected by the triumph of Henry VII and the Tudor dynasty, which united the Lancastrian and Yorkist lines. Since the 1970s critics have dismantled the monolithic ideology and rigid historical pattern of Tillyard's so-called 'Tudor myth' by observing the multiplicity of causal agencies and historical perspectives in this and other history plays. *Part 1* certainly endorses the idea that civil dissension and weak central authority—continually admonished in Elizabethan government writings—led to English losses in France during the Hundred Years War and the beginnings of the Wars of the Roses at home. But there is little in the play to connect these events with any metaphysical pattern of divine retribution. The focus is on secular history and personal agents making military and political decisions with predictable human consequences. Taking their cue partly from the conspicuous stage success the play has enjoyed in the past 50 years, theatre-minded critics have also observed how *Part 1* experiments with the full physical resources and configuration of the Elizabethan stage in boldly innovative ways, especially the use of the theatre gallery for vertically oriented assaults and multiply focused action on several levels. Stage productions have also pointed the way for feminist studies of Joan's subversion of traditional gender and social hierarchies. These critics have also noted the resemblance between Joan's various symbolic personae and public roles and those played by Elizabeth I.

STAGE HISTORY

Henslowe's diary entry indicates *1 Henry VI* was written for and performed by Lord Strange's Men at the Rose theatre, with London's leading actor, Edward Alleyn, probably taking the part of Talbot. Henry was probably played by a boy actor. No further records of performance exist until a revival at Covent Garden on 13 March 1738 'by desire of several ladies of quality'. The Temple Garden quarrel and several other scenes from *Part 1* were cannibalized by J. H. Merivale's romantic melodrama *Richard Duke of York* (1817), a star vehicle created for Edmund Kean. Osmond Tearle staged a fashionably spectacular production at Stratford in 1889, with himself playing Talbot. In Germany and Austria during this period, strong interest in Shakespeare's histories among Romantic critics stimulated many serious and innovative productions. F. R. Benson mounted all three *Henry VI* plays at Stratford in 1906. He played Talbot in *Part 1*, while Tita Brand played Joan la Pucelle. The play's opportunities for colourful pageantry were sumptuously exploited. Sir Barry Jackson and Douglas Seale's Birmingham Repertory Theatre production in 1953 launched the play's modern stage life and followed equally revelatory stagings of *The First Part of the Contention* and *Richard Duke of York*. Seale contextualized the opening funeral of Henry V by including the epilogue from Shakespeare's play, foreshadowing the darkening historical narrative: 'Henry the Sixth, in infant bands crowned king | ... Whose state so many had the managing | That they lost France and made [Henry V's] England bleed.' Alan Bridges played a gallantly chivalrous Talbot, but the surprise was Nancie Jackson's sympathetically engaging Joan, acted with 'a resolute pounce'. Seale's remounting of the trilogy at the Old Vic in 1957 was received with even more enthusiasm, although *Part 1* and *The Contention* were condensed into one play. This same approach characterized Peter Hall and John Barton's legendary *Wars of the Roses* for the RSC in 1963–4, later broadcast internationally in a 1965 television adaptation: *Part 1* was combined with much of *The First Part of the Contention* into *Henry VI*. Barton also added hundreds of lines of Shakespearian pastiche to clarify personal motives and story-lines. Janet Suzman played a zealously determined Joan la Pucelle, David Warner a vulnerably naive and movingly pious Henry. *1 Henry VI* was performed unadapted in Terry Hands's open and fast-paced 1977 RSC production of the whole trilogy, including a volcanic wooing scene between Helen Mirren as Margaret and Peter McEnery as Suffolk. In 1986 Michael Bogdanov and Michael Pennington reverted to Barton's condensed format—minus his invented lines—for their spiky 'post-Falklands' production, *The Wars of the Roses*, for the English Shakespeare Company, which toured internationally between 1986 and 1989. Adrian Noble followed their format but not their 'radical' ideology for his two-play version, *The Plantagenets*, for the RSC in 1988. In America, Pat Patton based his stirring 1991 Oregon Shakespeare Festival production on Noble's 'House of Lancaster'. Previous productions of *Part 1* at Ashland in 1953, 1964, and 1975 had employed strong ensemble acting and Shakespeare's full script. Michael Boyd's trilogy (see THE FIRST PART OF THE CONTENTION) represented one of the few occasions in recent decades in which *Part 1* has been staged as a discrete entity in its entirety. Edward Hall's much-lauded *Rose Rage* (2001), performed by the all-male Propeller company, followed the more usual practice of compressing three into two.

 ON THE SCREEN

Inspired by Brecht's self-conscious approach to theatricality, Jane Howell directed a playful but often intense production for BBC television, first broadcast in 1983. Trevor Peacock's Talbot and Brenda Blethyn's Joan were curiously matched as unheroic, down-to-earth, but knowing outsiders on their respective sides. Henry was played, as usual in modern productions, by an adult actor—the ascetic and benign Peter Benson, who succeeded in making Henry 'both pathetically ineffectual and truly saintly'.

Henry VI Part 2

see **First Part of the Contention of the Two Famous Houses of York and Lancaster, page 59**

Henry VI Part 3

see **Richard Duke of York, page 221**

Henry VIII

see **All Is True, page 1**

Julius Caesar

Shakespeare's most classical tragedy, as well as one of his most polished, was seen by a Swiss visitor, Thomas Platter, on 21 September 1599: since *Julius Caesar* is not mentioned among Shakespeare's works by Francis Meres the previous year, draws incidentally on two works published in 1599 (Samuel Daniel's *Musophilus* and Sir John Davies's *Nosce teipsum*), and is itself alluded to in a third (Ben Jonson's *Every Man in his Humour*), this is likely to have been an early performance. In vocabulary the play has links with Shakespeare's next tragedy, *Hamlet*, while in metre it is closest to *Henry V* and *As You Like It*: it was probably composed between the two latter plays, during 1599.

 TEXT

The play's only authoritative text is that provided by the First Folio (1623), for the most part an unusually good one, apparently prepared from a promptbook. It may record some alterations to the play made long after its première: 2.2 and 3.1, for example, seem to have been modified to allow an actor to double the roles of Cassius and Ligarius, while a line of Caesar's ridiculed as self-contradictory by Ben Jonson in his prologue to *The Staple of News* (1625) and again in *Discoveries* (c. 1630), 'Know Caesar doth not wrong but with just cause' (3.1.47), appears in the Folio with the offending last four words removed.

 SOURCES

This was Shakespeare's first play to use Plutarch's *Lives of the Noble Grecians and Romans*: it closely follows the relevant sections of Plutarch's biographies of Caesar, Brutus, and Antony, although Shakespeare compresses and transposes events at will. The Lupercal and the Ides of March, for example, which in the play seem to be successive days, are actually a month apart, while the battle of Philippi was actually two battles, the deaths of Cassius and Brutus separated by 20 days rather than the few hours which seem to intervene in the play. Plutarch, however, supplies only the barest summaries of the speeches made at Caesar's funeral by Brutus and Antony, the latter of which becomes the turning point of Shakespeare's play, as well as one of the most frequently quoted passages in the entire canon. Although here he adds material to Plutarch, in one crucial respect Shakespeare removes some: the play suppresses the detail that Brutus was suspected by many of being Caesar's illegitimate son (and that his 'unkindest cut' was delivered to Caesar's groin), exonerating him from parricide.

 CHARACTER LIST

Julius **Caesar**
Calpurnia *his wife*
Marcus **Brutus** *a noble Roman,*
    opposed to Caesar
Portia *his wife*
Lucius *his servant*

Caius **Cassius** ⎤
Casca   ⎟
Trebonius   ⎟
Decius Brutus   ⎟ *opposed to*
Metellus Cimber ⎟ *Caesar*
Cinna   ⎟
Caius **Ligarius**   ⎦

Mark **Antony**   ⎤ *rulers of*
Octavius Caesar ⎟ *Rome after*
Lepidus   ⎦ *Caesar's death*

Flavius   ⎤ *tribunes*
Murellus   ⎦ *of the people*

Cicero   ⎤
Publius   ⎟ *senators*
Popillius Laena ⎦

A **Soothsayer**

Artemidorus
Cinna the Poet
Pindarus *Cassius' bondman*
Titinius *an officer in Cassius'*
    army

Lucillius   ⎤
Messala   ⎟
Varrus   ⎟
Claudio   ⎟
Young Cato   ⎟ *officers and*
Strato   ⎟ *soldiers in*
Volumnius   ⎟ *Brutus' army*
Flavius   ⎟
Dardanius   ⎟
Clitus   ⎦

A **Poet**
Ghost of Caesar
A **Cobbler**
A **Carpenter**
Other **Plebeians**
A **Messenger**
Servants
Senators, soldiers, and attendants

:≡ SYNOPSIS

1.1 The tribunes Flavius and Murellus rebuke a group of commoners for celebrating Caesar's victory over Pompey in the civil wars.

1.2 At the festival of the Lupercal, Caesar reminds Antony to touch his wife Calpurnia while running the ceremonial race in the hopes of curing her infertility. A soothsayer urges him to beware the Ides of March, but is dismissed as a dreamer. Left together when Caesar's party leave for the race,

Brutus and Cassius discuss Caesar's increasing power, anxious, when they hear an offstage shout, that he may be proclaimed king: Cassius, working on Brutus, reminds him of his republican ancestor Lucius Junius Brutus. When Caesar returns with his followers he is angry, and asks Antony in private about the malcontented-looking Cassius: after their departure the sardonic Casca tells Cassius and Brutus how Antony offered Caesar a crown three times but he refused it, to the applause of the watching crowd, and that Murellus and Flavius have been condemned to death for removing festive decorations from images of Caesar. Brutus agrees to discuss the political situation further with Cassius, who resolves, in soliloquy, to have anonymous letters delivered to Brutus encouraging him to take an active part in a conspiracy against Caesar.

1.3 At night Casca speaks in terror of the prodigies he has seen, first to Cicero and then to Cassius, who welcomes them as omens commenting on Caesar's ambition and admits Casca to the conspiracy. Cassius sends Cinna to deliver further anonymous messages to Brutus before he and Casca go to Brutus' house to continue persuading him to join them.

2.1 In his orchard Brutus decides Caesar must be prevented from becoming a tyrant by assassination, a decision in which he is confirmed by reading the anonymous letters. His servant Lucius confirms that tomorrow is the Ides of March. Cassius, Casca, and other conspirators arrive, their faces hidden, and after a private discussion with Cassius, Brutus shakes their hands (declining to take a formal oath), ratifying their plan to kill Caesar the following day. Brutus overrules Cassius' suggestion that Caesar's close friend Antony should be killed too. Decius promises to flatter Caesar to ensure that he comes to the Capitol, where they will stab him. After the conspirators depart, Brutus' wife Portia implores him to tell her what has been on his mind, finally showing that she has wounded her own thigh to prove her stoicism: Brutus promises he will, but first admits the sickly Caius Ligarius, who is eager to join the conspiracy.

2.2 Caesar, alarmed by the omens, orders that augurers sacrifice an animal, which proves to have no heart. Calpurnia, who has dreamed of his murder, begs Caesar not to go to the Capitol, and he eventually agrees. Decius arrives, however, and persuades Caesar to change his mind, assuring him that the Senate means to crown him. Brutus and the conspirators, and Antony, arrive to accompany him to the Capitol.

2.3 Artemidorus has a letter for Caesar warning him against the conspirators.

2.4 Portia is desperately anxious for news from the Capitol.

3.1 Caesar and his party are met by the Soothsayer, who points out that the Ides of March are not yet over, and by Artemidorus, whose letter Caesar sets aside unread on the grounds that it concerns him personally. Cassius is worried that the conspiracy is about to be discovered, but Trebonius leads Antony out of the way as planned, and Metellus Cimber petitions Caesar for the repeal of his banished brother. The other conspirators kneel in his support, but Caesar insists that he is above being swayed from his purposes. Casca stabs him, followed by all the conspirators, lastly Brutus, and Caesar dies. The other senators and citizens flee: the conspirators wash their hands in Caesar's blood, planning to proclaim their act and its libertarian motives in the Forum. Antony arrives, and after asking whether they wish to kill him too, willing to die alongside Caesar, he shakes their hands, looking forward to hearing their reasons for the murder. Brutus, against Cassius' advice, permits Antony to speak at Caesar's funeral. Left alone with Caesar's body, Antony vows revenge. He tells the servant of Caesar's nephew Octavius that he means to see what his oratory can do to win over the people, after which he will discuss the future with Octavius.

3.2 Brutus ascends the pulpit before the plebeians and assures them, in prose, that though he loved Caesar he had to kill him to preserve their country's liberty: they hail him as a hero, but at his insistence they remain after his departure to hear Antony. Antony, praising the conspirators with an irony that becomes increasingly obvious, reminds the people of Caesar's virtues, shows a document he claims is his will, and, coming down from the pulpit, shows them Caesar's corpse and its wounds, inflaming them against the conspirators. Feigning unwillingness, he finally reads Caesar's will, in which according to Antony each Roman is left money and Caesar's private gardens will become public parks, upon which the crowd disperses to attack the conspirators. Hearing that Brutus and Cassius have fled the city, while Octavius and Lepidus are both at Caesar's house, he goes to join the latter.

3.3 Rioting citizens kill a poet called Cinna even though he insists that he is not the Cinna who was among the conspirators, before departing to burn the conspirators' houses.

4.1 Antony, Octavius, and Lepidus negotiate a proscription list, which includes Lepidus' brother and Antony's nephew. After Lepidus' departure Antony argues that he is not fit to share the government of Rome with them, but Octavius disagrees. They set about mustering allies and troops to meet those being raised by Brutus and Cassius.

4.2 At a private conference, Brutus accuses Cassius of betraying the conspiracy's ideals by accepting bribes: eventually they make up their quarrel, Brutus explaining his temper by revealing that he has just learned that Portia, distracted with anxiety, has killed herself. Their lieutenants Titinius and Messala are admitted to discuss strategy: Messala reports Portia's death, of which Brutus feigns a stoical acceptance. Brutus overrules Cassius, insisting that they should march immediately to Philippi to fight Antony and Octavius. After his colleagues' departure, when his staff have gone to sleep, Brutus is visited by Caesar's ghost, which promises to meet him at Philippi.

5.1 Antony and Octavius quarrel as to which shall lead the right flank of their attack before defying Cassius and Brutus to immediate battle at a parley. Cassius and Brutus part, resolved to kill themselves if defeated.

5.2-3 Brutus' forces assault those of Octavius, but leave Cassius' army at the mercy of Antony: Cassius sends Titinius to report from his camp. Seeing Titinius surrounded by cavalry, Cassius' servant Pindarus reports that all is lost, and Cassius has himself killed by him. The cavalry, however, were those of Brutus' army: finding Cassius' body, Titinius kills himself. Brutus, young Cato, and others find their bodies, but rally for another assault.

5.4 Young Cato is killed: Lucillius, claiming to be Brutus, is captured, but Antony is not deceived.

5.5 Brutus, among a few defeated followers, pauses to rest: one by one he asks three of them to kill him, saying he has seen Caesar's ghost again and knows his time has come, but each refuses. After the others fly, however, Strato agrees to hold Brutus' sword while he runs upon it, and Brutus dies saying he killed Caesar less willingly. Octavius and Antony find his body and speak of his virtues, distinguishing his high motives from those of the other conspirators.

ARTISTIC FEATURES

Julius Caesar is both a triumphant display of rhetoric and a stringent examination of its uses and abuses, its characters lucid and eloquent even when persuading others to adopt the most violent and primitive behaviour. It employs a much higher proportion of verse than any other play composed at this period of Shakespeare's career, determined to match its canonical classical subject with a consistently dignified style: the comic plebeians of 1.1 are swiftly dismissed, as is the comic poet who intrudes on Brutus and Cassius in 4.2.

CRITICAL HISTORY

For precisely these reasons, the play has often been more admired than loved, seen as representing Shakespeare rather self-consciously on his best artistic behaviour. It has often been chosen as a school set text, due to its edifying subject and absence of bawdy, and has consequently retained an unfortunate aura of the classroom for many readers and commentators. Nonetheless, the admiration *Julius Caesar* has enjoyed has been genuine, consistent, and well deserved. Praised by Margaret Cavendish, Duchess of Newcastle, during the Restoration, it became for the 18th century one of the most important plays in the canon, with Shakespeare seen as a sympathizer with Brutus' libertarian ideals: Francis Gentleman, commenting in Bell's edition in 1773, felt it should be a compulsory part of the syllabus at all major private schools and that all members of Parliament should be made to memorize it. (This wish was perhaps in part fulfilled by the election in 1997 of a Prime Minister, Tony Blair, who as a private schoolboy was aptly cast as Antony.) It has always been especially valued in the United States, where phrases from its text littered the rhetoric of colonists during the War of Independence. Discussions of this perennially topical play have traditionally centred on the question of where its political sympathies finally lie. Brutus has generally been taken as its tragic hero (Charles Gildon was the first critic to suggest the play should be renamed after him, in 1710), and he has been variously considered as an unambiguously endorsed personification of republican values, a Hamlet-like contemplative idealist too naive for public life, or a zealot committed to bloodless theories at the expense of flesh and blood. In the earlier 20th century the play's structural kinship with two plays about regicide, *Richard III* and, especially, *Macbeth*, was frequently noted. Since the Second World War *Julius Caesar* has enjoyed the attention of feminist critics interested in Portia's wound and the play's general relegation of women to the margins of a political world dominated by intense relationships between men, while poststructuralists have been fascinated by its interest in the interpretation and misinterpretation of signs and its dramatization of the relations between texts, bodies, and wills. Recent work has centred on the staging of the assassination and the psychologies of mob violence in the play.

STAGE HISTORY

The play remained in the theatrical repertory down to the closing of the theatres in 1642 (court performances are recorded in 1612–13, 1637, and 1638), and its power in the theatre is highly praised by Leonard Digges in his commendatory verse to Shakespeare's poems (1640). After the Restoration its potentially sympathetic depiction of an assassination easily read as regicide kept it from being revived at once, but it was back on the boards by 1671, and after 1684 Thomas Betterton took over the role of Brutus, with lasting success. Around 1688 the version of the play in use in London theatres was slightly rewritten to make Brutus more unambiguously sympathetic (adding, for example, a last defiant dialogue with Caesar's ghost at Philippi, which remained part of its text until the retirement of J. P. Kemble), but while it has frequently undergone minor cuts and transpositions the play was never supplanted by a full-scale adaptation (although the Jacobite statesman John Sheffield, Earl of Mulgrave, composed a heavily pro-Caesar version in two parts, *The Tragedy of Julius Caesar, Altered* and *The Tragedy of Marcus Brutus*, completed around 1716 but never performed). James Quin played Antony in 1718 but in later years was an important Brutus, first at Drury Lane and then, throughout the 1740s and 1750s, at Covent Garden: David Garrick, unsuccessful as Antony in *Antony and Cleopatra*, did not find any of the leading roles sufficiently commanding, and the play was not revived at Drury Lane during his entire management. Kemble's 1812 production was notable both for his upright Brutus and for its attention to the historical accuracy of the actors' togas: his most important immediate successor in the part was W. C. Macready, who had earlier played Cassius. The play had first been performed in America in 1774, in Charleston, but enjoyed its greatest vogue during the following century (when it was played in fifty-one different theatres in New York alone): most famously (and infamously), it was a favourite of the Booths, Edwin playing Brutus on tours throughout the States. A benefit performance of the play in 1738 had helped pay for Peter Scheemakers's statue of Shakespeare in Westminster Abbey, and another took place in New York in 1864 to pay for the statue of Shakespeare in Central Park. Edwin Booth played Brutus, Junius Booth was Cassius, and John Wilkes Booth played Antony; a year later he shot Abraham Lincoln. The play was less popular in England during the later 19th century, but enjoyed considerable success in Beerbohm Tree's lavish production of 1898, with himself as Antony. Thereafter it became a standard feature of the repertory at Stratford under Frank Benson, who played Caesar: it was chosen as the command performance to commemorate the tercentenary of Shakespeare's death in 1916, at the close of which Benson, still in costume, was knighted by George V. *Julius Caesar* also became a fixture at the Old Vic, where it was revived in every season from 1914 to 1923, and again in 1932, with Ralph Richardson as a much-praised Brutus. The most famous interwar production, however, took place at the Mercury Theatre in New York, when Orson Welles directed the play in modern dress, giving the conspiracy strong anti-fascist overtones: the idea was imitated at the Embassy Theatre in London soon after the outbreak of war. Notable post-war productions have included Anthony Quayle's in Stratford in 1950 (with Quayle as Antony and John Gielgud as Cassius), Minos Volanakis's production of 1962 (with Robert Eddison as Cassius), and Peter Hall's interval-free production for the RSC in 1996, with Hugh Quarshie as Antony. The play has remained popular on the stage, both as star vehicle and political think piece: Deborah Warner's modern-dress, politically unspecific 2006 production at the Barbican went for raw star power, with Ralph Fiennes as Antony, Simon Russell Beale as Cassius, and Anton Lesser as a tetchy Brutus. Harriet Walter played Brutus in opposition to Frances Barber's Caesar in Phyllida Lloyd's 2012 Donmar production, set in a high-security women's prison, while Gregory Doran's 2012 RSC production was set in an unspecified African nation with Jeffery Kissoon's Caesar its Mugabe-esque dictator. A worldwide slew of productions responded to the surge of populism registered in many states in 2016: in the UK, a 2017 production at the Sheffield Crucible (dir., Robert Hastie) saw Sam West's restrained and mournful Brutus contrast with the rabble-rousing Antony (Elliot Cowan) who delivered large parts of 'Friends, Romans, countrymen' from the stalls, while Nicholas Hytner's similarly modern-dress promenade version at his new Bridge Theatre in London the following year, with Ben Whishaw as a doomed, academic-looking representative of a defeated liberal elite, practically employed those who had paid least for their places as extras, having actors dressed as security guards fling them out of the way of the conspirators' pistols, and subsequently issue them with placards and brochures to wave at Caesar's funeral. The most discussed of these topical productions, though, was Oskar Eustis's for the New York Public Theatre in Central Park in 2017, in which the title role was given to Donald Trump lookalike Gregg Henry, an actor already known from his Trump-like turn as Hollis Doyle in the hit US television series *Scandal*. This controversial production saw Trump-Caesar bloodily assassinated in the state Capitol and was promptly defunded by its sponsors, Delta Airlines, for having 'crossed the line of … good taste'.

ON THE SCREEN

Nine silent versions (the first made by Georges Méliès) emerged between 1907 and 1914. Material from the play was among the earliest Shakespeare scenes broadcast on BBC television (1937) and in 1938 the BBC televised the Embassy's modern-dress production, reflecting the play's relevance to the political turmoil in 1930s Europe. The film with the strongest resonance remains the 1953 cinema film directed by Joseph L. Mankiewicz, with Louis Calhern (Caesar), James Mason (Brutus), John Gielgud (Cassius), and Marlon Brando as Mark Antony. The most recent screen version since the 1979 BBC TV production (which cast Charles Gray as Caesar and Richard Pasco as Brutus) is the BBC version of Gregory Doran's 2012 production, which combined scenes filmed in the original stage space with location shots. The lengthy clandestine dialogue between Paterson Joseph's Brutus and Cyril Nri's Cassius in 1.2, for example, moves off the stage into a deserted corridor, and thence to an equally deserted men's toilet as the need for conspiratorial privacy heightens.

King John

Perhaps the most modern in sensibility of all the history plays despite being set furthest in the past, *King John* was probably written between *Richard II* and *1 Henry IV* (with both of which, particularly the former, it shares some rare vocabulary), in 1596.

 TEXT

The play was first printed in the Folio in 1623, apparently from a scribal transcript of foul papers: the removal of profanities and the use of act divisions suggests that this manuscript was prepared for a projected revival after the Act to Restrain the Abuses of Players and after the King's Men acquired the Blackfriars theatre, although no such revival is recorded.

 SOURCES

The play is closely related to an anonymous two-part play, *The Troublesome Reign of King John*, published in 1591, which is itself based on Raphael Holinshed's *Chronicles* and on John Foxe's *Book of Martyrs*: although this play was attributed to Shakespeare in its 1611 and 1623 reprints, most scholars now believe that this was a source for Shakespeare's play rather than a derivative version of it. Shakespeare's condensation of *The Troublesome Reign* is marked chiefly by a toning down of its strident anti-Catholicism: the main point of the earlier play is to depict John as a fearless resister of the papacy, a comparatively incidental aspect of his presentation in Shakespeare's version.

 CHARACTER LIST

King John of England
Queen Eleanor
his mother

Lady Falconbridge
Philip the **Bastard**, later knighted as
Sir Richard Plantagenet

*her illegitimate son by King
Richard I (Cœur-de-lion)*
Robert **Falconbridge** *her
legitimate son*
James **Gurney** *her attendant*
Lady **Blanche** of Spain
niece of King John
Prince Henry *son of
King John*
Hubert *a follower of King John*
Earl of **Salisbury**
Earl of **Pembroke**
Earl of **Essex**
Lord **Bigot**
King Philip of France
Louis the Dauphin *his son*

Arthur, Duke of Brittaine
nephew of King John
Lady **Constance** *his mother*
Duke of **Austria** (Limoges)
Châtillon *ambassador from France to
England*
Count **Melun**
A **Citizen** of **Angers**
Cardinal **Pandolf** *a legate from
the Pope*
Peter of Pomfret *a prophet*
Heralds
Executioners
Messengers
Sheriff
Lords, soldiers, attendants

▤ SYNOPSIS

1.1 The ambassador Châtillon declares war on King John in the name of the French King Philip, who supports John's young nephew Arthur's claim to the throne: John promises to defend his title in a military campaign in France, though his mother Queen Eleanor privately admits to John that his deceased elder brother's son has the better right to the crown. The King is then asked to judge a dispute between one Philip (the Bastard) and his brother Robert Falconbridge: despite being the junior, Robert claims the lands of their father Sir Robert Falconbridge on the grounds that Philip is in fact the illegitimate son of John's late brother King Richard Cœur-de-Lion, who had sent Sir Robert away to Germany at the time the Bastard was conceived. The King, though recognizing by family likeness that the Bastard is indeed King Richard's son, points out that in law he is still rightful inheritor of Sir Robert's land, but Queen Eleanor gives her illegitimate grandson the choice between remaining a Falconbridge or renouncing his inheritance in order to be acknowledged illegitimate son of Cœur-de-Lion: he chooses the latter, and King John knights him as Sir Richard Plantagenet. Left alone, the ambitious Bastard is congratulating himself when his mother Lady Falconbridge arrives to reproach her sons for accusing her of adultery with King Richard, which she eventually admits: the Bastard thanks her for having chosen such a good father for him.

2.1 The French King Philip, besieging Angers with Geoffrey's widow Lady Constance and her son Arthur, welcomes the Duke of Austria, who wears a lion skin to commemorate his killing of King Richard Cœur-de-Lion, to their party. Châtillon brings the news that the English army is approaching, and King Philip and his allies are confronted by King John, the Bastard, John's niece Lady Blanche, and their army: the two sides taunt and defy one another, the Bastard singling out Austria for his attention. The citizens of Angers, summoned to the walls to see which of the two armies they will allow into the city, respond to the rival eloquence of King John and King Philip by saying they will recognize whoever wins a battle between the two as rightful king. The two armies battle offstage, but each returns and claims victory: the citizens of Angers are thus still unable to decide whom to favour. The Bastard, irritated with them, suggests that John and Philip should first combine to demolish Angers before settling their differences, and as the two sides prepare to take this advice a citizen of Angers, terrified, suggests that instead of further bloodshed the French and English should make peace by means of a marriage between the Dauphin and Lady Blanche. This proposal is accepted, King John offering a large dowry with his niece to assure himself against further trouble from Philip, and to pacify the absent Lady Constance and her son he declares Arthur Duke of Brittaine, Earl of Richmond, and lord of Angers. Left alone, the Bastard reflects on the calculating self-interest that governs all worldly affairs.

2.2 Lady Constance, with Arthur, is horrified to learn from the Earl of Salisbury that the French King has abandoned their cause: declining to appear before the two kings she sits on the ground in sorrow.

3.1 The new allies enter in state from the wedding between the Dauphin and Lady Blanche, and are cursed at length by Constance. She takes some comfort from the arrival of the papal legate Cardinal Pandolf, who has been sent to demand that King John allow the Pope's choice Stephen Langton to be Archbishop of Canterbury: when John defies him and the Pope, Pandolf excommunicates him and instructs King Philip to let go of his hand and declare war on him again. After much debate, the Bastard taunting Austria throughout, King Philip obeys Pandolf: Lady Blanche laments her divided loyalties.

3.2 In the ensuing battle the Bastard kills Austria and King John captures Arthur.

3.3 King John leaves Queen Eleanor in France, sends the Bastard to England to raise money from the Church, and appoints Hubert to kill Arthur.

3.4 The discomfited King Philip, the Dauphin, and Pandolf are further dismayed by the grief-stricken ranting of Constance, who unbinds her hair as a mark of her distraction. When Pandolf and the Dauphin are left alone, the Cardinal points out that King John is certain to have Arthur killed and that this, coupled with his assaults on the Church, will make him unpopular and vulnerable: he urges the Dauphin to claim the English crown through his marriage to Blanche, promising to gain Philip's support for an invasion.

4.1 Hubert has instructions to blind Arthur with hot irons, but the boy speaks so poignantly that he is unable to carry them out: instead he undertakes to protect Arthur but tell the King he has killed him.

4.2 King John has had himself crowned for a second time, an action which, as his nobles Pembroke and Salisbury point out, has made his claim to the throne look weaker rather than stronger. When the King, after hearing from Hubert, announces that Arthur has died, the nobles accuse him of murder, and leave, promising vengeance. A messenger brings the news that the Dauphin has landed with an army and that Queen Eleanor and Lady Constance are both dead. The Bastard arrives, reporting that the country is full of rumours of the King's impending fall: he has brought a prophet with him, Peter of Pomfret, who says John will give up his crown before noon on the next Ascension Day. John gives Hubert instructions to hang Peter of Pomfret at that time, and sends the Bastard to try to win the nobles back to his side. When Hubert brings news of further omens and prophecies John reproaches him for killing Arthur, eventually stinging him into confessing that Arthur is still alive, news which John instructs him to give to the nobles as soon as he can.

4.3 Disguised as a ship's boy Arthur leaps down from the walls and dies. Salisbury, Pembroke, and Bigot find the body just as the Bastard is trying to persuade them to rejoin the King instead of going over to the French, and just before Hubert arrives to tell them Arthur is still alive: they promise vengeance. Alone with Hubert, the Bastard accuses him of killing Arthur, but is eventually persuaded of his innocence: he fears John's reign cannot last.

5.1 On Ascension Day King John, making peace with the papacy, gives his crown to Pandolf, who restores it to him: he recognizes that Peter of Pomfret's prophecy has been fulfilled. The Bastard brings news that the nobles have joined with the Dauphin, who has entered London, and he chides King John for making peace with Pandolf, urging defiance.

5.2 The defecting English lords swear allegiance to the Dauphin, who refuses to make peace with King John even when Pandolf brings the news of his reconciliation to the Church. The Bastard defies the Dauphin on John's behalf and the two sides prepare for battle.

5.3 In the battle John, growing faint with fever, learns that French reinforcements have been wrecked on the Goodwin Sands: he retreats to the abbey at Swineshead.

5.4 Salisbury, Pembroke, and Bigot are dismayed to learn from the dying Count Melun that the Dauphin means to kill them if he wins the battle: at Melun's urging they set out to rejoin King John.

5.5 The Dauphin, close to victory, learns of the English lords' re-defection and of his shipwrecked reinforcements.

5.6 Hubert meets the Bastard and tells him the King has been poisoned by a monk: the Bastard, though pleased to hear of the nobles' return, reports that half his army has been drowned by the tide in the Wash.

5.7 The King's son Prince Henry has the dying King John, who has been singing in delirium, brought out into the open air, where he speaks of his longing to be cooled: he dies while the Bastard is telling him of the Dauphin's approach. The Bastard learns that Pandolf has negotiated a peace: he and the nobles kneel before Prince Henry, now King Henry III, who promises to honour his father's desire to be buried at Worcester. The Bastard observes that England is never conquered without the assistance of internal treachery but that, now the nobles have returned, it will remain invulnerable if the nation only keeps faith with itself.

🎭 ARTISTIC FEATURES

The play is perhaps most remarkable for the sardonic way in which it depicts the shifting allegiances of international power politics, most obviously by the set-piece mock-grandeur of 2.1, 3.1, and 5.2, in which monarchs ceremonially commit perjury in the ordinary pursuit of *realpolitik*. It is appropriate in this regard that the play's largest and most conspicuous role belongs not to King John but to the Bastard, a variously cynical and patriotic commentator on the play's action.

⭐ CRITICAL HISTORY

Although immensely popular in the theatre throughout the 18th and 19th centuries, *King John* has attracted little unmixed enthusiasm from literary critics: an anomaly among the English histories, it has often been ignored, like *All Is True* (*Henry VIII*), in favour of the two tetralogies. Commentators have usually found the play a mass of contradictions, whether between the defiant, potentially sympathetic King John of the early acts and the wavering would-be murderer of Arthur of the later (as did

Charles Knight), or between the psychological naturalism of some scenes (notably that of Constance's grief, 3.4) and the conventionality of others (as did Barrett Wendell). It is only since the advent of Bertolt Brecht and his view that historical dramas may exploit deliberate incongruities in the interests of concentrating an audience's mind on political ideas that the play's artistry has found defenders, although most discussions of the play remain centred on the question of Shakespeare's lack of Protestant zeal compared to that of his source.

STAGE HISTORY

The first recorded performances of the play took place at Covent Garden, under the auspices of the patriotic Shakespeare Ladies' Club, in 1737, and it held its own despite competition from a more anti-Catholic adaptation by Colley Cibber in the year of the second Jacobite uprising, 1745. David Garrick, successfully competing with this version, cast himself as John at Drury Lane to considerable applause. The role of Constance suited itself perfectly to the style of Sarah Siddons, who first took it in 1804, while her brother J. P. Kemble was much admired as John. Charles Kemble's lavish 1823 revival, designed by J. R. Planché, was a milestone in the staging of Shakespeare's histories, the first of many spectacular productions intended to animate the Middle Ages with as much antiquarian accuracy as possible. Kemble cast himself as the Bastard, and though his successor W. C. Macready played the King most Victorian actor-managers followed this choice of role, sometimes casting a girl as Arthur. More and more of the text disappeared, however, to make way for historical pageantry, Beerbohm Tree interpolating an entire dumb show of the signing of the Magna Carta in his 1899 revival.

In the 20th century the play's set pieces of pathos fell from favour, although periodic revivals rediscovered their power: among notable Constances have been Sybil Thorndike (1917–18, and again in 1941), while the Bastard has been played to great effect by Ralph Richardson (1931–2), Paul Scofield (1945), and Richard Burton (1953). The most critically admired production of the later 20th century was undoubtedly that of Deborah Warner for the RSC (1988). Gregory Doran directed Guy Henry as John in a briskly intelligent, intimate, and moving production in the RSC's Swan theatre (2001), the company tackling the play again in 2006 as part of the Complete Works Festival, with Richard McCabe and Joseph Millson as John and the Bastard respectively, in a psychologically probing and politically cynical vision by director Josie Rourke. Maria Aberg's inventive 2012 production (RSC), with Pippa Nixon as the Bastard, highlighted the more disturbing oddities of the play's power politics.

 ON THE SCREEN

Brief episodes from Beerbohm Tree's production, filmed in 1899, are the first recorded footage of Shakespearian material. Two subsequent British productions were made for television, one in 1952 and one in 1984 for BBC TV, with Leonard Rossiter as John.

King Lear

The third of the so-called 'great' tragedies, *King Lear* differs greatly in structure and tone from its predecessors, *Hamlet* and *Othello*. According to its entry in the Stationers' Register on 26 November 1607, it had been performed at court on 26 December 1606. This suggests composition no later than autumn 1606. The play is indebted to Samuel Harsnett's anti-Catholic pamphlet *A Declaration of Egregious Popish Impostures* and to John Florio's translation of Michel de Montaigne's *Essais*, both published in 1603. Gloucester's reference to 'late eclipses in the sun and moon' may or may not allude to actual eclipses of September and October 1605; possible debts to Ben Jonson, George Chapman, and John Marston's play *Eastward Ho* and to George Wilkins's *Miseries of Enforced Marriage* imply composition later than June 1605. The play was probably written late in 1605. Revision represented by the Folio text was made on a copy of the 1608 quarto, probably, judging by stylistic evidence, around 1610.

 TEXT

The play was first printed, badly, in 1608. The origin of this text has been much disputed but the current view is that it derives from Shakespeare's original manuscript. It was reprinted with minor but unauthoritative improvements in 1619. Editors from the early 18th century onwards, assuming that both texts derive from a single archetype, normally conflated them, but recent research indicates that the 1608 quarto represents the play as Shakespeare first wrote it, and the Folio a substantial revision, cutting some 300 lines and adding about 100, and with many other variations. The Oxford editors first disentangled the two texts under their original printed titles of *The History* and *The Tragedy of King Lear*. The synopsis given below is based on the *History* but indicates major variations in the *Tragedy*.

SOURCES

Lear's story had often been told and Shakespeare appears to have known several versions. He treats it with great freedom, especially by adding Lear's madness and giving it a tragic conclusion. He knew well *The True Chronicle History of King Leir and his Three Daughters*, a play published in 1605 but written at least fifteen years earlier. Echoes from it in many of Shakespeare's plays suggest that he may have acted in it, probably before 1594. The parallel story of Gloucester and his sons is based on episodes from Sir Philip Sidney's *Arcadia*. Details of, especially, Edgar's speeches as Mad Tom derive from Harsnett's *Declaration*, and Florio's *Montaigne* also influences the play's vocabulary.

CHARACTER LIST

Lear, King of Britain
Gonoril *Lear's eldest daughter*
Duke of **Albany** *her husband*
Regan *Lear's second daughter*
Duke of **Cornwall** *her husband*
Cordelia *Lear's youngest daughter*
King of **France** ⎤ *suitors of*
Duke of **Burgundy** ⎦ *Cordelia*
Earl of **Kent** *later disguised as Caius*
Earl of **Gloucester**
Edgar *elder son of Gloucester, later disguised as Tom o' Bedlam*

Edmund *bastard son of Gloucester*
Old Man *a tenant of Gloucester*
Curan *Gloucester's retainer*
Lear's **Fool**
Oswald *Gonoril's steward*
Three **Servants** of Cornwall
Doctor *attendant on Cordelia*
Three **Captains**
A **Herald**
A **Knight**
A **Messenger**
Gentlemen, servants, soldiers, followers, trumpeters, others

≔ SYNOPSIS

Sc. 1 (1.1) The Earl of Gloucester tells the Duke of Kent that King Lear is equally well disposed to each of his sons-in-law, the Dukes of Albany and Cornwall, in sharing out his kingdom. Gloucester introduces his bastard son Edmund to Kent, saying that the bastard is no less dear to him than the legitimate Edgar. Lear enters with his daughters, Gonoril, Regan, and Cordelia, and the elder sisters' husbands. Calling for a map, he declares his intention to divide his kingdom into three parts which he will share among his daughters. The King of France and the Duke of Burgundy are in waiting to learn which of them will win the hand of his youngest daughter, Cordelia. Lear asks each daughter for an expression of her love. Gonoril and Regan flatter him, but Cordelia refuses to take part in the competition. Infuriated, Lear banishes both her and Kent, who defends Cordelia. Lear announces that he will retain the name of king, and that, along with a retinue of 100 knights, he will live alternately month by month with each of his elder daughters. Burgundy refuses to marry the disinherited Cordelia, but France, perceiving her true value, accepts her. Left alone, Regan and Gonoril reveal jealousy of Cordelia and impatience with their father's weaknesses.

Sc. 2 (1.2) Edmund, declaring allegiance to the law of nature, reveals his determination to usurp his legitimate brother's inheritance. Producing a letter purportedly written by Edgar, he tricks Gloucester into believing that Edgar seeks to join with Edmund in seizing their father's estates. Edmund offers to demonstrate the truth of his allegation if Gloucester will conceal himself to overhear a conversation between the brothers. Gloucester blames recent eclipses of the sun and moon for overturning the natural order, but Edmund, in soliloquy, reveals a rationalist disposition. He tells the innocent Edgar that Gloucester is displeased with him.

Sc. 3 (1.3) Lear is staying with Gonoril. Complaining that he and his followers are riotous, she instructs her servant Oswald to treat them insolently. She will write to Regan advising her to follow a similar course.

Sc. 4 (1.4) Kent, disguised, declares unwavering loyalty to Lear, who admits him into his service. Oswald behaves insolently and Kent endears himself to Lear by mocking him. Lear's Fool warns his master in riddles and snatches of song against the consequences of his poor judgement. Gonoril complains to Lear of his retinue's behaviour; enraged, he calls for his horses, invokes a curse upon her, and leaves for Regan's home. Within moments he returns in even greater fury, having learned that 50 of his followers have been dismissed. Gonoril summons Oswald to carry a letter to Regan.

Sc. 5 (1.5) Lear also sends letters to Regan, by Kent. Lear meditates on his wrongs, punctuated by cryptic comments from his Fool.

Sc. 6 (2.1) In Gloucester's house, Curan, a servant, tells Edmund that Cornwall and Regan are approaching, and reports rumours of forthcoming wars between Cornwall and Albany. Edmund tricks Edgar, who is in hiding, into running away, convincing Gloucester by means of a mock fight that Edgar had been trying to persuade Edmund to murder their father. The duped Gloucester instigates a hunt to the death for Edgar. Cornwall and Regan join in enmity to Edgar, report receipt of Gonoril's letter, and commend Edmund, taking him into their service.

Sc. 7 (2.2) Kent threatens and insults Oswald; Cornwall orders Kent to be put into the stocks even though Gloucester points out that this will offend Lear. In soliloquy Kent tells of a letter he has received from Cordelia, in France, who knows of his course of action. He goes to sleep. The fugitive Edgar reveals to the audience his plan to assume the appearance and behaviour of a Bedlam beggar. Lear, entering with no more than his Fool and one follower, is appalled to find Kent in the stocks and goes off to question Regan. Speaking to Kent, the Fool reveals his continuing loyalty to Lear. Lear tells Gloucester of his anger that Regan and Cornwall have refused to see him. They enter, and Kent is released. Gonoril enters, and Lear is shocked that Regan welcomes her. Regan tells her father that he should return to Gonoril, dismiss half of his retinue, and then come to stay with her. Lear refuses to have anything more to do with Gonoril and says that he and his 100 knights will live with Regan. She prevaricates, saying she will accommodate no more than 25 followers, at which Lear decides he will go to Gonoril after all. When the sisters question his need for even a single follower, Lear, breaking down, threatens revenges on them both and expresses fear of madness. He departs into the night. Cornwall and Regan batten their gates against the coming storm.

Sc. 8 (3.1) A gentleman tells Kent that Lear, accompanied only by the Fool, is battling against the elements. Kent tells the gentleman of division between Albany and Cornwall and that an invasion force is on the way from France (not in *Tragedy*), and asks him to hasten to Dover to tell Cordelia of the King's plight (to give Cordelia, if he sees her, a ring which she will know comes from him (Kent, *Tragedy*).

Sc. 9 (3.2) Accompanied by the Fool, Lear rages against the storm. Kent tries to persuade him to shelter in a hovel, and they go off to look for it. (Before leaving the Fool speaks a mock prophecy, *Tragedy*.)

Sc. 10 (3.3) Gloucester, turned out of his own house, tells Edmund of division between Albany and Cornwall (and passes on news of the French invasion, *History*) (and that support for Lear's party is already on the way, *Tragedy*). Edmund, left alone, says he will instantly tell Cornwall of this and expresses determination to supplant his father.

Sc. 11 (3.4) Kent seeks to persuade Lear to enter the hovel. Before doing so, Lear prays for all who suffer in the storm, acknowledging that he has 'ta'en | Too little care of this'. The Fool, who has entered the hovel, emerges terrified by the presence of the disguised Edgar. Edgar vigorously acts the madman, and Lear assumes that Edgar has daughters who have 'brought him to this pass'. Edgar's near-nakedness provokes Lear to reflect on the basic state of 'unaccommodated man', and Lear tears off his own clothes in sympathy. Gloucester enters, shocked that Lear has 'no better company', and offers, in spite of the sisters' prohibition, to find shelter for Lear. Lear's wits are turning, and Gloucester fears for his own. They all go into the hovel.

Sc. 12 (3.5) Cornwall declares his determination to revenge himself on Gloucester. Edmund accuses his father of complicity with the powers of France, and Cornwall tells him that he will soon succeed his father.

Sc. 13 (3.6) Gloucester leaves the hovel to seek help. Lear, now fully mad, conducts a mock trial of Gonoril and Regan (not in *Tragedy*) then sleeps. Gloucester, reporting 'a plot of death' against the King, arranges for him to be carried in a litter to Dover. Edgar, left alone, reflects on the situation (not in *Tragedy*).

Sc. 14 (3.7) Preparing to take revenge on Gloucester, Cornwall sends Edmund away. Oswald reports that Lear, with a party of his knights, is on his way to Dover. Edmund leaves with Gonoril, and Cornwall gives orders for Gloucester to be bound and brought before him. Gloucester is tied to a chair and Regan plucks him by the beard as they interrogate him about the King's whereabouts. Provoked beyond endurance, Gloucester admits that he has sent Lear to Dover to protect him from his evil daughters. Sadistically, Cornwall puts out one of Gloucester's eyes. A servant who protests is stabbed to death by Regan, and Cornwall, injured in the fight, puts out Gloucester's other eye. When Gloucester calls on the absent Edmund for help, Regan reveals that it was he who told them of the help that Gloucester had given Lear. Gloucester now realizes that Edgar had been tricked. A horrified servant says he will get Tom o'Bedlam to lead Gloucester on his way to Dover, and another that he will fetch 'flax and whites of eggs | To apply to his bleeding face' (not in *Tragedy*).

Sc. 15 (4.1) The disguised Edgar encounters his father being led by an old man. Gloucester calls upon the supposedly absent Edgar for help. Edgar comes forward and his father asks him to lead him to the edge of Dover Cliff.

Sc. 16 (4.2) Gonoril welcomes Edmund. Oswald reports that her husband Albany, much changed, is refusing to oppose 'the army that was landed'. She sends Edmund to expedite Cornwall's opposition, giving Edmund a token of her love and kissing him. Albany enters and expresses horror at what the sisters have done to their father, prophesying that the heavens will take revenge. A gentleman brings news of Gloucester's blinding and reports that Cornwall has died of his wounds. Gonoril reveals fear that Regan may seduce Edmund.

Sc. 17 (not in *Tragedy*) Kent asks a gentleman why France has returned home and whether the letters describing Lear's plight moved Cordelia. The Gentleman describes Cordelia's sorrowful reaction. Kent remarks that Lear, in his more lucid moments, is too ashamed to see Cordelia.

Sc. 18 (4.3) Cordelia (entering with an army, *Tragedy*) sends soldiers to seek the mad King. A messenger brings news that the British armies are approaching. Cordelia declares that she is acting out of love for her father, not personal ambition.

Sc. 19 (4.4) The jealous Regan tries to persuade Oswald to reveal the contents of letters he is carrying from Gonoril to Edmund. She sends a token to Edmund by Oswald and offers promotion to anyone who will kill Gloucester.

Sc. 20 (4.5) Edgar persuades a suspicious Gloucester that they are close to the edge of Dover Cliff and invents a description of the view. Believing himself on the verge, Gloucester prays and leaps forward. Speaking in a different accent, Edgar approaches him as if he really had fallen. Gloucester repents his suicide attempt. Lear enters, madly reliving episodes from his past, inveighing against female sexuality and reflecting on justice and authority in a poignant mixture of reason and madness. Gloucester recognizes his voice and pays homage, and Edgar looks on, moved. Gentlemen arrive to take Lear to Cordelia, but he evades capture. Edgar asks about the impending battle and starts to lead Gloucester to safety. Oswald enters, recognizes Gloucester, and hopes to kill him so as to gain the promised reward, but Edgar fights and kills him. Dying, Oswald asks him to take the letters he is carrying to Edmund. Edgar searches his pockets and finds a letter in which Gonoril incites Edmund to kill her husband.

Sc. 21 (4.6) Kent, still in disguise, encounters Cordelia. A doctor (not in *Tragedy*) and gentleman ask if they may awaken Lear, and he is revealed (carried in, *Tragedy*) asleep, freshly arrayed. They wake him (to the accompaniment of music, *History*). At first Lear believes he is dead and that Cordelia is an angel, but slowly he comes to himself and recognizes her. He kneels to her in penitence, and she asks his blessing.

Sc. 22 (5.1) Amid preparations for war, Regan asks Edmund if he has seduced Gonoril. He replies evasively. Edgar, now disguised as a peasant, gives Albany a letter to open before the battle, claiming that, if Albany wins, Edgar will produce a champion who will bring to pass what the letter claims. Edmund admits to the audience that he has sworn love to both sisters and declares that he will have no mercy on Lear and Cordelia if they fall within his power.

Sc. 23 (5.3) The French (an, *Tragedy*) army, led by Cordelia with Lear, passes across the stage. Edgar, still disguised as a peasant, leaves his blind father in a safe place. Noises of battle are heard. Edgar, returning with news that Lear has lost and is captured with Cordelia, leads his father away.

Sc. 24 (5.3) Edmund enters with Lear and Cordelia captives, and they are led to prison. Edmund instructs a captain to follow them and to obey the orders in a note which he gives him. Albany instructs Edmund to hand over his captives. Edmund explains that he has sent them to prison. Albany says he had no right to make a decision. Regan and Gonoril vie in defending his action. Regan, saying that she is unwell, claims Edmund as her husband. Albany arrests Edmund and Gonoril on charges of high treason. Albany challenges Edmund. Regan becomes more sick, and Gonoril in an aside reveals that she has poisoned her. A herald reads a challenge on behalf of Edmund. The disguised Edgar answers it. They fight and Edgar wins. Gonoril opposes the decision but flounces off when Albany produces her letter to Edmund. Edgar reveals his identity and tells of his father's death (and of how Kent, finding them together, was so overcome with grief that he collapsed: not in *Tragedy*). A gentleman enters with news of Gonoril's suicide and Regan's death. Kent's entry in his own person to say farewell to Lear reminds Albany of Lear and Cordelia. The bodies of the evil sisters are brought on to the stage. Edmund, dying, repents and reveals that he has given orders for Lear and Cordelia to be killed. A servant is sent to try to countermand the order, but Lear enters with Cordelia in his arms. He seeks for signs that she is alive and reveals that he killed her murderer. Kent identifies himself. News arrives that Edmund is dead. Albany offers to give up the kingdom to Lear, who dies, grieving over Cordelia's body. Albany asks Kent and Edgar to rule, but Kent says he must follow his master. Albany (Edgar in *Tragedy*) rounds off the play, commending stoicism and integrity.

 ARTISTIC FEATURES

Though occasionally relieved by touches of humour, this is Shakespeare's most profoundly and philosophically intense drama, often dense in expression though with shafts of sublime simplicity, especially in Lear's reunion and reconciliation with Cordelia. It is his only tragedy with a fully developed sub-plot, or parallel story, the physical suffering of Gloucester, culminating in his blinding, running alongside the mental torment of Lear, culminating in madness. Shakespeare seems consciously to withdraw all sense of period, avoiding the Christian frame of reference which is notable in *Hamlet*, and of locality: even Dover is an idea rather than a place. The influence of the morality tradition is apparent in the exceptionally black and white characterization. Lear's Fool represents Shakespeare's most subtle and poignant development of this type of character. The play calls for acting of the highest quality but otherwise makes no exceptional demands; with doubling, it could be acted by thirteen men and three boys, and the staging calls for no special effects except an upper level at only one point.

CRITICAL HISTORY

Nahum Tate's adaptation *The History of King Lear*, a skilful piece of theatrical writing which evades the play's tragic issues, held the stage from 1681 to 1845, influencing the perceptions even of critics such as Samuel Johnson, William Hazlitt, Samuel Taylor Coleridge, and Charles Lamb, who acknowledged the original play's sublimity but doubted its theatrical validity. A. C. Bradley too, though he wrote eloquently on the play in *Shakespearean Tragedy* as 'the fullest revelation of Shakespeare's power', considered it '*not* his best play'. At the same time, Tolstoy vitriolically attacked *Lear*, eccentrically stating a preference for *King Leir*. Harley Granville-Barker's 'Preface', of 1927, successfully refutes Lamb's criticism of the play's actability. From G. Wilson Knight (*The Wheel of Fire*, 1930) onwards the play's literary qualities have provoked much fine criticism from critics including R. B. Heilman, W. H. Clemen, and Winifred Nowottny. Twentieth-century critics including J. F. Danby, Barbara Everett, W. R. Elton, Jan Kott, and many others concentrated on the question of whether the play embodies fundamentally Christian values or is fundamentally pessimistic. Other topics of discussion and, sometimes, controversy have included the play's structure, its relationship to the morality tradition, the credibility of, especially, the opening scene, whether the blinding of Gloucester and the death of

Cordelia are dramatically justifiable, and whether Lear dies happily or in despair. Critics such as Maynard Mack and Marvin Rosenberg have drawn on the play's performance history, and more recent criticism includes studies relating it to feminist, historicist, and materialist issues. It has also stimulated important scholarly studies feeding into criticism by, for example, W. W. Greg, Enid Welsford, Peter W. M. Blayney, Gary Taylor, and R. A. Foakes, along with numerous pictorial, dramatic, and fictional offshoots. Recent studies have re-evaluated *Lear*'s source material, its generic make-up, and its earliest dramatic contexts. New directions have likewise explored the play's ecological perspectives, its emotional range, and the interplay between human and animal.

PERFORMANCE HISTORY

The only recorded early performance is the one given at court on 26 December 1606. The play was acted after the Restoration, but from 1681 to 1838 in England, and to 1875 in America, all performances adopted or modified Nahum Tate's adaptation, which cuts around 800 lines, modernizes the language, omits the Fool and France, adds a love story between Edgar and Cordelia, and preserves the lives of Kent, Gloucester, and Lear. David Garrick triumphed as Lear, and the play was adapted into French and German during the 18th century. In the Romantic period J. P. Kemble and Edmund Kean were outstanding in the title role. W. C. Macready restored the Fool, played by a woman, in 1838, and the Italian Tommaso Salvini played in a shortened translation from 1882. Henry Irving, in 1892, cut nearly half of the text. The first French production of the unadapted text was acted in 1904. Theodore Komisarjevsky directed the play successfully at Stratford in 1936. Barker translated the principles of his 'Preface' into theatrical terms in an almost uncut text given in Elizabethan costume with John Gielgud as Lear at the Old Vic in 1940. Donald Wolfit was an admired Lear during the 1940s and 1950s. Peter Brook directed Paul Scofield in an austere and influential Stratford production of 1962; more recent outstanding British Lears have included Brian Cox (National Theatre, 1990), Robert Stephens (Stratford, 1993), Ian Holm (National, 1997), David Warner (Chichester, 2005), Ian McKellen (RSC, 2007), Derek Jacobi (Donmar, 2010), and Simon Russell Beale (National, 2014). The year 2016 was the year of *Lear*, with five major productions. Max Webster's for the Northampton Royal had Michael Pennington's tyrannical Lear stand off against Beth Cooke's defiant Cordelia, while Timothy West's Lear for Bristol Old Vic, saw in its title role a very foolish fond old man. At the RSC (dir., Gregory Doran), Antony Sher delivered a surprisingly dynamic and notably volatile Lear, and Don Warrington's turn at the Manchester Royal Exchange for Talawa (dir., Michael Buffong) stressed Lear's self-destructiveness and impending senility. When Glenda Jackson took on the role at the Old Vic in Deborah Warner's modern dress production, her scornful, regal Lear contrasted poignantly with Rhys Ifan's gently comic Fool. Ian McKellen reprised the role of Lear in 2017, bringing his arrogant, affecting King to Jonathan Munby's production at the Chichester Festival Theatre and the Duke of York's Theatre in London. Nancy Meckler's Globe debut in 2017 saw the director conceive of the play's 'unaccommodated man' in terms of home-lessness; a framing device in which the cast first appeared as squatters stressed the play's themes of exposure and eviction.

ON THE SCREEN

The most memorable film versions of *Lear* are the two made for cinema by Peter Brook (1971) and Grigori Kozintsev (1969), and Michael Elliott's production for Granada Television (1983). Both Brook and Kozintsev selected remarkably articulate locations to project the world of the play, Brook's landscape being one of ice and snow, Kozintsev's one of stony barrenness. While Brook infuses his film with moments of Brechtian alienation, remind-ing the viewer of the medium with written captions, Kozintsev's film explores, with no over-indulgence, the emotional dimensions of the play and (unlike Brook, who eschews it) gives music (composed by Shostakovich) a major function. There is, too, a great disparity in the portrayals of Lear. Brook's Lear (Paul Scofield) gives the impression of immense stature, and curtails the range of emotional expression in the lines. Kozintsev chose the Estonian Yuri Yarvet for his Lear. Physically small and unable to speak Russian, Yarvet impressed Kozintsev as ideal for Lear because of his eyes.

Michael Elliott's Granada production captures a rare side of Lear, played with compassion and a captivating autumnal radiance by the 75-year-old Laurence Olivier. Jonathan Miller's BBC TV production (1982) stressed the domestic dimensions of the tragedy, with Michael Hordern moving about the rather confined space like a father but not like a king.

Akira Kurosawa's *Ran* (1985) is a powerful and visually splendid adapta-tion of the play, with Lear's daughters transposed into the sons of the old warrior lord Hidetora. Cut to little over two hours, Anthony Hopkins's 2018 Lear for the BBC (dir., Richard Eyre) presented a man of extremes: angry and vulnerable, cruel and tender, and teeth-gnashingly mad.

A Lover's Complaint

Shakespeare's poetic depiction of a seduced and abandoned woman, the last and at 329 lines the shortest of his narrative poems, was published at the end of the Sonnets when they first appeared in quarto in 1609. Although it uses the same rhyme-royal stanza as *The Rape of Lucrece* (1593–4), the poem shares some imagery, phrasing, and rare vocabulary with *All's Well That Ends Well*, *Hamlet*, and *King Lear*, and was probably composed when Shakespeare was revising and completing his sonnet sequence, possibly while the theatres were closed by plague in 1603–4.

 TEXT

The whole of the 1609 volume appears to have been set from a transcript rather than from an authorial holograph. *A Lover's Complaint* is at times misleadingly punctuated, but otherwise the 1609 text poses few problems. The poem reappeared in 1640 in the printer John Benson's pirated *Poems: Written by W. Shakespeare, Gent.*, but this text merely reprints that of the 1609 quarto and has no authority.

SOURCES

A Lover's Complaint has no specific single source, but, like *The Rape of Lucrece*, draws on a well-established poetic tradition which goes back to Ovid's heroic epistles. The dramatization in verse of the sorrows of unfortunate women had more recently featured in *The Mirror for Magistrates* (1559, reprinted and augmented thereafter), a collection of poems in which historical figures lament their fates, and the form had been adopted by Samuel Daniel, whose *Complaint of Rosamond* (1592), the lament of Henry III's ill-fated mistress, employs the same rhyme-royal stanza.

SYNOPSIS

The narrator describes hearing the echoing voice of a woman lamenting in a valley, and then seeing her, wearing a straw hat, her beauty faded with time and grief. She sits beside a river, weeping, reading and tearing up love letters, throwing gifts of jewels into the water, and breaking rings (ll. 1–56). An old man grazing his cattle nearby comes and sits with her and asks what is the matter and whether he can help (ll. 57–70). The remainder of the poem, from line 71 onwards (the start of the eleventh of 47 stanzas), is given over to her reply. She first explains (ll. 71–84) that she is not as old as she looks: her beauty has in fact been damaged by sorrow as a consequence of her wooing by a young man she goes on to describe at length (85–133). Young and almost androgynously beautiful, with brown curling hair, eloquent, and a brilliant horseman, his gifts, especially of rhetoric, made him universally popular. She explains that though many women desired him and sought to own pictures of him, she did not pursue him herself, and at first was immune to his charms, recognizing that he was capable of perjury and had seduced others (ll. 134–75). She only fell when he made the speech she goes on to quote (ll. 176–280), in which he claimed that his previous amours had all been mere lusts of the flesh, while his vows to her were the first he had ever made sincerely. He showed her locks of hair different women had given him, together with gifts of jewels, which he then gave to her, tokens of conquest passed on to his conqueror: he even showed her a gift he had received from a love-struck nun. All these women were in love with him, but he only with her, he claimed, and they all share in his sorrow at her refusal and join in wishing her to accept him. At the close of this speech he wept (ll. 281–7), and the lady laments to her auditor that these dissembling tears overcame her, so that she wept too, seduced (ll. 288–301). She feels that he was such a skilled hypocrite, able even to preach chastity as part of a plot to seduce, that no one could resist him, and she is convinced that were he to repeat his attentions she would even now be persuaded to give up her repentance and be seduced again (ll. 302–29).

🎭 ARTISTIC FEATURES

The poem shares some of the formality, as well as some of the concerns, of *The Rape of Lucrece*, but this poem, its central woman seduced rather than raped, deliberately eschews the dramatic and conclusive ending of its predecessor. Part of its strength lies in its vivid depiction of a psychological state from which neither the woman nor the poem seems able to imagine an escape, condemned endlessly to re-enact to herself the drama of her own undoing. The 'complaint' of the title may be either the inset complaint of the woman, or the complaint of her seducer which it quotes: in either case, neither the rural old man to whom she speaks nor the narrator who overhears them is able to place the woman back into a wider world outside her own self-tormenting consciousness.

★★★ CRITICAL HISTORY

While the long-ignored Sonnets were rehabilitated at the end of the 18th century, *A Lover's Complaint* had to wait until the 1960s before many scholars were willing to concede that Shakespeare had even written it. Most editors of the Sonnets, considering their publication to have been unauthorized, omitted this poem, believing it to have been an inferior work foisted on Shakespeare by the printer Thomas Thorpe. It was only after Kenneth Muir and MacDonald P. Jackson independently vindicated the poem's authenticity in 1964 and 1965 that more commentators began to find the poem of interest, particularly in relation to the Sonnets it follows. It was pointed out that in placing this poem after the last of the Sonnets Shakespeare might have been following the examples of Thomas Lodge and Samuel Daniel, who had both appended poems in which seduced women lament their falls to their own sonnet sequences, and most modern criticism of *A Lover's Complaint* has taken up this suggestion. Although the poem's authorship continues to be debated, it is now usually regarded as a deliberate coda to the Sonnets, and critics have looked for ways in which it takes up their thematic concerns, particularly with the ethics of dissimulation (the seducer of *A Lover's Complaint* is, among other things, a consummate actor) and the use and abuse of praise.

Love's Labour's Lost

At once Shakespeare's most airy comedy and his most sustained discussion of language, *Love's Labour's Lost* was probably composed in 1594 and 1595. It is listed among Shakespeare's works by Francis Meres in 1598, and appeared in the same year in a quarto edition which boasts that the play was acted before Queen Elizabeth 'this last Christmas' (which may mean either 1597–8 or 1596–7). The play's heavy use of rhyme suggests it belongs to the 'lyrical' period initiated by *Venus and Adonis* (1592–3): in rare vocabulary it is closely linked to *Romeo and Juliet* (1595) and *A Midsummer Night's Dream* (1595), but stylistically it seems to be earlier.

Probable allusions in Act 5 to the Christmas revels at Gray's Inn in 1594 suggest that the play was composed, or at least completed, early in 1595.

 TEXT

The surviving 1598 quarto of the play claims to be 'Newly corrected and augmented', but in all probability this is an exaggeration and the edition is merely a reprint of a now lost earlier edition of the same year. The text seems to have been set, fairly carelessly to judge by certain passages which seem to preserve two successive drafts of the same speech (in 4.3), from Shakespeare's own foul papers. The play was reprinted in the Folio in 1623, directly from the quarto text, but with some corrections made apparently from a promptbook.

SOURCES

No specific source is known for the play's plot, although it clearly alludes to the historical French court: King Henri of Navarre did have two lords called the Maréchal de Biron and the Duc de Longueville, who served as commanders in the French civil war from 1589 to 1592. Biron was widely known in England, since he became an associate and adviser of the Earl of Essex when he led an English force to Henry's aid. It has been conjectured that the main story of *Love's Labour's Lost* may derive from a now-lost account of a diplomatic visit to Henry in 1578 made by Catherine de Médicis and her daughter Marguerite de Valois, Henry's estranged wife, to discuss the future of Aquitaine, but this is by no means certain. What is much clearer is that the play's sub-plot is peopled by Shakespeare's variants on familiar comic types from Italian *commedia dell'arte*, which abounds in pedants (like Holofernes), braggarts (like Don Armado), rustic priests (like Sir Nathaniel), rural clowns (like Costard), and pert pages (like Mote).

 CHARACTER LIST

Ferdinand, **King** of Navarre
Biron ⎤
Longueville ⎬ *lords attending on the King*
Dumaine ⎦
Don Adriano de **Armado** *an affected Spanish braggart*
Mote *his page*
Princess of France

Rosaline ⎤
Catherine ⎬ *ladies attending on the Princess*
Maria ⎦
Boyet ⎤ *attending on the Princess*
Two other **Lords** ⎦
Costard *a Clown*
Jaquenetta *a country wench*
Sir **Nathaniel** *a curate*

Holofernes *a schoolmaster*   **Mercadé** *a messenger*
Anthony **Dull** *a constable*   A **Forester**

:≡ SYNOPSIS

1.1 Ferdinand, the King of Navarre, has three of his lords, Biron, Longueville, and Dumaine, sign a declaration vowing that they will study with him for three years, not seeing a woman throughout that time: Biron is sceptical about the scheme, but eventually signs anyway. The rustic constable Dull, on the instructions of the Spaniard Don Armado (from whom he brings an affected letter), brings the country swain Costard to the King; Costard is condemned to a week's fasting for having been caught in the royal purlieus with the wench Jaquenetta.

1.2 Armado confesses to his punning page Mote that he is in love with Jaquenetta. Dull brings Costard with the King's instruction that Armado guard him and make him fast for a week. Armado undertakes to write poetry about his love.

2.1 The Princess of France arrives on an embassy to Navarre from her father, accompanied by three ladies, Maria, Catherine, and Rosaline, and three lords, one named Boyet: having heard of the King's vow she sends Boyet ahead to him, and while he is away the three respective ladies discuss the King's three respective fellow students. When the King and his three colleagues arrive the Princess presents him with a letter from her father, demanding back a share of Aquitaine in recompense for the full repayment of a loan: while the King reads it Biron is wittily rebuffed by Rosaline, with whom he attempts to flirt. The King agrees to accommodate the Princess while they await the arrival of documents which will establish whether or not the whole loan has already been repaid. Each of his lords privately asks Boyet the name of one of her ladies: Dumaine is attracted to Catherine, Longueville to Maria, and Biron to Rosaline, while Boyet tells the Princess he thinks the King himself is falling in love with her.

3.1 Armado sends Mote to fetch Costard, with whom he means to entrust a love letter to Jaquenetta. Costard, after a bantering quarrel with Mote about hurting his shin, is left with three farthings for delivering the letter. Biron arrives and gives Costard a shilling to deliver a letter to Rosaline; left alone, he reflects on the demeaning absurdity of his having fallen in love with her.

4.1 The Princess, out hunting with her ladies, meets Costard, who does not know which of them is Rosaline: he gives the Princess Armado's letter by mistake, which Boyet reads aloud to general amusement. Costard jests with Boyet and the ladies.

4.2 The schoolmaster Holofernes and the priest Nathaniel are being learnedly witty at the expense of Dull, and Holofernes is showing off his pedantry to Nathaniel, when the illiterate Jaquenetta and Costard arrive to ask Nathaniel to read them the letter Jaquenetta has received from Armado: unfortunately Costard has given her Biron's letter to Rosaline, which Holofernes tells her to take to the King.

4.3 Biron has been writing more poetry for Rosaline: hiding, he overhears the King reading aloud his own poem to the Princess. The King in turn hides when he sees Longueville approach, and both he and Biron overhear Longueville reading out a poem he has composed for Maria. Longueville then hides, and all overhear Dumaine sighing in rhyme for Catherine. Longueville steps forward and reproaches Dumaine: the King steps forward and reproaches Longueville for hypocrisy: then Biron steps forward and reproaches all of them. His triumph is short-lived, however, as Jaquenetta and Costard arrive with his own letter to Rosaline, which he at first tears up but then confesses to. Biron urges his colleagues to lay aside their unnatural vow and set about their wooing.

5.1 Nathaniel and Holofernes, discussing Armado's pretensions to linguistic style before a silent and uncomprehending Dull, are interrupted by Armado's arrival, with Costard and Mote: he has been sent confidentially by the King to commission an entertainment to be performed for the Princess. Holofernes decides they shall stage a pageant of the Nine Worthies.

5.2 The Princess and her ladies scoff at the respective love letters they have received. Boyet brings news that the King and his three lords are approaching, disguised as Muscovites: the women exchange masks, so as to trick their suitors into wooing the wrong people. The men arrive, posing as Muscovites, prefaced by a speech from Mote which, despite prompting, he forgets: all four are taken in by the trick and each is dashed by the witty rebuffs of his partner before they leave, discomfited. The women scoff behind their backs, and when they return undisguised they pretend not to have recognized them, lamenting that they have had their time wasted by foolish Russians. Biron forswears all affectation and pretence to wit in his future wooing, and finally understands how he and his companions have been ridiculed. Costard arrives to ask whether the Nine Worthies should perform, and despite the King's misgivings the Princess insists the pageant should proceed. Mocked by their spectators, speaking in archaic verse, Costard impersonates Pompey the Great, Nathaniel (who forgets his words) plays Alexander the Great, Mote plays the infant Hercules strangling snakes in his cradle, but Holofernes' performance as Judas Maccabeus is dashed by heckling. Armado appears as Hector, and is even more dashed by Costard's public claim that Jaquenetta is two months pregnant by him: the two nearly come to blows, but at this point the entertainment is interrupted by the coming of a messenger, Mercadé. He brings the news that the Princess's father has died. The women at last listen seriously to the men's love-suits, but will give no answer until they meet again in a year and a day: Rosaline makes Biron promise to spend the intervening period telling his jokes in a hospital. Armado returns, and before the King and his lords and the Princess and her ladies part he and the rustics perform a song of spring and winter, 'When daisies pied'.

 ARTISTIC FEATURES

The play is marked by long passages of sustained punning, and by a heavy use of rhyme: even when not reading aloud from love letters, the aristocratic characters sometimes speak in sonnets.

CRITICAL HISTORY

Until the 19th century very few critics found a good word to say about *Love's Labour's Lost*, which seemed to most commentators to represent Shakespeare simultaneously at his most self-indulgent and his most datedly Elizabethan. Francis Gentleman, relegating the play to the eighth volume of Bell's edition in 1774, called it 'one of Shakespeare's weakest compositions… he certainly wrote more to please himself, than to divert or inform his readers or auditors'. Enthusiasm grew over the following century, albeit often of a qualified sort. William Hazlitt, though admitting it had charm, found it pedantic, while Samuel Taylor Coleridge enjoyed the play primarily as an intelligent game at the expense of the ideals of Renaissance humanism. Victor Hugo initiated one enduring strand in the play's critical history in the preface to his translation of the play, when he attempted to show that it was a specific satire on Elizabeth's court, directly inspired by the relationship between the Earl of Southampton (according to Hugo, the original for Biron, as well as for the 'Fair Youth' of the Sonnets) with Elizabeth Vernon. (The quest for topical or allegorical significance in the play has been pursued more recently by Frances Yates and her latter-day followers). The play only came into its own critically with the dawning of the aesthetic movement at the end of the century, when commentators such as Walter Pater and Algernon Charles Swinburne began to celebrate the play's studied artifice and pose of insubstantiality instead of lamenting it. Since then critics have, however, looked for sterner things in the play, whether its questioning of the limitations of comedy (notably by the bereavement which cuts off its marital ending), its alleged attempt to beat the University Wits at their own game, its views of language, identity and social hierarchy, or its understanding of the pastoral and the festive.

🎭 STAGE HISTORY

The courtly tone of the play, together with its comparative brevity, has led some to speculate that it may have been written for performance at an annual revel of one of the Inns of Court, but there is no direct evidence for this beyond the possibility that the missing *Love's Labour's Won* was a sequel, played the following year and depicting the renewal of the courtships postponed for a year at the end of this play. The play was certainly acted before Elizabeth (see above), and a private performance took place at Southampton's house over Christmas 1604–5, according to a letter from Sir Walter Cope. After this, though, the play disappeared from the stage, regarded as the least rescuable of all Shakespeare's comedies (though the transplanted concluding song for many years adorned revivals of *As You Like It*): an anonymous adaptation published in 1762, *The Students*, was never performed, and when *Love's Labour's Lost* was finally staged by Elizabeth Vestris at Covent Garden in 1839 it enjoyed the distinction of being the last play in the canon to have been revived. Vestris was highly praised as Rosaline, but the play was not revived again until it flopped in 1857, with Samuel Phelps as Armado. (During the 19th century, however, an adaptation of the play in French sometimes served as a replacement libretto for Mozart's *Così fan tutte*, regarded at the time as immoral.) *Love's Labour's Lost* was chosen (partly for its obscurity) to be acted on Shakespeare's birthday at the Shakespeare Memorial Theatre in Stratford in 1885, but sporadic revivals there and elsewhere (including a musical version in 1919) failed to establish it in the repertory. The young Tyrone Guthrie produced it twice, first at the Westminster theatre in 1932 and then four years later at the Old Vic (with Michael Redgrave as the King), but neither production was a hit, though the play did become something of a favourite at the Open Air Theatre in Regent's Park in the mid-1930s. The first production really to establish the play was Peter Brook's delicate, bitter-sweet revival at Stratford in 1946, with Paul Scofield as a melancholy Armado and designs suggestive of the paintings of Watteau. Since then it has been revived much more frequently: notable RSC productions, for example, have included John Barton's, set in a wooded Elizabethan park, in 1977–8 (with Michael Pennington as Biron and Jane Lapotaire as Rosaline), Barry Kyle's in 1984 (with Josette Simon as Rosaline) and Ian Judge's in 1994–5, set in a *Zuleika Dobson*-esque Edwardian Oxford on the eve of the First World War. The Edwardian aesthetic, and, specifically, the evocation of the period as one of easy privilege and innocence on the eve of a devastating war, has been a surprisingly recurrent motif of subsequent professional productions; surprising mainly because there have been so few. Just as Judge's had ended to the sound of distant mortar explosions and gunfire, the spectre of the Great War appeared to bite with frosts the Edwardian summer of Trevor Nunn's production (National, 2003), starring Joseph Fiennes as Biron, and Christopher Luscombe's (RSC, 2014) was also set in the summer of 1914, in part to commemorate the centenary year. Greg Doran's RSC production of 2008, with David Tennant as Biron, stands out for retaining an Elizabethan mise-en-scène.

 **ON THE SCREEN**

The earliest of five silent films was made in 1912, unsuited as the medium seems to such a word-oriented play. The Bristol Old Vic production (1964) was recorded on television to mark the 400th anniversary of Shakespeare's birth. Elijah Moshinsky directed the BBC TV production in an 18th-century setting (1984). Kenneth Branagh's version, heavily cut and featuring song-and-dance routines to music by Cole Porter and others, which appeared in 2000, has so far been the least critically acclaimed of his films.

Love's Labour's Won

Francis Meres lists a play by this title among Shakespeare's works in 1598 and we know that it even got into print in quarto: *Love's Labour's Won* is listed in an extant bookseller's catalogue compiled in August 1603. Scholars have suggested that this may have been the original title of another Shakespeare play known by a different title after 1598 (one candidate is *Much Ado About Nothing*, which was performed under this title by the RSC in 2014 when paired with a production of *Love's Labour's Lost*), but no comedy written before 1598 and not mentioned by Meres really fits this title. It seems almost certain that before 1598 Shakespeare had written a comedy called *Love's Labour's Won*, possibly a sequel to *Love's Labour's Lost*, which for some reason failed to get into the Folio, but no copies of the quarto have yet come to light. Anyone finding one should contact the editors of this volume immediately.

Macbeth

Possibly Shakespeare's most intense tragedy, and certainly his most Jacobean—in that its interests in Scotland, in witches, and in the Stuarts' ancestor Banquo suggest that Shakespeare was here deliberately catering to the interests of his company's patron King James—*Macbeth* was probably first performed in 1606. The Porter's remarks about equivocation and treason appear to allude to the trial of the Gunpowder Plot conspirators, which took place from January to March of 1606, and the First Witch's undertaking to condemn a ship called 'the Tiger' to 81 weeks of storms (1.3.6–24) may allude to a real ship of that name which reached Milford Haven in June 1606 after a traumatic voyage of just that duration. Banquo's ghost may be glanced at in two plays written in 1607, the anonymous *The Puritan* and perhaps Beaumont and Fletcher's *The Knight of the Burning Pestle*. Internal evidence, moreover, particularly the play's metre, also suggests that *Macbeth* was composed in 1606, after *King Lear* but just before *Antony and Cleopatra*: Macbeth even mentions Antony (3.1.58) in a manner which suggests that Shakespeare was already revisiting Plutarch in preparation for the latter tragedy while composing his Scottish play.

 TEXT

Macbeth was first printed in the Folio in 1623, which provides its only authoritative text, unfortunately in many ways a defective one. The play is unusually short: many editors have suspected cutting, wondering, for example, whether the murderers' description of the killing of Banquo was originally a separate scene between 3.3 and 3.4, or whether King Edward the Confessor originally made an appearance in 4.3. More conspicuously, three episodes in which the goddess Hecate appears in person to the Witches (3.5, 4.1.38–60, 141–8), which have little or no effect on the plot and are different in style to the surrounding dialogue, seem to be non-Shakespearian interpolations. Since these episodes call for the performance of two songs found in Thomas Middleton's play *The Witch*, it is now generally believed that the text of *Macbeth* in the Folio derives from a promptbook of the play as adapted by Middleton for a later Jacobean revival.

 SOURCES

Shakespeare's principal source was Raphael Holinshed's account of the reigns of Duncan and Macbeth, supplemented by material borrowed from elsewhere in Holinshed's history of Scotland: Lady Macbeth, for example, is largely based on the wife of Donwald, who prompted her husband to kill King Duff. Shakespeare restructures Holinshed's material, however, making the historical Macbeth's long and peaceful reign look like a short-lived usurpation, and framing his play by the appearance of the three witches who tempt Macbeth and Banquo with their prophecies. Shakespeare may have consulted other accounts of Macbeth's reign too, including George Buchanan's *Rerum Scoticarum historia* (1582) and Andrew of Wyntoun's poem *The Original Chronicle of Scotland* (*c.* 1424), in which Macbeth is incited to kill Duncan by three women who appear to him in a dream. It is likely that Shakespeare also knew of a playlet by Matthew Gwinne, *Tres sibyllae*, performed before King James at St John's College, Oxford, in 1605. The three sibyls of the title reminded James that they had once prophesied endless dominion to Banquo's descendants, and saluted him in turn with the words 'Hail, thou who rulest Scotland!' 'Hail, thou who rulest England!' 'Hail, thou who rulest Ireland!' (cf. 1.3.46–8).

 CHARACTER LIST

King Duncan of Scotland

Malcolm
Donalbain } *his sons*

A **Captain** in Duncan's army
Macbeth, Thane of Glamis, later Thane of Cawdor, then King of Scotland
A **Porter** at Macbeth's castle
Three **Murderers** attending on Macbeth
Seyton *servant of Macbeth*
Lady Macbeth *Macbeth's wife*

A **Doctor** of Physic
A Waiting-**Gentle-woman** } *attending on Lady Macbeth*

Banquo *a Scottish thane*
Fleance *his Son*

Macduff, Thane of Fife
Lady Macduff *his wife*
Macduff's Son
Lennox
Ross
Angus
Caithness
Menteith } *Scottish Thanes*

Siward, Earl of Northumberland
Young Siward *his son*
An English **Doctor**
Hecate, Queen of the Witches
Six Witches
Three **Apparitions**, one an armed head, one a bloody child, one a child crowned
A **Spirit Like A Cat**

Other **Spirits**	**Servants**
An **Old Man**	A show of eight kings; Lords and
A **Messenger**	Thanes, attendants, soldiers,
Murderers	drummers

:= SYNOPSIS

1.1 Three witches agree to meet again on a heath in order to accost Macbeth after the day's battle.

1.2 King Duncan, fighting against the rebel Macdonald, receives a report from a bleeding captain about Macbeth's valiant deeds in the battle: Macbeth has killed Macdonald, and he and his comrade Banquo have met the fresh assaults of Macdonald's Norwegian allies. Ross brings the news that Macbeth has defeated the King of Norway and his associate, the traitorous Thane of Cawdor: Duncan condemns Cawdor to death and confers his title on Macbeth.

1.3 The three witches hail Macbeth by his current title, Thane of Glamis, and then as Thane of Cawdor and as future king: before vanishing they tell Banquo that though he will not be king his descendants will. Ross and Angus bring the news that Macbeth is now Thane of Cawdor: reflecting on the witches' prophecy, now partly fulfilled, Macbeth is already imagining the murder of Duncan.

1.4 Duncan, after hearing a report from his son Malcolm of the death of the former Cawdor, welcomes Macbeth and Banquo, before declaring Malcolm the Prince of Cumberland and his heir. Duncan means to be Macbeth's guest at Inverness, towards which Macbeth sets off to inform his wife, conscious that he must now remove both Malcolm and Duncan if the witches' prophecy is to be fulfilled.

1.5 Lady Macbeth reads a letter from Macbeth describing his meeting with the witches, and, aware of the conscience which may hold back his ambition, she is ready to urge him on to the murder of Duncan. A servant brings the news of Duncan's impending arrival: Lady Macbeth calls on the forces of darkness to make her cruel and unwomanly enough to be an instigator of Duncan's murder. When Macbeth arrives she urges him to dissemble with Duncan and promises to do her part.

1.6 Duncan and his nobles, including his sons Malcolm and Donalbain along with Macduff, the Thane of Fife, are welcomed to Inverness by Lady Macbeth.

1.7 Briefly alone while Duncan dines, Macbeth reflects in horror on the crime he is on the verge of committing, for no motive but ambition, and when Lady Macbeth comes to find him he renounces their plot to kill the

King. By taunting him for unmanliness and inconstancy, however, she persuades him to resume his original purpose, saying she will get Duncan's chamberlains drunk so that the Macbeths can make it appear that they are the culprits.

2.1 After midnight, Banquo and his son Fleance are met by Macbeth: Banquo opens the subject of the witches, but Macbeth says they will discuss them on another occasion. After the departure of Banquo and Fleance, Macbeth, awaiting the bell which will be Lady Macbeth's signal that it is time to kill Duncan, sees a vision of a dagger, at first clean but then bloodstained, beckoning him towards Duncan's chamber. The bell rings and he goes to commit the murder.

2.2 Lady Macbeth, having drugged Duncan's grooms and left their daggers ready for her husband to use, awaits Macbeth. When he arrives he is terrified by what he has done and fearful of discovery, convinced he has heard a voice cursing him with eternal insomnia: he is still clutching the bloodstained daggers, which Lady Macbeth has to take back to Duncan's chamber. Macbeth feels he will never be able to get his hands clean of the blood. He is frightened by the sound of knocking at a door: Lady Macbeth leads him away to wash his hands and change into a nightgown.

2.3 A drunken porter, also disturbed by knocking, indulges a fancy that he is the porter at the gates of Hell before finally admitting Macduff and Lennox, to whom he discourses about the effects of drink. Macbeth arrives and conducts Macduff, calling by appointment to awaken the King, to Duncan's door: Lennox describes the ominous storms of the past night. A horrified Macduff brings the news of Duncan's murder and awakens the household while Macbeth and Lennox go to the chamber: Lady Macbeth, Banquo, Macbeth, Lennox, Malcolm, and Donalbain assemble and learn both of Duncan's death and of Macbeth's sudden killing of the two apparently guilty chamberlains on reaching the fatal chamber with Lennox. While Macbeth is explaining that righteous anger overcame his judgement, Lady Macbeth faints. Banquo urges the others to dress and arm themselves: left alone, Malcolm and Donalbain, convinced that they too are intended victims, resolve to flee.

2.4 Ross is discussing further omens with an old man when Macduff arrives: he reports that it is thought the two chamberlains had been paid to kill Duncan by the fugitive Malcolm and Donalbain, and that Macbeth, chosen as Duncan's successor, has gone to Scone to be crowned. Although Ross means to attend the coronation, Macduff is on his way home to Fife.

3.1 Banquo recognizes that the witches' prophecies to Macbeth have been fulfilled, and suspects him of Duncan's murder; he wonders if their remarks about his own descendants will also come true. Macbeth, arriving with Lady Macbeth, Lennox, Ross, and other nobles, invites Banquo to a feast that evening and asks in detail about where he and Fleance mean to ride that afternoon. Dismissing his court, the insecure Macbeth summons two murderers, reflecting bitterly on the pointlessness of his crime if Banquo's descendants are destined to inherit the throne. He instructs the murderers to kill Banquo and Fleance.

3.2 Lady Macbeth also feels that their achievement of an anxious throne is worthless. When Macbeth arrives, envying the dead Duncan's freedom from fear, she urges him to feign cheerfulness at the feast. He hints darkly at the impending murder of Banquo and Fleance but does not confide that he has already commissioned it.

3.3 The two murderers, joined by a third, kill Banquo, but Fleance escapes.

3.4 Macbeth is called away from the feast by the two murderers, who report their partial success. Rejoining the party, he alone sees Banquo's ghost sitting in his place, and speaks in guilty horror. Taking him aside, Lady Macbeth rebukes him for his visible distraction, and after the ghost leaves he is able to compose himself and apologize to his guests for what he claims is merely an indisposition. The ghost returns, however, and Macbeth speaks to it in such terror that Lady Macbeth has to dismiss the company. Left alone with his wife, Macbeth comments on Macduff's absence from the feast, and resolves to consult the witches again.

3.5 The three witches are rebuked by Hecate for their dealings with Macbeth: Hecate is summoned away by spirits, with whom she sings.

3.6 Lennox, recognizing that Macbeth is responsible for the murders of Duncan and Banquo, talks with a Lord, who reports that Macduff has gone to the English court to join Malcolm and to urge the English king to provide military aid against Macbeth.

4.1 The witches, subsequently joined by Hecate, prepare a dreadful potion. Macbeth arrives and insists that they call forth their spirits to provide him with further insights into the future. An armed head warns him to beware of Macduff; a bloody child tells him he cannot be harmed by any man born of woman; and a crowned child holding a tree tells him he will never be defeated until Birnam Wood comes to Dunsinane. Encouraged, Macbeth insists that the witches tell him whether Banquo's descendants will indeed rule Scotland: to his horror he is shown a procession of eight kings, the last holding a mirror, with Banquo's ghost smiling and indicating that they are his descendants. After the witches vanish, Lennox brings the news that Macduff has fled to England. Alone, Macbeth resolves to have Macduff's family killed at once.

4.2 Lady Macduff laments her husband's absence to Ross, and speaks of it with her young son after Ross leaves. A messenger warns that they are in immediate danger, and flees: shortly afterwards murderers arrive, stab the boy to death, and pursue the screaming Lady Macduff.

4.3 In England Malcolm speaks warily with Macduff, professing a suspicion that he may have been sent by Macbeth, especially since he has left his family in Macbeth's power. Malcolm goes on to tell Macduff that he is unfit to be king in Macbeth's place, claiming to be lascivious, greedy, and generally vicious: when Macduff, despairing for Scotland, finally repudiates him, Malcolm says he is now convinced of Macduff's sincerity and is in fact innocent of all crimes, having maligned himself only as a test. He has indeed already secured English aid. A doctor tells of the English King's miraculous ability to cure scrofula. Ross brings the news that Macduff's wife, children, and servants have all been killed: overcome by grief and self-reproach, Macduff vows revenge on Macbeth.

5.1 A gentlewoman has brought a doctor to witness Lady Macbeth's habitual sleepwalking: Lady Macbeth duly arrives, obsessively washing her hands, and speaking guiltily of Duncan's murder and the deaths of Lady Macduff and Banquo.

5.2 Scottish nobles, including Lennox, go to Birnam to rendezvous with Malcolm's English army.

5.3 At Dunsinane Macbeth, convinced of his invulnerability, learns of the English army's approach: he reflects that he may as well die, however, having forfeited the respect and friendship that make life worth living. He asks the doctor about Lady Macbeth's health, but despairs of a cure for her sorrows. Angry and coarse with his staff, he dons his armour.

5.4 Malcolm instructs his army to carry boughs cut in Birnam Wood as camouflage.

5.5 Macbeth, with his servant Seyton and soldiers, learns that Lady Macbeth is dead: he feels life is futile. A messenger brings the news that Birnam Wood is apparently coming to Dunsinane: Macbeth feels that he is doomed, but resolves to fight defiantly.

5.6 Malcolm places the English nobleman Siward and his son in the vanguard of their army.

5.7 In the battle Macbeth, convinced he can only be killed by a man not born of woman, kills Young Siward.

5.8 Macduff seeks Macbeth.

5.9 Siward tells Malcolm Macbeth's castle has surrendered.

5.10 Macduff confronts Macbeth: they fight, but Macbeth tells Macduff of his presumed invulnerability. Macduff, however, tells Macbeth he was born by Caesarean section. Despairing, and cursing the witches' equivocation, Macbeth still refuses to surrender, and the two resume their combat. Macbeth is killed.

5.11 Malcolm and his nobles, knowing they have won the battle, await news of the missing. Siward stoically accepts the reported death of his son. Macduff brings Macbeth's head, and Malcolm is hailed as King of Scotland: he makes his nobles earls.

 ARTISTIC FEATURES

The structure of *Macbeth* resembles that of *Julius Caesar*—following the tense, suspense-filled preparations for an assassination, after which the perpetrators fall into discord and anticlimax—but Shakespeare's focus on the consciousness of Macbeth and his wife, achieved by a succession of extraordinarily dense and rich soliloquies, goes far beyond his comparatively dispassionate investigation of Brutus' more intellectual motivations. The vividness with which the play thus renders the psychological experiences not only of committing murder but of anticipating and remembering doing so, coupled with its depiction of the witches, make even reading the play seem a genuine engagement with the forces of evil, an effect no doubt partly responsible for the superstition according to which it is unlucky to mention *Macbeth* by name in the precincts of a theatre.

CRITICAL HISTORY

Macbeth has been of crucial importance not only to Shakespeare's reputation as a master of tragic pity and terror, possessed of uncanny psychological insight, but also to the work of subsequent artists, whether writers (from Lord Byron to the authors of countless Gothic novels and detective thrillers), musicians such as Verdi, painters such as Fuseli, or film-makers from Alfred Hitchcock (on whom the play exerted a palpable influence) to Orson Welles, Roman Polanski, and Akiro Kurosawa. In the modern theatre alone, the play's offshoots range from the American political skit *Macbird* (an attack on President Johnson, 1965, one of a long line of *Macbeth* burlesques and travesties) to Heiner Müller's radical adaptation *Macbeth nach Shakespeare* (1972) and Ionesco's *Macbett* (1972). Quite apart from anything else, the play has influenced all subsequent notions of ghosts and witches.

The force with which *Macbeth* depicts terror and the supernatural gave it a special place in the canon for 18th-century and Romantic commentators, with their interest in the sublime, while the density of its imagery has made it a perennially important test case for studies of Shakespeare's style. Although the success with which Sir William Davenant's verbally simplified adaptation displaced Shakespeare's text from the stage between the 1660s and the 1740s suggests that Restoration playgoers found this very density objectionable, *Macbeth* was by the mid-18th century one of the most highly regarded of the tragedies. Dr Johnson, who cites it more often than any other play in his *Dictionary*, found it more satisfactorily moral than most of Shakespeare's work. Romantic critics were less interested in the play's morality than in its intense theatrical and psychological effects; *Macbeth*, for example, inspired one of Thomas De Quincey's best literary essays, 'The Knocking at the Gate' (*London Magazine*, 1823). Following Samuel Taylor Coleridge, many 19th-century critics examined how Shakespeare created the play's distinctive atmosphere: A. C. Bradley, for example, in *Shakespearean Tragedy* (1904), pursued the play's recurrent references to darkness, anticipating 20th-century discussions (by Caroline Spurgeon and others) of its imagery of blood. This increased sense of the play's literary technique led to an impatience with earlier, realist accounts of its plot and characters, famously voiced in L. C. Knights's 1933 essay 'How Many Children Had Lady Macbeth?' The play has fascinated psychoanalytic criticism since the time of Sigmund Freud himself (who felt that the play resembled a dreamlike account of Elizabeth I's presumed guilt over the execution of Mary, Queen of Scots), with feminist critics in particular pursuing the connections between the uncertain gender of the witches, Lady Macbeth's imagined unsexing, and the mother-ripping birth of Macduff. Historically oriented critics, meanwhile, continue to muse on the play's relations to Jacobean politics. Unsurprisingly, perhaps, such studies are often invested in the Gunpowder Plot and the demonic. In addition to these interrelated concerns, recent critics have considered the play's domestic politics, particularly the overlap between witchcraft and the home—heath and hearth—in the Jacobean imagination.

STAGE HISTORY

Although *Macbeth* probably enjoyed its first performances in 1606, the first to be recorded took place in April 1611, when the astrologer and diarist Simon Forman saw it at the Globe. Forman was especially struck by the prophecies, Banquo's ghost, and the sleepwalking scene, but despite his interest in supernatural affairs he says nothing of the cauldron scene, or Hecate, and refers to the witches as 'fairies or nymphs'. It was probably a little after this, around 1613, that Middleton adapted the script, adding Hecate, and a tendency to elaborate on the witches' scenes would be even more spectacularly visible when the play enjoyed its next recorded revivals 50 years later. Sir William Davenant rewrote the play to suit the tastes and concerns of Restoration audiences and the scenic possibilities of Restoration playhouses in 1664. As well as developing its opportunities for music and special effects (with singing, flying witches, a cloud for Hecate to ride, and a disappearing cavern for the apparition scene), Davenant updated the play's interest in the Stuart monarchy, so that his usurping, regicidal Macbeth becomes a figure analogous to Oliver Cromwell and his Malcolm to the recently restored Charles II. More pervasively, Davenant simplified Shakespeare's diction, cut the indecorous Porter, and gave the play an unambiguous, symmetrical moral scheme by expanding the roles of Macduff and Lady Macduff to make them into virtuous counterparts to the Macbeths.

With Thomas Betterton and his wife Mary in the leading roles, this adaptation was immensely successful (Samuel Pepys saw it eight times in less than four years, describing it as 'a most excellent play in all respects, but especially in divertisement'), and Macbeth remained one of Betterton's greatest roles down to his retirement in 1709. His most important successor in the part as reshaped by Davenant was James Quin, who played it at different times from 1717 (at Drury Lane) until 1751 (by which time he had moved to Covent Garden), but by then his dignified, oratorical performance as Macbeth, and indeed the lucidly neoclassical script he was using, had been overshadowed by the arrival of David Garrick. In 1744 Garrick advertised *Macbeth* at Drury Lane 'as written by Shakespeare' ('What does he mean?', Quin is said to have remarked, 'don't I play Macbeth as written by Shakespeare?'), and though his own version retained Davenant's operatic witches and still excluded the Porter and the murder of the Macduffs' children (as well as supplying Macbeth with a longer and more penitent onstage dying speech), from Garrick onwards the great soliloquies of Shakespeare's script, and the unaltered dialogues between Macbeth and his Lady (played with particular success by Hannah Pritchard), were again the heart of the play.

Since Garrick's time, however, *Macbeth*, though one of Shakespeare's most regularly revived tragedies, has occasioned more conspicuous disasters in the theatre than successes (another factor, perhaps, contributing to actors' superstitions about the play), and the much shorter role of Lady Macbeth has been far luckier for performers than that of her husband. Charles Macklin was ahead of his time in his 1773–6 production at Covent Garden, which gave the play a consistent, 'authentic' old Scottish design, much ridiculed. Between 1777 and 1817 Lady Macbeth was by common consent Sarah Siddons's greatest role, but her brother J. P. Kemble's Macbeth was less successful. Edmund Kean cut some of Davenant's added witch material in 1814 (the rest disappeared finally from Samuel Phelps's revival of 1847), and he was followed by William Charles Macready, who played Macbeth (in tartans) between 1820 and 1848. Macready's performance, however, is remembered less vividly than that of his Lady Macbeth, Charlotte Cushman, just as Henry Irving's nervy and unwarlike Thane (Lyceum, 1875, 1888) was a critical flop compared to Ellen Terry's Lady

Macbeth. Cushman upstaged the American actor Edwin Forrest just as successfully during his visit to London in 1845, and Forrest's own Macbeth is remembered principally for its riot-provoking rivalry with that of Macready in New York in 1849, which further contributed to the play's evil reputation.

Unequivocally successful 20th-century revivals of the play were equally rare. Sybil Thorndike and Flora Robson were both praised as Lady Macbeth, but opinions were divided about the Macbeths offered by the most prominent Shakespearian actors of the time. John Gielgud, in 1930 at the Old Vic, was sensitive and introverted but unsoldierly; Donald Wolfit forceful but mannered (1937, 1945–6, 1953); Laurence Olivier was felt to be simplistic opposite Judith Anderson's operatic Lady at the Old Vic in 1937, but was more impressive in Glen Byam Shaw's Stratford production in 1955. Notable disasters include Barry Jackson's 'tweedy' modern-dress production (1928), Orson Welles's 'voodoo' design (1936), and Peter O'Toole's notoriously gory, melodramatic performance (1976). Perhaps the period's only legendary success was Trevor Nunn's studio production for the RSC in 1976, with Ian McKellen and Judi Dench. Further afield, meanwhile, the play inspired Welcome Msomi's popular Zulu adaptation *uMabatha*, premièred in Natal in 1972, which toured throughout the world between 1973 and 1998. In 1980, Yukio Ninagawa premiered his magisterial production. Dubbed the 'cherry blossom *Macbeth*' for its relocation of the play's action to feudal Japan, samurai protagonist, kabuki witches, and the butsudan set, Ninagawa's vision stood in stark contrast to the gloomy Scotlands of late 20th-century productions. Notable Macbeths in more recent years have been Sir Antony Sher (RSC, 1999), Greg Hicks (RSC, 2004), Patrick Stewart (Chichester, 2007), Jonathan Slinger (RSC, 2011), and James McAvoy (Trafalgar Studios, 2013). When Sir Kenneth Branagh took the title role in 2013, his and Rob Ashford's off-Broadway production—much expanded from its earlier incarnation in a deconsecrated church in Manchester—prioritized blood and mud, with Branagh a convincingly visceral warrior.

 ## ON THE SCREEN

The earliest recorded film of *Macbeth* is a one-minute scene shot in America (1905). The cinema adaptations of the play have had a more enduring impact than any television version. Still vigorously discussed are Orson Welles's *Macbeth* (1948), Kurosawa's *Throne of Blood* (1957), and Roman Polanski's *Macbeth* (1971). The places, the atmospheric dimensions, and the spatial detail referred to in the dialogue afford the cinematographer more elaborate opportunities than can effectively be accommodated on the television screen. Welles, Kurosawa, and Polanski each adopt different priorities in visualizing the drama; Welles dramatizes an amorphous universe, Kurosawa incorporates both Noh theatricalization and samurai realism, and Polanski counterpoises scenic realism with powerful acting and strong projection of dialogue. The play also provided the basis for two gangster films, *Joe MacBeth* (1955) and *Men of Respect* (1991), and an amusing adaptation set in a hamburger restaurant, *Scotland, PA* (2001), but its most interesting film version probably remains the one that got away, the film of *Macbeth* which Olivier planned after his stage performance in 1955 but was unable to finance. The most opulent big-screen adaptation to date has been Justin Kurzel's essentially medieval rendering (2015), forgoing more inventive interpretive strategies in favour of rich cinematography and two leads of acknowledged enigmatic power in Michael Fassbender and Marion Cotillard.

George Schaefer's American TV adaptation (1954, remade 1960) featuring Maurice Evans and Judith Anderson drew scant praise from the critics, though Michael Hordern's Banquo shone memorably in the later version. The television film (1979) of Trevor Nunn's famous RSC in-the-round production is historically interesting but suffers from the inevitable distancing which the camera brings to such a production, though it remains more effective than the foggy BBC TV production (1982) with Nicol Williamson and Jane Lapotaire. Gregory Doran produced an effective television adaptation of his RSC production of 2000, with Antony Sher and Harriet Walter: Rupert Goold followed suit after directing the play at Chichester in 2007, with Patrick Stewart and Kate Fleetwood. James McAvoy played Joe Macbeth, a chef in a Glaswegian restaurant who resorts to murder to take over the business in Peter Moffat's canny adaptation for the *Shakespeare Retold* series (BBC, 2005).

Measure for Measure

Shakespeare's ambivalently comic treatment of power, sexuality, and repression belongs very much to the early years of the Jacobean period. According to the Revels accounts for 1604–5, the first recorded performance of *Measure for Measure* took place at court on 26 December 1604. Several topical allusions in the text suggest a slightly earlier date of composition. A passing reference in the opening lines of 1.2 to the final stages of a war between the Duke of Vienna and the King of Hungary might be an allusion to the peace settlements with Spain which King James I signed at Hampton Court on 18 August 1604. It has been suggested that these lines might refer to the Duke of Holst, Queen Anne's brother, who levied an army in London in December 1604 to support the new Protestant ruler of Hungary. However, Mistress Overdone's complaint in the same scene provides another set of allusions to memorable events which occurred in London in the winter of 1603–4. The Overdone–Pompey exchange in 1.2 might also be another allusion to the King's proclamation of 16 September 1603 calling for the demolition of houses in the suburbs of London. The hypothesis that *Measure for Measure* was not a new play when it was staged at court in December 1604 is further reinforced by the fact that Shakespeare might have decided to write the play while performances at the Globe were suspended between 19 March 1603 and 9 April 1604 because of the plague.

 TEXT

Measure for Measure was entered in the Stationers' Register by Edward Blount and Isaac Jaggard on 8 November 1623: it was never printed in a quarto edition prior to its inclusion in the 1623 Folio. The Folio text was transcribed by Ralph Crane, probably from a promptbook. Crane is likely to have supplied the list of characters, where the Duke, who is otherwise never referred to by his proper name in the play, is called Vincentio.

The text shows some signs of adaptation: the Boy's song, 'Take, O take those lips away', at the beginning of Act 4 may be a late interpolation from Fletcher's *Rollo, Duke of Normandy* (1616–19), and the Duke's subsequent monologue 'O place and greatness' (too short to allow Isabella to inform Mariana about the Duke's plans) was probably transposed by the later adapter responsible for introducing the act division with the original monologue, 'He who the sword of heaven will bear', which is longer and more suitable as an act-break. More tampering must have occurred in 1.2, where the news of Claudio's arrest is divulged twice: the first part of 1.2 was probably added to the promptbook by a later adapter, probably Thomas Middleton. This later addition was probably meant to replace the original exchange, but Crane transcribed both by mistake. This late piece of adaptation may also be the source of some of the more obscure apparently topical references in 1.2. Some recent scholars have speculated that the play may originally have had an Italian setting rather than a Viennese one—'Verona' and 'Ferrara' would scan as well as does 'Vienna'—but the evidence is at best inconclusive.

 SOURCES

Of the three main plot-components upon which *Measure for Measure* is based—'the corrupt magistrate', 'the ruler in disguise', and 'the bed-trick'—only the first one derives from the play's main sources, the fifth *novella* of the eighth decade in Cinthio's *Hecatommithi* (1565), its dramatic rendition *Epitia* (1573), and George Whetstone's *Promos and Cassandra* (1578). The stock character of the ruler in disguise, which enjoyed sweeping popularity on the early Jacobean stage (see, for example, Middleton's *The Phoenix*, John Marston's *The Malcontent* and *The Fawn*, and Edward Sharpham's *The Fleer*), might derive from Elizabethan history plays, such as Thomas Heywood's *King Edward IV* (1600), the anonymous *Fair Em* (1590), or George Peele's *King Edward I* (1593), where the encounter between the disguised ruler and his subjects is the focus of the dramatic tension. The bed-trick, which Shakespeare used again in *All's Well That Ends Well*, has famous precedents in the Italian novelistic tradition but also in the Old Testament (Genesis 38), Plautus's *Amphitruo*, and Thomas Malory's *Le Morte d'Arthur*.

 CHARACTER LIST

Vincentio, the Duke of Vienna
Angelo *appointed his deputy*
Escalus *an old lord, appointed Angelo's secondary*
Claudio *a young gentleman*
Juliet *betrothed to Claudio*
Isabella *Claudio's sister, novice to a sisterhood of nuns*
Lucio *'a fantastic'*
Two other like gentlemen
Froth *a foolish gentleman*
Mistress Overdone *a bawd*
Pompey *her clownish servant*

A **Provost**
Elbow *a simple constable*
A **Justice**
Abhorson *an executioner*
Barnárdine *a dissolute condemned prisoner*
Mariana *betrothed to Angelo*
A **Boy** *attendant on Mariana*
Friar Peter
Francesca *a nun*
Varrius *a lord, friend to the Duke*
Lords, officers, citizens, servants

SYNOPSIS

1.1 The Duke leaves Vienna straight after appointing Angelo as his substitute. Angelo is younger and more inexperienced than the old councillor

Escalus and asks the Duke to test him before handing the rule of the city over to him. The Duke refuses to delay his departure any further.

1.2 Lucio's banter with two gentlemen is interrupted by Mistress Overdone's announcement that Claudio is being carried off to prison for getting Juliet with child. Mistress Overdone informs Pompey, the pimp, that because of a new proclamation her brothel and other houses of ill-repute in the suburbs will be pulled down. Lucio meets Claudio on his way to prison. The latter explains that although Juliet is 'fast' his wife, following a private exchange of vows between them, they have not been married in the church because Juliet's relatives oppose the match. Claudio will be sentenced to death as a result of Angelo's decision to revive an ancient law, which the Duke had failed to enforce for years. Claudio hopes that his sister Isabella will plead with the strict deputy for his life.

1.3 The Duke explains to Friar Thomas that he had to leave Vienna because of his failure to enforce the law and that Angelo was appointed to restore order on his behalf. The Duke will go back to Vienna disguised as a friar in order to keep an eye on his deputy.

1.4 Lucio goes to the convent where Isabella is about to take her vows and persuades her to plead with Angelo for Claudio's life.

2.1 Elbow, a constable, takes Pompey and Froth to court for attempting to corrupt his wife. Elbow's malapropisms bring the trial to an end and both Pompey and Froth are let off with a warning.

2.2 Isabella is brought before Angelo and she pleads for her brother's life. Her arguments grow stronger and Angelo is attracted both by the strength of her rhetorical powers and by her chastity. Angelo tries to repress his feelings for Isabella and wonders why he should be tempted by such a chaste creature as Isabella, since he has never been tempted by a woman before.

2.3 The Duke, disguised as a friar, goes to the prison and lectures Juliet about her share of responsibility for what has happened to her and Claudio, but fails to comfort her.

2.4 Isabella goes back for a second meeting with Angelo, who tells her that he will spare her brother only if she agrees to give up her virginity to him. Isabella threatens to report him, but Angelo is confident that his 'false' will overweigh her 'true', because of his spotless reputation and his privileged position as the Duke's deputy.

3.1 The Duke visits Claudio in prison pretending to be his 'ghostly father', a religious figure in charge of a penitent or one near death. His lesson in *ars moriendi* seems to persuade Claudio that life is not worth living after all, but as soon as Isabella hints at Angelo's indecent proposal, Claudio begs her to comply with Angelo's request. Isabella scolds Claudio for asking her to sacrifice her virtue. The Duke approaches Isabella and persuades her to trick Angelo into sleeping with his former fiancée Mariana, who had been spurned by Angelo a few years earlier following the loss of her dowry. They agree that Isabella will persuade Angelo to meet her in the dark, so that he will mistake Mariana for Isabella and spare her brother's life.

3.2 On his way out of the prison, the Duke meets Lucio, who slanders him. Because he is still in disguise, the Duke cannot refute Lucio's allegations.

4.1 Mariana, who is still in love with Angelo, welcomes the Duke's plans and agrees to go to Angelo pretending to be Isabella.

4.2 Pompey, who is now in prison himself, is appointed personal assistant to Abhorson, the executioner. The Duke realizes that Angelo has failed to keep his word and has ordered Claudio's execution. The Duke is therefore forced to inform the Provost that he is acting on the Duke's behalf and that he wishes him to delay Claudio's execution. He also suggests that the Provost should pretend that Angelo's orders have been carried out and that Claudio is dead, by sending Angelo the severed head of Barnardine, another prisoner who is shortly to be executed.

4.3 Barnardine spoils the Duke's plans by refusing to be executed. He claims to be too drunk and therefore unfit to die. The Duke instead sends Angelo the head of Ragozine, another prisoner who has fortunately just died in prison. The Duke lies to Isabella about Claudio's execution. She believes him dead and Lucio tries to comfort her, taking once more the opportunity to slander the Duke, by blaming him for leaving his subjects at the mercy of the strict deputy.

4.4 Angelo and Escalus learn of the Duke's imminent homecoming.

4.5 The Duke finalizes the arrangements for his homecoming, instructing Friar Peter to help Mariana and Isabella report Angelo to the Duke after his reinstatement as the supreme ruler in Vienna.

4.6 Still unaware of the friar's true identity, Isabella and Mariana are also instructed by the Duke.

5.1 The Duke meets Angelo and Escalus at the city gates. Isabella is brought before him and accuses Angelo of deflowering her. The Duke pretends to ignore the truth and, despite Lucio's interference, proceeds to have Isabella arrested for slandering his deputy. Friar Peter announces that a witness can corroborate Isabella's accusations. Mariana enters wearing a veil and promises to reveal her identity only when her husband bids her to do so. Mariana claims that Angelo is her husband and that they have already consummated their marriage. Angelo accuses Mariana of lying and the Duke pretends to side with him. Friar Peter asks that another witness be brought before the Duke. The Duke exits and re-enters wearing his disguise as a friar. When Lucio accidentally unmasks him, Angelo finally realizes that the Duke has known the truth all along. He begs to be executed but the Duke orders him to marry Mariana in order to restore her reputation, ordering his execution immediately after the ceremony. Mariana pleads for his life and asks Isabella to do the same. Isabella argues that Angelo should be spared because Claudio was at least punished for a crime he actually committed, while Angelo was in the event prevented from taking her virginity. Angelo is finally forgiven when the Duke orders the Provost to unmask a prisoner whose execution had been delayed and the prisoner turns out to be Claudio. The Duke asks Isabella to marry him.

🎭 ARTISTIC FEATURES

Measure for Measure has been perceived as an exceptionally complex and 'dark' comedy, or tragicomedy, mostly because of its peculiar structure and characterization. Whereas the first half of the play explores the moral issues raised by Claudio and Isabella's potentially tragic ordeal, the second half is largely devoted to the Duke's efforts to orchestrate the happy ending. The comic resolution, however, is remarkably fraught with tension, embarrassing silences (such as Isabella's failure to respond to the Duke's proposal) and disappointing reunions, and fails to provide an answer to the moral issues raised in the first half. The characters themselves are never single-mindedly evil or entirely sympathetic. Isabella is one of Shakespeare's most articulate heroines, but may seem harsh and self-righteous in her adamant conviction that 'more than our brother is our chastity'. Angelo is a hypocritical coward and yet he is also a self-conscious villain, who wonders at the mystery of his own fall from grace. The Duke aims to appear as a merciful ruler but resorts to spying, scheming, and acting as a meddling busybody throughout the play. Shakespeare seems therefore intent on systematically undercutting his characters' ideals so as to show them as painfully human and fallible.

⭐ CRITICAL HISTORY

Measure for Measure has always had a mixed critical reception: its moral complexity irritated Samuel Johnson but pleased William Hazlitt; the personal shortcomings of its characters alienated Samuel Taylor Coleridge but moved the German critic Hermann Ulrici. Twentieth-century critics have replicated this split by reading this comedy as either a problem play (as did E. M. W. Tillyard and Ernest Schanzer) or as a Christian allegory of mercy and forgiveness (as did Wilson Knight, 1930, Roy Battenhouse, and Nevill Coghill). Recent criticism is similarly divided in its assessment of this play in relation to the political and social institutions of its time. Some critics regard the low characters as ultimately subversive, while others argue that *Measure for Measure* exemplifies the systematic suppression of diversity. A feminist and a materialist critic have, for example, remarked that if 'feminist criticism… is restricted to exposing its own exclusion from the text' (Kathleen McLuskie, 1985), a materialist critic 'looking for evidence of resistance…[will] find rather further evidence of exploitation' (Jonathan Dollimore, 1985). Recent work on the play has explored *Measure* in terms of consent and in relation to other early modern rape narratives. The Duke's friar disguise has incited commentary on the play's religious politics, just as his surveillance tactics have continued to fuel discussions on the tension between Vienna's governmental authoritarianism and the loucheness of its sex trade.

STAGE HISTORY

The Revels accounts for 1604–5 report the only recorded performance prior to the closure of the London theatres in 1642. During the Restoration, *Measure for Measure* was revived in two heavily adapted versions, William Davenant's *The Law against Lovers* (1662) and Charles Gildon's *Measure for Measure; or, Beauty the Best Advocate* (1700), which cuts the low characters and instead fills out the play by having Angelo listen to Purcell's opera *Dido and Aeneas* in instalments in a fruitless bid to take his mind off Isabella. The Shakespearian original was restored to the stage in 1720, often understood as a warning against prime ministerial government, but most 18th-century productions were heavily cut. *Measure for Measure* disgusted the Victorians, but appealed to 20th-century audiences. Tyrone Guthrie's 1933 production at the Old Vic was only moderately successful, despite its star-studded cast, which included Charles Laughton as Angelo. The next remarkable production was Peter Brook's at Stratford-upon-Avon, remembered for Paul Scofield's foppish Lucio and for Barbara Jefford's dramatic pause before she knelt down to plead for Angelo's life in Act 5, which was never less than 30 seconds long and sometimes far longer. The cultural changes ushered in by the late 1960s led directors John Barton and Trevor Nunn to depart from Brook's optimistic interpretation of the Duke: their 1970 and 1990 productions emphasized the oppressive nature of the Duke's regime and Isabella's plight in Act 5. More sympathetic Dukes, however, have included Michael Pennington's in Barry Kyle's production (1978) and Daniel Massey's in Adrian Noble's (1984), opposite Juliet Stevenson's powerful Isabella. Nicholas Hytner's 1987 revival bucked this trend, focusing his RSC version on politics and sexual violence. Roger Allam's was a proto-fascist Vincentio, and Sean Baker's Angelo a terrifying predator; 2.4 shocked audiences with its brutality, as the Duke's deputy seemed almost to rape Josette Simon's Isabella. Trevor Nunn was the next to tackle the play for the RSC, this time in the small black-box theatre at The Other Place and with a determinedly happy ending. In 1994, the play returned to the company's main stage under the direction of Stephen Pimlott. Set in a modern-day prison, this production emphasized the play's theme of surveillance—a motif that would continue throughout the decade and into the next—and offered a counterpoint to Nunn's earlier treatment of Isabella's infamous silence. Stella Gonet's Isabella met the Duke's (Michael Feast) proposal with a slap across his face, a passionate embrace, and, finally, the sobs of the trauma- tized. Cheek by Jowl (dir., Declan Donnellan) rounded out this year of Measures (1994 also saw the release of David Thacker's film version—see below), with a production that stressed the dangers of sexual repression and the horrors of state authoritarianism. Set in late-Tsarist Russia, the Vienna of Michael Boyd's 1998 production for the RSC was on the brink of destruction: here, Angelo's ambition culminated in an attempted military coup. The noughties brought with them four major productions: by Sean Holmes, Simon McBurney, Jonathan Dove, and Peter Hall. Everyone, bar Emma Fielding's Isabella, was a cynic in Holmes's Third Man-ish Vienna, with its bureaucratic Angelo (Daniel Evans) and war-torn set. Played with- out interval for just over two hours, McBurney's production for Complicité at the National Theatre reignited interest in the play's religious politics, recognizing that, as well as sex and violence, this is a play about justice in an unjust state. Dove's version for the Globe rather palled in comparison to Complicité's Measure (which had caused quite a stir): Mark Rylance's clottish Duke and Sophie Thompson's sunny Isabella were felt by some critics to be more panto than problem play. Yuri Butusov's Vakhtangov Theatre produc- tion for the Globe to Globe Festival in 2012 made the innovative decision to cast the same actor (Sergey Epishev) as both Duke and deputy, drawing an equivalence between their indecent proposals to Isabella and the forms of coercion used to extort her. In 2013, Declan Donnellan tackled Measure again for Cheek by Jowl. With its emphasis on state surveillance and propaganda, this production seemed to evoke contemporary Russia. Josie Rourke offered an equally topical rendering of the play at the Donmar Warehouse in 2018: a heavily cut version of the play ran rapidly from begin- ning to end before Angelo (Jack Lowden) and Isabella (Hayley Atwell) swapped roles, restarting the story from the beginning. Designed to explore gender roles and their power structures, this decision nonetheless proved controversial.

ON THE SCREEN

The earliest film recorded was a 1913 Italian version. A 90-minute adaptation, again from Italy (1942), was followed by a more substantial German television film (1963). The BBC TV version (1978), though recognizing its Gothic elements, presented the play as a comedy. David Thacker's later BBC TV production (1994) is memorable for updating the play socially (into a world of televised courtrooms) and for taking a much more serious view of the action. Like John Barton's stage production, it left the question of Isabella's marriage unresolved, and, like a proliferation of American campus productions of the 1990s, it evoked the pre-#MeToo sexual harassment case between the US judge Clarence Thomas and his aide Anita Hill.

The Merchant
of Venice

Shakespeare's perennially popular, and perennially controversial, comedy of religious conflict was entered in the Stationers' Register on 22 July 1598, and is mentioned in Francis Meres's *Palladis Tamia* soon afterwards. *The Merchant of Venice* cannot have been more than two years old then: the passage in which Shylock cites the story of Jacob and Laban (1.3.70–89) shows the influence of Miles Mosse's tract *The Arraignment and Conviction of Usury* (1595), and the play is unlikely to have been written before 1596, since a reference at 1.1.27–9 to 'wealthy Andrew' probably alludes to a Spanish ship, the *St Andrew*, captured in the Cadiz expedition that summer. Internal, stylistic evidence links the play's metre and vocabulary to those of the *Henry IV* plays, and it was probably composed during the same period, around 1596–7.

TEXT

The Stationers' Register calls the play *The Merchant of Venice, or Otherwise Called The Jew of Venice*, possibly reflecting Shakespeare's original subtitle, but when it appeared in quarto in 1600 it did so as *The Most Excellent History of the Merchant of Venice. With the Extreme Cruelty of Shylock the Jew towards the Said Merchant, in Cutting a Just Pound of his Flesh: and the Obtaining of Portia by the Choice of Three Chests*. This remains the only authoritative text for the play, serving as the basis for a further quarto printed by the Jaggards for Pavier in 1619 (fraudulently dated '1600') and for the text published in the 1623 Folio, which adds, however, a number of stage directions (mainly musical cues) which may derive from the additional consultation of a theatrical manuscript. Fortunately it is a generally reliable text, deriving either from a fair copy in Shakespeare's own hand or from an accurate transcript of such a manuscript.

SOURCES

Shakespeare's play, as the quarto's subtitle suggests, brings together two widely known folk-tale motifs, the story of the pound of flesh and the story of the three caskets. Many of the play's most important elements are already present in the Florentine writer Ser Giovanni's version of the pound of flesh plot, a story known as 'Giannetto of Venice and the Lady of Belmont'. In this story a merchant borrows from a Jew in order to fund his protégé Giannetto's repeated attempts to woo the Lady of Belmont, who will only marry the man who can first pay a contestant's fee and then stay awake long enough to seduce her. Giannetto falls asleep on his first two attempts, before the Lady's maid warns him not to drink the wine which the Lady always offers her suitors before bed, which she drugs: he is thus enabled to win her. As in the play, the Jew is foiled in his attempt to exact a pound of flesh from the defaulting merchant. Shakespeare knew the pound of flesh story from other sources too, one of which, Alexander Silvayn's *The Orator* (translated in 1596), influenced his own trial scene. In rewriting the story of Giannetto as that of Bassanio, Shakespeare replaced the seduction test with the choice of the three caskets, a motif also available to him in many forms, in John Gower's *Confessio amantis*, in Boccaccio's *Decameron*, and in the anonymous *Gesta Romanorum*. It is possible that Shakespeare was not the first playwright to combine the pound of flesh and the casket plots: Stephen Gosson's *The Anatomy of Abuses* (1579) refers to a now lost play called *The Jew*, which represents, he reports, 'the greediness of worldly choosers and the bloody minds of usurers'. Whether or not this vaguely described play served as a source for *The Merchant of Venice*, Shakespeare must have been conscious as he wrote his own play about a Jew of another, Christopher Marlowe's black farce *The Jew of Malta* (*c*.1589). In Marlowe's play the titular Machiavellian villain-hero, Barabas, is betrayed by his daughter Abigail, who falls in love with a Christian, and becomes a nun after Barabas has her suitor killed. The elopement and conversion of Shylock's daugher Jessica, significantly, is an addition by Shakespeare to his chief, prose, sources. Marlowe's play had enjoyed a new lease of life in 1594, when it was revived by the Admiral's Men, apparently to capitalize on the anti-Semitism exacerbated by the execution that June of Elizabeth I's Jewish-Portuguese physician Roderigo Lopez on dubious charges of attempting to poison the Queen: some commentators regard Graziano's reference to 'a wolf…hanged for human slaughter' (4.1.132–7) as a punning allusion to Lopez's fate (*lupus* is Latin for 'wolf').

 CHARACTER LIST

Antonio *a merchant of Venice*
Bassanio *his friend and Portia's suitor*
Leonardo *Bassanio's servant*

Lorenzo
Graziano ⎤ *friends of Antonio and*
Salerio ⎦ *Bassanio*
Solanio

Shylock *a Jew*
Jessica *his daughter*
Tubal *a Jew*

Lancelot *a clown, first Shylock's servant and then Bassanio's*
Gobbo *his father*
Portia *an heiress*
Nerissa *her waiting-gentlewoman*

Balthasar ⎤ *Portia's servants*
Stefano ⎦

Prince of **Morocco** ⎤ *Portia's*
Prince of **Aragon** ⎦ *suitors*

Duke of Venice
Magnificoes of Venice
A jailer, attendants, and servants

SYNOPSIS

1.1 Antonio, a Venetian merchant, will not be cheered up by his associates, even the frivolous Graziano. Left alone with his friend Bassanio, who already owes him much money, he learns of Bassanio's desire to woo an heiress of Belmont called Portia, for which Bassanio will need further money. Antonio urges Bassanio to borrow money on his credit for this purpose.

1.2 In Belmont, Portia reflects on her late father's will, which obliges her to marry whichever suitor correctly chooses between three chests of gold, silver, and lead: she speaks disparagingly of the suitors listed by her waiting-woman Nerissa. Nerissa speaks of Bassanio, but they are interrupted by news that a fresh suitor has arrived, the Prince of Morocco.

1.3 Bassanio is negotiating a loan of 3,000 ducats, for three months, with the Jewish usurer Shylock. When Shylock sees Antonio approaching he speaks in an aside of his hatred of him, but when Antonio arrives, Shylock, though reminding him of many public insults, speaks affably in defence of usury, and despite Antonio's renewed profession of enmity offers to lend the 3,000 ducats at no interest, insisting only—professedly in fun—that Antonio should sign a bond specifying that if he defaults Shylock will be entitled to a pound of his flesh.

2.1 The Prince of Morocco agrees to vow, before making his choice of casket, that if he chooses wrongly he will remain unmarried forever.

2.2 Lancelot Gobbo debates the morality of running away from his master Shylock, finally deciding to do so. When his blind father arrives he pretends to be a stranger and announces his own death, before revealing his identity and announcing his intention of leaving Shylock's service. When Bassanio enters, the Gobbos beg that Lancelot may join his staff, to which Bassanio agrees. Bassanio is subsequently met by Graziano, whom he permits to accompany him to Belmont on condition that he behave soberly.

2.3 Shylock's daughter Jessica bids farewell to Lancelot, giving him a letter to Bassanio's friend Lorenzo, with whom she plans to elope.

2.4 Lorenzo, among his revelling friends, receives Jessica's letter, which directs him to take her from her father's house, disguised as a page, that night.

2.5 Shylock, invited out to dine with Antonio and associates, bids farewell first to Lancelot and then, despite misgivings, to Jessica.

2.6 Lorenzo, disguised among his friends, receives Jessica as she climbs from her window disguised as a boy, bringing much of Shylock's gold and jewellery. Antonio urges Graziano to join Bassanio on board their ship for Belmont.

2.7 Morocco chooses between the three caskets, which all bear mottoes: the lead 'Who chooseth me must give and hazard all he hath', the silver 'Who chooseth me shall get as much as he deserves', and the gold 'Who chooseth me shall get what many men desire'. To Portia's relief he chooses the gold casket, which contains a death's head bearing a poem, 'All that glisters is not gold...'

2.8 Salerio and Solanio, associates of Bassanio, discuss Shylock's anguish at the loss of his daughter, Antonio's tender parting from Bassanio, and rumours that a Venetian ship, possibly one of Antonio's, has been wrecked.

2.9 Portia's next suitor, the Prince of Aragon, chooses the silver casket, which contains a fool's head and another mocking poem. As he departs, news arrives that another, Bassanio, is approaching.

3.1 Solanio and Salerio are discussing the wreck of one of Antonio's ships when Shylock arrives and accuses them of complicity in Jessica's elopement: distraught, he is consoled only by the news of Antonio's losses, and promises to pursue his revenge against him as ruthlessly as would a Christian. Left alone with Tubal, Shylock learns of Jessica's extravagance with the money and jewels she took with her, alternating between grief at this and vengeful glee as he hears further of Antonio's impending bankruptcy.

3.2 Though Portia begs him to postpone his choice, Bassanio, to the accompaniment of a song ('Tell me, where is fancy bred...?'), reflects prudently on the caskets' mottoes and correctly chooses the lead one: within is a picture of Portia and a poem which instructs him to claim her with a kiss. Portia formally gives herself and her estate to him, with a ring which she urges him to wear forever. Graziano now announces that Nerissa has promised to marry him should Bassanio succeed; Portia and Bassanio give their blessing. Lorenzo and Jessica arrive, together with Salerio, who brings Bassanio a letter from Antonio: it tells him that, all his seaborne ventures having failed, he is at Shylock's mercy. Bassanio explains to Portia that Antonio incurred this lethal debt on his behalf, and she immediately postpones their marriage, sending him to Venice with money in the hopes of persuading Shylock to let Antonio live.

3.3 On the eve of the pound of flesh falling due, Shylock refuses to hear Antonio's pleas for mercy.

3.4 Portia hands over her house to Lorenzo's keeping, saying she and Nerissa will stay in a nearby convent while Bassanio and Graziano are in Venice, but after Lorenzo's departure she sends her servant Balthasar on an errand to her relative, the lawyer Bellario, and explains to Nerissa that the two of them will in fact go to Venice in male disguise.

3.5 Lancelot banters with Jessica about her conversion to Christianity. Jessica and Lorenzo speak admiringly of Portia and Bassanio.

4.1 Before the Duke, Shylock, though offered his 3,000 ducats, insists on his pound of flesh. Bassanio offers twice the sum, which Shylock also refuses. Antonio professes a stoical acceptance of death while Shylock sharpens his knife. The Duke threatens to adjourn the court until he has received legal advice from Bellario: instead he receives a letter sending a young expert in his place, Balthasar, who is really Portia in disguise, accompanied by Nerissa as clerk. Portia speaks eloquently to Shylock, urging him to show mercy, but he refuses, and she concedes his legal right to the pound of flesh. Bassanio and Graziano, in Portia and Nerissa's hearing, each tell Antonio they would sacrifice their wives to save him. Antonio has exposed his breast for Shylock's incision when Portia announces that since the bond mentions no blood, Shylock's estate will be forfeit to the state if he sheds any while cutting his pound of flesh. Baffled, Shylock accepts 9,000 ducats in place of the flesh, but Portia insists he is entitled only to the flesh, not even to the 3,000 ducats he originally loaned. Shylock is about to leave when Portia announces that as an alien who has sought to kill a Venetian he is liable to the death penalty, and his possessions must be divided between Antonio and the state. The Duke spares Shylock's life and offers to waive the state's claim to half Shylock's wealth, requiring only a fine. Antonio in his turn says he will only borrow half Shylock's estate and give it after Shylock's death to Lorenzo, to whom he insists Shylock bequeaths all his other possessions, and he further insists that Shylock should convert to Christianity. Shylock leaves, unwell. The disguised Portia and Nerissa, gratefully offered gifts by Bassanio and Graziano, demand their respective wedding rings: at Antonio's insistence the men hand them over.

5.1 Lorenzo and Jessica, outside Portia's house, listen to music by moonlight. Portia and Nerissa, no longer disguised, return home, followed separately by Bassanio, Antonio, and Graziano. Nerissa upbraids Graziano for giving her ring to the clerk, and Bassanio soon has to admit he gave his to the lawyer. Portia and Nerissa claim they will not sleep with their husbands, but only with the lawyer and his clerk: only when a penitent Antonio intercedes on Bassanio's behalf does Portia produce the ring again, at first claiming to have obtained it in bed from the lawyer before revealing her deception. Portia further gives Antonio news that three of his argosies have arrived safely, and gives Lorenzo the deed by which Shylock has made him his heir.

ARTISTIC FEATURES

Combining the logics of both the fairy tale and the financial market place—or perhaps revealing their secret kinship—*The Merchant of Venice* is one of Shakespeare's most tightly structured comedies, both narratively and thematically. The questions raised by the lead casket's motto, 'Who chooseth me must give and hazard all he hath', resonate throughout its two interwoven plots as they scrupulously weigh the competing claims of religion and civil society, justice and mercy, marriage and friendship. Shylock, the first of the mature comedies' great antagonists, owes some of his enduring impact not only to his formal status as the comedy's tragic scapegoat and his religious status as an embodiment of Judaic law in a Christian community nominally committed to love and mercy, but to the skill with which Shakespeare invests his comparatively short role with its own distinctive voice.

✯✯✯ CRITICAL HISTORY

Responses to this play have for most of its history been dominated by responses to Shylock. The question of Shakespeare's attitude to the Jews has been debated since the time of Nicholas Rowe, and from the early 19th century onwards many commentators have seen the play as essentially sympathetic to Shylock: William Hazlitt insisted that he was presented as, finally, an object of pity, while Heinrich Heine, remembering an English theatre-goer weeping 'The poor man is wronged!' at the end of Act 4 (in *Shakespeares Mädchen und Frauen*, 1839), opined that even if Shakespeare had consciously intended Shylock to be a monster his humanity had led him to write a vindication of the Jews. The argument between those who insist that Shakespeare was exposing his Christians' hypocrisy rather than attacking Judaism, and those who claim that all Elizabethans were automatically anti-Semitic and would have found Shylock's torments hilarious, continues to this day, though since the early 20th century accounts of Shylock's significance (such as that offered by W. H. Auden in 1948) have been more inclined to see him in thematic relation to the play's other outsider, Antonio. Antonio's erotically charged patron–client relationship with Bassanio has come under considerable scrutiny over the last century, while psychoanalytic criticism has been interested in the symbolism of the play's plots since Sigmund Freud's own remarks on the play (in *Psychopathology of Everyday Life*, 1914). Portia, meanwhile, offered as a role-model to the countless Victorian schoolgirls required to memorize her oration on mercy, has been studied in relation to the other cross-dressed heroines, and her successful replacement of Antonio as Bassanio's chief benefactor has been of much interest to recent feminist criticism. Drawing on critical race studies, more recent work has theorized Shylock's Jewishness, in terms of both his race and his religion. Queer studies has opened up new ways of reading Antonio and Bassanio's relationship; the interpretation of their friendship as homoerotic has become a mainstay of contemporary performance. Feminist criticism has redoubled its attention to Portia and the economies of gift-giving, trade, and justice that pervade the play.

▐ STAGE HISTORY

In the theatre, the history of *The Merchant of Venice* has largely been a history of great Shylocks. According to the quarto, the play was popular in its own time, and the Revels accounts record two court performances in 1605, but the play's next recorded performances were only in the form of George Granville's adaptation *The Jew of Venice* in 1701. It was only in 1741 that the original play returned to the stage, with Charles Macklin as a fierce, methodically prepared Shylock (a role he retained to his retirement in 1789). Macklin's most notable successors included J. P. Kemble (with Sarah Siddons as Portia), Edmund Kean, who played Shylock wholly sympathetically in 1814 (replacing his traditional red beard with a small black one), William Charles Macready, Charles Kean, and, most famously, Henry Irving, whose aristocratic, proud Shylock, first seen at the Lyceum in 1879 (with Ellen Terry as Portia), was a summit of his career. With actor-managers so frequently casting themselves as Shylock, the play sometimes finished at the close of his part, with Act 5 cut entirely. The 20th century, however, with its shift towards the director (well exemplified by Theodore Komisarjevsky's fantastically designed debut production at Stratford in 1932), saw a movement towards more balanced productions, using fuller texts. The period's troubled history, however, emphatically kept the spotlight on Shylock, whether played as an unsympathetic caricature (as he was by Werner Krauss in a 1942 Nazi production in Vienna specifically intended to celebrate the deportation and murder of the city's Jews, a performance for which Krauss was subsequently fined by a post-war de-Nazification court) or as a wronged victim (as he was by George C. Scott in New York in 1962, and by Laurence Olivier in Jonathan Miller's production of 1970). Although the play continues to divide Jewish audiences and actors (it has been much performed and discussed in Israel, and has inspired combative adaptations such as Arnold Wesker's *The Merchant*, 1976), the role of Shylock has increasingly attracted Jewish players, among them Dustin Hoffman, Warren Mitchell, Antony Sher, and Henry Goodman, whose meticulous performance dominated Trevor Nunn's National Theatre production, set in a just-pre-Nazi Central Europe, in 1999. F. Murray Abraham played the part to great acclaim in the Theater for a New Audience production that supplied the RSC's Complete Works Festival with its *Merchant* in 2007, and Patrick Stewart was a sympathetic and literally spat-upon Shylock in Rupert Goold's garish 2011 RSC version, colloquially known as the 'Merchant of Vegas'. The play was given a more conventional Renaissance setting at Shakespeare's Globe in 2015, with Jonathan Pryce as Shylock, a production which closed with an onstage representation of the usurer's brutal forced conversion. In contrast, by casting Makram J. Khoury, an actor celebrated in Israel and Palestine alike, as a stoical, patient, even gentle Shylock beset by thuggish Christians, Polly Findlay's modern-dress *Merchant* (2015, RSC) stressed ideas of a common humanity.

 ON THE SCREEN

Nine silent versions were made between 1902 and 1926. Of the memorable television versions, five were made for the BBC after 1947, culminating in the Jonathan Miller production (1980) with Warren Mitchell (Shylock) and Gemma Jones (Portia). Most impressive was Jonathan Miller's television adaptation of his National Theatre stage production (1970), with Laurence Olivier as an Edwardian Shylock whose off-screen wailing after his final exit gave his agony an indelible poignancy. Frank Finlay's Shylock for BBC TV (1972) was seen as significant in touching the role with comedy, so sharpening the question about the place of the play in the post-Holocaust world. Trevor Nunn's National Theatre production, with Henry Goodman as Shylock, was intelligently filmed for television. Michael Radford directed an opulently photographed Hollywood film in 2004, with Al Pacino as Shylock and Jeremy Irons as Antonio.

The Merry Wives of Windsor

Shakespeare's only comedy set in his homeland (with the exception of the Induction to *The Taming of the Shrew*), and his closest to the mainstream tradition of English farce, may also be his only play composed for a specific state occasion. According to a tradition first recorded by John Dennis in 1702, the play was personally commissioned by Queen Elizabeth, who, added Nicholas Rowe in 1709, particularly wished to see Falstaff in love. This unlikely piece of hearsay may have a kernel of truth, in that the play's last act alludes to the ceremonies of the Order of the Garter, to which Shakespeare's patron George Carey, Lord Hunsdon, the Lord Chamberlain, was admitted at Windsor early in 1597. These ceremonies were followed by a Garter Feast at the Palace of Westminster on St George's Day,

23 April, attended by the Queen, and the play's topical references to the Order of the Garter suggest that *The Merry Wives of Windsor* may have been composed expressly for performances associated with this event. The play may thus have enjoyed a royal première on Shakespeare's 33rd birthday: in any event its rare vocabulary, quite apart from its leading role, links it closely with the *Henry IV* plays (1596–8), and since it calls Sir John Falstaff throughout rather than Oldcastle it must post-date the censorship of *1 Henry IV*. Royal command performance or not, the play was almost certainly composed in 1597 or 1598.

 TEXT

The play was entered in the Stationers' Register in January 1602, and was printed in the same year in a quarto that was subsequently reprinted in 1619: a much fuller and more reliable text appeared in the Folio in 1623, and was itself reprinted in quarto in 1630. The two early quartos preserve an abbreviated and sometimes clumsily rewritten text of the play, apparently adapted from a memorial reconstruction prepared by an actor who had played the Host, but it is nonetheless a useful one, since the Folio text—visibly prepared from a transcript by the idiosyncratic scribe Ralph Crane—is apparently based on a promptbook which had undergone both expurgation (in compliance with the Act to Restrain the Abuses of Players, 1606) and censorship. Lord Cobham, who had already complained about Shakespeare's treatment of his ancestor Oldcastle, seems to have objected to Ford's alias as 'Brooke' (the Cobhams' family name), which the Folio text alters to 'Broome' (though preserving, meaninglessly, some of the puns occasioned by the original pseudonym). The confusing incident involving the theft of the Host's horses, apparently incorporating allusions to the German Count Momplegard (finally elevated to the Garter *in absentia* in 1597 after much embarrassing importunity), also seems to have been censored, but is irrecoverably truncated in both extant texts.

SOURCES

No single source for this play is known, though its plot draws on widespread literary traditions, most obviously that of the Italian novella (exemplified, for example, by the work of Ser Giovanni). With its good-natured plot of a comic elopement in a realistic English provincial setting, the play resembles Henry Porter's *Two Angry Women of Abingdon*, published in 1599, but Porter's comedy may have been influenced by Shakespeare's rather than vice versa. A long-standing tradition regards Justice Shallow as a hostile portrait of Sir Thomas Lucy, alleged to have prosecuted the young Shakespeare for deer-poaching, though Leslie Hotson (in *Shakespeare versus Shallow*, 1931) claimed him more plausibly as a hit at the Surrey justice William Gardiner.

 CHARACTER LIST

Mistress Margaret **Page**
Master George **Page**
   her husband
Anne Page *their daughter*
William Page *their son*
Mistress Alice **Ford**
Master Frank Ford
   her husband

Citizens of Windsor

John
Robert *their servants*

Sir John Falstaff

Bardolph
Pistol *Sir John's followers*
Nim

Robin *Sir John's page*

The **Host** of the Garter Inn
Sir Hugh **Evans** *a Welsh parson*
Doctor **Caius** *a French physician*
Mistress Quickly *his housekeeper*
John **Rugby** *his servant*
Master **Fenton** *a young gentleman, in love with Anne Page*
Master Abraham **Slender**
Robert **Shallow** *his uncle, a Justice*
Peter **Simple** *Slender's servant*
Children of Windsor, appearing as fairies

SYNOPSIS

1.1 Justice Shallow calls at Master Page's house in Windsor, hoping to recommend his foolish nephew Slender as a suitor to Page's daughter Anne: he is incensed against Sir John Falstaff, also a dinner guest at the Pages', who has been poaching his deer. The Welsh parson Evans attempts to make peace between Shallow, Sir John, and Sir John's followers Bardolph, Nim, and Pistol, who have earlier got Slender drunk and robbed him. Finally left alone with Anne, Slender is socially inept.

   1.2 Evans sends a letter, via Slender's servant Peter Simple, to Mistress Quickly, housekeeper to the French physician Dr Caius and a friend of Anne, urging her to promote Slender's suit.

   1.3 Sir John, staying at the Garter Inn, successfully recommends Bardolph to his Host as a tapster. Sir John then explains to Nim and Pistol that he means to gain money by seducing Mistress Ford and Mistress Page, and gives them love letters to deliver: when they refuse this dishonourable errand he dismisses them, entrusting the letters instead to his page Robin. Nim and Pistol decide to avenge themselves by warning Ford and Page.

1.4 Mistress Quickly is telling Simple she will recommend Slender to Anne when Dr Caius returns unexpectedly: she hides Simple in a closet, where Caius finds him. Furious to learn of Simple's errand—since he himself wishes to marry Anne—Caius sends a challenge to Evans. After Caius' departure, the well-born Fenton arrives, also hoping to be recommended to Anne.

2.1 Mistress Page is affronted by the letter she has received from Sir John: Mistress Ford arrives, similarly agitated by her own letter, and when the two women compare notes they discover Sir John has written identically to each. They decide to avenge themselves on him by feigning compliance only to delay him at the Garter until he is bankrupt, deliberately arousing Ford's causeless jealousy at the same time. Ford and Page arrive, receiving their warnings from Pistol and Nim: Page laughs his off, but the jealous Ford is troubled. The two wives leave with Mistress Quickly, whom they intend to use as go-between to Sir John. Ford arranges with the Host to visit Sir John under the alias of Brooke: he, the Host, Page, and Shallow leave in the hopes of seeing the intended duel between Evans and Caius.

2.2 At the Garter Mistress Quickly tells Sir John that both wives, ignorant of each other's affairs, are in love with him, and that Mistress Ford sends word her husband will be absent from his house tomorrow between ten and eleven: she enlists Robin to act as a go-between for Mistress Page. Ford, sending Sir John a bottle of sack, subsequently arrives as Brooke, and privately explains that he has long desired Mistress Ford himself but despairs of overcoming her virtue unless she is first seduced by a more accomplished lover. Sir John delightedly accepts the money Brooke offers him to seduce Mistress Ford, and tells him gleefully of his appointment with her the following morning. Alone, Ford, horrified that his worst fears are apparently justified, rejoices that at least he now stands a chance of averting his cuckolding.

2.3 Caius and his servant John Rugby are waiting for Evans to arrive and fight: the Host, Shallow, Page, and Slender arrive, and the Host promises not only to lead Caius to where Evans is but to bring him to a farmhouse where he may woo Anne.

3.1 Evans is also waiting, with Simple, for Caius, trying to maintain his courage by singing: when Shallow, Slender, and Page and at last the Host and Caius arrive, the jovial Host reveals that he has deliberately been averting the duel by sending the would-be combatants to separate places. Caius and Evans, reconciled, plan to avenge themselves on the Host for this indignity.

3.2 Ford, learning that Mistress Page now employs Sir John's page, is astonished at Page's unsuspicious nature. Page arrives, assuring Slender that he supports his suit with Anne although Mistress Page favours Caius, and though the Host thinks that Anne herself will prefer Fenton. Ford takes Caius and Evans with him towards his house, expecting to surprise Sir John with his wife.

3.3 Mistresses Ford and Page are preparing for Sir John's arrival, having their servants bring a large laundry basket and hiding Mistress Page in another room. Sir John arrives and woos Mistress Ford, swearing that her suspicion that he is also courting Mistress Page is groundless: on a pre-arranged cue from Robin, Mistress Page enters, announcing that the jealous Ford is on his way with armed men to search the house, and the two women hide Sir John in the laundry basket, in which he is carried out by two servants just as Ford, Page, Caius, and Evans arrive. When their combined search of the house fails to find Sir John, the baffled Ford has to apologize to the company.

3.4 Fenton is reassuring Anne that although at first, as her father suggests, he only wooed her for her money, he now loves her truly, when Shallow, Slender, and Mistress Quickly arrive: Slender is as incompetent a wooer as ever. Page and Mistress Page arrive: Page rebukes Fenton for his persistence, favouring Slender, whom Anne tells her mother she does not wish to marry. Left alone, Mistress Quickly admits she has been accepting gifts from all three of Anne's rival suitors.

3.5 A chilled Sir John, who has been tipped from the basket into the Thames with the laundry, orders some mulled sack. Mistress Quickly apologizes on Mistress Ford's behalf and tells him to come again between eight and nine, when Ford will be out birding. Ford then arrives as Brooke for a progress report, and learns both how Sir John escaped him among the laundry and of his next impending appointment with his wife.

4.1 Mistress Page's young son William is given a Latin lesson by Evans, much misconstrued by Mistress Quickly.

4.2 Sir John is again wooing Mistress Ford when Mistress Page again brings news that the jealous Ford is approaching: Sir John refuses to enter the laundry basket again, and the women instead arrange to dress him as Mother Prat, a suspected witch. Before Page, Caius, Evans, and Shallow, Ford triumphantly ransacks the laundry basket, baffled not to find Sir John, and himself unwittingly drives Sir John, disguised as Mother Prat, out of the house, beating him with a cudgel. After the men depart, the wives agree to inform their husbands of the whole story, hoping this will have cured Ford's jealousy forever, and resolve to punish Sir John further only with their husbands' co-operation.

4.3 Bardolph requests three horses from the Host for a mysterious German duke, who has apparently booked the Garter for a week already, obliging the Host to turn away his other guests.

4.4 The Pages and the Fords, laughing over Sir John's misadventures to date, plot that the two wives should invite Sir John to meet them, disguised as the legendary horned spirit Herne the Hunter, at Herne's Oak in Windsor Park at midnight, where Sir John can be ambushed by Anne, William, and other children disguised as fairies and then exposed to public ridicule. It is agreed that Anne Page will be dressed as the queen of the fairies: Page plans secretly to arrange Slender's elopement with her, though his wife still prefers Caius.

4.5 Simple has come to the Garter, hoping to consult Mother Prat, supposedly seen entering Sir John's rooms, about Anne Page's fortune. The Host learns from Bardolph, Evans, and Caius that the German duke was a hoax and his horses have been stolen. Mistress Quickly brings Sir John the letter appointing his midnight rendezvous.

4.6 Fenton arranges with the discomfited Host for a vicar to be ready to marry him to Anne between midnight and one: she has feigned compliance with both her father's plot that she should elope with Slender and her mother's that she should elope with Caius, but really plans to run away with Fenton.

5.1 Sir John agrees to the rendezvous, and tells Ford as Brooke of his escape and sufferings in the guise of Mother Prat.

5.2 Page and Shallow check that Slender knows how he is to identify the figure with whom he is to elope: he and Anne will both be dressed in white.

5.3 Mistress Page similarly briefs Caius, who expects Anne to be in green. Anne, Evans, and the other pretended fairies are already lying in wait in a pit near Herne's Oak.

5.4 Disguised as a satyr, Evans marshals his fairies.

5.5 The amorous Sir John, wearing horns, awaits Mistress Ford: she arrives, with Mistress Page, and he is delightedly preparing to enjoy both when, hearing a noise, they flee in pretended panic. Evans and the fairies appear, with Anne dressed as a fairy and Mistress Quickly as the fairy queen: Sir John hides, convinced he is witnessing fairy revels and in grave danger, as they recite verses blessing Windsor and the Garter emblems. The fairies find Sir John, testing his purity with lighted tapers, then pinching him as a punishment for his sins (to the song 'Fie on sinful luxury...'): meanwhile Caius steals away with a fairy in green, Slender with one in white, and Anne leaves with Fenton. The pretended fairies disperse at a sound of hunters, and are replaced by the Pages and the Fords, who confront Sir John and reveal their various stratagems. Evans joins in their sermonizing. Slender arrives, indignant at discovering that the fairy in white was a boy, followed by Caius, whose fairy in green was also a boy: the newly-weds Fenton and Anne then arrive, and on Ford's advice the Pages accept their new son-in-law. All, including Sir John, set off for Windsor to laugh about the night's events.

 ## ARTISTIC FEATURES

The play uses less verse than any other Shakespeare play, and features more devices familiar from later situation comedies, such as comic stage accents (Welsh and French) and malapropisms (or, less anachronistically, Quicklyisms). Nonetheless its harmonious, magic-haunted conclusion is recognizably akin to the worlds of *A Midsummer Night's Dream* and *As You Like It*.

CRITICAL HISTORY

Apart from a long-running argument about whether the Sir John of this play lives up to his appearances in the *Henry IV* plays, *The Merry Wives of Windsor* has occasioned very little critical discussion, although some modern criticism has related it usefully to the city comedies favoured by some of Shakespeare's younger colleagues, such as Ben Jonson and Thomas Middleton.

STAGE HISTORY

As its multiple early editions suggest, the play was popular before the Civil War (played at court in 1604 and in the 1630s), and it was revived in unadapted form soon after the Restoration in 1660. Despite John Dennis's short-lived adaptation *The Comical Gallant* (1702), the original play has remained popular ever since, often starring actors already established as Sir John in *Henry IV* (from Thomas Betterton to James Quin to Beerbohm Tree and beyond), though many important performers have also been attracted to the role of Ford (including J. P. Kemble and Charles Kean), and to those of the wives themselves (including Anne Bracegirdle and Elizabeth Barry, Madge Kendal and Ellen Terry, the Vanbrugh sisters, Peggy Ashcroft and Edith Evans). Modern directors have found possibilities in the play too: Theodore Komisarjevsky gave it a Viennese setting at Stratford in 1935, Terry Hands has directed it twice, and in 1985 Bill Alexander successfully staged the play for the RSC in a kitsch, mock-Tudor 1950s setting, the wives comparing letters under adjoining hairdryers. It remains true, however, that this unabashedly middlebrow play has enjoyed its greatest acclaim as an opera, its musical transformations including Otto Nicolai's *Die lustigen Weiber von Windsor* (1848) and Verdi's last masterpiece *Falstaff* (1893). Gregory Doran added a minor footnote to this tradition in 2006 when he directed *Merry Wives—The Musical* for the Royal Shakespeare Company, with Judi Dench as Mistress Quickly.

 ON THE SCREEN

Historically interesting screen versions include the BBC TV transmission of Glen Byam Shaw's Christmassy Stratford production (1955), with Anthony Quayle, and the 1982 BBC TV production with Ben Kingsley (Ford) and Richard Griffiths (Sir John).

A Midsummer Night's Dream

One of Shakespeare's most perfect achievements in comedy, and perhaps in any other genre, *A Midsummer Night's Dream*—with its exuberant range of poetic styles, metres, and rhyme-schemes—clearly belongs to the lyrical period of his career that also produced *Love's Labour's Lost*, *Richard II*, and *Romeo and Juliet*. It has close links with the latter play (which in Mercutio's 'Queen Mab' speech displays a similar conception of fairies), of which the play-within-the-play staged by the 'mechanicals', 'Pyramus and Thisbe', is almost a burlesque. Indeed, Shakespeare's departures here from Ovid's version of the Pyramus and Thisbe story seem to be shaped by the plot of *Romeo and Juliet*, suggesting that *A Midsummer Night's Dream* was written soon after it, in 1595. Other evidence, too, ties the play to the 1594–6 period: it was certainly extant by 1598, when it is listed by Francis Meres, and its references to disrupted weather (2.1.88–114) suggest composition between mid-1594 and late 1596, a disastrous period for English agriculture. A familiar hypothesis that the play was specifically written for performance at an aristocratic wedding seems implausible (elaborate courtly entertainments were more prevalent in the Jacobean period, and the earliest known example of a play commissioned for a wedding is Samuel Daniel's *Hymen's Triumph*, 1614), but if the play were acted privately in association with such a function the likeliest candidates are the nuptials of the Earl of Derby with Elizabeth Vere (1595) and those of Thomas Berkeley with Elizabeth Carey (1596).

 TEXT

The play, entered in the Stationers' Register in October 1600, appeared in quarto in the same year, and this quarto was reprinted in 1619 (though this second quarto is fraudulently dated '1600'). The quarto text seems to have been set from Shakespeare's foul papers: some of its mislineation probably results from confusion over revisions jotted in their margins. The text printed in the Folio in 1623 was set from a copy of the second quarto (reproducing some of its errors), but one which had been supplemented by reference to a promptbook. This promptbook had clearly been used in relatively late revivals of the play: one stage direction mentions the musician William Tawyer; a cut of 'God warrant us' and 'God bless us' at 5.1.314–15 suggests compliance with the 1606 Act to Restrain the Abuses of Players; and the newly imposed act divisions suggest the introduction of intervals, not used by the King's Men before around 1609. But the bulk of the Folio's amendments to stage directions and the attributions of speeches may date from early in the play's performance history, and are probably authorial.

SOURCES

Most of the plot is Shakespeare's own invention, though the play draws on a number of literary sources. The most important is Geoffrey Chaucer's 'The Knight's Tale,' from *The Canterbury Tales* (c.1400), to which Shakespeare would return, with John Fletcher, nearly 20 years later, dramatizing it as *The Two Noble Kinsmen*. Chaucer's story provides the basis for Shakespeare's depiction of Theseus and Hippolyta's marriage, which it juxtaposes, furthermore, with a rivalry between two men for the same woman, source for the competition between Lysander and Demetrius over Hermia. Shakespeare, however, adds a second woman, Helena, who has earlier been jilted by Demetrius, and thereby repeats the pattern of love intrigues he had deployed in *The Two Gentlemen of Verona*. *A Midsummer Night's Dream* is pervasively indebted to Ovid, most obviously for Pyramus and Thisbe, but also for the name Titania, an alternative name for Diana (hence the fairy queen's reference to the Indian boy's mother as 'a vot'ress of my order', 2.1.123) and also for Circe (who transformed her lovers into beasts, a habit echoed in Titania's infatuation with the 'translated' Bottom). The name Oberon for the fairy king derives from the French romance *Huon de Bordeaux*, and also appears in Robert Greene's *James IV* (*c*.1591). Robin Goodfellow was well known in folklore, and Shakespeare may also have read about him in Reginald Scot's *Discovery of Witchcraft* (1584). The transformation of Bottom owes much to Apuleius' *The Golden Ass*, written in Latin in the 2nd century and translated into English in 1566, while Bottom's anxiety about bringing a lion among ladies (3.1.25–30) may derive from a real incident at the Scottish court (reported in a pamphlet, *A True Reportary*, 1594) when a lion was excluded from the entertainments at Prince Henry's baptismal feast because its presence 'might have brought some fear to the nearest'.

 CHARACTER LIST

Theseus, Duke of Athens

Hippolyta, Queen of the Amazons *betrothed to Theseus*

Philostrate *Master of the Revels to Theseus*

Egeus *father of Hermia*

Hermia *daughter of Egeus, in love with Lysander*

Lysander *loved by Hermia*

Demetrius *suitor to Hermia*

Helena *in love with Demetrius*

Oberon, King of Fairies

Titania, Queen of Fairies

Robin Goodfellow *a puck*

Peaseblossom
Cobweb
Mote   *fairies*
Mustardseed

Peter **Quince** *a carpenter*

Nick **Bottom** *a weaver*

Francis **Flute** *a bellows-mender*

Tom **Snout** *a tinker*

Snug *a joiner*

Robin **Starveling** *a tailor*

Attendant lords and fairies

SYNOPSIS

1.1 Four days before their wedding, Theseus, Duke of Athens, and the Amazonian Queen Hippolyta whom he has conquered are visited by Egeus, accompanied by his daughter Hermia and her two suitors: Egeus complains that Hermia refuses to marry his choice, Demetrius, because she has been wooed by Lysander, and demands that she be put to death, as Athenian law allows, unless she marries Demetrius. Lysander points out that Demetrius formerly wooed Helena, who still loves him, but despite this Theseus supports Egeus, declaring that unless Hermia agrees to marry Demetrius she must accept either death or a vow of eternal celibacy. Left alone, Lysander and Hermia arrange to meet in nearby woods the following night and flee to his aunt's house beyond Athens' borders, where they may marry. They confide this in Helena, who arrives bewailing Demetrius' preference for Hermia, and who decides to betray their elopement to Demetrius and accompany him when he goes in pursuit.

1.2 Led by Quince the carpenter, a team of artisans meet to cast the play of 'Pyramus and Thisbe' which they hope to perform at Theseus' wedding: Bottom the weaver has ambitions to play most of the roles, but finally agrees to confine himself to Pyramus. They arrange to rehearse privately in the woods.

2.1 In the woods Robin Goodfellow, a puck who serves the fairy king Oberon, meets a fairy servant of their queen, Titania, with whom Oberon has fallen out because she will not part with an Indian changeling boy she keeps as an attendant. Oberon and Titania meet, accusing one another of over-familiarity with Hippolyta and Theseus respectively, and Titania recounts how their quarrel has affected the climate, confusing the seasons. Oberon urges her to make peace by yielding up the boy, but she refuses, explaining that she loved his mortal mother, and departs with her train. Oberon resolves to defeat her by applying the magic juice of a flower, love-in-idleness, to her eyes as she sleeps, which will make her fall in love with the next creature she sees: he sends Robin to fetch it. Meanwhile he watches Demetrius, unable to find Hermia and Lysander, rebuking Helena, who follows him off despite his disdain, and when Robin returns with the love-juice, Oberon, determined to punish Demetrius, instructs Robin to find a man wearing Athenian clothes and apply some of the love-juice to his eyes when the woman he scorns is nearby.

2.2 Titania's fairies sing her a lullaby, 'You spotted snakes…': while she sleeps Oberon drops the love-juice on her eyelids. Lysander and Hermia arrive, benighted, and settle themselves to sleep (apart, at her insistence): Robin, assuming Lysander to be the Athenian Oberon intended, applies the love-juice to his eyes. Lysander is awakened by the arrival of Helena, whom Demetrius flees, and falls in love with her: although she is outraged at what she thinks is his mockery, Lysander pursues her off. Hermia awakens from a nightmare and finds herself alone.

3.1 The artisans meet, and Bottom insists that they alter their script to point out that Pyramus and Thisbe do not really die and the lion is only Snug the joiner dressed up: after further discussion they agree that the play's characters must include the moonshine by which the lovers meet and the wall through whose cranny they speak. As they rehearse, Robin arrives, and mischievously transforms Bottom's head into that of an ass. Bottom cannot understand why his colleagues flee, assuming they are playing a joke, and sings to keep up his courage. Titania awakens, sees Bottom, and falls in love with him: she appoints four fairies to be his attendants and leads him away to her bower.

3.2 Robin tells a delighted Oberon of Titania's love for the transformed Bottom, but when Hermia arrives, accusing Demetrius of killing the missing Lysander, it becomes clear that Robin has enchanted the wrong Athenian. While Demetrius, eluded by Hermia, sleeps, Oberon sends Robin to fetch Helena and applies the love-juice to Demetrius' eyelids. Helena arrives, pursued by the besotted Lysander, and when Demetrius awakes and also falls in love with her she concludes that both are mocking her. When Hermia arrives, lamenting Lysander's defection, Helena decides she too must be a participant in this cruel game, and accuses her of betraying their childhood friendship. The incensed Hermia decides Helena must have lured Lysander away by pointing out her superior height, and after the two rival men leave to fight, Helena has to run away from her. Oberon accuses Robin of negligence and instructs him to lead Demetrius and Lysander astray and use the love-juice to restore Lysander's love for Hermia before day breaks. Robin, feigning the respective would-be duellists' voices, keeps them apart.

3.3 Misled by Robin, Lysander and Demetrius, still hoping to fight, independently settle to sleep: Helena arrives too, and also sleeps, as does Hermia. Robin applies the love-juice to Lysander's eyes, with a spell to restore his affection to Hermia.

4.1 Titania arrives with Bottom and his fairy attendants: after these have been dismissed, the two sleep. Oberon reports to Robin that the enchanted Titania has given him the changeling, and proceeds to undo the spell: waking, Titania at first thinks her passion for Bottom was a dream before seeing him asleep. Robin removes Bottom's ass-head: Oberon and Titania, reconciled, dance, and leave, as does Robin. Theseus, Hippolyta, and Egeus arrive, hunting, and find the four lovers, who awaken, restored to themselves and to each other, and attempt to explain what has been happening. Theseus overrules Egeus, declaring that Hermia may marry Lysander, and Helena Demetrius, when he marries Hippolyta. The lovers, uncertain as to whether they are dreaming, follow Theseus and his party towards Athens. Bottom awakes, awestruck at the recollection of experiences which he too thinks must have been a dream, which he hopes to have Quince make into a ballad.

4.2 The artisans are distraught at Bottom's absence and their missed opportunity to perform, but to their delight he rejoins them and they leave for the palace.

5.1 Hippolyta and Theseus discuss the lovers' reported experiences, which Theseus puts down to overactive imagination. As the two other newly married couples join them, Theseus considers what entertainment should while away the time before bed, and despite being warned how amateurishly bad 'Pyramus and Thisbe' is he chooses the artisans' play. Quince duly mis-recites a prologue, and his cast enact the story of Pyramus and Thisbe in dumb show. Punctuated by derisive comments from its audience, the play, written in archaic and comically inept rhyme, proceeds. Snout the tinker explains that he is playing the Wall through which Pyramus and Thisbe converse. Bottom as Pyramus and Flute the bellows-mender as Thisbe arrange to meet at Ninus' tomb. After Starveling, bearing a lantern, has finally explained that he represents the man in the moon, Thisbe arrives and flees from Snug as the lion, who worries her dropped mantle. Pyramus finds the mantle, concludes that Thisbe has been eaten by the lion, and kills himself: Thisbe returns, finds his body, and kills herself too. Theseus declines their offered epilogue, and Bottom and Flute dance a bergomask instead before leaving. After the three couples have retired to bed, Robin arrives, sweeping with a broom, followed by Oberon, Titania, and their train, who bless the house and the three married couples, warding off birth defects from their children. Left alone, Robin speaks an epilogue, advising the audience to dismiss the play as a dream if they have not enjoyed it, but promising to improve if the audience applauds.

ARTISTIC FEATURES

As well as showing off some of Shakespeare's most dazzling dramatic poetry—which, with its evocation of the minutely detailed woodland world of Robin Goodfellow and his colleagues, has shaped all subsequent notions of fairies—A Midsummer Night's Dream offers some of his most piercing reflections on the nature of theatre and the imagination themselves. The Mozartian interweaving of its different layers of plot and artifice has never been equalled: it is understandable why the play should have attracted not only painters and illustrators (from Henry Fuseli to William Dadd and beyond) but operatic composers, from Henry Purcell to Benjamin Britten.

CRITICAL HISTORY

Popular in its own time and beyond ('Pyramus and Thisbe', for example, profoundly influenced the pioneer of English nonsense poetry John Taylor),

A Midsummer Night's Dream fell from favour after the Restoration, dismissed as a self-indulgent novelty for most of the 18th century: Dr Johnson called it 'wild and fantastical', while Francis Gentleman, annotating Bell's edition in 1774, spoke of 'a puerile plot, an odd mixture of incidents, and a forced connexion of various styles'. The Romantics, however, completely revalued the play's elements of fancy, and over the course of the 19th century *A Midsummer Night's Dream* was taken ever more seriously by literary critics: Georg Brandes, recognizing its seminal importance to his Romantic precursors, identified the play as a bridge between the mental worlds of Edmund Spenser and Percy Bysshe Shelley. Twentieth-century critics variously mined the play for elements of folk May-games (treating its comedy as a sort of fertility ritual), pursued its lines of thought about the nature of theatrical make-believe, and considered its potentially troubling representations of the relations between the sexes. Louis Montrose, in one of the most influential of new historicist essays, related the play's animus against virginity and its depictions of the tamed Amazon Hippolyta and the defeated Titania to imputed male anxieties about the dominance of England's real-life fairy queen, Elizabeth I. Recent work has highlighted the play's racial politics, focusing particularly on Hippolyta's silence(s), the function of the Indian changeling boy, and the intercultural exchanges between human and fairy worlds. So, too, have critics been keen to unpack the language of impression that pervades the play and its class relationships, while a fine-grained understanding of the boy-player has lent greater weight to discussions of children and childishness.

 STAGE HISTORY

A range of allusions suggest that the play was frequently revived in Shakespeare's own time and afterwards: it was acted at court in 1604, and was popular enough to survive even during the Interregnum in the form of Robert Cox's abbreviated version *The Merry Conceited Humours of Bottom the Weaver*. After the Restoration the play was revived in London and also at the Smock Alley theatre in Dublin, but seemed suddenly dated and artificial in a theatrical repertoire now dominated by contemporary satirical comedy: Samuel Pepys, seeing it in 1662, called it 'the most insipid ridiculous play that ever I saw in my life'. Thereafter its stage history for most of the next century and a half is one of successive adaptations: the anonymous semi-opera *The Fairy Queen* (with music by Purcell, 1692), David Garrick's *The Fairies* (1755), George Colman's *A Fairy Tale* (1763), and the independent fortunes of 'Pyramus and Thisbe', transplanted into Charles Johnson's *Love in a Forest* (1723) and made into separate mock-operas by

Richard Leveridge (1716) and Frederick Lampe (1745). An attempt by Garrick, in collaboration with Colman, to revive the whole play in 1763 was, instructively, a flop: the play was too various, and too much of an ensemble piece, to fit the 18th-century theatre. Regarded as too poetical for the stage by William Hazlitt—disappointed by Frederick Reynolds's pantomime-like musical version of 1816—the play had to await the displacement of the actor-manager by the designer and the director before coming into its own. The most important revival of the Romantic period took place in Germany in 1843, supervised by the translator, Ludwig Tieck, who used Felix Mendelssohn's famous incidental music (1826–42). At last seized upon by designers, the play was ever more lavishly staged by Elizabeth Vestris, Samuel Phelps (self-cast as Bottom, the favourite role of actor-managers), and Charles Kean, whose production included an 8-year-old Ellen Terry entering as Robin Goodfellow on a pop-up mushroom. This tradition of spectacle peaked in Beerbohm Tree's production (1900): his wood featured real live rabbits. More indicative of 20th-century *Dreams* to come was Harley Granville-Barker's controversial 1914 production at the Savoy, with its gilded, other-worldly, puppet-like fairies. Since then the play has been both immensely popular (one of the most frequently revived in the canon, especially in outdoor venues: it appeared every year at the Open Air Theatre in Regent's Park between 1932 and 1940 and has nearly done so ever since) and a directors' playground, successive productions veering between spectacle and minimalism, nostalgia and eroticism. Notable revivals have included Max Reinhardt's eclectic spectacular of the 1920s (the basis for his later film), Tyrone Guthrie's gauzily Victorian production of 1937 (with Vivien Leigh as Titania and Ralph Richardson as Bottom), the successive incarnations of Peter Hall's Elizabethan production of 1959 (also filmed), and, most famously, Peter Brook's 'white box' production for the RSC in 1970, the play's magic translated into the terms of the circus. Brook's influence has haunted subsequent directors of the play, notably Adrian Noble (1994), whose red-room reimagined Brook's set. Robert LePage acknowledged his debt to Brook's *Dream* in his own 1992 production for the National; set in a swamp, with a contortionist Puck and white-pyjama-clad lovers, this *Dream* explored the Athenians' subconscious desires. *Dream* remains one of the most-revived plays in English: its depiction of amateur drama, coupled with its equal balance of roles and indestructibly comic plotting, has made it a perennial favourite of amateur companies—hence Erica Whyman's semi-professional RSC production of 2016, which toured Britain using a different set of local amateurs to play the local amateurs wherever it went. It is also one of the most important Shakespearean comedies in translation (one of the recognized highlights of the 2012 'Globe to Globe' festival in London was a visit from Yohangza's ingeniously naturalized Korean production, with its athletic native spirits). Its continuing vigour in popular culture has been demonstrated by two recent revivals, Emma Rice's exuberant production at Shakespeare's Globe in 2016 (with a gay Helenus replacing Helena, and a voluptuous burlesque artiste as Titania) and Nicholas Hytner's comparably vigorous promenade production at the nearby Bridge Theatre (2019), which featured aerial displays reminiscent of Brook's acrobatic *Dream*, a musical score augmented by the aural resplendence of Beyoncé's 'Love on Top', and, in another bid to restore the balance between the sexes, a punitive swapping of Oberon for Titania as Bottom's bed-mate in the bower.

 ON THE SCREEN

The play clearly offers attractive possibilities for visual realization. The earliest version was an eight-minute sequence shot in America (1909). The year 1935 brought to the screen the Max Reinhardt film featuring Olivia de Havilland as Hermia, Mickey Rooney as Puck, and James Cagney as Bottom, so asserting a claim by Hollywood film actors for Shakespearian roles. Between 1937 and 1981 there were eight British television productions based on the play, the last being the visually elaborate BBC TV version produced by Jonathan Miller (with Elijah Moshinsky as director), some of its framed compositions alluding to 17th-century Dutch paintings. A subsequent BBC version of 2016, directed by Russell T. Davies, with Nonso Anozie as Oberon, controversially killed off Theseus at the end instead of reinstating his normative patriarchal marriage to Hippolyta.

Peter Hall's film (1968), based on his earlier stage production, had a mixed reception. It juxtaposes in an arresting way expressionism and realism, and boasts an impressive cast (including Diana Rigg, Helen Mirren, Judi Dench, Ian Richardson, and Ian Holm), but its documentary camera techniques can seem at odds with the illusory worlds of the play. In 1984 Celestino Coronado made a memorably imaged film of the Lindsay Kemp London stage production. Adrian Noble's film (1996), based on his own RSC production, uses a boy's dream as a central narrative device, linking the cinematic world of Theseus' court with the more theatrically minimalist woods. Michael Hoffman's less intellectually cogent Hollywood film (1999) sets the play in 19th-century Italy, punctuating its soundtrack with famous operatic arias.

Much Ado About Nothing

Shakespeare's popular comedy of reputation and repartee is not listed among his works by Francis Meres in mid-1598, but it must have been written by early 1599, when the comedian Will Kempe, accidentally mentioned in the quarto edition of 1600 as the original Dogberry, left Shakespeare's company. It was probably composed in 1598 and first performed that autumn, a dating confirmed by internal evidence: in rare vocabulary it is closely related to *2 Henry IV* and *Henry V* (1597–8, 1598–9) and the incidence of colloquialisms in its verse places it before *As You Like It* (1599).

 TEXT

The 1600 quarto was clearly set from Shakespeare's own foul papers. This authorial draft was apparently fairly untidy: as well as sometimes preserving the names of actors Shakespeare had in mind as he wrote (Kempe for Dogberry and Richard Cowley for Verges), the speech prefixes are often inconsistent, while entrances and exits are often omitted, and one mute character, Leonato's wife Innogen, is mentioned in the opening stage directions to the first two acts but never says or does anything and is never mentioned. The Folio text (1623) reprints the play from a copy of the quarto supplemented, here and there, by the consultation of a promptbook, from which certain stage directions have been added or elaborated.

SOURCES

The main plot of *Much Ado About Nothing*—the story of Hero's defamation—derives from one of the most widely disseminated narratives in European Renaissance culture, which Shakespeare probably knew in many different forms. It appears as the story of Ginevora in Ariosto's *Orlando furioso* (1516, translated into English by Sir John Harington in 1591), and as the story of Fenicia in Bandello's *Novelle* (1554, translated into French in

Belleforest's *Histoires tragiques*, 1559), while English versions include those of George Whetstone (in *The Rock of Regard*, 1576) and Edmund Spenser (in book 2 of *The Faerie Queene*, 1590). The story had already been dramatized in English at least twice, once as *A History of Ariodante and Genevra*, acted at court in 1583, and once as *Fedele and Fortunio* (1585), an adaptation, probably by Anthony Munday, of Luigi Pasqualigo's *Il Fedele* (1579). The more comical story of Beatrice and Benedick, however, seems to be Shakespeare's own invention (though some commentators feel that their repartee shows the influence of the exemplary witty dialogues between courtly ladies and gentlemen supplied in Castiglione's *Il libro del cortegiano*, 1528, translated by Sir Thomas Hoby as *The Book of the Courtier*, 1561), as do the doings of Dogberry and Verges.

 CHARACTER LIST

Don Pedro, Prince of Aragon

Benedick, of
   Padua
Claudio, of
   Florence
} *lords, companions of Don Pedro*

Balthasar *attendant on Don Pedro, a singer*

Don John *the bastard brother of Don Pedro*

Borachio
Conrad
} *followers of Don John*

Leonato *Governor of Messina*

Hero *his daughter*

Beatrice *an orphan, his niece*

Antonio *an old man, brother of Leonato*

Margaret
Ursula
} *waiting-gentlewomen attendant on Hero*

Friar Francis

Dogberry *the Constable in charge of the Watch*

Verges *the Headborough, Dogberry's partner*

A **Sexton**

Watchmen

A **Boy**, serving Benedick

Attendants and messengers

:≡ SYNOPSIS

1.1 Leonato, Governor of Messina, together with his daughter Hero and niece Beatrice, learn of the approach of Don Pedro, Prince of Aragon, who has just defeated his illegitimate half-brother Don John (to whom he is now reconciled) in a military campaign: among his party are the young Count Claudio and his friend Benedick, about whom Beatrice, Benedick's long-time conversational adversary, makes disparaging jokes. Leonato welcomes Don Pedro, and Beatrice and Benedick, both scorners of romantic love, exchange witty insults. The bashful Claudio, left with Benedick, confides despite his friend's disdain for marriage that he means to woo Hero. Don Pedro promises to assist by courting Hero while disguised as

Claudio at the evening's masked ball and winning Leonato's consent to the match.

1.2 Leonato is told by his brother Antonio that he has heard that Don Pedro seeks to marry Hero.

1.3 The malcontented Don John, with his companion Conrad, learns from Borachio of his brother's plan to woo Hero for Claudio, and hopes to thwart it.

2.1 At the masked ball, Don Pedro (whom Hero has been advised to accept if he proposes) speaks in disguise to Hero. Beatrice speaks to a disguised Benedick, whom she feigns not to recognize, of his faults. Don John, pretending to take the masked Claudio for Benedick, tells him Don Pedro is wooing Hero for himself. Claudio, cast down, laments this apparent betrayal. Benedick is more affronted at the account of himself he has heard from Beatrice, whom he describes scornfully to Don Pedro: when Beatrice reappears, with Claudio, Hero, and Leonato, he rudely leaves. Don Pedro reassures Claudio that he has wooed Hero only on Claudio's behalf, and the match is agreed, to mutual satisfaction. Don Pedro banters with Beatrice. After her departure, he undertakes that, with the help of Leonato, Claudio, and Hero, he will trick Benedick and Beatrice into falling in love during the week that intervenes before Claudio and Hero marry.

2.2 Borachio promises Don John he will prevent the marriage between Claudio and Hero by arranging that on its eve Claudio shall see him courting Margaret, Hero's gentlewoman, in Hero's clothes at Hero's window and thus think Hero unfaithful. Don John promises him 1,000 ducats as a fee.

2.3 In the orchard Benedick, reflecting on Claudio's transformation from soldier to lover, hides to overhear a conversation between Don Pedro, Leonato, and Claudio. After hearing a song by Balthasar, 'Sigh no more, ladies', Don Pedro, pretending not to have noticed the concealed Benedick, asks Leonato whether it is true that Beatrice is in love with Benedick. He and Claudio confirm and elaborate this story and, praising Beatrice, the three say they will not tell Benedick because he would only scorn her. Satisfied that Benedick has heard, they leave to initiate a corresponding stratagem against Beatrice, whom they send to call Benedick to dinner. Left alone Benedick, completely taken in, repents of his earlier attitude and promises to reciprocate Beatrice's imputed love. After she bids him in to dine, Benedick, alone, twists her straightforward and unenthusiastic remarks into subtle messages of love.

3.1 Hero arranges for Beatrice, apparently unperceived, to overhear a conversation with her gentlewoman Ursula in which Hero reports that Benedick is deeply in love with Beatrice and deserves better than the insults he would receive if he told her of it. Alone, the deceived Beatrice undertakes to reciprocate Benedick's love.

3.2 The day before the wedding Don Pedro and Claudio banter with Benedick, who will not admit that he has fallen in love, but nonetheless leaves for a private conference, presumably about the possibility of marrying Beatrice, with Leonato. Don John tells Claudio and Don Pedro that Hero is disloyal, promising to show them a man entering her chamber window that night: Claudio says that if this proves true he will shame Hero at the intended wedding.

3.3 The constable Dogberry, with his partner Verges, gives the Watch comically ill-worded advice as to how to discharge their duties during the night. After Dogberry and Verges leave, the Watch overhear Borachio boasting to Conrad about how he has been wooing Margaret at Hero's window, successfully persuading the watching Claudio and Don Pedro (placed at a distance by Don John) that Hero is false. The Watch arrest both men.

3.4 Hero, Beatrice, Ursula, and Margaret are dressing on the morning of the wedding, Margaret joking at the expense of the apparently converted Beatrice and Benedick.

3.5 Dogberry and Verges come to tell a preoccupied Leonato about the arrested Borachio and Conrad, whom they hope to interrogate in his presence, but are so long-winded and inept that he dismisses them to proceed on their own.

4.1 At the wedding service, conducted by Friar Francis, Claudio gives Hero back to her father, accusing her, with the support of Don Pedro and Don John, of falsehood, and recounting that he saw her entertain a lover at her chamber window the previous night. Hero faints before her three accusers leave. Leonato, convinced of her guilt, wishes she were dead, but Friar Francis, questioning her as she revives, is persuaded of her innocence. Leonato and Benedick agree, on the Friar's advice, to conceal Hero, giving out that she has died. Left together, Beatrice and Benedick admit they love one another. Beatrice asks Benedick to prove his love by avenging the slander of Hero: he agrees to challenge Claudio to a duel.

4.2 The inept and self important Dogberry and Verges, with the Sexton and the Watch, question Borachio and Conrad. The Sexton realizes that the supposedly dead Hero was slandered by Don John, who has stolen away, and goes to tell Leonato. Dogberry, insisting when Conrad calls him an ass that this too should be written down, brings his prisoners after him.

5.1 Leonato refuses Antonio's attempts to comfort him: when they meet Don Pedro and Claudio, they accuse Claudio of killing Hero by his defamation, but he declines to fight with either, and they leave, Don Pedro still maintaining the truth of Claudio's accusation. Benedick arrives and, despite flippant remarks from Don Pedro and Claudio, challenges Claudio to a duel, and leaves. When Dogberry, Verges, the Watch, and their prisoners Borachio and Conrad arrive, Don Pedro and Claudio are appalled to learn how they have been deceived. Brought by the Sexton, Antonio and Leonato join them, and a penitent Borachio confesses to Leonato his share in Hero's supposed death. Don Pedro and Claudio beg Leonato to impose what penance he will for theirs: Leonato instructs Claudio to vindicate Hero's reputation to the people of Messina, to bring an epitaph to her tomb that night, and to be ready the following morning to marry a daughter of Antonio's, said to resemble Hero, in her place. Borachio assures Leonato that Margaret was unaware of the malicious plan in which she was a participant.

5.2 Benedick has been trying to write love poems for Beatrice: the two are talking when Ursula brings the news that Hero has been cleared and the slanderous Don John has fled.

5.3 At Leonato's family tomb Claudio reads out and places an epitaph for the wronged Hero, and a hymn is sung, 'Pardon, goddess of the night'. Claudio and Don Pedro leave to change out of mourning in time for the planned wedding.

5.4 At Leonato's bidding Antonio is ready to present a veiled Hero to Claudio as if she were his daughter. Friar Francis, his faith in Hero vindicated, agrees to marry Beatrice and Benedick at the same time. Don Pedro and Claudio arrive: Antonio brings Hero, Beatrice, Margaret, and Ursula, all veiled, and shows Claudio which he is to marry. Claudio vows to marry the veiled Hero, thinking she is Leonato's niece: she then reveals her face, asserting her innocence. The Friar promises to explain everything to the overjoyed Claudio after the wedding ceremony. Meanwhile Beatrice and Benedick, beginning to realize how they were tricked, come close to disowning their mutual affection before their friends produce a love sonnet written by Benedick and a love letter by Beatrice as evidence of it, and they agree to wed, Benedick disavowing his former opposition to marriage. Benedick calls for music that all the reconciled friends and lovers may dance before the wedding, and when news arrives that Don John has been captured and brought back to Messina Benedick urges Don Pedro to postpone all thoughts of him and his due punishment until the following day.

🎭 ARTISTIC FEATURES

Less lyrical than the other mature comedies, with the exception of *The Merry Wives of Windsor*, *Much Ado About Nothing* nonetheless looks forward, in the depiction of Hero's 'resurrection', to the late romances (particularly *The Winter's Tale*). Its closest kinship, however, is with the early *The Taming of the Shrew*, with which it shares a structure contrasting naive, romantic attitudes to love (such as those of Lucentio or Claudio) with more pragmatic and sceptical ones. Benedick and Beatrice, quarrelling in prose all the way to the altar, often resemble Petruccio and Katherine: Beatrice, for example, admitting to herself that she loves Benedick, promises to reform her character in terms of which Petruccio would certainly approve: 'I will requite thee, | Taming my wild heart to thy loving hand' (3.1.111–12).

⭐ CRITICAL HISTORY

Although their relationship occupies what is nominally only the sub-plot, it is the more protesting and reluctant couple who have dominated responses to the play, which seems to have been nicknamed 'Beatrice and Benedick' (the title Hector Berlioz would use for his operatic version) from early in its stage history (by, for example, Charles I). Combining the play with elements of *Measure for Measure* in 1662 (as *The Law against Lovers*), William Davenant borrowed only Beatrice and Benedick from this play, their repertee decisively influencing the subsequent development of Restoration comedy. The play has been one of the most popular of the mature comedies since the mid-18th century, though it has never inspired as rich a critical literature as *The Merchant of Venice*, *As You Like It*, or *Twelfth Night*. William Hazlitt praised Dogberry, regularly hailed since as an all too convincing depiction of petty officialdom, but from his day to this the main plot of the play has elicited little but apologies, with criticism on the subject mainly dedicated to exploring or explaining Claudio's inadequacies as a comic protagonist. His behaviour towards Hero, variously excused and vilified as wholly conventional, and the play's suggestions of a woman-centred world which finally prevails against the barrack-room assumptions of the soldiers, have, however, recommended the play to the attention of feminist critics, while others have found in Friar Francis's stratagem not only an anticipation of the last plays but glimpses of Shakespeare's views on religion.

🎭 STAGE HISTORY

Much Ado About Nothing was one of the plays acted at court in May 1613 to celebrate the marriage of Princess Elizabeth, and according to Leonard Digges's commendatory poem (1640) was one of Shakespeare's most popular comedies. Beatrice and Benedick reappeared at the Restoration only as the laughing cavaliers of William Davenant's adaptation, but the original made brief returns to the stage in the 1720s and 1730s (displaced between 1737 and 1741 by another adaptation, the Reverend James Miller's *The Universal Passion*, which crosses the play with Molière's *La Princesse d'Élide*). It was finally established in the repertory forever when David Garrick wittily chose the role of Benedick for his first performances on returning to the stage after his honeymoon in 1748, opposite Hannah Pritchard's Beatrice. Since then the bantering couple's most notable representatives have included J. P. Kemble and Dorothea Jordan (1798), Mr and Mrs Charles Kean (1858), Mr and Mrs Charles Calvert (1865), Henry Irving and Ellen Terry (1882), Lewis Casson and Sybil Thorndike (1927), John Gielgud and Peggy Ashcroft (1931, 1950, 1955), and, in John Barton's production of 1976 (set in the British Raj), Donald Sinden and Judi Dench. Dench herself directed the play for Kenneth Branagh's Renaissance company in 1988–9 (with Branagh as Benedick and Samantha Bond as Beatrice), a production which anticipated many elements of his subsequent film. Modern productions of the play, like Barton's, have often stressed the military world inhabited by its male characters: this was especially true of Cheek by Jowl's award-winning 1998 production, which followed Barton in dressing Don Pedro's officers in uniforms of the British colonial period. Notable *Much Ados* in recent years have tended towards big-name charisma in the Beatrice and Benedick pairing to ensure full houses, as with Gregory Doran's verdant, post-Second World War RSC production (2002) with Harriet Walter and Nicholas le Prevost as the reluctant lovers. Zoë Wanamaker and Simon Russell Beale headed Nicholas Hytner's successful production at the National Theatre in 2007, while Catherine Tate and David Tennant led a sell-out run at Wyndham's Theatre in 2011. Christopher Luscombe's Edwardian-style production for the RSC in 2014, with Michelle Terry and Ed Bennett as Beatrice and Benedick, paired the play with *Love's Labour's Lost* and retitled it *Love's Labour's Won*.

🎬 ON THE SCREEN

The earliest recorded screen version was an American silent film of 1909. Scenes from the play were among the earliest Shakespeare television extracts to be transmitted (1937). Russian films were made in 1956 and 1973. Zeffirelli directed an impressive British cast (including Maggie Smith, Derek Jacobi, and Frank Finlay) in a stage production later adapted for television (1967), followed by a BBC TV version (1978) with Michael York as Benedick, originally scheduled to open the complete BBC series but replaced in 1984 by Stuart Burge's TV production. On a grander scale Kenneth Branagh filmed the play (1993) in a lavish Italian setting, with himself and his then wife Emma Thompson as Benedick and Beatrice among a part-Hollywood cast. Joss Whedon eschewed star names in his low-budget, modern-day version, shot in black-and-white in and around the director's house in 2012: unusually among film versions, its Dogberry and Verges were generally regarded as funnier than its Beatrice and Benedick.

Othello

Shakespeare's claustrophobic tragedy of jealousy and slander belongs to the same period of his career as three plays with equally dark views of sexuality, *Troilus and Cressida*, *Measure for Measure*, and *All's Well That Ends Well*: it is close in its use of rare vocabulary to the former tragedy, and similar in its versification to the two comedies. According to the Revels accounts, it was acted at court in November 1604, and it is apparently echoed in a play by Thomas Dekker and Thomas Middleton, *The Honest Whore, part 1*, composed in the same year. It is just possible that *Othello* was already in the King's Company's touring repertoire towards the end of 1603 (some commentators find echoes of its phrasing in the 1603 quarto of *Hamlet*, a reported text compiled by an actor perhaps influenced by recollections of *Othello*), but it seems likeliest that the play was composed in late 1603–4 and first acted in 1604, especially since its account of the Turkish navy is informed by Richard Knolles's *History of the Turks*, published only in autumn 1603.

 TEXT

The play first appeared in quarto in 1622, and reappeared in the Folio the following year. The differences between these two texts make *Othello* one of the most complicated plays to edit in the canon, and they are compounded by the fact that both seem to have been set from manuscripts that had already been transcribed by fairly independent-minded scribes. The quarto, the only Shakespearian quarto divided into acts, seems to derive from a presentation copy of the play prepared from Shakespeare's foul papers by a scribe who sometimes had trouble making sense of their details, and who sometimes intervened to expand and clarify stage directions for the benefit of readers. The Folio text, 160 lines longer and different in wording at over 1,000 points, seems to have been set from a later manuscript incorporating Shakespeare's subsequent revisions, prepared by an even more intrusive scribe with different tastes. As well as having been expurgated in compliance with the Act to Restrain the Abuses of Players (1606), the Folio has fewer and less detailed stage directions, and more punctuation, and insists on spelling out in full some words and expressions contracted in the quarto. The Oxford edition, favouring Shakespeare's revisions, incorporates the new passages found only in the Folio (which include Desdemona's Willow Song, and an increased emphasis on Emilia's role in the last act), but in other respects follows the unexpurgated and less scribally sophisticated quarto.

📖 SOURCES

Shakespeare derived most of the plot for *Othello* from a story in Giraldi Cinthio's *Hecatommithi* (1565), which he must have read either in the original Italian or in a French translation published in 1584. In this rather squalid prose tale, an ensign lusts after his Moorish captain's Venetian wife Disdemona, and avenges her rejection of his advances by persuading the Moor that she has committed adultery with his friend, a captain. The ensign substantiates his allegation by stealing a handkerchief from Disdemona while she is fondling her baby, planting it in the captain's room, and showing the Moor the captain's wife copying its embroidery. Convinced of his wife's guilt, the Moor collaborates with the ensign to beat her to death in her chamber with a sand-filled stocking, and they then pull down the ceiling in order to make the murder look like an accident. Disdemona's relatives, though, learn the truth and eventually kill the Moor in revenge, and the ensign dies horribly under torture. Shakespeare both promoted and ennobled the Moor to create the first black tragic hero in Western literature, though the name he gave him may consciously echo a comedy: in Ben Jonson's *Every Man in his Humour* (1598), the obsessively (and groundlessly) jealous husband is called Thorello (later renamed Kitely when Jonson rewrote the play to set it in London instead of Italy). Shakespeare moved the action to the earliest days of Othello and Desdemona's marriage, adding the characters of Brabanzio and the gullible disappointed suitor Roderigo, and he set this relationship between a Moor and a Venetian against the backdrop of Venice's wars against the Ottoman Empire. Cyprus was attacked by the Turks in 1570 and fell the following year, but in the play martial conflict gives place to marital once the characters reach Cyprus. Exotic details in Othello's speeches suggest a familiarity with Pliny's *Natural History* (translated by Philemon Holland in 1601).

 CHARACTER LIST

Othello *the Moor of Venice*
Desdemona *his wife*
Michael **Cassio** *his lieutenant*
Bianca *a courtesan, in love*
with Cassio
Iago *the Moor's ensign*
Emilia *Iago's wife*
A **Clown** *a servant of Othello*
The **Duke** of Venice
Brabanzio *Desdemona's father, a*
Senator of Venice

Graziano *Brabanzio's brother*
Lodovico *kinsman of*
Brabanzio
Senators of Venice
Roderigo *a Venetian gentleman, in*
love with Desdemona
Montano *Governor of Cyprus*
A **Herald**
A **Messenger**
Attendants, officers, sailors,
gentlemen of Cyprus, musicians

SYNOPSIS

1.1 The ensign Iago, enraged that the Moorish general Othello has made Cassio his lieutenant instead of him, has Roderigo awaken the Venetian senator Brabanzio and inform him that his daughter Desdemona has eloped with Othello. Horrified, Brabanzio raises a hue and cry.

1.2 Iago, concealing his enmity, warns Othello against Brabanzio's wrath. Cassio brings Othello a summons to the Duke. Brabanzio arrives with officers, accusing a calm Othello of having seduced his daughter by sorcery: all depart for the palace, Brabanzio confident that the Duke will support him.

1.3 The Duke learns that a hostile Turkish fleet is bound for Cyprus. When Othello arrives the Duke says he must be sent immediately against the Turks, before Brabanzio makes his accusation against the Moor. Sending for Desdemona as a witness, Othello eloquently describes how she fell in love with him when, invited by her father, he related his past military escapades and exotic adventures. Challenged by Brabanzio on her arrival, Desdemona says her first duty is now not to him but to her husband Othello: heartbroken, Brabanzio refuses the Duke's consolation. The Duke sends Othello to defend Cyprus: neither Brabanzio nor Othello wishes Desdemona to stay at her father's house during his absence, and she herself insists on accompanying her husband. Othello gives order that she shall travel to Cyprus in the conduct of Iago. Left with Iago, Roderigo despairs of ever enjoying Desdemona, but Iago, promising that her marriage to Othello will prove fragile, urges Roderigo to provide himself with money and come to Cyprus, undertaking to help him cuckold the Moor as part of his own revenge. Alone, Iago speaks of his hatred of Othello and a rumour that the Moor has cuckolded him, and hatches a plan to persuade Othello that his wife is unfaithful with Cassio.

2.1 Montano, governor of Cyprus, awaits news of the Turkish fleet, soon reported to have been wrecked in continuing storms. Cassio arrives from Venice, anxious for the safety of Othello's ship. Iago, his wife Emilia, Desdemona, and Roderigo arrive on another vessel, and receive a courtly welcome from Cassio. Iago banters misogynistically with Desdemona as she awaits Othello's arrival, and watches as she speaks with Cassio, certain he can use their friendship to their undoing. Othello arrives and is blissfully reunited with Desdemona before confirming the destruction of the Turkish fleet. Left with Roderigo, Iago tells him Desdemona is in love with Cassio, and outlines a scheme by which this new rival may be discredited: placed in charge of the watch that night, Roderigo will provoke Cassio into a brawl. Alone, Iago claims he too desires Desdemona, to avenge his own alleged cuckolding by Othello, and hopes that by convincing the Moor she is false with Cassio he may enjoy Othello's favour.

2.2 A herald announces feasting in honour of Othello's marriage.

2.3 Leaving Cassio in charge, Othello retires to bed with Desdemona. Iago gets Cassio drunk among members of the Cypriot garrison, singing 'And let me the cannikin clink' and 'King Stephen was a worthy peer'. Iago alleges that Cassio is a drunkard, a story apparently confirmed when Cassio drives in Roderigo, who has succeeded in provoking him to fight. Montano tells Cassio he is drunk, and they also fight. An alarm bell summons Othello to quell this brawl: he interrogates the participants, and Iago, feigning to defend Cassio, blames the incident on the lieutenant. Othello cashiers Cassio before leading Desdemona, roused by the fray, back to bed. Alone with Iago, Cassio laments the loss of his reputation: Iago advises him to woo Desdemona to plead for his reinstatement. Alone, Iago reflects with satisfaction on his hypocrisy. A bruised Roderigo arrives, dissatisfied with Iago's progress on his behalf, and is reassured. Alone again, Iago plans to have his wife advise Desdemona to support Cassio's suit, and to arrange for Othello to find Cassio soliciting Desdemona.

3.1 The next morning Cassio has musicians play outside Othello's apartments: they are dismissed by a clown, whom Cassio sends to fetch Emilia. Iago arrives and undertakes to lead Othello away while Cassio speaks with Desdemona. A sympathetic Emilia promises to bring Cassio to her.

3.2 Othello arranges to meet Iago at the citadel.

3.3 Desdemona and Emilia promise Cassio to do all they can to persuade Othello to reinstate him: he takes his leave when he sees Othello and Iago approaching, a departure to which Iago insinuatingly draws Othello's attention. Desdemona speaks on Cassio's behalf, but Othello postpones the subject and asks to be left alone for a while. Iago, alone with the Moor, questions him about Cassio's role in his courtship, and at Othello's increasingly anxious and impatient promptings suggests that Othello should watch Desdemona carefully lest she be engaged in an affair with Cassio, warning against jealousy, and promising to help Othello investigate the situation. Alone, Othello, trusting Iago's supposed honesty, is convinced of Desdemona's infidelity, though when she returns his faith revives: nonetheless he complains of a headache, for which she offers a handkerchief to bind his brow, which he drops. When the troubled couple leave Emilia picks the handkerchief up, recognizing it as Othello's first gift to Desdemona, for which Iago has been asking, and which she gives him on his return. Iago, alone, plans to leave it in Cassio's lodging. Othello returns, already visibly distracted with jealousy, and demands that Iago prove the truth of his allegations. Iago claims he has overheard Cassio dreaming of illicit encounters with Desdemona and has seen him with the handkerchief. Othello vows revenge: Iago vows to serve it. Othello commands Iago to kill Cassio and means to kill Desdemona himself.

3.4 Desdemona sends the clown to fetch Cassio. She is troubled about the loss of the handkerchief, which Emilia denies having seen. Othello arrives, and Desdemona tells him she has summoned Cassio: he feigns a cold and asks for the handkerchief. When she says she has lost it he tells her it was magically charmed to ensure the continuance of mutual love, given to his mother by a sorceress, and that its loss is ominous: as his questioning about it grows more urgent, she attempts to change the subject back to Cassio, which enrages him further until he leaves. Desdemona and Emilia are alarmed by this unwonted behaviour. Cassio arrives with Iago, but Desdemona explains that Othello is uncharacteristically vexed and will not hear his suit. Desdemona decides Othello must be anxious about state affairs, and the two women go to seek him. Cassio is accosted by his mistress Bianca, who is suspicious when he asks her to copy the embroidery on Desdemona's handkerchief, which he has found in his chamber.

4.1 Othello, told by Iago that Cassio has admitted sleeping with Desdemona, falls into a fit. While Iago gloats, Cassio arrives: Iago has him wait nearby. When Othello recovers, Iago hides him where he may watch Cassio talking, as Iago claims, about his liaison with Desdemona: he then converses flippantly with Cassio about the doting Bianca. Othello, watching, is convinced Cassio is laughing about Desdemona, and is even more enraged when he sees Bianca give Cassio back the handkerchief. Alone again with Iago, Othello asks Iago to fetch him poison for Desdemona: Iago persuades him instead to strangle her in bed, and promises to kill Cassio before midnight. Desdemona arrives with Lodovico, a Venetian senator who has brought letters: Othello, with increasing fury, reads that he is to return to Venice, leaving Cassio in his place, and strikes Desdemona. She is leaving in tears, but he calls her back before dismissing her again, eventually storming off himself. Lodovico is astonished.

4.2 Emilia tells Othello Desdemona is innocent, but he dismisses her as a bawd, telling her to keep the door while he speaks with Desdemona. He accuses his wife of whoredom, discounts her denials, and insultingly gives Emilia money as he leaves. Desdemona, weeping, speaks with Iago and Emilia, vowing eternal fidelity despite Othello's mistreatment. After the women leave, Roderigo comes to accuse Iago of merely leading him on: Iago promises he will soon enjoy Desdemona so long as he is prepared to kill Cassio.

4.3 After supper, Othello, leaving to walk with Lodovico, bids Desdemona prepare for bed and dismiss Emilia. Undressing with Emilia's help, Desdemona sings the Willow song ('The poor soul sat sighing by a sycamore tree'). The two women discuss infidelity, which Desdemona can hardly believe any woman would commit: Emilia, however, argues that wives should revenge themselves in kind against unfaithful husbands.

5.1 Iago sets Roderigo on to kill Cassio in the dark, but Cassio wounds Roderigo, and Iago, attacking unseen from behind, is able to wound Cassio only in the leg. Hearing his cries, Othello is satisfied that Cassio is dying and, inspired by Iago's example, goes to kill Desdemona. Lodovico, with Brabanzio's brother Graziano, hears the wounded men: Iago, feigning to help, stabs Roderigo, then pretends horror on finding him dead. When Bianca arrives Iago accuses her of being behind the incident, and when Emilia comes he sends her to tell Othello of what has happened.

5.2 Othello comes, with a light, to the sleeping Desdemona and kisses her tenderly, though convinced of her guilt. When she awakens he tells her to pray, as he is about to kill her. Desdemona protests her innocence and that of Cassio, weeping when Othello tells her he is dead: he smothers her and conceals her body behind the bed curtains as Emilia calls for admittance, bringing the dismaying news that Roderigo is dead and Cassio wounded. Desdemona, regaining consciousness, tells Emilia she has been falsely murdered but insists Othello was not her killer before dying. Othello, however, admits killing her, explaining to a horrified Emilia that he did so because he learned from Iago that she had committed adultery with Cassio. Emilia calls for help and confronts Iago, who arrives with Montano and

Graziano. Graziano says the sight of Desdemona's body would drive Brabanzio to despair had he not already died of grief over her marriage. Othello says he saw Cassio with Desdemona's handkerchief: aghast, Emilia declares how she gave the handkerchief to her husband. Realizing the truth, Othello runs at Iago, but Montano disarms him: Iago stabs Emilia before fleeing, pursued by Montano. Emilia, still reproaching Othello with Desdemona's innocence, dies. Othello produces another sword and laments over Desdemona's body, intending suicide. Lodovico, Montano, and a crippled Cassio enter with Iago under guard, whom Othello wounds before being again disarmed: Othello asks forgiveness of Cassio, and asks why Iago has so conspired against him. Iago says he will never speak again. Cassio and Lodovico, with the help of letters found on Roderigo, unravel Iago's machinations: Lodovico says Othello must be taken to Venice. Othello, however, asking to be remembered fairly, along with his services to the state, stabs himself, just as he once stabbed a Turk who had beaten a Venetian. He dies kissing Desdemona. Lodovico, leaving to report these tragic events in Venice, urges Cassio, now governor of Cyprus, to have Iago tortured to death.

 ARTISTIC FEATURES

The diction of *Othello* is unusually polarized between the glamorous, exotic music of the Moor's poetry and the harsh cynicism of his ensign's soliloquies: this has contributed to the play's attractiveness to operatic composers such as Verdi, who translated Othello into a tenor and Iago into a baritone. Partly through these soliloquies, *Othello* exploits dramatic irony more relentlessly than any other play in the canon, letting us know of 'honest' Iago's treachery from its opening scene onwards but denying that knowledge to the rest of the cast until the final act. The play's intensity is assisted by the absence of any sub-plot, and by the skill with which Shakespeare compresses the narrative he found in Cinthio: it is this compression which gives rise to the famous 'double time' effect, whereby the play's events seem at once to take place with terrible swiftness over only two or three days (so that there is no time for Othello to realize the truth) and yet to encompass enough time for Iago's allegations to be plausible.

CRITICAL HISTORY

The subject of more 17th-century allusions than any other Shakespeare play except *The Tempest*, *Othello* was already established as one of

Shakespeare's greatest achievements long before Thomas Rymer made his ineffectual attack on it in 1693 (describing it as 'a bloody farce', a view which would be developed more sympathetically in W. H. Auden's account of Iago's scheme as a terrible practical joke). Samuel Johnson and William Hazlitt alike praised the rich contrasts between its characters and the skill of its design. Iago influenced Milton's dramatization of Satan, and would fascinate the Romantics, Samuel Taylor Coleridge finding in his soliloquies (with their excess of potential rationalizations for his crimes) 'the motive-hunting of motiveless malignity'. Although some 19th-century Americans (including Joseph Quincy Adams) found the play's depiction of interracial marriage objectionable (and even Coleridge refused to see Othello as black, preferring to envisage him as an aristocratic Arab), most 19th-century critics found Othello convincingly noble. It was only in the 20th century, when T. S. Eliot took issue with A. C. Bradley's account of the play, that some began to adopt Iago's view of Othello as a bombastic self-deceiver. This argument between pro- and anti-Othello factions has now been largely displaced by the discussion of Shakespeare's attitude to Moors, and whether Othello's unquestioning assumption that adulterous wives should die is intended to be seen as confirming the racist views expressed by Brabanzio and Iago. Iago's interconnected obsessions with class, race, and gender have indeed helped to keep the play central to much current critical discourse, whether feminist, Marxist, or psychoanalytic. Critical race studies has produced field-changing work on *Othello*, particularly in relation to its sources and to Elizabethan understandings of the meanings of cosmetics: in 2015, for instance, the scholar Ian Smith demonstrated the handkerchief, 'dyed in mummy', would have been black (rather than, as per the stage tradition, white), and thus more closely aligned with Othello than with Desdemona.

STAGE HISTORY

The quarto reports that the play was acted at both the Blackfriars and the Globe, and an eyewitness account of a performance in Oxford in 1610 confirms the power the play exerted on the Jacobean stage. Still in the repertory through the 1630s, it was revived in unadapted form at the Restoration (so that Desdemona was one of the first roles to be played by a woman on the English professional stage) and few seasons have gone by without a revival since. Outside the English-speaking world, the play has been especially popular in Russia, which from Ira Aldridge's visits onwards prided itself on being exempt from the racism which supposedly distorted interpretations of the play in the Anglo-American world. Great Othellos have included Thomas Betterton, James Quin, Spranger Barry, J. P. Kemble, and Edmund Kean, whose frightening, animalistic performance in the role was one of his greatest from 1814 until his death (after collapsing onstage in Act 4) in 1833. The American Ira Aldridge was the first black actor to play Othello, a role he played almost everywhere except in his own country between 1826 and 1865 (he is even depicted in the role on his gravestone, in Łódź, Poland), but the role remained predominantly a blackface one (from Edwin Forrest and Edward Booth to Tommaso Salvini and Johnston Forbes-Robertson) until the advent of Paul Robeson, who first played it at the Old Vic in 1930 and last in Stratford in 1958 and whose record-breaking Broadway run in the role in 1943 greatly distressed white supremacists. Laurence Olivier's Othello for the National Theatre in 1963, a magnificent egotist who reverts to barbarism, was in retrospect the last possible flowering of the blackface tradition: non-black actors who have played the role since (such as Anthony Hopkins and Ben Kingsley) have preferred to make the role less African or at least less sub-Saharan. Patrick Stewart even played a white Othello among an otherwise all-black cast in Washington in 1998. Nowadays some black actors refuse the part on the grounds that in making an exotic spectacle of Othello's blackness the play is innately racist, but it has elicited towering performances from the likes of James Earl Jones and Willard White, and Janet Suzman's production at the Market Theatre in Johannesburg in the late 1980s, with John Kani in the title role, made an eloquent protest against apartheid. The casting of the South African actors Sello Maake ka-Ncube and Sir Antony Sher—who played Iago as an uncharismatic and sexually warped middle ranking careerist in a Suez-era military setting (RSC, 2004)—summoned an apartheid context, though militarism and psycho-sexual motives were heavily foregrounded to defuse somewhat the play's racial divisiveness. Nonetheless, the production's intimate, austere sorrows, heightened by the use of the Swan space, reconfirmed the deservedness of the play's particular reputation for inflicting emotional wounds. In the late 1990s, Hugh Quarshie argued that Othello is the only Shakespearean character that should not be played by a black man, such is the risk that their performance in the role reinforces racist stereotypes. In 2015, however, Quarshie was persuaded to take on the title role for Iqbal Khan's production for the RSC, partly on condition that Lucian Msamati (an actor of colour) should play Iago, thereby avoiding the troubling dynamic, so common to productions of this play, in which the audience watches a cunning white man duping an all-too gullible black man.

This example has not deterred white star actors from continuing to wish to play Iago, as in the case of Mark Rylance, who did so for Shakespeare's Globe (opposite André Holland) in 2018.

 ## ON THE SCREEN

The most interesting silent film is the 93-minute German *Othello* (1922) directed by Dmitri Buchowetzki, with Emil Jannings as the Moor. The four best-known sound cinema films are those made by Orson Welles (1952) and Sergei Yutkevich (1955), Stuart Burge's film with Olivier as Othello (1965), and the Hollywood *Othello* directed by Oliver Parker (1995). Pre-eminent among those filmed for television are Janet Suzman's Johannesburg production (1988) and Trevor Nunn's RSC production with Willard White as the Moor (1990).

Despite its unimpressive Venice sequences, Welles's film, with its Moroccan location brilliantly exploited for dramatic contrasts, stands in a class of its own. Yutkevich's *Othello*, shot in colour and originally with Russian dialogue, is profoundly memorable for its visual impact, with stone, sea, and sky as elements in the film's language. Burge's film of John Dexter's National Theatre production is historically important for its capturing of Olivier's immense performance, though his stage projection is somewhat overpowering for the camera, and it is hard to watch the film now except as a period piece. While Jonathan Miller's BBC TV *Othello* (1981) featuring Anthony Hopkins was criticized for its failure to give Othello the necessary dramatic weight, the two stage productions filmed for television focus well on characters other than the Moor. Parker's Othello was Laurence Fishburne, an American black actor whose portrayal has been seen as capitalizing on the then recent media dramatization of the O. J. Simpson trial. Kenneth Branagh played Iago. The play's plot, if not its language, has attracted other American directors wishing to dramatize their country's troubled race relations: Tim Blake Nelson's *O* (2001), for instance, starred Mekhi Phifer as Odin James, captain of the school basketball team, and Josh Hartnett as Hugo, the embittered, steroid-addicted son of the team's coach, overshadowed by James both on court and in his father's attentions.

Pericles

Conclusive external evidence shows that the first and most deceptively simple of Shakespeare's late romances was written no later than 1608. A manuscript copy of the play, most probably the promptbook used by the King's Men at the Globe, was entered in the Stationers' Register by Edward Blount on 20 May 1608. In the same year, George Wilkins published a novel called *The Painful Adventures of Pericles Prince of Tyre*, which is clearly based on the play. The Italian ambassador Giorgio Giustinian saw a production of *Pericles* during his visit to London between January 1606 and November 1608, and it is referred to as 'new' in a pamphlet, *Pimlico*, of 1609.

 TEXT

The only extant text of *Pericles* is a pirate quarto edition published by Henry Gosson in 1609. The text of the play was reconstructed either by one of the actors playing a minor role or by two reporters, who transcribed the text of the play surreptitiously, as it was being performed at the Globe. The 1609 quarto is a very poor text, where verse is printed as prose and prose as verse, the stage directions are few and sketchy, and blatant mistakes abound. Perhaps because of the textual shortcomings of this edition, *Pericles* was not included in the 1623 Folio, although it was added to the Third Folio, along with several apocryphal plays. Although the original quarto does not divide the play into acts (and is followed in this respect by the Oxford edition), later editions conventionally break it up into five, starting Act 2 at Scene 5 (after the Antioch incidents and the relief of Tarsus), Act 3 at Scene 10 (after the wedding of Pericles and Thaisa), Act 4 at Scene 15 (after the storm and its immediate consequences), and Act 5 at Scene 20 (after Marina's release from the brothel).

A considerable amount of effort has gone into establishing the origins of Wilkins's 1608 *The Painful Adventures*. The theory that Wilkins's novel served as a source for the play has been repeatedly confuted, although the assumption that the novel contains passages from an earlier play on the subject has found some supporters. Many modern editions, including the Oxford, take the view that the novel in part derives from the play, and use it to emend the defective quarto text.

 SOURCES

The story of Pericles derives from the Greek romance of Apollonius of Tyre, which had already been retold several times, most importantly in John Gower's *Confessio Amantis* (1393): Gower himself features as the Chorus in Shakespeare's play. The other main source, which Shakespeare followed as closely as Gower, is Laurence Twine's *The Pattern of Painful Adventures* (1576). Twine's influence is especially noticeable in the brothel scenes in Act 4. Given that the main hero is called Apollonius in both sources, editors since George Steevens have argued that Shakespeare may have borrowed the name 'Pericles' from a character in Sir Philip Sidney's *Arcadia*.

 CHARACTER LIST

John **Gower** *the Presenter*
Antiochus King of Antioch
His **Daughter**
Thaliart *a villain*
Pericles Prince of Tyre
Helicanus ⎤ *two grave*
Aeschines ⎦ *counsellors of Tyre*
Marina *Pericles' daughter*
Cleon *Governor of Tarsus*
Dioniza *his wife*
Leonine *a murderer*
King Simonides of Pentapolis
Thaisa *his daughter*

Three **Fishermen** *his subjects*
Five **Princes** *suitors of Thaisa*
A **Marshal**
Lychorida *Thaisa's nurse*
Cerimon *a physician of Ephesus*
Philemon *his servant*
Lysimachus *Governor of Mytilene*
A **Bawd**
A **Pander**
Boult *a leno*
Diana *goddess of chastity*
Lords, ladies, pages, messengers, sailors, gentlemen

:≡ SYNOPSIS

1 The presenter Gower introduces himself and the main characters involved in the Antioch episode, namely King Antiochus the Great, who is having a secret incestuous affair with his daughter, and Pericles, the King of Tyre, who has travelled to Antiochus' court to woo the fair Princess. The King has devised a riddle, which his daughter's suitors must solve in order to gain her hand. If they fail they lose their lives. Pericles is brought before Antiochus: professing his love for the Princess, he is granted the opportunity to solve the riddle. Pericles deciphers the riddle, which reveals the King's incest. Knowing that either revealing this secret or pretending not to have solved the riddle will bring about his death, Pericles gives a riddling answer, whereby he warns the King without exposing him. The King grants Pericles more time to solve the riddle only in order to arrange to have him murdered by Thaliard. Pericles, conscious of the danger, flees.

2 Pericles confides his troubles to Helicanus, who urges him to leave Tyre.

3 Thaliard arrives at Tyre straight after Pericles' departure.

4 Pericles arrives at Tharsus, formerly a rich town, whose resources have been wasted by its proud citizens, and delivers them from famine by giving them corn. The rulers Cleon and Dioniza swear allegiance to Pericles in return for his generosity.

5 As Gower, with the help of a dumb show, explains, Pericles receives word of Thaliard's mission and decides to resume his travels, which are brought to an end by a sea-storm. Pericles suffers shipwreck and is cast ashore near Pentapolis among fishermen. After offering Pericles food and shelter, they recover his father's armour from the sea. Pericles decides to wear it and take part in a joust which Simonides, King of Pentapolis, has organized to test the valour of his daughter's suitors.

6 The joust is preceded by a parade and the interpretation of the emblematic shields and mottoes carried by the six suitors. Pericles is mocked for his modest apparel. The joust takes place offstage.

7 Pericles wins but looks melancholic and refuses to eat at the banquet. Simonides and his daughter Thaisa also lose their appetite: Thaisa is charmed by the mysterious knight and her father is too keen to discover his origins to care about food. Simonides sends his daughter over to Pericles to enquire about his identity. Pericles refrains from disclosing his real identity and introduces himself as a lord from Tyre.

8 In Tyre, Pericles' lords complain about the protracted absence of their King and offer Helicanus the crown. Helicanus asks them to wait and search for their King for another year.

8a Pericles, brought to a bedchamber, requests a stringed instrument on which to play.

9 Simonides dismisses the other suitors, then tests Pericles by confronting him with a forged love letter to Thaisa. He pretends to be angry while Pericles begs Thaisa to tell her father that he has never importuned her with love. Simonides, now certain of his daughter's feelings and Pericles' virtue, suddenly grants them his consent to marry.

10 Gower describes the joyful celebration of their wedding, and with the help of a dumb show narrates its sequel: Thaisa is pregnant when a second letter reaches Pericles, announcing that Helicanus will be crowned king should Pericles fail to return within the following six months. Pericles discloses his real identity and although Simonides is happy to find out that his son-in-law is a king, he is sad to see him and his daughter depart for Tyre.

11 The sea journey to Tyre is interrupted by another storm. Thaisa apparently dies in childbirth: at the superstitious sailors' insistence, Pericles casts her body overboard, sealed in a box. He decides to take Marina, his newly born baby, to Tharsus.

12 Cerimon, a lord of Ephesus, manages to revive Thaisa, washed up on his coast, from her deathlike slumber.

13 Pericles arrives at Tharsus and hands Marina over to Cleon and Dioniza.

14 Cerimon takes Thaisa, unable to remember Marina's birth, to the temple of Diana in Ephesus.

15 Gower tells how after Marina grows into a charming and talented young woman, Dioniza, forgetful of her debt to Pericles, plans to have her murdered in order to enhance her own daughter's chances of an advantageous marriage. Leonine, hired to kill Marina while she is walking along the seashore, is interrupted by the arrival of pirates, who kidnap Marina.

16 In Mytilene, a pander and a bawd complain that they are short of healthy young women to initiate to their trade. Their man Boult is sent to the market to search for female slaves. Boult comes back with the pirates who agree to sell Marina to the Bawd. Marina regrets that Leonine was too slow to dispatch her. The Bawd attempts to let Marina into the secrets of the sex trade, but Marina refuses to collaborate.

17 Cleon arraigns his wife for betraying Pericles' trust.

18 Gower describes Pericles' arrival at Tharsus and his suffering following the discovery of Marina's death, on which he swears to spend the rest of his life mourning the loss of his wife and daughter, his hair unshorn.

19 Virtuous Marina converts the Bawd's customers. Lysimachus, the Governor of Mytilene, apparently a regular client despite a subsequent claim that he is there solely to gather evidence against the Bawd, visits the brothel and is left with Marina, who persuades him she is genuinely a virgin and no prostitute: he leaves promising to help. The Bawd, outraged by Marina's behaviour, orders Boult to deflower her, but she persuades him she will be more profitably employed in respectable activities such as sewing, weaving, and dancing.

20 Gower narrates Marina's establishment as a singer and embroiderer, and the arrival of Pericles' ship at Mytilene.

21 Lysimachus enquires after Pericles' distemper and suggests that Marina might be able to cure him. Marina is sent for and sings to the silent Pericles. He initially pushes her away, but his interest is aroused by her defiant reaction: Marina claims to have suffered as much as he and to have royal ancestors. Pericles finally looks at her and notices her resemblance to Thaisa. Marina reveals her name and father and daughter are finally reunited. Diana appears to Pericles in a dream and directs him to Ephesus.

22 Gower narrates the arrival of Pericles and his party at Diana's temple, where Thaisa is among the vestals.

23 When Pericles narrates his story, Thaisa faints, and, reviving, is reunited with Pericles and Marina. Gower's epilogue recommends endurance in the face of adversity.

 ## ARTISTIC FEATURES

The most prominent, and most vilified, feature of *Pericles* is the uneven quality of its dramatic and poetic diction, often mock-medieval in style. The differences in style, characterization, and structure between Acts 1 and 2 and the second half of the play are remarkable, even allowing for the short-comings of the reporters of the first pirate edition of 1609 and the idiosyncrasies of its compositors. Critics and editors have therefore argued that *Pericles* was either hastily revised by Shakespeare or written collaboratively with William Rowley, Thomas Heywood, John Day, or, more plausibly, George Wilkins. Both hypotheses help to account for the rambling plot and the scanty characterization in Acts 1 and 2 and the sudden improvement at the beginning of Act 3. Particularly admired for its psychological and dramatic complexity is the reunion between Pericles and Marina in Act 5. Although neither the revision nor the collaboration theory have been convincingly confuted, critics now tend to emphasize the structural unity of the play, which is reinforced by the constant presence of the sea and the re-emergence of the incest motif, and Shakespeare's reliance on music, magic, and supernatural intervention, which is typical of the late romances.

CRITICAL HISTORY

In his *Ode to Himself* (1629), Ben Jonson famously referred to *Pericles* as a 'mouldy tale'. Many critics after him criticized the 'absurdity' of its plot and the lack of consistency of its characterization. In *An Essay on the Dramatic Poetry of the Last Age* (1672), Dryden remarked on the 'lameness' of the plot and the 'ridiculous' and 'incoherent' qualities of the story: fooled by the play's conscientiously naive style and manner, he thought *Pericles* must have been Shakespeare's first play. This view was even endorsed by Edmond Malone, who dated the play *c.* 1592. Because *Pericles* abounds in what Neoclassical critics regarded as serious formal flaws, its authorship was regularly contested. Nicholas Rowe included it in his 1709 edition of Shakespeare's *Complete Works*, but Alexander Pope, Lewis Theobald, Thomas Warburton, Samuel Johnson, Edward Capell, and others omitted it from the canon. Malone, who believed that Shakespeare wrote at least some parts of the play, reintroduced it in his 1780 edition. Many critics have remarked on Shakespeare's unusual reliance on his sources. Malone noticed that Shakespeare 'pursued the story exactly as he found it'. In 1898, Albert Henry Smyth defined *Pericles* as the 'most singular example in Elizabethan literature of a consistent copying of a venerable and far-travelled story'. In 1956, J. C. Maxwell observed that the 'complicated episodic narrative of the sources is followed in a fashion unparalleled in Shakespeare'. In 1976, Northrop Frye reached a similar conclusion: '*Pericles* seems to be a deliberate experiment in presenting a traditional archetypal sequence as nakedly and baldly as possible.' After almost two centuries of critical neglect, the play is now praised for its power to move. The reunion between father and daughter in Act 5, which is often compared to the climactic reunion between Lear and Cordelia at the end of *King Lear*, Act 4, was T. S. Eliot's main source of inspiration for his poem 'Marina'. More generally, critics now tend to regard *Pericles* as the first of the last plays, in that, despite the obvious flaws of its text, it anticipates several elements of the romances. Shakespeare, for example, uses Gower to bridge the temporal gaps between adjacent episodes in *Pericles* in ways which parallel the use of Time as chorus in *The Winter's Tale*.

 ## STAGE HISTORY

Pericles was an immense theatrical hit in 1608, possibly Shakespeare's largest: its first quarto was printed twice in 1609 and four new reprints were published before the outbreak of the Civil War in 1642. *Pericles* was the first of Shakespeare's plays to be revived when the London theatres reopened in 1659–60: the young Thomas Betterton was highly praised for his performance in the leading role. The play was not performed again until George Lillo adapted it as *Marina* in 1738, omitting the first two acts, but it then disappeared until Samuel Phelps produced it as a rarity at Sadler's Wells in 1854. After that it enjoyed few stage revivals until Robert Atkins's 1921 production at the Old Vic. In 1939 Robert Eddison played Pericles at the Open Air Theatre in Regent's Park: after the war, Paul Scofield played the title role twice (in 1947 and 1950), and Douglas Seale directed a successful production at the Birmingham Repertory Theatre (1954). This revival established an enduring directorial tradition of emphasizing the fairy-tale qualities of the plot and Shakespeare's unusual use of pageantry, followed, for example, by Glen Byam Shaw's Stratford production the following year, with Geraldine McEwan as Marina. It remained, however, one of Shakespeare's least-revived plays, a situation unimproved by Phyllida Lloyd's short-lived production at the National Theatre's Olivier auditorium in 1991, until a wave of revivals in the early 21st century by directors including Adrian Noble and Yukio Ninagawa. Cardboard Citizens, a theatre troupe run by and for the homeless, produced the play in collaboration with the RSC in 2003, and Dominic Cooke's 2006 promenade production as part of the RSC's Complete Works Festival was a potent reminder of the play's disarming power to move. Ninagawa's production (2003), framed as a story enacted by refugees, anticipated several successors in finding resonances between the wanderings of Pericles and the sufferings of those displaced by war.

 ON THE SCREEN

The only extant screen version is a slightly literal-minded BBC TV production of 1983, with Mike Gwilym as Pericles and Juliet Stevenson as Thaisa.

The Phoenix and Turtle

This enigmatic lyric poem—also known as 'The Phoenix and the Turtle'—was ascribed to Shakespeare when it appeared, untitled, as one of the 'Poetical Essays' by various authors, including the playwrights Ben Jonson, George Chapman, and John Marston, in Robert Chester's *Love's Martyr; or, Rosalind's Complaint* (1601, repr. 1611). It was later included in John Benson's 1640 edition of Shakespeare's poems.

Chester's *Love's Martyr* is a long poem described as 'allegorically showing the truth of love in the constant fate of the phoenix and turtle' (i.e. turtle dove).

The 'poetical essays' appended to it are called 'Divers poetical essays on the former subject, viz. the turtle and phoenix, done by the best and chiefest of our modern writers, with their names subscribed to their particular works; never before extant'. How Shakespeare came to be involved in the enterprise is not known; he appears to have read Chester's poem before writing his own, a 67-line allegorical elegy which mounts in intensity through its three parts. First it summons a convocation of benevolent birds, with a swan as priest, to celebrate the funeral rites of the phoenix and the turtle dove, who have 'fled / In a mutual flame from hence'. Then the birds sing an anthem in which the death of the lovers is seen as marking the end of all 'love and constancy'.

> So they loved as love in twain
> Had the essence but in one,
> Two distincts, division none.
> Number there in love was slain.

Their mutuality was such that 'Either was the other's mine'. Finally Love makes a funeral song

> To the phoenix and the dove,
> Co-supremes and stars of love,
> As chorus to their tragic scene.

This threnos—funeral song—is set off by being written in an even more incantatory style than what precedes it; each of its five stanzas has three rhyming lines, and the tone is one of grave simplicity.

The poem, often regarded as one of the most intensely if mysteriously beautiful of Shakespeare's works, is usually assumed to have been composed not long before publication, though at least one scholar has dated it as early as 1586. Its affinities and poetical style seem to lie rather with Shakespeare's later than his earlier work. In subject matter it appears to have irrecoverable allegorical significance. Various scholars have identified one or other of the phoenix and the turtle with the dedicatee Sir John Salisbury and his wife, with Queen Elizabeth, with her collective subjects, with the Earl of Essex, with Shakespeare himself, and even with the Italian philosopher Giordano Bruno (who died at the stake in 1600). G. Wilson Knight, one of the poem's most passionate advocates, supposed that 'the Turtle signifies the female aspect of the male poet's soul'. The topic has been intelligently sifted by James Bednarz in *Shakespeare and the Truth of Love: The Mystery of 'The Phoenix and Turtle'* (2012).

The Rape of Lucrece

Presumably the 'graver labour' promised in the dedication to *Venus and Adonis* (1593), Shakespeare's narrative of rape and suicide was entered in the Stationers' Register in May 1594 (as *The Ravishment of Lucrece*) and published in quarto in the same year. In rare vocabulary it is linked with *Titus Andronicus*, *1 Henry VI*, and *Richard III*: it was probably the next work Shakespeare composed after *Venus and Adonis*, in 1593–4.

 TEXT

The quarto is well printed, presumably from Shakespeare's own manuscript, by Richard Field, the Stratford-born printer also responsible for the first edition of *Venus and Adonis*: six further editions followed during Shakespeare's lifetime, and another three had appeared by 1655. The title page of the first edition calls the poem *Lucrece*, but the head title and running titles call it *The Rape of Lucrece*.

SOURCES

Like *Venus and Adonis*, this poem derives from the work of Shakespeare's favourite classical author Ovid, but for this tragic narrative Shakespeare turned from the mythological *Metamorphoses* to Ovid's historical *Fasti* ('chronicles'), which he probably consulted in the original Latin. He also shows a familiarity with the earliest account of the Lucrece story, written by Livy around 25 BC (five centuries after Lucrece's death), which had been translated in William Painter's *Palace of Pleasure* (1566). Two earlier English versions of this semi-legendary material lie behind his own, that of Geoffrey Chaucer (in *The Legend of Good Women*) and perhaps that of John Gower (in *Confessio Amantis*). Shakespeare's literary treatment of the story shows the influence of the 'complaint' tradition exemplified by the *Mirror for Magistrates* (1559), in which the ghosts of historical figures bemoan their fates in verse. This tradition had recently been developed by Samuel Daniel in *The Complaint of Rosamond* (1592), which uses the same rhyme-royal stanza, and Shakespeare would return to this genre with his own *A Lover's Complaint* (c. 1603–4).

:≡ SYNOPSIS

A dedication, signed 'William Shakespeare', commends the poem to the attention of 'the Right Honourable Henry Wriothesley, Earl of Southampton and Baron of Titchfield' in unusually affectionate terms: 'The love I dedicate to your lordship is without end…[w]hat I have done is yours; what I have to do is yours, being part in all I have, devoted yours.' The Argument which follows, summarizing the content of the poem in Latinate prose, supplies many details of the story which the poem itself either omits or mentions only fleetingly, particularly the events leading up to the rape and its political consequences. (Assuming it to be authorial, it is the longest specimen extant of Shakespeare's non-dramatic prose.) It recounts how during the reign of King Tarquinius Superbus, who had obtained the throne unelected through the murder of his father-in-law, a group of Roman noblemen were engaged in the siege of Ardea, among them the King's son Sextus Tarquinius (the poem's Tarquin) and Collatinus (the poem's Collatine). They fell to discussing the virtues of their wives, which they resolved to test by riding quickly back to Rome together to see how they were occupied in their husbands' absence: all were amusing themselves except Collatinus' wife Lucretia (Lucrece), who was virtuously spinning among her maids. Sextus Tarquinius, desiring her, subsequently returned privately to her house at Collatium ('Collatia' in the sources, which Shakespeare seems erroneously to have thought a suburb of Rome), where he was welcomed and lodged: during the night he crept to Lucretia's chamber, raped her, and fled. The following morning Lucretia summoned her father and husband, told them what had happened, and stabbed herself to death after vowing them to revenge: with the assistance of Junius Brutus, they used Lucretia's death to incense the Roman people against the Tarquins, who were banished, and the monarchy was replaced by a consular republic.

The first section of the poem focuses primarily on Tarquin's consciousness. At its opening he is already speeding alone towards Collatium (ll. 1–7), the origins of his lust recounted briefly in flashback (ll. 8–49): Lucrece welcomes him, unsuspecting, and later he retires to bed (ll. 50–126). Alone, he reflects on his intended crime before rising and lighting a torch (ll. 127–89): the next thirteen stanzas (ll. 190–280) are his soliloquy, dilating on the danger and dishonour of his intentions but finally resolving to pursue them nonetheless. Stealing through the house, he forces each lock which intervenes on the way to Lucrece's chamber, ignoring the reproaches constituted by these, by a draught that nearly extinguishes his torch, and by the evidence of Lucrece's virtuous sewing (ll. 281–336): at last he forces his way into her room (ll. 337–71). There follows a set-piece description of Lucrece asleep as Tarquin sees her (ll. 372–420), before she is awakened by his hand at her breast (ll. 421–69). Challenged, he tells her, drawing his sword, that if she refuses him he will kill her and a slave, making it appear he caught them in bed together, whereas if not she can keep his violation a secret (ll. 470–539). She pleads in vain (ll. 540–666), and Tarquin, extinguishing the light and silencing her with her nightdress, forces her (ll. 667–86). He immediately experiences a revulsion of feeling, and creeps away in shame, longing for the morning which Lucrece wishes would never come (ll. 689–749).

From here the poem concentrates on Lucrece's perspective. Embarking on her lengthy, rhetorical complaint, she apostrophizes night, time, and opportunity (ll. 750–966), and curses Tarquin (ll. 967–1022), before resolving on suicide, as much for Collatine's sake as for her own: she will tell him everything (ll. 1023–78). As morning approaches, she rebukes the sun for rising and the birds for singing, comparing herself to the ravished Philomel who was transformed into the nightingale (ll. 1079–148), and finally concludes that suicide (which, with an anachronistically Christian perspective, she regards as a sin against her soul) is preferable to a shamed life (ll. 1149–76). She decides that suicide will save her reputation, and that her husband can vindicate her through revenge on Tarquin (ll. 1177–211). She calls her maid, who weeps to see her mistress's grief: after Lucrece asks about Tarquin's departure, the maid asks the cause of her sorrow, but Lucrece will not tell, sending for ink and paper (ll. 1212–95). Lucrece writes briefly to Collatine, summoning him home (ll. 1296–365). Awaiting his return, she meditates on a painting of besieged Troy, described at length, which she apostrophizes, finally tearing its likeness of the traitorous Sinon because reminded of Tarquin (ll. 1366–568). When her husband arrives, with other lords, she describes what has happened, withholding the name of her rapist until all the men have vowed to avenge her, then stabs herself to death (ll. 1568–729).

Lucrece's bleeding corpse is described, and the lamentation of her father Lucretius, with whose grief that of Collatine competes (ll. 1730–806). Junius Brutus, however, abandoning the folly he has assumed as a disguise, rallies the men to renew their vow of vengeance (ll. 1807–48). The poem's final stanza briefly recounts that they subsequently displayed Lucrece's corpse in Rome, thereby winning the Roman people to agree to the banishment of the Tarquins (ll. 1849–56).

ARTISTIC FEATURES

The discrepancies between the Argument and the poem itself—which shows very little interest in the public consequences of Tarquin's crime, preferring to dramatize the private experiences of rapist and victim—have led some commentators to conclude that the Argument was not written by Shakespeare, but the differences probably reflect its function, to provide the standard account of the story on which the poem offers an artistic variation. The poem proper is intensely dramatic, and would frequently be recalled by Shakespeare in his subsequent writings for the stage, primarily his Roman tragedies but in other plays too: Hamlet, like Lucrece, reflects in grief on the represented sufferings of Hecuba, and both Macbeth and Cymbeline's Giacomo liken themselves to Tarquin. Modern readers, however, who have generally preferred Venus and Adonis, often find that its drama is dissipated rather than enhanced by its forceful display of rhetoric.

CRITICAL HISTORY

The popularity reflected by the proliferation of early editions of The Rape of Lucrece is confirmed by allusions and imitations: it was praised by Thomas Freeman in 1614 ('Who loves chaste life, there's Lucrece for a teacher'), and imitated by Thomas Middleton (in The Ghost of Lucrece, 1600), Thomas Heywood (in his play The Rape of Lucrece, published in 1608), and John Quarles, whose 'Tarquin Banished; or, The Reward of Lust' was appended to the 1655 edition of Shakespeare's poem. After this, though, the poem fell from favour, ignored throughout the 18th century, and despite Samuel Taylor Coleridge's grudging admission of its eloquence most 19th-century readers were more interested in the Dedication's hints at the nature of Shakespeare's relationship with Southampton than in the poem's literary qualities. In the 20th century, however, it was at least partly rehabilitated, although much criticism has concentrated on its anticipation of later works. Its subject matter has attracted both feminists and their opponents. Perhaps predictably, it was a favourite poem of Ted Hughes, who found in it a key to Shakespeare's entire output as a tragedian. One notable staging of the poem combined narration and song in a performance of stunning power and originality by Camille O'Sullivan (RSC, 2012–14). Accompanied by Feargal Murray on the piano, with whom O'Sullivan composed the original music, and directed by Elizabeth Freestone, the voices given to both Lucrece and Tarquin in O'Sullivan's electrifying delivery helped audiences see with fresh eyes the dramatic potency of Shakespeare's supposedly non-dramatic writing.

The Reign of King Edward the Third (*Edward III*)

 TEXT AND AUTHORSHIP

Edward III was entered into the Stationers' Register in 1596 and was printed anonymously later that year. In 1656, the play was attributed to Shakespeare in a catalogue of plays appended to an edition of *The Careless Shepherdess*, a Jacobean tragicomedy written by Thomas Goffe. Just over a century later, Edward Capell advanced the idea that Shakespeare had a hand in the play in *Prolusions, or, Selected Pieces of Ancient Poetry* (1740). Nonetheless, the nature of *Edward III*'s authorship remained disputed, conferring upon it an apocryphal status. Now, however, textual and attribution scholars largely agree that Shakespeare collaborated on the play, suggesting that he was responsible for the *Measure for Measure*–esque 'Countess Scenes' (scenes 2 and 3) and Audley's meditation on death in scene 12. The identity of Shakespeare's collaborator remains unknown, but George Peele, Thomas Kyd, and Christopher Marlowe (who must, however, have completed his share before his death by stabbing in 1593) have all been mooted.

 CHARACTER LIST

The English
King Edward III
Queen Philippa *his wife*
Edward, **Prince of Wales**
  their eldest son
The **Earl of Salisbury**
The **Countess of Salisbury** *his wife*
The **Earl of Warwick** *the*
  Countess's father

Sir William de **Montague**
  Salisbury's nephew
The **Earl of Derby**
Sir James **Audley**
Henry, **Lord Percy**
John **Copland** *an esquire,*
  later knighted
Lodowick *King Edward's secretary*
Two Squires

A **Herald** to King Edward
from the Prince of Wales
Four **Heralds** who bear the
Prince of Wales's armour
Soldiers

Allied with the English
Robert, **Comte d'Artois** and
Earl of Richmond
Jean, **Comte de Montfort**,
later Duc de Bretagne
Gobin de Grâce *a French prisoner*

The French
Jean II de Valois, **King of France**
Prince Charles, Jean's eldest son,
Duc de Normandie, the **Dauphin**
Prince Philippe *Jean's
younger son*
The **Duc de Lorraine**
Villiers *a prisoner sent as an
envoy by the Earl of Salisbury
to the Dauphin*

The **Captain of Calais**
Another **French Captain**
A **Mariner**
Three **Heralds** to the Prince
of Wales from the King of
France, the Dauphin, and
Prince Philippe
Six **Poor Men** *residents
of Calais*
Six **Supplicants** *wealthy merchants
and citizens of Calais*
Five other **Frenchmen**
A **Frenchwoman** with two children
Soldiers

Allied with the French
The **King of Bohemia**
A **Polish Captain**
Polish and Muscovite soldiers
David II, **King of Scotland**
Sir **William Douglas**
Two Scottish **Messengers**

≔ SYNOPSIS

1. The banished Comte d'Artois, made Earl of Richmond by King Edward, explains to the English court the grounds of Edward's claim to the French crown, and, when the Duc de Lorraine arrives to demand that Edward pays homage to King Jean of France, Edward, his son the Prince of Wales, and others defy the Duc and declare war. Lorraine has no sooner departed than Sir William Montague brings news from the Scottish border, where the Scottish king, David, breaking a peace treaty, has taken Berwick and Newcastle and besieged the Countess of Salisbury, whose husband is serving in France, in Roxburgh Castle. Edward disposes his warlords and troops for what are now two battlefronts.

2. The Countess of Salisbury, besieged, overhears the Scottish king promising the Duc de Lorraine that he will continue to harry the English and then discussing with Douglas whether he or the King will take the Countess, her jewels, or both when the castle surrenders; but when a messenger brings the news that Edward is coming at the head of a large army, they prepare to flee, mocked by the Countess. Edward, Artois, and Warwick, the Countess's father, arrive: Edward finds the Countess's welcome captivating and postpones pursuing the Scots. Left alone, a courtier, Lodowick, comments on the King's evident sudden infatuation. The King returns and, after soliloquizing about his new passion, first sends Lodowick to fetch pen and paper and then commissions him to write a love letter to the Countess, but he is dissatisfied with his efforts. The Countess returns, and Edward dismisses Lodowick and attempts to woo her, but she refuses his advances and leaves; when her father Warwick arrives, the King instead orders Warwick to command his daughter to agree to his suit. Left alone, Warwick reflects on his horror at this errand, but, on the Countess's arrival, he nonetheless propositions her on Edward's behalf, as instructed. He expresses relief, however, when her virtue remains unshaken.

3. Derby, returning from France with the news that the Emperor has agreed to assist with Edward's campaign in France, meets Audley, who has mustered Edward's troops: Derby reports that Edward and his court are all so reclusive and discontented that he has yet to communicate his news to the King. When Edward arrives, Derby tells him of the Emperor's support, but the King is unable to concentrate on his military affairs, continually speaking of the Countess by mistake. Lodowick reports privately that the Countess will give the King her final decision before nightfall. The Prince of Wales, his troops ready for the campaign, arrives, and his resemblance to his mother briefly recalls the King to himself, but, just when he is about to set forth at the head of his army, renouncing his passion for the Countess, he learns that she wishes to see him alone, and he abruptly dismisses the Prince. Alone with the King, the Countess tells him that she will be his on condition that he kills both her husband and his wife; when the King agrees to this, she shows him her two wedding knives, offering him one with which to kill the Queen but assuring him that she will kill herself with the other unless he abandons his suit. The King, finally brought to his senses by this, promptly summons his military leaders and embarks on his campaign, making Warwick Warden of the North, sending the Prince and Audley to sea via Newhaven, and undertaking to lead his own force, with Audley, Artois, and Derby, through Flanders.

4. King Jean of France, his sons the Dauphin and Prince Philippe, and the Duc de Lorraine encamp near the coast, awaiting news of the impending sea battle and discussing the prospects of the campaign. The French army is reinforced by the arrival of the King of Bohemia with Danish troops, and a Polish captain with Polish and Muscovite troops. A French mariner reports on the appearance of the English fleet; while Jean and Philippe dine, he is sent to report on the progress of the battle. He returns with a detailed account of an English victory at sea, and a discomfited Jean and Philippe hurry away to rally and unite their troops.

5. French citizens, some with baggage, some with their children, are fleeing from the war zone, full of appalling reports of English victories and civilian casualties.

6. King Edward and Derby reward Gobin de Grâce for showing the English where to ford the Somme. They are joined by Artois, Audley, and Prince Edward, and the Prince reports that his army has captured Harfleur, Lô, Crotoy, and Carentan and that the French king is massing his army near Crécy in preparation for battle. King Jean, the Dauphin, Prince Philippe, the Duc de Lorraine, and the King of Bohemia arrive at the head of their soldiers: the rival kings, backed by their princes and lords, defy one another and dismiss one another's claims to the throne of France before turning to rally their own forces for the imminent battle. After the French leave, Edward solemnly arms his son the Prince, who is ceremonially presented with armour, a helmet, a lance, and a shield by successive peers and vows to fight with valour and loyalty. The King appoints him and Audley as leaders of the vanguard.

7. In the battle, retreating French troops are pursued by Prince Edward. The Duc de Lorraine explains to King Jean that the French army, though superior in numbers, has been demoralized by the premature retreat of a Genoese garrison.

8. Artois, Derby, and Audley successively report to King Edward that his son is surrounded, urging him to send troops to rescue him, but the King refuses to do so, expressing confidence in the Prince's valour and a desire not to hinder him from earning a famous unassisted victory. Trumpets are heard sounding what turns out to be a French retreat, and Prince Edward arrives, with the shattered remains of his lance and the body of the King of Bohemia. The King knights him. The Prince reports that the French have lost 11 princes, 80 barons, 120 knights, and 30,000 common soldiers, whereas the English have lost only 1000. The King sends the Prince to pursue King Jean towards Poitiers while he and Derby besiege Calais.

9. The Comte de Montfort pledges allegiance to King Edward, giving his coronet to the Earl of Salisbury to take to the King. Salisbury employs a French prisoner, Villiers, to obtain a passport from the Duke of Normandy that will enable him to join the King at Calais, trusting Villiers not to flee.

10. The King and Audley meet six poor citizens of Calais, no longer fit to serve in its defence, who have been sent out of the besieged city to reduce the demands on its food supply: the King receives them charitably. Lord Percy brings news that, under the leadership of his pregnant Queen, the English army at home has defeated the Scots: King David has been taken prisoner by a squire, John Copland, who, to the displeasure of the Queen, now on her way to Calais to join her husband, refuses to hand him over save to the King. A Captain of Calais arrives to tell the King that the town has at length decided to surrender to him, on condition that he spares their lives and their property, but the King tells him that, since they refused his earlier offer of such clemency, he will destroy the city unless its six richest burghers prostrate themselves before him with nooses around their necks.

11. The Dauphin refuses to grant Villiers a passport for Salisbury, but when he sees how true Villiers is to his vow to return to Salisbury as his prisoner, he relents. After Villiers has departed, King Jean arrives, saying his forces have Prince Edward surrounded and urging the Dauphin to join their attack; the Dauphin is reluctant, having heard a prophecy at Crécy to the effect that the French army will be defeated when it is frightened by birds and attacked with flints and that the French king will be taken to England.

12. Prince Edward and Audley, surrounded and outnumbered, are visited by a herald from King Jean offering their lives if they and a hundred of their most important soldiers will surrender and be ransomed, but they refuse. A herald from the Duke of Normandy offers the Prince a horse on which to escape, which he also refuses; a herald from Prince Philippe gives the Prince a prayer book, but he mockingly sends it back to Philippe, who he fears will be unable to pray without it. Audley comforts the Prince with reflections on the inevitability of death.

13. King Jean, the Dauphin, and Philippe are dismayed by a sudden darkness and by a flock of ravens hovering over their army. Salisbury is brought to them as a prisoner: the King wishes to execute him, but the Dauphin remembers that he bears Salisbury's passport, obtained by Villiers, and saves his life, sending him on to Calais to tell King Edward of his son's impending death.

14. In the battle, Prince Edward tells Artois that, since they have run out of arrows, they must gather and fire flintstones at the French.

15. King Jean, the Dauphin, and Philippe are horrified at the rout of their army, who are terrified by the fulfilment of the prophecy.

16. Audley, mortally wounded, asks to be taken to Prince Edward.

17. Prince Edward has King Jean and the Dauphin prisoner; they are joined by Artois, who brings the captive Philippe. The dying Audley is brought by two squires; when Prince Edward rewards his service with land worth 3,000 marks a year, Audley bequeaths it to the squires. Hoping to stay alive long enough to say farewell to the King, Audley is transferred to a litter for the journey to Calais.

18. Six citizens of Calais surrender to King Edward and Queen Philippa; the King orders their execution but is persuaded to spare them by the Queen. Copland brings his prisoner King David before them; the King, overruling the Queen's displeasure, knights and rewards Copland. Salisbury brings de Montfort's coronet but also the news of his own capture and release and of what he regards as Prince Edward's certain death. The King vows revenge on the French, but a herald then brings the news that the Prince is at hand with the French king as his prisoner. The Prince arrives with

Jean and Philippe as his captives, along with Artois, and Audley, borne in a litter by the two squires, and he is joyously welcomed by his parents. King Edward tells Jean he will be taken to England before being ransomed, and he recognizes the fulfilment of the prophecy. Prince Edward wishes his martial hardships had been even greater, so as to inspire future Englishmen to defeat not only the French but also the Spanish, the Turks, and others. The King declares a peace, looking forward to the royal party's return to England.

✯✯✯ CRITICAL HISTORY

Unacknowledged as Shakespeare's for centuries, *Edward III* has only a limited history of critical discussion, but in recent times it has occasioned rich discussions on the intertwined issues of its authorship and its apocryphal status. When not subject to these discussions, criticism on the play has tended to focus on its rhetorical schemes and the representation of conflict and family relations.

🎭 PERFORMANCE HISTORY

By 1596, *Edward III* had been 'sundry times played about the city of London', but it is not easy to see the play today. In 1911 William Poel directed an abridged version, titled *The King and the Countess* for the Elizabethan Stage Society, as part of a double bill with the Calvinistic sixteenth-century interlude *Jacob and Esau*. One critic expressed delight that 'two interesting relics of the past' had been briefly resurrected, but it was fifty years before the play was performed again, this time in an abridged radio version, produced by the BBC in 1963 and starring Stephen Murray as the King and Googie Withers as the Countess. Just over a decade later, in 1977, *Edward III* hit the airwaves again, this time as part of the BBC's *Vivat Rex* series, where it was narrated by the boomingly mellifluous tones of Richard Burton. The year 1987 saw two fully mounted productions, staged by the Shakespeare Society of America in the Globe Playhouse of Los Angeles and by Theatr Clwyd in Mold, Wales. It took until 1999, however, for the play to be produced by a major national theatre. Directed by Edward Hall in the RSC's Other Place theatre, the production starred Rupert Penry-Jones as the Prince and Malcolm Storry in the title role. In 2002, the RSC gave the play another outing, this time on the Swan stage, where it was directed by Anthony Clark, with David Rintoul as the King. Critics tended to admire the play's Countess (Caroline Faber) scenes but were rather less impressed by the French conflict that dominates so much of the play. The play's best-received production to date may well have been its staging at the National Theatre of Romania in 2008, in a translation by George Volceanov, with Ion Caramitru as the King.

Richard Duke of York (*3 Henry VI*)

Shakespeare's darkest history play, detailing the worst civil chaos of the Wars of the Roses, was originally known and performed as *The True Tragedy of Richard Duke of York, with the Death of Good King Henry the Sixth, with the Whole Contention between the Two Houses Lancaster and York*. This title derives from the first text of the play, published in octavo (small-format book) in 1595. The alternative title is almost certainly editorial and comes from the better-known version of the play, longer by about 1,000 lines, published in the 1623 First Folio. Like the titles of the other plays concerned with the events of Henry's reign, *3 Henry VI* was substituted when the Folio presented all the English histories in chronological order of their contents, even though Shakespeare did not compose the plays in this order. *Richard Duke of York* was apparently written in 1591 as the continuation of *The First Part of the Contention*, which dates from 1590–1 and was published in 1594. It followed the publication of the second edition of Holinshed's *Chronicles* (see below) in 1587, and probably the first instalment of Edmund Spenser's *The Faerie Queene* (printed in 1590). It must have been written before September 1592, when the playwright Robert Greene parodied a line from *Richard Duke of York* (1.4.138) in an attack on Shakespeare in *Greene's Groatsworth of Wit*, referring to his 'Tiger's heart wrapped in a player's hide'. *Richard Duke of York* must also have been performed before an outbreak of the plague closed the theatres on 23 June. On 3 March in the same year the manager-owner of the Rose theatre, Philip Henslowe, records a 'new' performance of 'Harry the VI' in his diary. This probably refers to *Part 1*, which must have been performed by August 1592, when Thomas Nashe admired it in *Piers Penniless his Supplication to the Devil*. This would leave the period between March and June for *Richard Duke of York* and *The First Part of the Contention* to have been written and performed. But this period has struck some, but not all, scholars as unrealistically brief, in which case Shakespeare must have written *Richard Duke of York* before *1 Henry VI*.

TEXT

The play was attributed to Shakespeare prior to the 1623 Folio by the title page of the unauthorized Pavier quarto of 1619 (the third quarto). Beginning in the late 18th century, however, Shakespeare's whole or part authorship began to be questioned. While the view that Shakespeare revised a play by Greene has been discounted, the Oxford editors leave open the possibility that certain scenes might not be wholly by Shakespeare. Some degree of collaboration in this or (more likely) the other *Henry VI* plays might explain Francis Meres's failure to mention them in *Palladis Tamia* (1598), which lists other—but not all—known Shakespeare plays. Other recent editors, however, believe Shakespeare was the sole author. *Richard Duke of York*'s poetic tone and dramatic structure are the most unified of the trilogy, and its action integrally looks forward to *Richard III*.

Publication of the octavo text (O) of *Richard Duke of York* in 1595 was probably covered by the Stationers' Register entry for *The First Part of the Contention* on 12 March 1594. A second edition based on O was published in 1600 (Q2), as was the Pavier edition (Q3) in 1619. O's origins have been questioned since the 18th century. Edmond Malone first argued that it was written by Greene and later revised by Shakespeare as the Folio version. Alternatively, Dr Johnson and Edward Capell speculated that O was a report of the Folio made from memory or shorthand. Building on this idea, Peter Alexander demonstrated in 1929 that O was reconstructed from memory by actors (probably Pembroke's Men, named on O's title page). This remains the accepted explanation for O, notwithstanding corrective challenges to the universal applicability of memorial reporting. In 1928 Madeleine Doran suggested that O was also deliberately abridged for fewer players, though Randall Martin, in his Oxford edition, has shown that the personnel requirements of O and F are virtually identical. This edition revives Malone's idea that O is a first version of the play which Shakespeare revised and expanded in the Folio text.

The Folio text, which is generally clear, is based on Shakespeare's manuscript, since several missing, imprecise, or discretionary stage directions, and uncertainty over the historical figures represented by Montague, point to a draft in progress rather than a fair copy or finished state. Shakespeare's hand is also indicated by the names of several real contemporary actors, whom he had in mind to play characters in 1.2 and 3.1.

 **SOURCES**

Richard Duke of York's two documentary sources are Edward Halle's *Union of the Two Noble and Illustrious Families of Lancaster and York* (1548), and the compilation edited by Raphael Holinshed, *Chronicles of England, Scotland, and Ireland* (2nd edn. 1587). Halle is traditionally regarded as the dominant—and more ideologically conservative—influence, but recent scholarship has shifted the balance towards Holinshed. The Folio text sometimes stages Holinshed's version of events, whereas the octavo prefers Halle (e.g. at 5.4–5). Sir Thomas More's *History of King Richard III*, included by both chronicles, influences Gloucester's soliloquies (the one in 3.2 being the longest in the canon). Shakespeare alludes several times to Thomas Sackville and Edward Norton's play *Gorboduc* (1561), as well as *The Mirror for Magistrates*, Thomas Kyd's *The Spanish Tragedy*, and Christopher Marlowe's *Tamburlaine*. The Folio's expanded version of Margaret's Tewkesbury oration in 5.4 draws on Arthur Brooke's *The Tragical History of Romeus and Juliet* (1562). Shakespeare's portrayal of York's torment in 1.4 seems to allude to Passion scenes dramatized in various mystery cycles: he might himself have seen such a cycle performed in Coventry in his youth.

CHARACTER LIST

Of the King's Party
King Henry VI
Queen Margaret
Prince Edward *their son*
Duke of **Somerset**
Duke of **Exeter**
Earl of **Northumberland**
Earl of **Westmorland**
Lord **Clifford**
Lord **Stafford**
Somerville
Henry, young Earl of **Richmond**
A **Soldier** who has killed
    his father
A **Huntsman** who guards
    King Edward

The Divided House of Neville
Earl of **Warwick** *first of York's*
    party, later of Lancaster's
Marquis of **Montague** *his brother,*
    of York's party
Earl of **Oxford** *their brother-in-law,*
    of Lancaster's party

Lord **Hastings** *their brother-in-law, of*
    York's party

Of the Duke of York's Party
Richard Plantagenet, Duke of **York**
Edward, Earl of March, his
    son, later Duke of York and
    King Edward IV
Lady Gray *a widow, later Edward's*
    wife and queen
Earl **Rivers** *her brother*
George, Edward's brother, later
    Duke of **Clarence**
Richard, Edward's brother, later
    Duke of **Gloucester**
Earl of **Rutland** *Edward's*
    brother
Rutland's **Tutor** *a chaplain*
Sir **John** Mortimer *York's uncle*
Sir Hugh Mortimer *his brother*
Duke of **Norfolk**
Sir William Stanley
Earl of Pembroke
Sir John **Montgomery**

A **Nobleman**

Two **Gamekeepers**

Three **Watchmen**, who guard King
   Edward's tent

Lieutenant of the Tower

The French

King Louis

Lady Bona *his sister-in-law*

Lord Bourbon *the French*
   High Admiral

Others

A **Soldier** who has killed his son

Mayor of Coventry

Mayor of York

Aldermen of York

Soldiers, messengers, and attendants

⫶☰ SYNOPSIS

1.1 The victorious Yorkists seize the throne and are confronted by Henry and his supporters. They dispute each other's title to the crown. Under threat, Henry agrees to disinherit his son Prince Edward in favour of York and his heirs on condition that York ceases the civil war and allows Henry to remain King for his lifetime. Margaret denounces Henry's decision and vows to defend her son's rights, marching against York.

1.2 York's sons Edward and Richard persuade him to break his oath and seize the crown immediately.

1.3 At the battle of Wakefield, Clifford pitilessly murders York's young son Rutland.

1.4 York is captured and derisively set on a molehill by Margaret and Clifford. He passionately deplores their torment before they kill him.

2.1 Edward and Richard learn of their father's death, while Warwick and Montague report a further Yorkist defeat. They rally to proclaim Edward Duke of York and future King.

2.2 Henry spurns Clifford's counsel for revenge. He dubs his son Prince Edward a knight. The Yorkists and Lancastrians exchange a violent parley.

2.3–4 At the battle of Towton, an exhausted Warwick is spurred to revenge his brother's death. A single combat between Clifford and Richard is broken off by Warwick's arrival.

2.5 Sent away from the battlefield by Margaret, Henry contrasts the fulfilling natural simplicity of the shepherd's life with the emotional stresses and empty ostentation of kingship. He laments the country's destruction by civil war, joined by a grieving son who has killed his father in battle, and a father who has killed his only son. Margaret, Prince Edward, and Exeter flee with Henry to Scotland.

2.6 Clifford faints and dies from his wounds, while the Yorkists verbally abuse his body. Edward heads to London to be crowned.

3.1 Returning secretly to England, Henry is captured and turned in by two gamekeepers.

3.2 Edward sexually blackmails Elizabeth, Lady Grey, a widow petitioning for repossession of her husband's lands. She insists upon marriage, to which he agrees. His choice of a commoner astonishes George, newly elevated Duke of Clarence, and Richard, Duke of Gloucester. Henry is reported captured and sent to the Tower. Alone on stage, Gloucester reveals his contempt for Edward and burning ambitions for the crown. Freed from ethical responsibility by his physical deformities, Gloucester turns to role-playing and Machiavellian policy to achieve his goals.

3.3 Margaret seeks the French King's aid. Warwick begins to negotiate the marriage of the King's sister Lady Bona to Edward. But letters arrive announcing Edward's marriage to Lady Grey, buoying Margaret and humiliating Warwick, who switches loyalties and vows to depose Edward.

4.1 Clarence, Gloucester, and others sneer at Edward's impolitic marriage. Clarence and Somerset leave Edward to join Warwick.

4.2–4 At night Warwick and Clarence surprise Edward in his camp-tent. Warwick uncrowns him and sends him under arrest to the Archbishop of York.

4.5 Queen Elizabeth laments Edward's capture and takes sanctuary to protect her unborn child.

4.6 Richard, Hastings, and Stanley rescue Edward while he is hunting and depart for Flanders to seek aid.

4.7 Henry is released from the Tower and appoints Warwick and Clarence joint protectors. Henry prophesies that the young Richmond—future Henry VII—will one day become king.

4.8 The Yorkists land in England ostensibly to claim Edward's dukedom at York. The Mayor is intimidated into granting them entry into the city, and Edward is proclaimed King.

4.9–10 Warwick and Clarence take leave of Henry, who is captured with Exeter by Edward and Gloucester and sent to the Tower.

5.1 The Yorkists confront Warwick at Coventry. Oxford, Montague, and Somerset arrive to support him, but Clarence switches sides back to his brothers.

5.2 During the battle of Barnet, a fatally wounded Warwick dies after learning of Montague's death.

5.3 Edward marches towards Tewkesbury to meet Margaret.

5.4 Margaret rallies her dispirited troops.

5.5 Edward defeats her and captures Prince Edward, who is impetuously killed by Edward, Gloucester, and Clarence. Gloucester rushes away to the Tower. Margaret curses the others over her son's body.

5.6 Gloucester visits Henry, who intuits his son is dead and prophesies Gloucester's future slaughter by recalling the evil omens of his birth.

Gloucester kills him but continues Henry's story of his destiny, vowing to kill his brothers and everyone else who stands in his way.

5.7 Edward relishes the fall of his enemies and, with Queen Elizabeth, delights in their new infant prince. Gloucester gives the child a Judas kiss. Edward banishes Queen Margaret to France, and announces Yorkist celebrations.

✭✭✭ CRITICAL HISTORY

Richard Duke of York has often been better appreciated on the stage than in academic criticism because much of its dramatic interest centres on intense battle scenes, which materialize its discursive themes of civil war's destruction of familial and social bonds. Nineteenth-century commentators, preoccupied with heroic character, had little use for Henry's pacifism and viewed Margaret simply as a she-wolf. But German Romantic critics situated the play in the wider context of Shakespeare's histories as part of a national epic. E. M. W. Tillyard's influential *Shakespeare's History Plays* (1944) adopted this interpretation but emphasized the providential triumph of the Tudors, foreshadowed by Henry's prophecy over Richmond in 4.7. But Tillyard and others depressed critical interest in *Richard Duke of York* by claiming that Shakespeare was uninspired when writing it. The modern stage has dispelled this view, while revisionist critics have observed how little *Richard Duke of York* supports Tillyard's unifying vision of controlling providential order. More apparent is an early modern focus on the dangers of divided succession and dynastic factionalism, and the vision of an amoral universe of power-seeking individuals associated with the new philosophy of Niccolò Machiavelli that explicitly inspires Gloucester. Feminist critics have also learnt from stage performances, investigating the multiple social dimensions in Margaret's role as militant mother upholding her son's rights against a disordered patriarchy.

🎭 STAGE HISTORY

Richard Duke of York was probably first written for and performed by Lord Strange's Men, and then certainly staged by Pembroke's Men after they came into existence in May 1591. There is no further stage evidence until John Crowne's Royalist adaptation, *The Misery of Civil-War* (1680, staged 1681), whose sensationalizing climax is the battle of Towton (2.2–6). From this point until the beginning of the 20th century, *Richard Duke of York* was performed in England only in inferior adaptations. Much of its final act and Gloucester's soliloquies were cannibalized by Colley Cibber's hugely successful and long-lived adaptation of *Richard III* (1700). In Germany and Austria, however, strong interest in Shakespeare's histories among 19th-century critics stimulated many innovative productions. F. R. Benson mounted *Richard Duke of York* at Stratford-upon-Avon in 1906, when all three *Henry VI* plays were first performed as a cycle (another idea borrowed from Germany). Benson's exuberant Gloucester was matched by his wife Constance's Margaret, played with 'unflagging force and spirit' despite heavy cuts. Sir Barry Jackson and Douglas Seale's Birmingham Repertory Theatre production in 1952 launched the play's modern stage life. Seale successfully alternated attention between still and lucid passages of formal verse, and energetic clashing armies. Barbara Jeffrey's fully humanized interpretation as Queen Margaret drew new attention to the role's tragic grandeur, as did Barbara Jefford's when the production reappeared at the Old Vic in 1957. Their moving performances were surpassed only by Dame Peggy Ashcroft's 'revelation' in Peter Hall and John Barton's *Wars of the Roses* for the RSC in 1963–4. The condensed *Edward IV* began with Cade's rebellion and continued into *Richard Duke of York*. Barton also added hundreds of lines of Shakespearian pastiche to clarify personal motives and story-lines. *Richard Duke of York* was performed unadapted in Terry Hands's well-received 1977 production of the whole trilogy. In 1986 Michael Bogdanov and Michael Pennington reverted to Barton's condensed format—minus his invented lines—for their eclectic 'post-Falklands' production, *The Wars of the Roses*, for the English Shakespeare Company, which toured internationally between 1987 and 1989 (and is preserved on videotape). Adrian Noble followed their abridgement in *The Plantagenets* in 1988, but with more traditional spectacle in the second play, 'House of York'. Katie Mitchell's stand-alone production at the RSC's Other Place in 1994, 'Henry VI: The Battle for the Throne', underlined the play's religious ritual and natural imagery to heighten its anti-war themes. In America, Pat Patton, recalling the experiences of Vietnam, chose Noble's 'House of York' for his stirring Oregon Shakespeare Festival production in 1992. Previous productions of *Richard Duke of York* at Ashland in 1955, 1966, and 1977 employed strong ensemble acting and Shakespeare's full script. Michael Boyd's haunting, semi-abstract realization of the three plays for the RSC (2000), part of the 'This England' history cycle, won enormous critical acclaim. Boyd's trilogy was revived in 2006 for the company's Complete Works Festival in which he also directed the other five parts of the First and Second Tetralogies, staging the entire sequence together in 2007–8 as 'The Histories'. Edward Hall's gory, all male, abattoir-set *Rose Rage* (2001) was, like the *Henry VI* chapter in his father Peter's *Wars of the Roses* (RSC 1963–4), a two-part adaptation of the three plays.

 ON THE SCREEN

BBC TV broadcast the play as an episode in the series *An Age of Kings* (1960), but it appeared more memorably in 1965 when the BBC transmitted the RSC's *The Wars of the Roses*. No mere recording of the stage production, the action was filmed by twelve cameras on an extended acting area. Inspired by Brecht's self-conscious approach to theatricality, Jane Howell directed an equally playful and moving production for BBC television, first broadcast in 1983. Battle scenes were effectively varied in appearance, and speeches personalized by being spoken directly to the camera.

Richard II

The most lyrical of Shakespeare's history plays, *Richard II* marks an enormous change from its predecessor in the genre, *Richard III*. It is written entirely in verse, as are *1 Henry VI*, *Richard Duke of York* (*3 Henry VI*), and *King John*, but neither these plays nor the three histories which continue the story of Bolingbroke's usurpation and its consequences (*1 and 2 Henry IV* and *Henry V*) match *Richard II*'s tragic plangency. In its heavy use of rhyme it is recognizably akin to *Romeo and Juliet* and *A Midsummer Night's Dream* (1595), and an invitation from Sir Edward Hoby to Sir Robert Cecil dated 7 December 1595 to come to supper and see 'King Richard present himself to your view' has usually been identified as alluding to a private performance of *Richard II*, presumably then new. The dating of the play to 1595 is confirmed by its indebtedness to Samuel Daniel's epic poem *The First Four Books of the Civil Wars*, entered in the Stationers' Register in October 1594 but apparently only published in 1595.

 TEXT

The play was entered in the Stationers' Register in 1597 and appeared in a quarto apparently set from Shakespeare's foul papers in the same year. This text was reprinted twice in 1598, and a fourth quarto followed in 1608, this one, however, with 'new additions of the Parliament Scene, and the deposing of King Richard', passages omitted from the earlier editions. This fuller text was reprinted in 1615, and, annotated by reference to a promptbook, provided the basis for the text reproduced in the Folio in 1623. The Folio's text was itself reprinted as a quarto in 1634. Although deprived of oaths in compliance with the Act to Restrain the Abuses of Players (1606), the Folio text is at some points superior to the quarto, particularly in its stage directions.

SOURCES

The large number of early editions, and the omission of the deposition scene, suggest a play, or at least a subject, of considerable topical interest: depicting the feasibility of dethroning a childless English monarch was clearly felt to be controversial during Elizabeth I's later years, and the episode depicting Richard's abdication was evidently a victim of political censorship, probably removed in performance as well as in print until after the Queen's death. Sensitive as the play proved, however, Shakespeare's modifications to his historical material suggest, if anything, a toning-down of its potential for seditious application, though this did not deter the Earl of Essex from having it revived as part of the preparations for his abortive attempted coup in 1601, any more than it mitigated Queen Elizabeth's wrath, reported by William Lambarde, at the parallel this implied between her and King Richard. In particular, Shakespeare suppresses some of the justifications for Bolingbroke's usurpation: according to Holinshed's *Chronicles*, the play's chief source, although Mowbray had not himself killed the Duke of Gloucester (but had merely allowed his murderers access to him), he had been directly ordered to do so by Richard. Shakespeare had read widely around his subject, not only in Samuel Daniel and Holinshed but in *The Mirror for Magistrates*, and his depiction of John of Gaunt (the character most altered from Holinshed's version) owes something to an anonymous chronicle play about the earlier part of Richard's reign, *Thomas of Woodstock* (*c.* 1592?), which may conceivably have had a now-lost sequel dramatizing the same events as Shakespeare's play. The most important dramatic precedent for *Richard II*, however, is Christopher Marlowe's *Edward II* (*c.* 1592), structurally similar in its depiction of an at once tyrannous and ineffectual English king who, achieving tragic pathos in defeat, is deposed, imprisoned, and murdered.

 CHARACTER LIST

King Richard II
The **Queen** *his wife*
John of Gaunt, Duke of Lancaster
  Richard's uncle

Harry **Bolingbroke**,
  Duke of Hereford, John
  of Gaunt's son, later
  King Henry IV

Duchess of Gloucester
  widow of Gaunt's and
  York's brother
Duke of **York** *King*
  Richard's uncle
Duchess of York
Duke of **Aumerle** *their son*
Thomas **Mowbray**,
  Duke of Norfolk

Green ⎤
Bagot ⎱ *followers of*
Bushy ⎦ *King Richard*

Percy, Earl of
  Northumberland ⎤ *of Boling-*
Harry Percy, his son ⎱ *broke's*
Lord **Ross** ⎦ *party*
Lord **Willoughby**

Earl **of Salisbury** ⎤ *of King*
Bishop of Carlisle ⎱ *Richard's*
Sir Stephen **Scrope** ⎦ *party*

Lord **Berkeley**
Lord **Fitzwalter**
Duke of **Surrey**
Abbot of **Westminster**
Sir Piers **Exton**
Lord Marshal
Heralds
Captain of the Welsh army
Ladies attending the Queen
Gardener
Gardener's **Men**
Exton's **Men**
Keeper of the prison at Pomfret
Groom of King Richard's stable
Lords, soldiers, attendants

▤ SYNOPSIS

1.1 Before King Richard II, Bolingbroke, the Duke of Hereford, accuses Thomas Mowbray, the Duke of Norfolk, of killing the Duke of Gloucester, which he denies: the two challenge one another, and Richard, unable to command them to peace, concedes that they must fight a judicial combat.

1.2 Gloucester's widow rebukes her brother John of Gaunt, the Duke of Lancaster, for tamely accepting her husband's murder, praying that his son Bolingbroke may kill Mowbray, and bidding what she fears will be a last farewell.

1.3 After formal preliminaries, the judicial combat is stopped by Richard, who briefly consults his nobles before decreeing that both would-be combatants must be banished, Bolingbroke for ten years and Mowbray forever. After Mowbray's departure, however, the King shortens Bolingbroke's sentence to six years in exile, though Gaunt laments that he will certainly be dead before his son returns. Bolingbroke refuses Gaunt's attempts to console him.

1.4 Lord Aumerle brings Richard a mocking account of Bolingbroke's tearful departure: the King speaks scornfully of Bolingbroke's cultivation of popular opinion. One of his favourites, Green, urges Richard to put down a rebellion in Ireland, to which the King agrees. Another, Bushy, brings news that Gaunt is sick, and they leave to visit him, Richard hoping

Gaunt will soon die so that his confiscated possessions may fund their Irish expedition.

2.1 With his brother the Duke of York, the dying Gaunt laments the King's extravagance and the fallen state of the country. When the King arrives with his followers Gaunt rebukes him with this and with the death of Gloucester before being carried off. Northumberland brings the news of Gaunt's death, upon which Richard, despite York's protests on behalf of Gaunt's heir Bolingbroke, seizes his entire estate. Left with Willoughby and Ross, Northumberland laments Richard's degeneracy, and announces that Bolingbroke is only awaiting Richard's departure for Ireland to land in the north with an army: all three hasten to join him.

2.2 The Queen is dismayed to hear of Bolingbroke's landing and of the nobles who have sided with him, as is York, regent in Richard's absence, whose loyalties are divided between Richard and Bolingbroke and who is further distressed by news of the Duchess of Gloucester's death. The King's favourites disperse to seek safety.

2.3 Near Berkeley Castle, Bolingbroke and Northumberland are joined by Northumberland's son Harry Percy, who brings news that Worcester has joined their cause, and by Ross and Willoughby. York accuses Bolingbroke of treasonously defying his sentence of banishment, but admits he has not sufficient force to arrest him: mollified by Bolingbroke's claim that he seeks only the due inheritance of his father's estate and title and to rid the court of parasites, he allows Bolingbroke's party to enter the castle.

2.4 To the dismay of Salisbury, the King's Welsh forces disperse, convinced Richard is dead.

3.1 Bolingbroke sends Bushy and Green to execution for denying him his inheritance and misleading the King.

3.2 Richard, back from Ireland, greets his native soil, urging it to repel Bolingbroke. Dismayed by Salisbury's news, he is rallied by Aumerle, but when Scrope brings word that Wiltshire, Bushy, and Green are all dead Richard sits on the ground and laments the mortality of kings. The Bishop of Carlisle urges him to fight, and Aumerle reminds him that York still has an army, but when Scrope reveals that York too has joined with Bolingbroke Richard despairs.

3.3 Bolingbroke and his supporters are outside Flint Castle: Richard appears on the walls, and Northumberland assures him that Bolingbroke wants only Gaunt's title and lands. Richard agrees to this demand, but in his lament at being forced to concede admits that he is utterly powerless and can himself ask only for a grave. Descending, he meets Bolingbroke, whose kneeling does not convince Richard of his fealty, and who at Richard's prompting agrees that they should leave for London.

3.4 The Queen learns that Richard's deposition is inevitable when she overhears a conversation between her gardeners.

4.1 In Parliament, Bolingbroke questions Bagot about the murder of Gloucester: Bagot accuses Aumerle, who denies the charge and challenges him. Fitzwalter and Harry Percy take Bagot's part, Surrey Aumerle's: Bolingbroke hopes to settle these arguments by recalling and trying Mowbray, but learns he has died. York arrives and announces that Richard has yielded his royal title to Bolingbroke. Bolingbroke is about to ascend the throne when the Bishop of Carlisle warns him that this usurpation can only lead to civil war: Northumberland arrests the Bishop for treason. Bolingbroke summons Richard so that he may abdicate in public: Richard does so, but in a performance that is both mocking and intended to excite pity, and he refuses to recite a list of the crimes which have justified his deposition. He accuses the assembled lords of treason and demands a mirror which, studying his reflection, he smashes, saying he has given away even his identity. After Bolingbroke sends Richard to the Tower and leaves, giving orders for his own coronation, Carlisle, the Abbot of Westminster, and Aumerle conspire together against him.

5.1 The Queen meets Richard on his way to the Tower: he bids her fly to France. Northumberland brings word that Richard is instead to be sent to Pomfret: Richard prophesies that in time Northumberland will turn against Bolingbroke. Richard and the Queen part.

5.2 York tells his Duchess of Bolingbroke's eager reception from the London crowds and their jeering at Richard. York finds that his son Aumerle is carrying a letter which reveals that he has plotted to assassinate Bolingbroke: despite his wife's pleas he hurries to betray this conspiracy to Bolingbroke, pursued by Aumerle and the Duchess.

5.3 Bolingbroke, now crowned as King Henry, longs for news of his dissolute son Harry. Aumerle arrives and, insisting on a private conference with the King, implores pardon. York arrives to warn of his son's treason, followed by his wife, who kneels with Aumerle to implore mercy: York in turn kneels to implore Bolingbroke not to spare his treacherous son, but Bolingbroke pardons Aumerle.

5.4 Sir Piers Exton is sure Bolingbroke wants him to kill Richard, and leaves for Pomfret.

5.5 Alone in his cell, Richard reflects on his past follies. A former groom has obtained permission to visit him, and tells how Bolingbroke rode Richard's favourite horse at his coronation. A keeper dismisses the groom: he has brought Richard's food but for once will not taste it before Richard eats. Exton arrives to kill Richard: Richard kills two of his helpers before dying, cursing Exton for killing a true king. Exton, preparing to carry the body to Bolingbroke, already regrets his deed.

5.6 King Henry hears of the defeat of various rebels against him, and pardons the Bishop of Carlisle. When Exton brings Richard's body he banishes him, vowing a pilgrimage to the Holy Land to expiate the crime of Richard's murder.

 ARTISTIC FEATURES

The play is remarkable among the histories for the carefully planned symmetry of its structure (by which, in effect, Richard and Bolingbroke exchange places) and for the formality, rhetorical and ceremonial, by which it evokes a lost medieval world. Many of its set-piece speeches, much anthologized, have become classics in their own right, most famously Gaunt's 'This royal throne of kings, this sceptred isle...' (2.1.40–68), and Richard's 'Let's talk of graves, of worms and epitaphs...' (3.2.141–73).

CRITICAL HISTORY

The play was little valued by Enlightenment critics, who found it merely laboured and archaic, but the Romantics, particularly Samuel Taylor Coleridge, were more in sympathy with its depiction of the eloquently helpless Richard. It appealed even more strongly to their 19th-century successors among the nostalgic Pre-Raphaelite Brotherhood and the aesthetic movement, such as Walter Pater, and in a famous essay ('At Stratford upon Avon', 1901) W. B. Yeats wrote of his conviction that as a true poet Shakespeare of course preferred Richard II to the merely efficient Henry V. Modern criticism has explored the many analogies the play draws between royal power and the theatre, as its self-dramatizing King upstages his usurper, and has analysed the sacramental and ultimately sacrificial notion of kingship Richard espouses, often in relation to the late medieval doctrine of 'the king's two bodies'. Many commentators have also found in the play the first movement of a pattern of fall and redemption played out across the whole of Shakespeare's second tetralogy of histories. Recently critics have paid greater attention to the role of Queen Isabella, especially in relation to gender and girlhood. A wider turn towards the study of the history of the emotions has also resulted in work on the play's representation of sympathy and grief.

STAGE HISTORY

Richard II remained current after its notorious revival at the request of Essex in 1601 (the actor Augustine Phillips's description of it under interrogation as 'an old play' thereafter may have been disingenuous): it was reportedly performed on board Captain Keeling's ship the *Dragon* in 1607 and at the Globe as late as 1631. Though archaic by the later 17th century, it was still controversial: when it was next revived, in Nahum Tate's adaptation (1680), it was banned by the Crown after only two performances. Tate's attempt to avoid this prohibition by giving all the characters Italian names and retitling the play *The Sicilian Usurper* failed: he was especially chagrined by the ban, as his adaptation had been designed to turn Bolingbroke into a caricature of Charles II's populist political enemies and to make Richard a blameless martyr. The play was again rewritten in 1719, this time by Lewis Theobald, who tried to make it fit contemporary tastes in pathos by supplying a love plot between Aumerle and Northumberland's daughter (both of whom die) and by developing the relationship between Richard and his Queen, who witnesses her husband's murder and remains onstage to speak an epilogue. This version at least avoided a ban, but soon disappeared from the repertory. Shakespeare's original was revived at Covent Garden in 1738, but after that had to wait until the 19th century before achieving anything like popularity. Edmund Kean played Richard in 1815 (in a text adapted by Richard Wroughton), and the role was occasionally taken by W. C. Macready, but the most successful production for many years was Charles Kean's in 1857, staged with much medieval pomp which included an onstage presentation of Bolingbroke's procession into London with Richard in his wake, complete with large crowds of extras and real horses. After that, though William Poel produced an experimental revival in 1899 (with Harley Granville-Barker as Richard) and the play was taken up by Frank Benson and Herbert Beerbohm Tree in the years preceding the First World War, the play had to wait until the 1920s to achieve real prominence. George Hayes played Richard at the Old Vic in 1924 (and again at Stratford thereafter), but the performance that really established the play was that of John Gielgud, first at the Old Vic in 1929–30 (joined by Ralph Richardson as Bolingbroke), then in the West End in 1937 (with Michael Redgrave), and subsequently on international tours and on radio. The role was widely regarded as one of Gielgud's finest, and his lyrical delivery of the great speeches, preserved on sound recordings, has influenced all the many Richards who have followed since the Second World War, among them Alec Guinness, Michael Redgrave, Ian McKellen, Alan Howard, and, alternating the roles of Richard and Bolingbroke in John Barton's celebrated RSC production of 1973, Richard Pasco and Ian Richardson. The play was also much revived, often with considerable supplementary spectacle, in post-war festivals in Italy, France, and Germany, including Jean Vilar's performance in the title role for the inaugural production of the Avignon Festival (1947). Two notable revivals since have further extended the play's possibilities. Deborah Warner directed Fiona Shaw in the title role at the National Theatre in 1995, claiming this showy role for actresses (and paving the way for Adjoa Andoh and Lynette Linton's all-female, all-black production at the Sam Wanamaker Playhouse in 2019), while Stephen Pimlott made a rare departure from the play's pageantry-dominated performance tradition by directing it in modern dress, with hints of both Brecht and Beckett, for the RSC in 2000, with Samuel West as Richard. This production was echoed both by Trevor Nunn's modern-dress production at the Old Vic (with Kevin Spacey as Richard) and by Joel Hill-Gibbins's stripped-back, eight-person production at the Almeida (2018), in which Simon Russell Beale was an unusually older (and consequently Lear-like) Richard. Thanks to its digital relay to cinemas worldwide, however, the most-seen *Richard II* of the early 21st century was Gregory Doran's more convention-ally medieval RSC spectacle of 2013, starring a conspicuously bewigged, effete David Tennant.

 ON THE SCREEN

The post-war popularity of the play was reflected by television versions screened by the BBC in 1950 and in the USA in 1954, but it was more sub-stantially treated as two parts of the BBC series *An Age of Kings* (1960). A later BBC production (1970) starred Ian McKellen and Timothy West, and the BBC transmitted the play again in 1978, this time with Derek Jacobi as King Richard and his great predecessor in the role, John Gielgud, as Gaunt. Deborah Warner's impressive National Theatre production was videotaped for television in 1996. More recently, Ben Whishaw took the title role in the opening chapter of the BBC's grand retelling of the Second Tetralogy, *The Hollow Crown* (2012).

Richard III

The action of *Richard III* directly follows that of *Richard Duke of York* (*3 Henry VI*), written in 1591, and so may date from later that year to the temporary closure of the London theatres in June 1592. However, if the

Henry VI plays were not composed in historical order, as some scholars believe, and Shakespeare wrote *1 Henry VI* after *The First Part of the Contention* (*2 Henry VI*) and *Richard Duke of York* but before *Richard III*, the latter was probably written after June 1592. *Titus Andronicus*, which shares features of neo-Senecan tragedy with *Richard III* and came before it, may also have been written after the *Henry VI* plays for performance outside London, which makes a date of 1592–3 for *Richard III* more likely. This time frame would explain the absence of any documentary evidence referring to the play before the plague closed the theatres, a silence that seems telling in view of its later manifest popularity. While it has a large number of roles, Elizabethan doubling practices allow it to be performed with a smaller cast than that required by the earlier *Henry VI* plays. A date of 1592–3 also supports the theory that publication of the anonymous *True Tragedy of Richard the Third* (1594)—a very different dramatization of events from Richard's reign—was intended to capitalize on the success of Shakespeare's play, which was subsequently listed in Francis Meres's *Palladis Tamia* (1598).

 TEXT

The play first appeared in a quarto edition in 1598 (known as Q1), after being entered in the Stationers' Register on 20 October. This was followed by five more editions derived successively from Q1, which most scholars believe was reconstructed from memory by players who originally performed it (probably the Chamberlain's Men, Shakespeare's company, when they went on provincial tour in summer 1597 but left their promptbook in London). Another text of the play was published in the 1623 First Folio: this version is longer than Q1 and requires a larger cast and more onstage equipment. It is based on a scribal copy of Shakespeare's manuscript draft, but relies for certain details on one or more of the previously printed quarto texts. It also lacks a major passage found only in Q1, the so-called 'clock dialogue' (4.2.102–18). Thus, although the Folio version of the play is earlier overall and more rhetorically elaborate than the version preserved by Q1, it also contains elements which derive from Q1, as well as later agencies: for example, the Folio copy was censored to eliminate certain religious oaths, as required by the Act to Restrain the Abuses of Players (1606), which sought to banish profanity from the stage. Some scholars have speculated that the Folio text may be Shakespeare's revision of the play first represented by Q1, but the opposite is more likely—that the play underlying Q1 probably represents a streamlined adaptation of the Folio text (the longest play in the canon other than *Hamlet*), better accommodated to actual conditions of stage performance.

SOURCES

Richard III synthesizes a diverse range of facts and contexts from historical, literary, and dramatic sources. The main documentary events derive from Edward Halle's *Union of the Two Noble and Illustrious Families of Lancaster and York* (1548), and the compilation edited by Raphael Holinshed, *Chronicles of England, Scotland, and Ireland* (2nd ed. 1587). In Halle, for example, Shakespeare found accounts of Richard's nightmare before Bosworth and the suggestion for his famous call for a horse (5.7.7). In Holinshed he read about the bleeding of Henry's corpse (1.2.55–6) and Richard's ominous pairing of 'Rougemont' and 'Richmond' (4.2.105–9). Both these chronicles incorporate an earlier source, Sir Thomas More's *History of King Richard III*, which begins with Edward IV's death and ends with Buckingham's flight. More's account is biased against Richard to the point of making him mythically evil, but it also highlights his witty theatricalizing irony—traits that clearly attracted Shakespeare's interest. Richard's jaunty sangfroid and conspiratorial self-disclosure are also indebted to the dramatic traditions of the morality play Vice, and his Elizabethan heir, the Machiavel, who villainously parodies the pragmatic political philosophy of Niccolò Machiavelli. The play was also influenced by the rhetorical conventions of Senecan tragedy, particularly Lycus' wooing of Megara in *Hercules Furens* for Richard's seduction of Lady Anne in 1.2, and *Troades* for the lamenting women in 4.4. Clarence's dream draws on Spenser's *The Faerie Queene* (printed 1590), Kyd's *The Spanish Tragedy*, and *The Mirror for Magistrates* (1559 and later editions), the last a well-known series of politically moralizing tragedies of princes and other public figures. In 2018, verbal parallels detected through the use of anti-plagiarism software suggested that Shakespeare had also read George North's 1576 essay 'A Brief Discourse of Rebellion'.

CHARACTER LIST

King Edward IV
Duchess of York *his mother*
Prince Edward ⎤
Richard, the young ⎟ *his sons*
  Duke of York ⎦

George, Duke of ⎤
  Clarence ⎟
Richard, Duke of ⎟ *his brothers*
  Gloucester, later ⎟
  King Richard ⎦

Clarence's **Son**
Clarence's **Daughter**
Queen Elizabeth *King*
   Edward's wife
Anthony Woodville, Earl **Rivers**
   her brother

Marquis of **Dorset** ⎤
Lord **Gray** ⎦ *her sons*

Sir Thomas **Vaughan**
Ghost of King Henry IV
Queen Margaret *his widow*
Ghost of Prince Edward *his son*
Lady Anne *Prince Edward's widow*
William, **Lord Hastings**,
   Lord Chamberlain
Lord **Stanley**, Earl of Derby *his friend*
Henry Earl of Richmond, later **King**
   Henry VII *Stanley's son-in-law*

Earl of **Oxford** ⎤
Sir James **Blunt** | *Richmond's*
Sir Walter **Herbert** ⎦ *followers*

Duke of ⎤
   Buckingham | *Richard*
Duke of **Norfolk** | *Gloucester's*
Sir Richard **Ratcliffe** | *followers*
Sir William **Catesby** |
Sir James **Tyrrel** ⎦

A **Page**
Cardinal
Bishop of **Ely**
John, a **Priest**
Christopher *a priest*
Sir Robert **Brackenbury**,
   Lieutenant of the Tower
   of London
Lord **Mayor** of London
A **Scrivener**
Hastings, a **Pursuivant**
Sheriff
Aldermen and citizens
Attendants, two bishops,
   messengers, soldiers

☰ SYNOPSIS

1.1 Richard, Duke of Gloucester, spurns the new opportunities for peace and leisure made possible by the triumph of his brother Edward IV and the House of York. Secretly he plots the downfall of those who stand between him and the throne. He turns Edward against his other elder brother George, Duke of Clarence, by libelling him with the suspicion of plotting to kill Edward, who imprisons him in the Tower. Richard meets Clarence on his way there, feigning sympathy.

1.2 Richard interrupts Lady Anne's mourning over the coffin of her father-in-law Henry VI, who was killed by Richard. Richard woos her, saying he killed Henry and her husband, Prince Edward, for the sake of her beauty, and that she must now charitably believe his motives were sincere. At first Anne scorns his claims, but ultimately, though still reluctantly, she yields.

1.3 Queen Elizabeth and her sons Dorset and Grey worry about Edward IV's illness and the prospect of Gloucester becoming protector over Prince

Edward. Gloucester questions her family's loyalty to the Yorkists. Queen Margaret curses everyone with predictions of misfortune and death. Richard sends two murderers to dispatch Clarence.

1.4 Clarence recounts a nightmare in which he drowned after being inadvertently pushed overboard by Gloucester. He was then judged in the underworld for temporarily switching loyalties to the Lancastrians. After sleeping, he is awakened by the murderers, whom he tries but fails to talk out of killing him. The Second Murderer flees away remorsefully.

2.1 Edward reconciles the Queen and her family with the other lords, but the news of Clarence's death shatters this peace and grieves the King, who thought Clarence's death warrant had been cancelled.

2.2 The Duchess of York tries to conceal her grief for Clarence's death from his two children. Queen Elizabeth laments the death of Edward and fears for her children's safety. The lords prepare to bring Prince Edward from Ludlow to London.

2.3 Citizens fear the outbreak of factionalism while the Prince is still a child.

2.4 On hearing of Rivers's and Grey's imprisonment, Queen Elizabeth takes sanctuary with her young son the Duke of York, accompanied by the Duchess of York.

3.1 Prince Edward is welcomed to London by the lords and Mayor but misses his absent mother and brother. Against his better judgement, the Cardinal is persuaded to fetch the Duke of York out of sanctuary. The young princes reluctantly submit to Gloucester's advice to lodge temporarily in the Tower. Catesby is sent to find out Hastings's opinion about the idea of Gloucester becoming king. Gloucester promises Buckingham the earldom of Hereford for his support after he is crowned.

3.2 Lord Stanley's messenger reports to Hastings his master's dreams of Gloucester's malevolence, but Hastings dismisses his fears. Catesby reports the execution of Hastings's enemies Rivers, Grey, and Vaughan that day at Pomfret, but Hastings rejects his suggestion that Gloucester should become king. Stanley and Buckingham travel with Hastings to London.

3.3 Ratcliffe escorts Rivers, Grey, and Vaughan to execution.

3.4 The council gathers to plan the coronation. Richard accuses Hastings of keeping Mrs Shore who has bewitched his arm, and demands his execution.

3.5 Gloucester and Buckingham elaborate Hastings's alleged conspiracies to the Mayor to justify their summary execution of him to the populace.

Buckingham rumours Edward's uncontrollable lust and his children's bastardy.

3.6 A scrivener observes that the indictment for Hastings's death was commissioned hours before he was accused of any crime, but nobody dares to speak openly about such state ruses.

3.7 The citizens refuse to believe Buckingham's stories about the princes' illegitimacy. The Mayor and citizens watch Gloucester's show of religious devotion with two bishops. Buckingham urges him to accept their faint request to become king, to which Richard consents after making a pretence of refusing.

4.1 Elizabeth is denied access to her sons in the Tower. Distressed at Lord Stanley's news of Richard's impending coronation, she sends Dorset overseas to join Richmond, while Lady Anne laments her misery as Richard's wife and future Queen.

4.2 Richard is enthroned. Buckingham hesitates to consent to killing the young princes and loses Richard's confidence. When he later agrees, claiming the earldom of Hereford as he was promised, Richard rebuffs him. Buckingham flees to Wales. Richard hires James Tyrrell to kill the princes. Tyrrell recounts the murderers' abhorrence of their deed, and reports the princes' deaths. Richard reveals Anne's death, Buckingham's revolt, and Ely's military alliance with Richmond. Rumours of Richmond's plans to marry Elizabeth of York spur Richard to woo her for himself.

4.4 The surviving women, led by Margaret, agonize their griefs and curse Richard. He asks the Queen to woo Princess Elizabeth on his behalf. She resists his threats and cajoling, ambiguously agreeing to write to him with her decision, which he interprets as submission. News arrives of Richmond's imminent invasion. Richard holds Stanley's son for assurance of his loyalty. Further reports of growing support for Richmond, Buckingham's capture, and Richmond's arrival at Milford Haven.

4.5 Stanley pledges to support Richmond and relates the Queen's consent to her daughter's marriage to him.

5.1 Buckingham is led to execution, recalling how Margaret's curse has come true.

5.2 Richmond and his army march towards Leicester.

5.3 Richard pitches his tent in Bosworth field and prepares for battle next day.

5.4 Richmond encamps himself, sends word to Stanley, and plans for battle.

5.5 Richard retires and sleeps. Stanley promises Richmond aid covertly, to safeguard his son. Richmond prays and sleeps. The ghosts of Richard's victims—Prince Edward, Henry VI, Clarence, Rivers, Grey and Vaughan, Hastings, the two princes, Lady Anne, Buckingham—curse him in his sleep, while wishing Richmond victory. Richard starts awake, fearful and despairing; Richmond rises refreshed, and cheers his soldiers in an oration.

5.6 Richard plans his battle strategy, and rallies his army in an oration.

5.7 During the battle, Richard's horse is killed but he continues fighting.

5.8 Richmond defeats him in single combat. Stanley presents Richard's crown to Richmond, who proclaims a general pardon and looks forward to ending the country's civil wars by marrying Elizabeth and uniting the houses of Lancaster and York.

 ARTISTIC FEATURES

Although the play is dominated by Richard's Marlovian vigour and his gleeful manipulation of dramatic irony, it is notable, too, for the lyricism and formal rhetoric which characterize his victims, from Clarence's dream through the rival laments of the bereaved women.

CRITICAL HISTORY

A number of allusions confirm the play's impact on Shakespeare's contemporaries and near-contemporaries (notably John Milton), and even during the long ascendancy of Colley Cibber's stage adaptation Shakespeare's depiction of Richard was regularly cited as a startling example of the range and depth of his characterization. Dr Johnson, however, felt that widespread praise for the play was undeserved: 'some parts are trifling, others shocking, and some improbable.' Along with Iago, though, Richard became a favourite with Romantic writers interested in creating their own Gothic, Satanic villains. Modern studies of the play have tended to divide between those which approach it as a self-contained tragedy focused on the titular character and those which see it as the final instalment of the larger historical drama played out across the *Henry VI* plays. One area of interest from the first perspective is the play's structural and rhetorical affinities with Greek and neo-Senecan tragedy, with Margaret, Elizabeth, and the Bosworth ghosts ritually invoking forces of nemesis and revenge, and Richmond acting as an agent of divine retribution. Feminist critics have focused on the women's undeluded opposition to Richard—their collective agency, especially in 4.4, arguably transcending their individual moral positions. Psychoanalytic theory has focused on the relationship between Richard's physical deformities and his deviant behaviour, initially disclosed in his two major soliloquies in *Richard Duke of York* (3.2, 5.6). Sigmund Freud argued that Richard exemplified the pathology of 'exceptional' persons who flaunt their physical limitations to excuse their antisocial desires, which serve as compensation: 'Nature has done me a grievous wrong in denying me the beauty of form which wins human love. Life owes me reparation for this, and I will see that I get it. I have a right to be an exception, to disregard the scruples by which others let themselves be held back. I may do wrong myself, since wrong has been done to me.' Richard's inner motives have also been discussed in terms of various sexual pathologies. Key scenes are his seduction of Lady Anne in 1.2 and proxy wooing of Elizabeth in 4.4. Historical scholarship has investigated Richard's Machiavellian dynamics of power, the dramatic origins of his theatrical flamboyance in the morality play Vice, and the play's encoding of contemporary political debate over royal authority. The last of these crosses over to the second major critical perspective introduced by German Romantic critics such as A. W. Schlegel, who interpreted *Richard III* as an evolutionary political epic stretching back through the preceding chronicle plays. In 1944 E. M. W. Tillyard's *Shakespeare's History Plays* situated *Richard III* as the culmination of a national *commedia*: Richard is God's final scourge for the wrongful deposition of Richard II, which eventually led to the Wars of the Roses. Richmond's victory restores national order and redeems the country's political transgression. Since then, critics have moved away from Tillyard's providential reading, observing that the chronicles emphasize the practical benefits brought by Richmond's reconciliation of the warring houses of Lancaster and York as Henry VII. They also challenge Tillyard by highlighting elements of non-elite and popular culture (e.g. the citizens) that problematize claims for any single official ideology or traditional moral design.

STAGE HISTORY

The play's initial popularity is attested by the number of early editions and the frequency of contemporary allusions and anecdotes, the most famous of which—in which Shakespeare pre-empts Richard Burbage at an assignation made by an eager female spectator of the play—is found in John Manningham's diary, 1602. Beyond this apocryphal tale—an allegory about the rivalry between playwright and actor as to which is responsible for the role's seductive power—actual performance details from this period are rare. If the play dates from 1591–2, it was probably written for Lord Strange's Men, but if from 1592–3, then for Pembroke's Men (as the preceding reference to Burbage, their leading actor, suggests). In 1594 the play passed into the hands of the Chamberlain's Men, and then of their successors the

King's Men, with Eliard Swanston succeeding Burbage after 1624, including a performance at court on 16 November 1633. The play was revived after the Restoration without conspicuous success until Colley Cibber's melodramatic adaptation in 1700, only half of whose lines were by Shakespeare. Cibber cut Edward IV, Clarence, Margaret, and Hastings, but the simplified historical narrative appealed to actors and audiences, as David Garrick's performances from 1741 onwards confirmed. Edmund Kean's intelligently expressive and emotionally intense interpretation was praised by Byron in 1814. W. C. Macready tried briefly to revive Shakespeare's play in 1821, but Cibber continued to dominate until Henry Irving's productions in 1877 and 1896–7. Yet these also severely cut and rearranged the text. Even after the staging of Shakespeare's original became commonplace, bits of Cibber ('Off with his head—so much for Buckingham') continued to be interpolated into performances of *Richard III*, including John Barrymore's popular appearances in America in the 1920s, and Sir Laurence Olivier's deliberately stagey film version. In Germany and Austria, however, strong interest in Shakespeare's histories stimulated integral and innovative performances from the mid-19th century, most notably by the Polish actor Bogumil Dawison at Dresden in the 1850s and 1860s. F. R. Benson's *Richard III* appeared nearly every other season at Stratford-upon-Avon between 1894 and 1915, and a twelve-minute silent film (1911) still conveys Benson's ruthless exuberance. Laurence Olivier followed Benson's example by transferring his celebrated 1944 Old Vic performance to the screen in 1955. As with Olivier's other films, this expanded audiences for Shakespeare enormously, while also creating a permanently visible interpretation later actors have sometimes found oppressive. Ian Holm successfully avoided comparisons with Olivier's 'limping panther' in Peter Hall and John Barton's three-part *Wars of the Roses* for the RSC in 1963–4, by making Richard's deformities more psychological than physical: reviewers described him as 'manic-depressive', 'schizophrenic', and 'psychopathic', while Dame Peggy Ashcroft completed her triumphal performance as Margaret, now haggard and chilling. In 1984 the RSC's Antony Sher recreated Richard as a 'bottled spider': a pair of crutches and a medieval gown with hanging sleeves gave the impression of six legs, as Sher scuttled rapidly about. Michael Bogdanov and Michael Pennington reverted to Barton's condensed cycle format for their eclectic and politicized production in 1986–9 for the English Shakespeare Company, in which a strikingly bald and northern-accented Andrew Jarvis, initially in 1930s dress, finally appeared in a pinstriped suit before a computer screen. This production influenced Richard Eyre's 1990 National Theatre revival, in which Ian McKellen caricatured Richard as a fascist dictator in a 1930s Britain; his performance became more flexible in

Richard Loncraine's visually stylish 1996 film version. Al Pacino's 1996 film-documentary *Looking for Richard* conveys a credibly updated interpretation freed from Olivier's jokester-villainy, as does Ron Cook's largely unironic performance in Jane Howell's BBC television production, first broadcast in 1983. In the United States and Canada, *Richard III* has remained very popular on stage. The Oregon Shakespeare Festival, to take just one example, has mounted successful productions every decade since the 1950s. Tyrone Guthrie staged *Richard III* with Alec Guinness to open the Ontario Stratford Festival in 1953, while Brian Bedford gleefully indulged audiences there in Robin Phillips's memorable 1977 production. Kevin Spacey chose the role for his farewell to the Old Vic in 2011. *Richard III*, as a depiction of a paradigmatic tyrant, has been the most consistently popular of Shakespeare's histories outside the Anglophone world, with notable 21st-century Richards including Lars Eidinger (in Thomas Ostermeier's production for the Schaubühne in Berlin, 2015–) and Hans Kesting (in Ivo van Hove's adaptation *Kings of War*, Toneelgroep Amsterdam, 2015–).

ON THE SCREEN

Two very different films were produced early in the 20th century, F. R. Benson's (1911) recording his stage production, while Frederick B. Warde acted the role in a highly spectacular American cinematic adaptation (1912) which included the arrival of a ship bringing the forces under the Earl of Richmond.

No significant sound version appeared until in 1955 Laurence Olivier directed his third Shakespeare film, taking the role of Richard himself. Many of his established team worked with him, notably William Walton, whose music strikes a note of solemnity, reminding the viewer (as does an opening title) that Richard's ascent to the throne and reign are a mere episode in the history of the English Crown. Filmed in colour, the jaunty manipulations of Olivier's Richard amid the moral paralysis of the court have been seen as a counterpoise to both the triumph of the English in his *Henry V* (1944) and the dark, nostalgic brooding of *Hamlet* (1948). As part of its funding demanded, the film was broadcast on American television at the time of its release.

Olivier's film has overshadowed most of its successors: though Jane Howell's *Richard III* for BBC TV (1983) drew critical acclaim—as had her productions of the *Henry VI* plays—for finding inventive ways to use the medium, many found Ron Cook disappointingly lacking in camp as Richard. Richard Loncraine's *Richard III* (1996) imitates many of Olivier's procedures, notably an opening which introduces the cast during Edward's coronation festivities, though Loncraine preceded this with a violent episode owing more to the opening sequences of James Bond films. Ian McKellen's characterization has as much of Oswald Mosley in it as of Shakespeare's 'crookback' King, and the film is shot through with heavy irony. Memorably inventive is the use of familiar English locations to create a composite political world, ranging from power stations and derelict hotels to the Long Gallery of the Brighton Pavilion. It drew a divided critical reception, generally judged as clever rather than profound.

Romeo and Juliet

Shakespeare composed his definitive version of what is often called 'the greatest love story ever told' during the lyrical period of his career which also produced *Richard II* and *A Midsummer Night's Dream*, probably in the same year as these two plays, 1595. The play first appeared in print in 1597, in an unlicensed quarto edition apparently produced from a reported text assembled by actors who had played Romeo and Paris. The title page proclaims that *Romeo and Juliet* has 'been often (with great applause) played publicly, by the Right Honourable Lord Hunsdon his servants': since Shakespeare's company was renamed the Lord Chamberlain's Men as of 17 March 1597, this edition must have gone to press before then. Furthermore, the work of producing it was interrupted by the seizure of its original printer's presses, an event which took place between 9 February and 27 March 1597, by which time the first four sheets had already been printed. Allowing time for the play's reportedly numerous performances and the compilation from memory of the manuscript, *Romeo and Juliet* could not very well have been written before late 1596. Its influence on *A Midsummer Night's Dream*, particularly visible in the changes Shakespeare made to his source for 'Pyramus and Thisbe', would place it just before that play. In any event the play cannot be earlier than 1593, since it shows the influence of English translations of two poems by Du Bartas only published in that year (in John Eliot's *Ortho-Epia Gallica*). The dating of *Romeo and Juliet* to 1595 is perhaps confirmed by the Nurse's remark that "'Tis since the earthquake now eleven years' (1.3.25), which may be a topical allusion to the earthquake which shook England in 1584.

 TEXT

A second quarto, which calls the play *The Most Excellent and Lamentable Tragedy of Romeo and Juliet*, appeared in 1599, fuller and more reliable than the first: its variations in speech-prefixes, permissive stage directions, and accidental preservations of deleted false starts show that it was produced from Shakespeare's rough draft of the play, which its compositors, unfortunately, had trouble deciphering, sometimes resorting to the illicit first quarto for guidance. This edition was reprinted in 1609, 1623, and 1637, and a copy of the 1609 reprint served as the basis for the text published in the Folio in 1623, though some improvements to speech prefixes and stage directions suggest that this copy had been annotated by reference to a promptbook. Most recent editions of the play are based on the second quarto, but supplement it by reference both to the first quarto and to the Folio, particularly over details of staging.

SOURCES

Although it is undeniably more romantic to pretend that Shakespeare either made up the plot of *Romeo and Juliet* or transcribed it more or less directly from his own experience (as did the popular film *Shakespeare in Love*, 1998), the story of Verona's star-crossed couple had been popular throughout Europe for half a century before Shakespeare's dramatization. Tales of unfortunate aristocratic lovers proliferated in the Italian Renaissance: one early anticipation of the Romeo and Juliet story is that by Masuccio Salernitano, published in *Il novellino* (1474), but the first to use the names Romeo and Giulietta, and to set the tale in Verona against the backdrop of a feud between Montagues and Capulets, is Luigi da Porto's *Istoria novellamente ritrovata di due nobile amanti* (1535). This story was adapted by Bandello, whose version appeared in *Le novelle di Bandello* (1560): his novella was translated into English in William Painter's *Palace of Pleasure* (1566–7), and was the source of a French version by Pierre Boaisteau, published in François de Belleforest's *Histoires tragiques* (1559–82).

This French prose tale supplied the basis for Shakespeare's principal direct source, an English poem by Arthur Brooke, *The Tragical History of Romeus and Juliet* (1562), which Shakespeare had already used when composing an earlier play with the same setting, *The Two Gentlemen of Verona*. (Brooke's preface refers to a now-lost English play on the same subject, but there is no evidence to suggest that Shakespeare knew this dramatic precedent.) Shakespeare follows Brooke's poem quite closely, retaining the emphasis on fate which Brooke had imitated from Geoffrey Chaucer's *Troilus and Criseyde*, reusing some of Brooke's imagery, and denying the lovers the last interview in the tomb which they enjoy in most other versions of the story. Shakespeare, however, greatly develops some of the poem's minor characters—most spectacularly, Mercutio, the Nurse, and Tybalt—and fundamentally alters its perspective. Brooke's poem is mainly on the side of the lovers' parents, moralizing against 'dishonest desire' and disobedience: his Juliet, for example, is a 'wily wench' who takes pleasure in deceiving her mother into thinking she prefers Paris to Romeo, and the lovers' deaths are represented as righteous punishments for their own sins. As well as returning the story's principal sympathies to Romeo and Juliet, Shakespeare greatly compresses its action, to produce a fast-moving, tightly plotted play (punctuated by urgent references to the passage of time, and formally organized around the three successive interventions of the Prince at 1.1, 3.1, and 5.3) whose events take place over days rather than months. Within this controlled structure, Shakespeare produces some of his most exuberant poetry, for details of which he draws at times on other sources: these include Geoffrey Chaucer's *The Parliament of Fowls* for Mercutio's Queen Mab speech (1.4.53–94), a poem by Guillaume Du Bartas (1544–90) for the discussion of the nightingale and the lark in the 'aubade' scene (3.5.1–36), and Samuel Daniel's *Complaint of Rosamond* (1592) for Romeo's description of Juliet's apparently dead body in the tomb (5.3.92–6).

 CHARACTER LIST

Chorus
Romeo
Montague *his father*
Montague's Wife
Benvolio *Montague's*
   nephew
Abraham *Montague's*
   servingman
Balthasar *Romeo's*
   man
Juliet
Capulet *her father*
Capulet's Wife
Tybalt *her nephew*

His **Page**
Petruccio
Capulet's Cousin
Juliet's **Nurse**

Peter
Samson   *servingmen of the*
Gregory   *Capulets*

Other **Servingmen**
Musicians
Escalus, Prince of Verona

Mercutio
County **Paris**   *his kinsmen*

Page to Paris

Friar Laurence
Friar John
An **Apothecary**
Chief Watchman

Other **Citizens of the Watch**
Masquers, guests, gentlewomen,
    followers of the Montague and
    Capulet factions

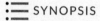 SYNOPSIS

Prologue: a Chorus outlines the story, requesting a patient hearing.

1.1 Servants of the Capulet family provoke a quarrel with their Montague counterparts, which, with the Capulet Tybalt's encouragement, develops into a full-scale brawl involving Capulet and Montague themselves, despite attempts by Benvolio, members of the Watch, and the wives of Capulet and Montague to restore order. The fighting is stilled by the arrival of the Prince, who threatens that if the feud breaks out once more Capulet and Montague will be executed. Left with Benvolio, Montague and his wife ask after their absent son Romeo, and employ Benvolio to investigate the cause of his solitary melancholy. Romeo reveals to Benvolio that he is suffering from unrequited love.

1.2 Capulet, bound to the peace, tells the Prince's kinsman Paris that if he can win his 13-year-old daughter Juliet's acceptance he may marry her. He invites Paris to a feast that night, and gives a list of the other intended guests to his servant Peter. Alone, Peter admits he cannot read, and when Romeo and Benvolio arrive he seeks their help. Learning of Capulet's feast, Benvolio hopes to cure Romeo's melancholy by taking him there and showing that his beloved Rosaline has no monopoly on beauty.

1.3 Capulet's wife, much interrupted by the digressive Nurse, tells Juliet of Paris' suit: they are called to the feast.

1.4 Romeo, Benvolio, and their friend Mercutio have masks and torches ready for their uninvited arrival at the Capulets' feast. Romeo has dreamed the occasion will be fatal to him, but Mercutio ridicules this notion, attributing dreams to the fairy Queen Mab.

1.5 During the dancing at the feast, Romeo is captivated by Juliet's beauty, renouncing his infatuation with Rosaline. Despite his mask he is recognized by Tybalt, whom Capulet has to restrain from challenging him. Romeo accosts Juliet and begs a kiss, subsequently learning her identity from the Nurse before he and his friends depart. Juliet similarly learns his.

2.0 The Chorus speaks of the mutual love of Romeo and Juliet, which they will pursue despite the dangers posed by their parents' enmity.

2.1 Returning from the feast, Romeo doubles back, concealing himself despite the mocking summons of Benvolio and Mercutio. Hidden, he sees

Juliet emerge at a window: when she sighs his name, wishing he were not a Montague, he reveals himself, and in the lyrical conversation which follows they exchange vows of love. Juliet promises to send by nine the following morning to Romeo, who is to arrange their marriage.

2.2 Friar Laurence is gathering medicinal herbs early the following morning when Romeo tells him of the night's events: at first chiding Romeo for so quickly abandoning his passion for Rosaline, he agrees to marry him to Juliet in the hope of ending the feud between Montagues and Capulets.

2.3 Benvolio and Mercutio at last meet Romeo, and Mercutio banters with him against love. The Nurse arrives with Peter, and after much mockery from Mercutio is able to speak privately with Romeo: Juliet is to come to Laurence's cell that afternoon, and Romeo will send a rope-ladder by which she may later admit him at her window to consummate their secret marriage.

2.4 The Nurse teases an impatient Juliet before passing on Romeo's message.

2.5 Friar Laurence warns Romeo against immoderate love before Juliet arrives to be married.

3.1 Benvolio and Mercutio are accosted by Tybalt, who wishes to challenge Romeo: when Romeo arrives, however, he refuses to be provoked to fight, to the disgust of Mercutio, who draws his own sword. As Romeo tries to part the combatants, Mercutio is mortally wounded by Tybalt: incensed, Romeo fights and kills Tybalt before fleeing, aghast at what he has done. The Montagues and Capulets gather, with the Prince, Mercutio's kinsman, who, learning what has happened from Benvolio, sentences Romeo to immediate banishment.

3.2 Juliet's eager anticipation of her wedding night is cut short by the Nurse, who brings the news of Tybalt's death and Romeo's banishment: moved by her grief, the Nurse promises to find Romeo and bring him despite everything.

3.3 Friar Laurence brings Romeo, hidden at his cell, the news of his sentence, to his inconsolable despair. The Nurse arrives, and has to prevent Romeo from stabbing himself: the Friar reproaches Romeo for his frenzy, telling him to go to Juliet as arranged but leave for Mantua before the setting of the Watch.

3.4 Capulet agrees with his wife and Paris that Juliet shall marry Paris the following Thursday.

3.5 Early the following morning Romeo reluctantly parts from Juliet, descending from her window. Her mother brings Juliet the news that, to dispel the sorrow they attribute to Tybalt's death, she is to marry Paris: Capulet arrives and, angry at Juliet's refusal, threatens to disown her unless she agrees to the match. After her parents' departure, the Nurse advises

Juliet to marry Paris. Juliet feigns to agree, but resolves that unless Friar Laurence can help her she will kill herself.

4.1 Paris is with Friar Laurence when Juliet arrives: after his departure, the Friar advises Juliet that she should pretend to agree to the marriage, but that on its eve she should take a drug which he will give her, which will make her seem dead for 24 hours. She will be laid in the Capulets' tomb, where Romeo, summoned from Mantua by letter, can await her waking before taking her back with him.

4.2 The Capulets and the Nurse are making preparations for Juliet's wedding to Paris, to which she, returning, pretends to consent. Capulet brings forward its date to the following day.

4.3 Left alone in her chamber that night, Juliet, despite her apprehension at the prospect of awakening in the tomb, takes the Friar's potion.

4.4 The Capulets' busy preparations on the wedding morning are laid aside when the Nurse finds Juliet apparently dead: in the midst of their grief Friar Laurence takes charge of funeral arrangements. Hired musicians, no longer needed, jest with Peter.

5.1 In Mantua Romeo has dreamed he died but was awakened by Juliet when his servant Balthasar brings the news that Juliet is dead: intending to return to Verona and kill himself, Romeo buys poison from a needy apothecary.

5.2 Friar Laurence learns that his colleague Friar John has been prevented by plague quarantine restrictions from delivering his explanatory letter to Romeo: he hurries towards the Capulets' tomb.

5.3 Paris is strewing flowers at the tomb and reciting an epitaph for Juliet when Romeo arrives, sending an apprehensive Balthasar away: Paris attempts to arrest Romeo and is killed in the fight that ensues, asking, as he dies, to be laid with Juliet. Romeo opens the tomb and brings Paris' body inside. He speaks to the apparently dead Juliet, bidding her a last farewell, drinks the poison, kisses her, and dies. Friar Laurence arrives as Juliet begins to awaken: frightened by the approach of the Watch, he attempts to persuade her to fly with him and enter a nunnery, but she will not leave. She finds that Romeo has taken poison, but there is none left for her: hearing the Watch approaching, she takes his dagger and stabs herself. The Watch, finding the bodies, summon the Prince, the Capulets, and the Montagues (though Lady Montague has just died, in grief at her son's exile) and arrest Balthasar and Friar Laurence, who are able to explain the whole story to the assembled families. The Prince regards the deaths of Romeo, Juliet, Paris, and Mercutio as the families' punishments for their feud and his own for failing to quell it. Montague and Capulet shake hands, promising to build statues of the dead lovers.

 ARTISTIC FEATURES

Romeo and Juliet is, among much else, Shakespeare's greatest dramatic contribution to the boom in love sonnets which swept literary London in the late 1580s and early 1590s. The play teems with sonnets including its Chorus speeches and, most famously, the first dialogue between Romeo and Juliet, 1.5.92–106. Mercutio aptly observes of the enamoured Romeo that 'Now is he for the numbers that Petrarch flowed in' (2.3.36–7), and the play's entire plot brilliantly reanimates the clichéd Petrarchan oxymoron whereby the adored mistress is referred to as a 'beloved enemy' (cf. 1.5.116–17, 137–40). Like a Petrarchan sonnet, too, the entire play changes in mood at a key turning point, resembling a romantic comedy during its ebullient early scenes but modulating decisively into tragedy with the death of Mercutio in 3.1.

CRITICAL HISTORY

By now the impact of *Romeo and Juliet* extends across most artistic media (particularly ballet, opera, and film) and across most of the world. It was sufficiently well thought of, in some circles at least, for an Oxford divine, Nicholas Richardson, to quote it in a sermon in 1620, though it was sometimes criticized over the next two centuries for an over-indulgence in punning and rhyming. Because of the citizen status of its protagonists and the generic blending of its construction—its hospitality to the Nurse's comic garrulity and Mercutio's bawdy wordplay as well as to Romeo's sense of fate and the Prince's moralizing—the play was less acceptable than the other tragedies to Neoclassical tastes during the Restoration, but it was decisively restored to critical favour thereafter. Although John Dryden reported a tradition that Shakespeare had once remarked that he had been obliged to kill Mercutio in the third act 'lest he would have been killed by him', Dr Johnson, who regarded *Romeo and Juliet* as one of Shakespeare's best plays, rejected this story, praising the death of Mercutio as an integral part of the play's structure. Romantic writers and artists across the English-speaking world and continental Europe, from Samuel Taylor Coleridge to Hector Berlioz, regarded the play as an unqualified presentation of an ideal love too good for the corrupt world. It was only later in the 19th century that some commentators began to express misgivings that the play was not sufficiently tragic, its conclusion produced too much by malign coincidence rather than character, and from the time of F. S. Boas onwards various attempts were made to prove the lovers as properly blameworthy as they are in Brooke's poem. Others, meanwhile, insisted that the play's main theme was really the feud rather than the relationship between the innocent

Romeo and Juliet. Since the later 20th century, critical writing about *Romeo and Juliet*, while still interested in the question of its genre, has concentrated more heavily on the play's notions of sexuality, on its account of Veronese society and family structure, and on its language.

STAGE HISTORY

Although the early quartos attest to the play's popularity in the theatres, no specific performances of *Romeo and Juliet* are recorded before the Restoration. When it reappeared in 1662, with Thomas Betterton as Mercutio, both its style and its fusion of the comic and the tragic were hopelessly out of fashion ('It is a play of itself the worst that ever I heard in my life', opined Pepys), and it was subsequently rewritten by Sir James Howard, who gave it a happy ending (though the tragic ending was performed on alternate nights). Howard's version, sadly, does not survive, but it had in any case been set aside by the time *Romeo and Juliet* was supplanted by Thomas Otway's successful adaptation *The History and Fall of Caius Marius* (1679). Otway returned to the play's earlier sources to have his Juliet (Lavinia) awaken before Romeo (Young Marius) has finished dying of the poison, and a final dialogue between the lovers was retained when *Romeo and Juliet* returned to the stage in the 1740s, first as Theophilus Cibber's heavily Otway-based *Romeo and Juliet: A Tragedy, Revised and Altered from Shakespeare* (acted at the Haymarket from 1744 onwards and printed in 1748) and then in David Garrick's adaptation of 1748. Garrick's version was closer to the original, though he increased Juliet's age to 18 and eliminated much of what he dismissed as 'jingle and quibble', cutting puns, simplifying diction, and rewriting rhyme as blank verse (shortening even Romeo and Juliet's sonnet on meeting at the feast). In 1750 he further removed Romeo's initial crush on Rosaline and added an elaborate funeral procession for Juliet. In one of the most famous theatrical rivalries of all time, Garrick's Romeo at Drury Lane competed with Spranger Barry's at Covent Garden for twelve successive nights in 1750 (ending only when Susannah Cibber, Covent Garden's Juliet, fell ill), and the play was rarely out of the repertory of either theatre thereafter, acted more often than any other Shakespeare play during the remainder of the 18th century.

Garrick ceased to play Romeo in 1760, considering himself too old for the part, and the youth and naivety of the role deterred many subsequent actor-managers from attempting it at all, though the many actresses who made successful debuts as Juliet were rarely in any hurry to forsake the role, easily one of the longest and most attractive in Shakespearian tragedy. J. P. Kemble and Sarah Siddons gave up the parts after 1789, passing them on to Charles Kemble and Dorothea Jordan (later succeeded by Fanny Kemble): Edmund Kean failed as Romeo in 1815, and two of the most successful Romeos of the ensuing decades were women, Priscilla Horton (1834) and Charlotte Cushman (1845–6, 1855), whose production was the first to abandon Garrick's added dialogue in the tomb. (Lydia Kelly had played the role in New York in 1829: the last major female Romeo was Fay Templeton in 1875.) Henry Irving failed to convince opposite Ellen Terry in a scenically elaborate production in 1882, which was better received when William Terriss and Mary Anderson took over the leads during Irving's absence in America in 1884. (Terry later excelled as the Nurse.) Since then the play has remained immensely popular despite the continuing difficulties leading actors have experienced with the lyrical but comparatively unreflective leading role: John Gielgud, for example, was criticized for relying on his voice at the expense of his body when he played Romeo at 20 in 1924, but he returned to it repeatedly, in 1929, for Oxford University Dramatic Society in 1932 (with Peggy Ashcroft, and Edith Evans as the Nurse), and finally at the New Theatre in 1935, playing Mercutio to Laurence Olivier's Romeo (again with Ashcroft and Evans). During this record-breaking production, Gielgud and Olivier exchanged roles, Olivier finally more comfortable as Mercutio, although he would play Romeo again (disastrously) in America in 1940. Juliet, however, has been a success for actresses including Claire Bloom (1952, 1956), Dorothy Tutin (1958), and Judi Dench (in Franco Zeffirelli's production, 1960). Directors, meanwhile, have increasingly shied away from Romeo's traditional tights and short tunic to set the play in modern dress (sometimes glibly translating the feud as a recognizable, topical equivalent), particularly since the success of *West Side Story*. Rupert Goold's RSC production of 2010, the first new show to be seen in the remodelled Royal Shakespeare Theatre, compromised by dressing Romeo and Juliet in modern dress and the rest of the cast in Elizabethan.

 ON THE SCREEN

Romeo and Juliet has been more filmed than any other Shakespeare play except *Hamlet*, and in more languages: the earliest film (1902) was followed by a number of other silents including one from Italy (1911), the first to use Veronese locations, which anticipated later films in delivering both impressive spectacle and athletic sword-fights. George Cukor's 1936 sound version included Leslie Howard (Romeo), Norma Shearer (Juliet), Basil Rathbone (Tybalt), and John Barrymore (Mercutio) among the cast, on a lavishly constructed set. Renato Castellani's colourful film (1954) aimed at a neo-realist style at the expense of dramatic impact.

Franco Zeffirelli's *Romeo and Juliet* (1968) caught the fashionable waves of the 1960s and, championing the sincere innocence of the young amid inflexible parental attitudes, was immensely attractive to an adolescent viewing public. Zeffirelli used young inexperienced actors, Olivia Hussey (Juliet) and Leonard Whiting (Romeo), giving the action its visual youthfulness but losing poetic weight in the lines. Notwithstanding some gratuitous sentimentality, the screen is filled with colour, atmospheric contrasts, and passionate energy.

Alvin Rakoff's production for BBC TV (1978), a disappointing opening to the BBC/Time Life complete plays, set out to make the closeness of the Capulet family a dominant motif, thereby challenging the youth-centred priorities of Zeffirelli's. Forbidden by the series' commitment to full texts to sacrifice long speeches in the interests of dramatic pace, this production compensates for the inadequacy of the young performers in its leads by its detailed and sensitive exploration of family relationships, projecting an unusual sympathy for the older generation (notably Michael Hordern's Capulet). As such it strives intelligently to use the medium to dramatize feeling rather than athletic action.

Baz Luhrmann's 1996 *William Shakespeare's Romeo+Juliet*, commercially the most successful of all films based on Shakespeare, is both disturbing and clever in juxtaposing the controlled manipulation of the world as the mass media deliver it with the confused but essentially sacrificial love of the teenage Romeo (Leonardo DiCaprio) and Juliet (Claire Danes). The film presents, with the speed and energy of MTV, images which reflect a postmodern American society and environment choked with the obsolescent and the discarded, including a good deal of religious kitsch. Encapsulating the dislocated action within the ephemerality of television news presentations highlights the confusion between a world in which order has disintegrated and one which is presented as managed. Although the play's script is heavily cut and sometimes almost inaudible over the film's pop music soundtrack, this is a witty and compelling attempt to translate the story into the terms of contemporary culture and the play into those of contemporary popular cinema. Carlo Carlei's 2013 film returned to Zeffirelli's Renaissance Italian aesthetic and cast two leads unmistakably reminiscent of Hussey and Whiting in Hailee Steinfeld and Douglas Booth. Worse than the sense of aesthetic retread, however, was a frequently cringeworthy script by Julian Fellowes that attempted—sometimes subtly, sometimes blockishly, always inexplicably—to modernize the play's language.

Sir Thomas More

In the British Library is an undated dramatic manuscript, in several hands, catalogued as BL MS Harleian 7368, and bearing the title 'The Booke [i.e. playscript] of Sir Thomas Moore'. The general consensus among the many scholars who have studied this document since the 19th century is that the story behind it runs roughly as follows. In the early to mid-1590s Anthony Munday, assisted by Henry Chettle, composed an episodic play about the rise and fall of Thomas More and submitted a fair copy of it (largely in Munday's hand) to the Master of the Revels, Sir Edmund Tilney. Tilney refused to approve it for performance as it stood, partly on the grounds that its depictions of rioting against foreign immigrants made it potentially inflammatory at a time when such disturbances were breaking out again, and he annotated the manuscript to demand revisions which would have involved losing as much as half of the play. Some time later— probably soon after the death of Queen Elizabeth (1603), which would have made some of the play's depiction of her father Henry VIII's court less sensitive—a number of additions were made to the script, though they do not meet Tilney's objections (the play was never acted in Shakespeare's lifetime or for centuries thereafter, in either its revised or unrevised state). The additions are in several different hands, among them 'Hand B' (Thomas Heywood?), 'Hand E' (Thomas Dekker), and 'Hand D', which bears a close resemblance both to the handwriting of Shakespeare's attested signatures on legal documents and to the habits of spelling and of handwriting implied by printed editions of his works.

It is now generally agreed that Shakespeare wrote the section of the manuscript known as Addition II.D, which is the only specimen we have of writing for the stage in his own hand, and probably Addition III, though this has been copied by a scribe ('Hand C'). Addition II.D is a scene some 164 lines long, in which More single-handedly quells the xenophobic 'Ill May Day' riot of 1517, and was probably based on a comparable scene in Munday and Chettle's first draft: III is a 21-line soliloquy in which More reflects on his promotion to Lord Chancellor. Shakespeare does not seem even to have read Munday and Chettle's drama in its entirety, and consequently even some editions of his complete works which accept the two additions as his (such as the Riverside) print only Shakespeare's small contribution to the play rather than the whole text.

The manuscript of II.D is of immense interest for the light it can shed on Shakespeare's working practices: if nothing else, its messy appearance—with deletions, false starts, and every appearance of speedy composition—both confirms the account his colleagues John Heminges and Henry Condell supply, in their preface to the First Folio, of Shakespeare's facility and calls into question their assertion that they scarce found 'a blot in his papers'. Beyond the question of its palaeography and authorship, the Ill May Day scene, close in imagery and thematic concerns to other work from Shakespeare's early Jacobean period, provides one of Shakespeare's most sustained attacks on bigotry. Though *Sir Thomas More* has little stage history in its entirety (its principal full-scale production to date was staged by the Royal Shakespeare Company in its Swan auditorium in 2005, with Nigel Cooke in the title role), More's speech to the crowd has featured powerfully in Shakespearian recitations and one-man shows, notably that of Sir Ian McKellen, who played More in a Nottingham production of 1964.

Sonnets

Despite his contemporaries' preference for *Venus and Adonis* and *The Rape of Lucrece*, the Sonnets have long been regarded as Shakespeare's most important and distinctive contributions to non-dramatic poetry, as well as the most profoundly enigmatic works in the canon. In certain select circles Shakespeare already had a reputation as a sonneteer by 1598, when Francis Meres wrote of 'his sugared sonnets among his private friends', but although two of his sonnets reached print the following year (in

The Passionate Pilgrim) his whole sequence only appeared in 1609, with *A Lover's Complaint* as its coda. (A Stationers' Register entry of 1600 for a book called *Amours* by I.D., 'with certain other sonnets by W.S.', could conceivably refer to some of Shakespeare's sonnets, but the issue is clouded by the existence of another sonneteering W.S., William Smith, who had published a collection of his own in 1596). The title page of the 1609 quarto is dominated by Shakespeare's surname, and implies that the sonnets of this by-now celebrated dramatist and narrative poet have long been eagerly desired by the reading public: it offers 'Shake-Speares Sonnets. Never before Imprinted'.

Although the subsequent history of the Sonnets suggests that this book failed at first to excite as its printer clearly hoped it would, its implication that these poems had been awaiting publication for some time by 1609 is borne out by their style. It is probable that Shakespeare had begun writing sonnets some fifteen years before this quarto appeared, in the mid-1590s, during the boom in the form that extended from the posthumous publication of Sir Philip Sidney's *Astrophil and Stella* in 1591 through Samuel Daniel's *Delia* (1592), Michael Drayton's *Idea's Mirror* (1594), and Edmund Spenser's *Amoretti* (1595), among many other English sonnet sequences. Suggestively, Shakespeare's sonnets share rare vocabulary with *Love's Labour's Lost* (a play which includes no fewer than seven sonnets in its text), *A Midsummer Night's Dream*, and *Richard II*, all of them composed around 1594–5. But Shakespeare was still writing in this form after Meres's report of the existence of some of his sonnets in manuscript: Sonnet 107, for example, appears to allude to the death of Queen Elizabeth in early 1603 ('The mortal moon hath her eclipse endured'). Variants between the 1609 texts of Sonnets 2 and 106 and versions transcribed in 17th-century manuscripts, and between the 1609 texts of 138 and 144 and the versions published in *The Passionate Pilgrim*, suggest that Shakespeare revised some of the earlier-composed poems when organizing his collected sonnets into the book published in 1609. The positioning of *A Lover's Complaint* as the tailpiece to the collection—itself convincingly dated to around 1603–4—suggests that Shakespeare finished assembling the book at around that time.

 TEXT

The 1609 text of the Sonnets, published by Thomas Thorpe, is on the whole a good one, though its punctuation is demonstrably not authorial (two recognizably different compositors display quite different preferences) and an unusual recurrent misprint of 'their' for 'thy', found nowhere else in the canon, suggests that the edition was printed from a manuscript not in Shakespeare's own handwriting. *Shakespeare's Sonnets*, however, was Shakespeare's least reprinted quarto: its contents reappeared only in 1640, in John Benson's pirated volume *Poems: Written by W. Shakespeare, Gent.*, which includes most of the sonnets along with *A Lover's Complaint*, 'The Phoenix and Turtle', *The Passionate Pilgrim*, and various non-Shakespearian poems by the likes of Ben Jonson and John Milton. Benson reordered the sonnets and gave them titles, running some of them together, and, antici-pating subsequent anxieties about their content, he made verbal changes to make some refer to a woman rather than a man.

The question hanging over the belated 1609 quarto of *Shakespeare's Sonnets* has always been whether it too, like Benson's opportunistic reprint, was unauthorized, a question hardly simplified by its notoriously baffling dedication to 'Mr W.H'.:

> TO.THE.ONLY.BEGETTER.OF.
>
> THESE.ENSUING.SONNETS.
>
> MR.W.H. ALL.HAPPINESS.
>
> AND.THAT.ETERNITY.
>
> PROMISED.
>
> BY.
>
> OUR.EVER-LIVING.POET.
>
> WISHETH.
>
> THE.WELL-WISHING.
>
> ADVENTURER.IN.
>
> SETTING.
>
> FORTH.
>
> T. T.

'T.T'. is presumably the printer Thomas Thorpe, but beyond that no wholly convincing explanation of what this dedication is supposed to imply—or any clue as to whether Thorpe transcribed it from the manuscript or composed it himself—has ever been found. Does 'begetter', for example, mean the person who inspired the poems, or the person who wrote them, or the person who obtained the manuscript? Like so much else about the Sonnets, this dedication has provoked endless biographical speculation, and it is admittedly different in kind from the authorial dedications Shakespeare supplied when he published *Venus and Adonis* and *The Rape of Lucrece*. However, the view that the publication of the Sonnets was

Thorpe's own unauthorized 'adventure' has usually been based on the questionable assumption that the poems themselves are so compromisingly autobiographical that Shakespeare must have actively sought to prevent their being made public, and while this view certainly invests the appearance of the 1609 quarto with ample drama (exemplified by the relevant episode of John Mortimer's biographical novel *Will Shakespeare* (1977), which imagines the poet smashing the type of a projected second edition after his wife has complained about the first) it is a very difficult one to substantiate. Given Thorpe's otherwise untarnished reputation and the lack of any evidence that Shakespeare took offence at the appearance of this book (compared to his reported displeasure over *The Passionate Pilgrim*), it seems reasonable to assume that the publication was legitimate. The most recent theory about the dedication, aired in 2015, suggests unglamorously that Thorpe was dedicating the project as a memorial to an obscure fellow publisher, William Holmes, who had died in 1607.

SOURCES

Beyond their general debt to the entire European tradition of the sonnet back to Francesco Petrarch, Shakespeare's Sonnets are among his least obviously derivative or allusive works. In form, however, they are specifically indebted to the sonnet's chief English importers, Sir Thomas Wyatt (1503–42) and Henry Howard, Earl of Surrey (1515–47), who had generally translated their Italian originals not only into English but into a different shape of sonnet, replacing the Petrarchan division of the sonnet's fourteen lines into sense-units of eight and six (the octave and the sestet, often rhymed *abbacddc efgefg*) into the simpler 'English' (and subsequently 'Shakespearian') pattern of three quatrains and a couplet (usually rhymed *abab cdcd efef gg*). This form of sonnet had been employed by other English sonneteers between Wyatt's time and Shakespeare's, but rarely as exclusively. Some specific literary borrowings can be traced: Shakespeare's first few sonnets echo a specimen from Erasmus' widely known treatise *De conscribendis epistolis*, a model letter advising a young man to marry, and his last two are variations on an anacreontic epigram from *The Greek Anthology*, while in between different commentators have detected thematic and sometimes verbal debts to Ovid, Sidney, Spenser, Christopher Marlowe, and Henry Constable (whose *Diana*, 1594, assuming it pre-dates Shakespeare's poem, anticipates Sonnet 99, 'The forward violet thus did I chide'). However, Shakespeare, in common with his most successful fellow sonneteers, seems for most of the collection to be writing without specific literary models, a fact which, coupled with the poems' very few references to mythology, has contributed to the willingness of many readers to treat the sonnets as unmediated autobiography. Indeed Shakespeare is strikingly original in the uses to which he puts the sonnet form: instead of wooing a chaste mistress on the grounds that she ought to be producing beautiful children, the first group of sonnets attempts instead to persuade a beautiful young man to marry on the same grounds, and when the sonnets do turn their attentions to a female addressee they do so with a contemptuous bitterness unequalled by any previous anti-Petrarchan writer. Although Richard Barnfield's *Cynthia* (1595) includes 20 homoerotic sonnets addressed to a boy, no other English sonnet collection of its time is as preoccupied as Shakespeare's with an intense relationship between two men.

≔ SYNOPSIS

Attempts to read the Sonnets as a single consecutive narrative are controversial: the following summarizes what has been the most common way of so doing over the last century.

The first seventeen sonnets, the most uniform group in the sequence, are apparently addressed to the 'Fair Youth', urging him to marry and beget an heir. Down to Sonnet 126, the poems which ensue appear to chart a developing relationship with this man, who the poet promises will be rendered immortal by his verses (verses which neglect, however, to specify his name); different sonnets celebrate the mutuality of their love, or lament the young man's mortality, or regret temporary separations. Others suggest events within this relationship: 41 and 42 seem to record that the young man has been seduced by the poet's mistress, 78–86 express jealousy over his relationship with a 'rival poet', 87–90 lament that the friend has forgotten the poet, 91–6 suggest a friendship renewed despite doubts as to the friend's constancy, and 117–20 apologize for a lapse in the poet's own fidelity.

Sonnet 126, 'O thou my lovely boy'—unusually, a poem in six rhymed couplets rather than a sonnet proper—marks a turning point: the last poem addressed to the young man, it offers a final warning to him of his inescapable mortality. The next sonnets, 127–52, are known as the 'Dark Lady' group, addressed to or concerned with an unfashionably dark-haired, dark-eyed, and dark-complexioned mistress. For the most part, these poems reproach her: she is a tyrant, black in deeds as well as in looks (131), and an adultress (152); she has seduced the poet's friend (133–4); the poet is foolish to love anyone so obviously unworthy (137, 147–52) and is clearly deceiving himself (138), asking her in one sonnet to confess her infidelity (139) and in the next to say she loves him even though this is not true (140). The poet, aware of the delusions of lust but unable to avoid its trap (129), woos his mistress regardless with a series of sexual puns on the name 'Will' (135–6, 143); he is torn between 'a man right fair' and 'a woman coloured ill', suspecting they are lovers (144).

Among this latter group of sonnets, however, are two which seem incongruous. Sonnet 145 (unusually, in octosyllabics), with its apparent pun on 'Hathaway' ('"I hate" from hate away she threw, | And saved my life, saying "not you"'), may date from Shakespeare's courtship in the early 1580s, while Sonnet 146 is more conventionally Christian than the rest of the sequence, resolving to cherish the soul rather than the mortal body. The whole sequence ends with 153 and 154, two sonnets allegorizing the poet's love by means of fables about Cupid. In the 1609 quarto it is then followed by A Lover's Complaint.

🎭 ARTISTIC FEATURES

To read Shakespeare's sequence in the hopes of decoding an implied story, keen though some of these poems seem to be to encourage this strategy, is inevitably to do violence to the lyric compression and self-enclosure of the individual sonnets which compose it, and to the rich variety of tone and technique they achieve despite or rather through the formal limitations of their strict fourteen-line structure. Perhaps the most characteristic feature of Shakespeare's Sonnets is their fine poise between the idea developed over the three quatrains and its qualification or repudiation in the final couplet: it is impossible to decide, for example, whether in Sonnet 30, 'When to the sessions of sweet silent thought', the concluding assertion that 'all losses are restored' by the thought of the friend constitutes a triumphant repudiation of the three quatrains' preceding evocation of life's inevitable costs or a poignantly unconvincing defiance.

⭐ CRITICAL HISTORY

Although some of the Sonnets were transcribed in manuscript collections during the early 17th century (particularly Sonnet 2), Benson's pirated, doctored edition offered their only 17th-century reprint: out of date by the time of their publication, Shakespeare's Sonnets were in his own age his least popular poems. Most 18th-century editions were based on

Benson, and while the sonnet form was itself out of fashion Shakespeare's experiments with it were felt to be particularly embarrassing. George Chalmers, writing in 1796, refused to accept that 'Shakespeare, a husband, a father, a moral man, addressed a hundred and twenty, nay, a hundred and twenty-six *Amorous* Sonnets to a *male* object!', and claimed that the Young Man poems, advocating marriage and procreation, were really addressed to the Queen ('Elizabeth was often considered as a man', he insisted). It was Edmond Malone who first singled out the Sonnets as reliable (and uncompromising) clues to Shakespeare's inner life, a development which coincided with the revaluation of the sonnet form among the Romantic poets: William Wordsworth, indeed, revised his low opinion of the sequence to produce his influential sonnet 'Scorn not the sonnet' in 1827, claiming that 'with this key | Shakespeare unlocked his heart'. The bulk of 19th-century comment on the Sonnets, though, is preoccupied with their alleged biographical content at the expense of their artistry, seeking to identify the originals for the Fair Youth, the Dark Lady, and Mr W.H. rather than to explicate the poetry *per se*. The first attempt to make unambiguous confessional sense of Shakespeare's sequence by putting the poems into a different order was made by Charles Knight in 1841, and many more followed. Nineteenth-century discussions of the young man sequence extend from Samuel Taylor Coleridge's attempt to excuse the Sonnets' apparent homoeroticism to Oscar Wilde's celebration of it (in his story 'The Portrait of Mr W.H'. and at his notorious trial in 1895, an event which effectively 'outed' Shakespeare and paved the way for the Sonnets' subsequent presence in gay subculture). Only with the rise of modernism in the early 20th century—with its delight in complexity, irony, and ambiguity—did the Sonnets at last appear to belong in the mainstream of English poetry, valued and emulated by exponents of the art from Robert Graves to W. H. Auden, and cherished, in particular, by the academic new critics of the mid-century and their structuralist successors. Outstanding and influential readings include William Empson's account of Sonnet 94, Roman Jakobson and Lawrence Jones's meticulous dissection of Sonnet 129, and the work of Stephen Booth and Helen Vendler. While much criticism remains preoccupied with the question of whether these poems can be read as confessional and whether they constitute evidence about Shakespeare's own sexuality (with Sonnet 20 a particular bone of contention), the Sonnets are now more widely enjoyed than ever as triumphs of Shakespeare's art as well as potential glimpses of Shakespeare's life.

The Taming of the Shrew

The most enduringly popular of the early comedies, if also the most potentially offensive, *The Taming of the Shrew* has sometimes been regarded as Shakespeare's first play—partly on the sentimental grounds that its Induction's allusions to Warwickshire reflect the homesickness of a Stratford man newly arrived in London. Although the sophistication of its dramatic structure and scenic technique compared to those of *The Two Gentlemen of Verona* make this placing in the chronology unlikely, the play does belong to the very first phase of Shakespeare's writing career: while evidence as to its date is complicated by the existence of a similar play, *The Taming of a Shrew*, published anonymously in 1594, it seems certain that *The Taming of the Shrew* was already extant by 1592, when passages without any equivalent in *A Shrew* were echoed in another anonymous play, *A Knack to Know a Knave*. In 1593 Shakespeare's play was remembered again, this time by the poet Antony Chute, whose poem *Beauty Dishonoured* includes the line 'He calls his Kate, and she must come and kiss him.' *The Taming of the Shrew* requires a similar size of cast to *The First Part of the Contention* (*2 Henry VI*) and *Richard Duke of York* (*3 Henry VI*), and shares rare vocabulary with both plays: it is likely that it was composed at around the same time as Shakespeare's earliest histories, *c.* 1590–1.

 TEXT

Although *The Taming of a Shrew* appeared in quarto in 1594, 1596, and 1607, *The Taming of the Shrew* was not printed until the publication of the Folio in 1623. Its text is among the most puzzling in the canon: for one thing it lacks a completion to the frame-narrative of Christopher Sly, which disappears after 1.1 (though one possible ending is preserved by *The Taming of a Shrew*, which is probably a garbled plagiarism of Shakespeare's play). In incidentals the Folio text is a mess, and an inconsistent mess at that: some speech-prefixes preserve the names of actors rather than characters ('Sinclo' for one of the players, 'Nick' for a messenger in 3.1), consistent with a text derived from foul papers, while some speech-prefix errors suggest a scribe who has been misled by authorial use of an abbreviated alias to designate a character currently in disguise. Some passages suggest the Folio text derives from foul papers, in which Shakespeare's process of initial composition is still visible (4.4, for example, suggests indecision as to whether the location is outside Baptista's house or outside Tranio's lodging), others—notably 'Sinclo's' reference to 'Soto', apparently an interpolated allusion to John Fletcher's *Women Pleased* (*c.*1620?)—suggest a manuscript which has been altered for a late Jacobean revival, perhaps in conjunction with Fletcher's sequel *The Woman's Prize; or, The Tamer Tamed*. This last hypothesis, however, is itself rendered problematic by the fact that the Folio text has not been expurgated to comply with the Act to Restrain the Abuses of Players of 1606. It seems impossible to decide whether the Folio text derives from foul papers or from a transcript which has undergone some theatrical adaptation: some of its inconsistencies have been explained by the hypothesis that Shakespeare may have been working with a collaborator, but this theory has not been generally accepted.

 SOURCES

The Taming of the Shrew has an impeccably literary sub-plot—the Bianca–Lucentio story is derived from George Gascoigne's pioneering prose comedy *Supposes* (1566), itself a translation of Lodovico Ariosto's *I suppositi* (1509)—but its main plot belongs more to folklore than to high culture. Although countless ballads depict a husband disciplining an unruly wife (among them *A Merry Jest of a Shrewd and Cursed Wife*, 1550), most of these are far more brutal than Shakespeare's play (in *A Merry Jest*, for example, the shrew is beaten up and wrapped in the skin of a dead horse), and none is close enough in detail to the Petruccio–Kate story to be cited as a specific source, though the play clearly belongs in the same general tradition. Some commentators, however, have detected the influence of a relatively humane colloquy by the Dutch humanist Erasmus (*c.* 1466–1536), translated in 1557 as 'A Merry Dialogue, Declaring the Properties of Shrewd Shrews and Honest Wives'. The Induction, too, detailing the adventure of a peasant duped into believing himself a lord, derives from a story widespread through folklore and told in various earlier ballads, and Shakespeare does not seem to have had any single precedent in mind as he composed his own Warwickshire variant on the theme.

 CHARACTER LIST

In the Induction
Christopher Sly *beggar*
  and tinker
A **Hostess**
A **Lord**
Bartholomew *his page*
Huntsmen
Servants
Players
  In the play-within-the-play
Baptista Minóla *a gentleman*
  of Padua
Katherine *his elder daughter*
Bianca *his younger daughter*
Petruccio *a gentleman of Verona,*
  suitor of Katherine

Grumio⎤
         ⎟ *his servants*
Curtis⎦

Gremio *a rich old man of*
  Padua, suitor of Bianca

Hortensio *another suitor,*
  who disguises himself as Licio,
  a teacher
Lucentio *from Pisa, who disguises*
  himself as Cambio,
  a teacher

Tranio   ⎤
             ⎟ *his servants*
Biondello⎦

Vincentio *Lucentio's father*
A **Pedant** (schoolmaster), from
  Mantua
A **Widow**
A **Tailor**
A **Haberdasher**
An **Officer**
Servingmen, including
  Nathaniel, **Philip**,
  Joseph, and **Peter**
Other servants of Baptista and
  Petruccio

SYNOPSIS

Induction 1 Christopher Sly, a beggarly tinker, falls asleep after being ejected from a tavern for breaking glasses, and is found by a lord out hunting, who instructs his men to take Sly to his house, put him to bed, and persuade him when he wakes that he is its lord, who has been suffering from delusions. The Lord welcomes a troupe of players, and gives order that his page Bartholomew shall be dressed for the role of Sly's lady.

Induction 2 As instructed, the servingmen tell Sly he is a lord who has been mentally ill for fifteen years, to the grief of his lady: accepting the story, Sly is eager to resume conjugal relations with the cross-dressed Bartholomew, but is put off, and instead agrees to watch the players perform a comedy.

1.1 Lucentio, arriving in Padua to study, falls in love with Bianca when he sees her with her father Baptista, her elder sister Katherine, and two rivals for her love, Gremio and Hortensio. Baptista declares that Bianca may be courted only after the angry and disdainful Katherine is married, and that meanwhile Bianca will be tutored at home. Hortensio and Gremio agree that they must find some man willing to marry Katherine. Lucentio, over-hearing all this, hits upon a strategy with his servant Tranio: he will gain access to Bianca by disguising himself as a schoolmaster while Tranio, seconded by his other servant Biondello, fills the role of Lucentio. They exchange clothes. (Above, Sly is apparently bored by the play.)

1.2 Petruccio, arriving from Verona with his servant Grumio, calls on his friend Hortensio, and, learning of Katherine's dowry, agrees to woo her despite her reported shrewishness: he also agrees to recommend a dis-guised Hortensio to Baptista as Bianca's music teacher. Gremio arrives with the disguised Lucentio, whom he will present to Baptista as a tutor for Bianca: he agrees with Hortensio to co-sponsor Petruccio's wooing of Katherine. Tranio arrives, disguised as Lucentio, and announces his own intention of courting Bianca: he too agrees to fund Petruccio's suit, and Petruccio and the rivals repair to a tavern.

2.1 Katherine has tied Bianca's hands, and is interrogating her about her suitors when Baptista arrives, separates them, and sends them indoors. The company arrive from the tavern: Petruccio offers himself as a suitor for Katherine (confirming that her dowry is 20,000 crowns and half of Baptista's land in reversion) and presents Hortensio, disguised as Licio, as a music master. Gremio offers Lucentio, disguised as Cambio, as a tutor: both supposed teachers are accepted and sent to the two women, though Hortensio soon returns, after Katherine has broken his head with a lute, and is sent to Bianca instead. At Petruccio's insistence he is left alone and Katherine sent to him: in the wrangling conversation which follows Petruccio affects to disregard the contempt she displays, declares that he was born to tame her, and tells the returning Baptista that she has agreed to marry him the following Sunday. Despite Katherine's protests Baptista agrees, and Petruccio leaves to prepare for the wedding. Gremio and the disguised Tranio now attempt to outbid one another for Bianca's hand, Tranio promising all Lucentio's father Vincentio's wealth, an offer Baptista accepts on condition that Vincentio confirms it. Tranio realizes he will need to produce a surrogate Vincentio.

3.1 Hortensio and Lucentio, furious rivals, each declare their identities and purposes to Bianca under cover of teaching her: she seems to favour Lucentio, and Hortensio is disgusted at the idea that she might welcome the courtship of a mere tutor.

3.2 After keeping his bride and the company waiting, Petruccio arrives for his wedding in grossly tattered and absurd clothes.

3.3 Gremio tells Lucentio and Tranio of Petruccio's rough and swagger-ing behaviour during the marriage service: when the company arrive from the church, Petruccio refuses even to stay for the wedding breakfast, despite Katherine's protests, and takes her away immediately.

4.1 Grumio, arriving at Petruccio's country house to prepare his master's welcome, tells the servant Curtis of the foul and uncomfortable journey Katherine has suffered. When Petruccio and Katherine arrive, Petruccio abuses the servants, rejects the food they bring, and insists that Katherine goes to bed hungry: alone, he explains that his strategy is to break her spirit by depriving her of food and sleep, always pretending that he is doing so for her own good, and he asks whether anyone in the audience knows of a better way of taming a shrew.

4.2 Hortensio leads Tranio where he may see the mutual courting of Bianca and Lucentio: Tranio feigns shock and abandons his pretended suit, while Hortensio, forswearing Bianca, leaves to court a wealthy widow he means to marry instead, intending to call on Petruccio on the way. Lucentio, Bianca, and Tranio agree on their strategy for obtaining Baptista's consent by producing a false Vincentio to assure a marriage portion. Tranio persuades a passing Mantuan pedant that he is in mortal danger in Padua because of fictitious hostilities between the two city-states, and must disguise himself for safety: he explains that the Pedant can easily pass for Vincentio if he only goes through some formalities about a marriage settlement, in which Tranio will brief him.

4.3 At Petruccio's house Grumio loyally refuses to let Katherine have any food, and assists Petruccio, watched by Hortensio, in rejecting the new cap and gown ordered from a haberdasher and a tailor for Katherine to wear on her bridal visit to her father. Petruccio insists the clothes are not good enough, abuses the tradesmen, and tells Katherine they will go only when she shows complete obedience.

4.4 Tranio presents the Pedant, dressed as Vincentio, to Baptista, and they agree to sign the marriage settlement between Lucentio and Bianca at Tranio's lodgings over supper.

4.5 Biondello, on Tranio's instructions, advises Lucentio to marry Bianca privately while her father is busy over the pretended marriage settlements.

4.6 On their way to Baptista's house, Petruccio makes Katherine humour him by calling the sun the moon, and when they meet the real Vincentio he at first makes her greet him as if he were a young girl. Learning Vincentio's identity, Petruccio congratulates him on his son's marriage to Bianca, news which is confirmed by Hortensio before he leaves to woo the Widow.

5.1 Lucentio and Bianca hasten from his lodging towards their surreptitious wedding. Petruccio and Katherine arrive, bringing Vincentio, who knocks and is answered by the Pedant. The Pedant insists that he is Vincentio, supported by Biondello, who denies having ever seen the real

Vincentio before (and is beaten by him), and when Tranio arrives in Lucentio's clothes, Vincentio becomes convinced that his son has been murdered by his servants. Baptista is trying to have Vincentio taken to prison as an impostor when the newly-wed Lucentio and Bianca arrive (at which Tranio, Biondello, and the Pedant flee), and Lucentio confesses all. Petruccio agrees to follow them all and see how the affair turns out on condition that Katherine kisses him in the street: she does so.

5.2 The entire reconciled cast are assembled at Lucentio's banquet, celebrating his wedding to Bianca and Hortensio's to the Widow; after the three brides leave the chamber, each husband bets 20 crowns that his wife will return most obediently when summoned. Bianca and the Widow refuse to come, but Katherine comes immediately, and at Petruccio's bidding fetches the other two wives, throws off her hat, and preaches a long homily on wifely obedience, thereby winning him the wager. A delighted Baptista adds another 20,000 crowns to Petruccio's winnings. (In *The Taming of a Shrew*, Sly, now asleep, is put back into his own clothes and returned to where the Lord found him: awakened at dawn by a tapster, he says he has had a wonderful dream, and since he now knows how to tame a shrew has no fear of returning home to his wife.)

🎭 ARTISTIC FEATURES

The Taming of the Shrew is the first of Shakespeare's comedies to hint at his power to pursue a serious idea across a whole range of comic plots and situations, taking up the notions of identity, education, and persuasion initiated by the Induction (which has already modelled the production of an 'ideal' wife through the transformation of Bartholomew), and developing them through each of the intrigues of the play proper.

✮ CRITICAL HISTORY

Long dismissed as a simple-minded, robust farce (Samuel Johnson's verdict, though he was impressed by Shakespeare's interlinking of the two main plots, was merely that the play was 'very popular and diverting'), *The Taming of the Shrew* has been taken ever more seriously since the early 20th century, and not only because that period has seen the emergence of modern feminism. As with its stage history, the play has divided interpreters between those who wish to excuse or celebrate Petruccio's behaviour towards Kate and those who wish to condemn it—essentially, between those who regard the 'taming' as a benign piece of psychic or social therapy inflicted in the cause of mutual love, and those who see it as simply an expression of the naked power of Elizabethan men over Elizabethan women. Many commentators have related Katherine's speech on marriage to wider Elizabethan doctrines of authority and social subordination (notably E. M. W. Tillyard in *The Elizabethan World Picture*, 1943), but opinion on the play remains profoundly divided as to whether her submission is to be accepted and welcomed at face value or whether the play suggests it is to be viewed with scepticism, irony, or even revulsion. Recent studies have continued to focus upon the play's sexual politics, reading the central relationship in terms of violence, coercion, and the patriarchy.

STAGE HISTORY

Partly because of this very controversy over how we are to take Petruccio's triumph, the play has been inspiring adaptations and spin-offs ever since *The Taming of a Shrew*: around 1611, for example, John Fletcher produced a sequel (in which the characters have all miraculously become English), *The Woman's Prize; or, The Tamer Tamed*, in which Petruccio's second wife Maria proves much less tractable than the now-dead Kate. Although Shakespeare's original was performed at court in the 1630s and in the early 1660s, *The Taming of the Shrew* was rewritten by John Lacy in 1667 as *Sauny the Scot*, a largely prose version of the play, anglicized to match *The Woman's Prize*, and dominated by Lacy's performance as the caricatured Scottish servant Sauny (Grumio, 'Sander' in *A Shrew*). Despite two topical rewritings of the Induction (both as *The Cobbler of Preston*, 1716, and a 1735 ballad opera, *A Cure for a Scold*), this was the version that held the stage until the mid-18th century, when it was supplanted by David Garrick's three-act afterpiece *Catharine and Petruchio* (1754). Garrick's version, eliminating the Bianca plot and insisting that Petruchio loves Catharine all along and only feigns his various tactical brutalities, was not finally replaced until after Augustin Daly's production of the original in 1887–8, with Ada Rehan as Kate, though the original had been revived twice in the 1840s, by Benjamin Webster (once in a precociously quasi-Elizabethan staging by J. R. Planché, 1844) and by Samuel Phelps in 1856. The play has enjoyed frequent revivals ever since, with great Kates including Violet Vanbrugh, Laurence Olivier (his debut, in a school production, 1922), Edith Evans, Barbara Jefford, and Vanessa Redgrave (at Stratford in 1961, and in London 25 years later). Since feminism's second wave in the 1970s, the tradition of playing Petruccio and Kate as a couple who fall happily in love in between their less happy lines has often given place to more critical productions, which have sometimes overcompensated by rendering Petruccio more brutal: Charles Marowitz's 1973 adaptation *The Shrew* has Petruchio (as the role was then known) sodomizing Kate onstage, and in Michael Bogdanov's 1978 RSC production Jonathan Pryce, a loutish, set-demolishing Sly, burst into the play-within-the-play as Petruchio on a phallic motorbike. He was finally slightly abashed, however, by Paola Dionisotti's submission speech, which many successive actresses have sought to reclaim as an act of perverse defiance. Barry Kyle's exuberant 1982 production for the RSC, on the other hand, positioned Kate's (Sinead Cusack) taming as an act of liberation. While some directors have continued to find redeeming qualities in the relationship between Petruccio and Katharina (notably Gregory Doran, whose 2003 RSC production, cross-cast with Fletcher's *Tamer Tamed*, depicted both as equally damaged and in the end equally therapeutic for one another, a strategy broadly followed by Lucy Bailey in 2012), recent productions have attempted to complicate the question between the two by casting, whether by using all-female casts (as in Phyllida Lloyd's production at Shakespeare's Globe in 2002) or all-male (as in Edward Hall's for Propeller, 2006, 2013). Justin Audibert's 2019 gender-flipped RSC production, set as if in a lavishly dressed Renaissance matriarchy, played entertainingly with the play's mainstream performance tradition, transforming *Shrew* into a play about a pair of constrained male heirs, often ignored or believed, who are comprehensively upstaged by a range of middle-aged female character parts.

🎬 ON THE SCREEN

The earliest film (1908) is of historical interest in being the work of D. W. Griffith. Five silent versions followed before Sam Taylor's adaptation (1929), the first Shakespeare film to have a soundtrack with English dialogue. Two television productions followed, one for BBC TV (1939) by Dallas Bower, and George Schaefer's American production (1956) with Maurice Evans as Petruchio. Franco Zeffirelli's film (1966) filled the screen with colour and captivatingly robust action, with Elizabeth Taylor as Kate and Richard Burton as a powerful, swaggering, though unsubtle Petruchio. Jonathan Miller's production for BBC TV (1980), criticized for failing to give Katharina sufficient dramatic weight in her own right, tackled the play along surprisingly unorthodox lines, casting John Cleese as a Puritan Petruchio. Shirley Henderson played Katherine Minola as an abrasive politician advised to marry in order to soften her public image in Sally Wainwright's adaptation for the *Shakespeare Retold* series (BBC, 2005), with Rufus Sewell the rhinoceros-skinned, penniless nobleman happy to oblige. The play provided a good deal of material for the Cole Porter musical *Kiss Me Kate*, filmed in 1953, and for the Hollywood teen rom-com *Ten Things I Hate About You* (1999).

The Tempest

Printed as the first play in the Folio, *The Tempest* has always enjoyed a special prominence in the Shakespeare canon. Its first recorded performance took place at James I's court on 1 November 1611, and it cannot have been much more than a year old then. *The Tempest* is indebted to three texts unavailable before the autumn of 1610, namely William Strachey's *True Reportary of the Wrack and Redemption of Sir Thomas Gates* (completed in Virginia in July 1610, and circulated in manuscript before its eventual publication in 1625), Sylvester Jourdan's *Discovery of the Bermudas* (printed in 1610, with a dedication dated 13 October), and the Council of Virginia's *True Declaration of the Estate of the Colony in Virginia* (entered in the Stationers' Register in November 1610 and printed before the end of the year). An apparently irresistible urge to identify Prospero with Shakespeare (visible since the 1660s) has led many commentators to think of *The Tempest* as the playwright's personal farewell to the stage, and while this view seems both sentimental and slightly inaccurate (since Shakespeare was yet to co-write *Cardenio, All Is True (Henry VIII),* and *The Two Noble Kinsmen* with Fletcher), this probably was his last unassisted work for the theatre, completed in 1611. Its position in the Folio may reflect his colleagues' recognition of this fact.

 TEXT

The Folio provides the only authoritative text of the play: it was prepared with care, apparently from a literary transcript by the scribe Ralph Crane. The text's unusually detailed stage directions were probably elaborated by Crane for the benefit of readers from briefer indications in his copy, but they may well reflect his accurate recollections of seeing the play staged. *The Tempest* calls for an unusual quantity of music, and the words of its songs are preserved in a number of 17th-century manuscripts. These all seem to derive from the Folio text, but some may supplement it by accurately recording where breaks came between verses and refrains.

 SOURCES

The three texts from late 1610 which lie behind this play supplied Shakespeare with the story of a much-discussed shipwreck in the West Indies. The *Sea-Adventure*, flagship of a nine-strong flotilla taking 500 colonists from Plymouth to Virginia, struck the coast of Bermuda in a storm on 29 July 1609 and was presumed lost, but in May 1610 the bulk of its crew and passengers reached Jamestown, having wintered on Bermuda and built themselves pinnaces. The accounts Shakespeare read, which gave hints for details in the play such as the St Elmo's fire with which Ariel adorns the storm (1.2.197–204), represent the preservation of the survivors as the work of Providence (just as Gonzalo regards the outcome of the play's story, 5.1.204–16). It may be significant to the play's depictions of authority and subordination that these texts are almost as interested in the suppression of potential mutiny as they are in the unfamiliar climate and natural history of Bermuda, and it is probably relevant to the play that before their landing there the mariners had regarded the island as a haunt of evil spirits.

Beyond these local sources, the play is indebted to Shakespeare's other reading about travel, trade, and colonialism, notably in Robert Eden's *History of Travel* (1577), from which he derived the name of Sycorax's god Setebos, and in Michel de Montaigne's essay 'Of the Cannibals', the source for Gonzalo's vision of an ideal commonwealth (2.1.149–74). Caliban's name may be related to 'Carib' as well as to 'Cannibal', suggesting that Shakespeare had read early accounts of Caribbean native cultures. Other important debts are to Ovid's *Metamorphoses*, from which Shakespeare took Prospero's farewell to his magic (5.1.33–57) almost verbatim (tellingly, from a speech by the sorceress Medea), and to Virgil's *Aeneid*, particularly its depiction of Aeneas' dealings with Dido, Queen of Carthage, whom Shakespeare remembered often during this play about a ship wrecked between Tunis and Italy. The main plot of the play, though—unusually, largely told in retrospect, the play neoclassically confining itself to showing the last few hours of the story in a single location—is Shakespeare's own.

 CHARACTER LIST

Prospero, the rightful Duke of Milan

Miranda *his daughter*

Antonio *his brother, the usurping Duke of Milan*

Alonso, King of Naples

Sebastian *his brother*

Ferdinand *Alonso's son*

Gonzalo *an honest old counsellor of Naples*

Adrian ⎤
         lords
Francisco ⎦

Ariel *an airy spirit attendant upon Prospero*
Caliban *a savage and deformed native of the island, Prospero's slave*
Trinculo *Alonso's jester*
Stefano *Alonso's drunken butler*
The **Master** of a ship

Boatswain
Mariners
Spirits
The Masque
Spirits appearing as:
Iris
Ceres
Juno
Nymphs, reapers

 SYNOPSIS

1.1 Alonso, King of Naples, his son Ferdinand, their ally Antonio, Duke of Milan, and a number of courtiers are returning to Italy from Alonso's daughter's wedding to the King of Tunis when their ship is driven aground in a violent storm, the sailors struggling in vain to preserve it between the interruptions of their aristocratic passengers. All are convinced they are about to drown.

1.2 After the storm, Prospero reassures his daughter Miranda that no one has perished in the shipwreck, which he caused and controlled by magic. For the first time he tells her of how, twelve years earlier, they came to this island. The rightful Duke of Milan, Prospero was usurped by his brother Antonio, who, governing the state while Prospero studied magic, promised that Milan would pay tribute to Naples in return for Alonso's military backing for his coup. Prospero and the 3-year-old Miranda were set adrift far out to sea in a small boat provisioned and supplied with Prospero's books only at the insistence of a humane Neapolitan courtier, Gonzalo. Since then Prospero has brought Miranda up on the island where they came ashore, in ignorance of his royalty, but now his enemies have been brought to the island and their future depends on the next few hours. While Miranda falls into a magically induced sleep, Prospero summons his spirit Ariel, who describes how he executed the storm and how he has left the mariners and passengers, the former asleep on the safely harboured ship, Ferdinand alone, and the rest dispersed around the island. When Ariel reminds Prospero of his promise to free him from his labours, the enchanter reminds him of his twelve-year confinement in a pine at the hands of the banished Algerian witch Sycorax (now dead, though survived by her son Caliban), and threatens to renew such an imprisonment if Ariel complains again. Promising to free him after two days, Prospero commands Ariel to reappear as a sea-nymph, visible only to him. Miranda awakens and Prospero summons their slave Caliban, who curses them, remembering their kinder treatment when they first came to the island, which he insists is rightfully his. He has been enslaved since an attempt to rape Miranda, which he unrepentantly remembers. Prospero sends him to fetch fuel, threatening him with torments. After Caliban's departure, the invisible Ariel leads Ferdinand to them with the song 'Come unto these yellow sands', confirming the Prince's belief that his father has drowned with another, 'Full fathom five thy father lies'. Ferdinand and Miranda fall in love instantly, and he proposes to her: this is just as Prospero has planned, but he feigns displeasure, offering to imprison Ferdinand, who is magically paralysed when he attempts to draw his sword.

2.1 Elsewhere on the island, Gonzalo tries to comfort Alonso, who is convinced Ferdinand has drowned: Antonio and Alonso's brother Sebastian, however, ridicule Gonzalo and reproach Alonso for marrying his daughter to an African. Gonzalo, further mocked by Antonio and Sebastian, speaks of the utopian community he imagines establishing on the island. The invisible Ariel plays music and all sleep except Antonio and Sebastian: Antonio persuades Sebastian he should seize the opportunity to make himself King of Naples by violence, and they both draw swords to kill Alonso and Gonzalo. Ariel, however, rouses Gonzalo with a song, 'While you here do snoring lie', and the whole party awakens, obliging the two would-be assassins to pretend they have drawn because alarmed by a noise as of lions.

2.2 Caliban, seeing the jester Trinculo, thinks he is one of Prospero's tormenting spirits, and lies hiding under his gaberdine: Trinculo, finding him, at first thinks him a monstrous fish whom he wishes he could exhibit lucratively at English fairs, but decides he must be a thunder-struck native. When it begins to rain, he too takes shelter under the gaberdine. Alonso's drunken butler Stefano, drinking sack preserved from the wreck and singing, thinks the gaberdine is a four-legged monster, then a two-headed one too, before he realizes the truth and is reunited with Trinculo. Caliban, given some of Stefano's sack, thinks him a god, swears allegiance to him, and sings in joy of his deliverance from Prospero's slavery.

3.1 Concealed, Prospero watches with approval as Ferdinand, enslaved and bearing logs for him, speaks with Miranda and the two vow to marry.

3.2 Increasingly drunk, Caliban begins to fall out with Trinculo, a quarrel exacerbated by Ariel, who invisibly simulates Trinculo's voice and contradicts Caliban as he speaks of Prospero. Caliban proposes that Stefano should murder Prospero during his afternoon nap and marry Miranda, a scheme to which he and Trinculo agree. They sing a catch, the tune of which Ariel invisibly plays on a tabor and pipe. Caliban reassures the Italians that the island is full of harmless magical sounds.

3.3 Alonso and his hungry fellows are astonished when spirits lay out a banquet before them, inviting them to dine. As Prospero watches invisibly from above, Alonso, Antonio, and Sebastian are about to eat when Ariel appears in the shape of a harpy, makes the banquet disappear, and speaks of the three's sinfulness, reminding them of the banishment of Prospero. Prospero congratulates Ariel on his performance. Alonso, convinced Ferdinand has died in punishment for his own role in Antonio's usurpation, is stricken with guilt.

4.1 Prospero, explaining that Ferdinand's servitude was only a test of his love, blesses his engagement to Miranda, though he warns the Prince severely against premarital sex. To celebrate the occasion, Prospero's spirits perform a masque in which Iris, at Juno's behest, summons Ceres (played by Ariel) to help bless the couple, in the welcome absence of Venus and Cupid. During a dance of nymphs and reapers, however, Prospero remembers Caliban's plot, and hastily terminates the unfinished masque, apologizing to Ferdinand for his distraction but pointing out that all the world is as mortal and fragile as was the spirits' performance. After the couple have gone, Ariel tells Prospero how he has led Caliban, Stefano, and Trinculo through thorns and a filthy pool on their way to seek him: at Prospero's bidding he hangs out fancy clothing, and while Stefano and Trinculo are distracted by the task of stealing it—to Caliban's impatience—Prospero and Ariel drive the three of them away to more torment with spirits in the shapes of hunting dogs.

5.1 Prospero, in his magic robes, listens to Ariel's compassionate description of the sufferings of Alonso and his party (imprisoned by magic on Prospero's instructions), and resolves that since they are penitent he will not pursue vengeance against them. While Ariel goes to release them, he draws a circle with his staff, remembering the magnificent achievements of his magic powers but vowing to renounce them. Alonso and his followers are led into the circle by Ariel, still charmed, and Prospero speaks to them. Ariel sings 'Where the bee sucks', a song of his imminent freedom, as he dresses Prospero in his former clothes as Duke of Milan. Alonso, Gonzalo, and the others recover their wits and are astonished to be greeted by Prospero. Prospero forgives Antonio, but demands the restoration of his dukedom, pointing out privately that he knows of the earlier assassination attempt against Alonso. When Alonso speaks in grief about the presumed death of Ferdinand, Prospero says he too lost a child in the recent storm, and draws a curtain to reveal Miranda and Ferdinand playing chess together. Alonso and Ferdinand are happily reunited. Miranda is astonished at the beauty of mankind, and Alonso and Gonzalo bless her engagement to Ferdinand. Ariel brings the Master and Boatswain, who are amazed to report that the ship and crew are perfectly intact. Ariel then brings Caliban, Stefano, and Trinculo, whose conspiracy Prospero describes. Caliban, admitting he was foolish to believe his drunken companions gods, is sent to tidy Prospero's cell while his former confederates return their stolen clothing. Prospero promises he will tell his whole story before they set sail for Italy the following morning, and assures Ariel that he will be free as soon as he has provided a wind which will enable them to catch up with the rest of Alonso's fleet. Alone, Prospero speaks an epilogue, in rhyme, saying that now that he has no magic powers he needs the audience's indulgent applause to free him.

 ARTISTIC FEATURES

As even the above synopsis may suggest, *The Tempest* works less as a straightforward narrative than as a series of rich but profoundly enigmatic images, often arranged in symmetrical patterns: the parallel servitudes of Caliban and Ariel, Caliban and Ferdinand; the paired younger brothers Antonio and Sebastian; Prospero's magical control of the sea and of the spectacle; Ariel's performances as sea-nymph, as harpy, and as Ceres. As such it is closer to lyric, as well as more crammed with lyrics, than any other Shakespeare play, a haunting sea-poem in which celebration over what can be restored and sorrow over what must be lost are inextricably intertwined.

CRITICAL HISTORY

The mysterious qualities of *The Tempest*—the sense that the play reveals only glimpses of its purposes, quite apart from dramatizing only a few hours of its characters' lives—have given it a richer afterlife in drama, literature, and the other arts than almost any other Shakespeare play, as subsequent writers and artists have sought to explain, supplement, and extend it. Versions of Prospero the master illusionist have haunted the theatre (F. G. Waldron composed the first of several sequels, *The Virgin Queen*, in 1796) and, especially, film (allusions to *The Tempest* have, for example, become almost *de rigueur* in science fiction, from the 1956 outer-space version *Forbidden Planet* onwards). The play's interpreters in other media include William Hogarth, Henry Fuseli (who based his drawings of Prospero on portraits of Leonardo da Vinci), Iris Murdoch, Aimé Césaire (anticolonialist author of *Une tempête*), and W. H. Auden, a list which very nearly included Mozart.

From the Restoration onwards the play was regarded as a display of imaginative liberties not possible (or permissible) for lesser writers:

John Dryden, for example, cited both Caliban and Ariel as specimens of Shakespeare's abilities to go beyond nature. His critical observations on the play, though, are perhaps less revealing as comments on it than the adaptation he co-wrote with Davenant in 1667, *The Tempest; or, The Enchanted Island*. William Davenant, according to Dryden, 'found that somewhat might be added to the design of Shakespeare…and therefore to put the last hand to it, he designed the counterpart to Shakespeare's plot, namely that of a man who had never seen a woman'. In the adaptation, which elaborates on the symmetries of Shakespeare's original, Prospero is also responsible for a naive male ward, Hippolito, doomed to die if he ever meets a woman, and Miranda has a sister, Dorinda: in a coyly Edenic scene Dorinda and Hippolito do meet, despite Prospero's prohibitions, and when Hippolito (uninstructed in the monogamous codes of civil society) finds himself just as enthusiastic about Miranda as he is about her sister he is killed in a duel by Ferdinand. Meanwhile Caliban, too, has a sister (confusingly, called Sycorax) whom he pairs off with Trinculo (though she is just as keen on Stefano), and the rival attempts by the mutineers to claim the island by marriage displace their attempted coup against Prospero. Prospero's role, meanwhile, is greatly reduced: he never renounces his magic, which is in the event exceeded by that of Ariel, who is able to provide a magic cure to revive the dead Hippolito and permit a happy ending. Davenant and Dryden make *The Tempest* more orderly, and a good deal lighter, but their invention of the Hippolito plot makes fully visible the fears of sexuality, women, and death which seem to trouble Prospero in the original.

The identification of Prospero with *The Tempest*'s author is already visible in the prologue to Davenant and Dryden's adaptation, and it became a commonplace of 18th-century poetry and prose about Shakespeare (made fully explicit by Thomas Campbell in 1838), which generally regarded the Duke of Milan as a figure of serene wisdom. The 19th century in general maintained this view, seeing the play as an autumnal work about a magician who comes to terms with the renunciation of his powers and the marriage of his only child: according to Victor Hugo, for whom *The Tempest* was a powerfully mythic text which completed the Bible, this 'last creation of Shakespeare' has 'the solemn tone of a testament' and offers 'the supreme denouement, dreamed by Shakespeare, for the bloody drama of Genesis. It is the expiation of the primordial crime.' Even Hugo, though, had some misgivings about Prospero (calling him 'the master of Nature and the despot of destiny'), and in time the univocally pro-Prospero reading of the play came under pressure, especially from commentators who found Caliban as potentially sympathetic as his master. The play had already come to function for some as an allegory about slavery and colonialism by the 1840s, when the Brough brothers' burlesque *The Enchanted Isle* depicted Caliban as a black abolitionist who sings the 'Marseillaise', and Charlotte Barnes hybridized the play (in *The Forest Princess*, 1844) with the story of Pocahontas. During the 20th century this view would be developed by many anti-colonial writers, particularly Octave Mannoni in East Africa, and would become a commonplace of cultural materialist and new historicist criticism from the 1970s onwards. The extent to which the play, though set in the Mediterranean, is in any sense 'about' the New World (and a colonial enterprise which in Shakespeare's time barely existed) has been a contentious question throughout the post-war period (not coincidentally, a period when Shakespeare studies have been increasingly dominated by North American critics). Discussions of the play in recent years have often been dominated by the question of Shakespeare's level of approval for Prospero and the related question of the nature, black or white, of his magic.

🎭 STAGE HISTORY

After its court performance in November 1611, *The Tempest* was again played for the royal family in 1613 during the celebrations of Princess Elizabeth's wedding. No further performances of the original are recorded until the mid-18th century: from 1667 the play was displaced by Davenant and Dryden's adaptation (supplied with further operatic embellishments in 1674, including a masque of Neptune and a girlfriend for Ariel), which became the most popular show of its time (popular enough, for example, to be wickedly parodied by Thomas Duffett). Regularly revived at Christmas, its cast including an actress as Hippolito, a middle-aged comedian as Sycorax, and Ariel as the perfect good fairy, this play is one of the ancestors of English pantomime. David Garrick experimented with his own drastically shortened *The Tempest: An Opera* (1756), but after its failure he instead revived a conservatively abridged text of Shakespeare's original. To 18th-century audiences, however, Shakespeare's play lacked 'business', and the Dryden–Davenant version returned, first as the puppet play *The Shipwreck* (1780). John Philip Kemble (a righteously authoritarian Prospero) restored Hippolito and Dorinda to the stage proper in 1789, though he gradually included more of Shakespeare's text over the next decade. Frederick Reynolds's musical version in 1821 was again based on the Dryden–Davenant adaptation, and it was not until 1838 that the original play (though supplemented with lavish special effects) was again restored, by W. C. Macready. Spectacle characterized subsequent revivals by Charles Kean (1857), whose production employed 140 stagehands, Samuel Phelps (1871), and Beerbohm Tree, whose 1904 production centred on Caliban, played by himself, who was left alone to watch the Italians' ship departing in a wistful final tableau.

In the 20th century the play was revived more frequently, with major Prosperos including Robert Atkins (1915) and, especially, John Gielgud, who played Ferdinand in 1926 but had already graduated to a Dantesque Prospero at the Old Vic in 1930 (with Ralph Richardson as Caliban). Gielgud repeated the role in 1940, in 1957 (for Peter Brook at Stratford), and in 1973 (for Peter Hall at the National), and his intellectual, mellifluous, exquisitely spoken rendering of the part (particularly its rhetorical set pieces) has been immensely influential (and, through sound recordings and the film *Prospero's Books*, is likely to remain so). Even within Gielgud's performances as Prospero, however, there was an increasing sense that the Duke of Milan could no longer be played as a benign, Father Christmas-like magus: Brook's production stressed Prospero's obsessive brooding, while Hall had Gielgud present him as puritanically vengeful, successfully acting out his plan but not with meditative detachment. These directions have been pursued by others, too: at the RSC, Derek Jacobi was a young and passionate Prospero in 1983, John Wood an unpredictably irritable one in Nicholas Hytner's production of 1988, Alec McCowen a frail, patronizing showman finally spat upon by Simon Russell Beale's freed Ariel in Sam Mendes's production of 1993. A fine specimen of postcolonial interpretations of the play was provided by Janice Honeyman's 2009 production, a collaboration between the RSC and the Baxter Theatre of Johannesburg, with Antony Sher as Prospero and John Kani as Caliban. At the same time the play has continued to inspire theatrical adaptations and variations, among them Philip Osment's *This Island's Mine* (Gay Sweatshop, 1987–8), while Prospero's power was memorably digitized in Gregory Doran's 2016 production for the RSC, with Simon Russell Beale as a virtual-reality-enhanced magus. The further opening up of the play's text to contemporary questions of gender and power visible in recent criticism has continued to expand the theatrical possibilities of this haunting, conflicted, and mysterious play.

 ON THE SCREEN

Dallas Bower's BBC TV production (1939) with Peggy Ashcroft as Miranda was one of the last Shakespeare broadcasts before the BBC closed its television service for the length of the war. The American Hallmark television series produced a memorable *The Tempest* (1960) with Maurice Evans (Prospero), Lee Remick (Miranda), and Richard Burton (Caliban). Michael Hordern's Prospero for BBC TV (1979) was judged dignified but undisturbing, whereas Derek Jarman's *The Tempest* (1980) aroused fierce critical response since it resonates with an underlying agenda which seeks to subvert heterosexual orthodoxy. Jarman presents a dark view of the relationships in the play, Heathcote Williams's Prospero crushing Caliban's fingers underfoot and Toyah Willcox's Miranda displacing innocent winsomeness with brazen and compulsive sexuality. The priorities in this film are more readily understood when viewed in the context of the whole Jarman *œuvre*. Peter Greenaway's *Prospero's Books* (1991), using highly sophisticated technology, bases a rewriting of the play's action on the books that Gonzalo packs to accompany Prospero in his exile, John Gielgud taking on the multiple personality of Shakespeare, Greenaway, and Prospero, so that the film is essentially about the process of writing, filming, and experiencing simultaneously. The last of the books is Shakespeare's First Folio with blank pages waiting for Shakespeare's *The Tempest* to cover them. Julie Taymor's *The Tempest* (2011) starred Helen Mirren as 'Prospera'.

Timon of Athens

This bitter, schematic fable of bankruptcy and misanthropy—which long enjoyed the dubious distinction of being perhaps the least popular play in the Shakespeare canon—shares many concerns, and a good deal of rare vocabulary, with *King Lear* and was probably written shortly before it, in 1604–5. It may have been influenced by an anonymous academic play, *Timon* (acted at one of the Inns of Court *c.* 1602), and by the depiction of Timon found in William Painter's *Palace of Pleasure* (1566), a work on which Shakespeare drew for the plot of *All's Well That Ends Well* (1604–5). However, there is no external evidence to help date the play, which went unmentioned in any extant document until its appearance in the First Folio in 1623.

 TEXT

It is quite possible that *Timon of Athens* would have been omitted from the Folio had its compilers not experienced last-minute difficulties in obtaining *Troilus and Cressida*: Charlton Hinman's study of the Folio's printing showed that this play occupies space originally intended for *Troilus and Cressida*. The reasons for the play's near-exclusion are not known, but they may relate to its status as a collaboration. The Folio text is a highly unusual one, full of loose ends of plot (notably the virtually irrelevant episode in which Alcibiades pleads in vain on behalf of a soldier guilty of manslaughter, 3.6), and anomalies in its lineation and in its use of pronouns. Although some commentators have preferred to think of it as an 'unfinished' work by Shakespeare alone, many editors since Charles Knight in the 1830s have regarded it as a collaborative work, and it is now widely accepted that about a third of the play was composed by the young Thomas Middleton. Careful independent studies of language, oaths, spelling, rare vocabulary, and other forensic details have identified Middleton's share as 1.2, all of Act 3 except Timon's devastating appearance at his mock-feast in 3.7, and the dialogue between Timon and Flavius at the end of 4.3. It is clear from the Folio text that the play was set from foul papers, with each playwright's share written in his own hand and betraying quite different habits with incidentals.

SOURCES

The principal source for *Timon of Athens* is a digression in Plutarch's life of Mark Antony, from which the play takes Timon's epitaph almost verbatim. Shakespeare and Middleton must also have known Lucian's dialogue *Timon misanthropus* (either directly or indirectly, perhaps through the anonymous *Timon* play), which supplies Timon's discovery of gold during his self-imposed exile in the woods and its consequences.

CHARACTER LIST

Timon of Athens
A **Poet**
A **Painter**
A **Jeweller**
A **Merchant**
A **Mercer**
Lucilius *one of Timon's servants*
An **Old Athenian**
Lords and **Senators** of Athens
Ventidius *one of Timon's false friends*
Alcibiades *an Athenian captain*

Apemantus *a churlish philosopher*
One dressed as **Cupid** in the masque
Ladies dressed as Amazons in the masque
Flavius *Timon's steward*
Flaminius
Servilius } *Timon's servants*
Other **Servants** of Timon
A **Fool**
A **Page**

Caphis	⎤ servants
Isidore's Servant	⎟ to
Two of **Varro's Servants**	⎦ Timon's creditors

Titus' Servant	⎤ other
Hortensius' Servant	⎟ servants to
Philotus' Servant	⎦ Timon's creditors

Lucullus' Servant
Lucius' Servant
Three **Strangers**, one called
  Hostilius

Phrynia	⎤ whores with
Timandra	⎦ Alcibiades

The banditti, **Thieves**
Soldier of Alcibiades' army
Messengers, attendants,
  soldiers

≔ SYNOPSIS

1.1 Outside the rich Timon's house a jeweller, a merchant, a mercer, a poet, and a painter cluster in hopes of his patronage, and he is visited by senators; the Poet, discussing all this with the Painter, has composed an allegory warning Timon that Fortune is fickle. Timon, arriving, speaks courteously to all his suitors, pays his friend Ventidius' debt to free him from prison, and gives his servant Lucilius money to enable him to marry an old Athenian's daughter. He accepts the offerings of the Poet, the Painter, and the Jeweller, and welcomes Alcibiades, 20 of his fellow knights, and even the snarling philosopher Apemantus, who rails at his fellow guests as parasites.

1.2 At Timon's great banquet Apemantus continues to satirize the flatterers around him, who shower Timon with gifts but receive larger ones in return. A masque of Amazons is performed. Flavius, Timon's steward, knows his coffers are almost exhausted.

2.1 A senator is calculating the sums Timon owes, and hurriedly sends his factor Caphis to call in his own debts before Timon is bankrupt.

2.2 Flavius is besieged by Timon's creditors, on whom Apemantus vents his satirical wit while Flavius is finally able to convince Timon that he has given away his entire estate. Timon confidently sends servants to three of his friends, Lucius, Lucullus, and Sempronius, in order to borrow money from them. Flavius reports that the senators have already declined to make such a loan, but Timon sends him to borrow from Ventidius, who has recently inherited a fortune.

3.1 Lucullus at first assumes Timon's servant has come to bring him another gift, but when he learns he has come for money he attempts to bribe him to tell Timon he has not seen him. The servant throws back the bribe and curses him.

3.2 Lucius, hearing from three strangers of Lucullus' conduct, is indignant on Timon's behalf, but when he is himself asked for money he makes elaborate excuses: the strangers reflect on his hypocrisy.

3.3 Sempronius, too, refuses to lend Timon money, affecting to be too offended at not having been asked first.

3.4 Timon's house is besieged by his creditors' servants: eventually he himself emerges and rants at them.

3.5 The furious Timon tells an uncomprehending Flavius to invite Lucius, Lucullus, and Sempronius to dinner once more.

3.6 Alcibiades pleads with the senators for the life of one of his soldiers, who has committed manslaughter, and grows so angry at their refusal that they banish him: he vows to rally his troops and attack Athens in revenge.

3.7 Timon's friends, convinced his apparent bankruptcy must have been a test of their loyalty, gather eagerly for the feast. Covered dishes are brought in: Timon recites a satirical grace before their lids are lifted, revealing only stones in lukewarm water. He rants at his guests and beats them, vowing eternal misanthropy.

4.1 Outside Athens Timon curses the city, tearing off his clothes to live in the woods as a beast.

4.2 Flavius bids a poignant farewell to his fellow servants, sharing his remaining money with them: he sets off loyally to find and assist Timon.

4.3 Timon, still cursing mankind, digs for roots but finds gold. When Alcibiades arrives with two courtesans, Phrynia and Timandra, Timon gives them gold, to encourage the women to infect the world with venereal diseases and to help Alcibiades destroy Athens and then himself. After their departure, Apemantus arrives, and in a long philosophical dialogue points out that Timon's extreme misanthropy is merely the inverse of his former pride. After Timon finally drives Apemantus away, three thieves arrive, to whom Timon gives gold in order to sponsor their profession, but his sermon and his money in fact convert them to a love of peace. When Flavius arrives, however, Timon is moved by his fidelity, though he nonetheless insists that he stay away in future.

5.1 The Poet and the Painter also come in the hopes of obtaining gold from Timon: he drives them away with blows and curses.

5.2 Flavius brings two senators to Timon's cave, who beg him to return to Athens in honour and lead their defence against Alcibiades, but he professes indifference to his country's fate and suggests that to avoid death at Alcibiades' hands the citizens should all hang themselves. He says he has been writing his epitaph, and means to be buried between high and low tides on the beach.

5.3 The news of Timon's refusal to help Athens reaches the city.

5.4 A soldier, seeking Timon, finds only a gravestone: unable to read its inscription, he takes an impression of it for Alcibiades to interpret.

5.5 The senators surrender to Alcibiades, who promises to kill only his own enemies and those of Timon. The Soldier brings the news of Timon's death and seaside burial, and Alcibiades reads the misanthropic poem he composed as his epitaph. Though he knows Timon would scorn his grief, Alcibiades mourns Timon, and enters Athens with promises of peace.

ARTISTIC FEATURES

Constructed more as a series of emblems than as a narrative, and falling sharply into two very distinct halves—the first three acts depicting Timon's fall from grace, the last two his invective and death outside Athens—*Timon of Athens* is more remarkable for its poetry than for its drama, in this, perhaps, resembling the late romances. Timon's final vision of the tide washing his grave (5.4.99–108) certainly suggests a near-religious perspective beyond the reach of an ordinary play—let alone one so cynical about human motivation as this otherwise appears to be.

CRITICAL HISTORY

Although Samuel Johnson valued the play for its clear moral lesson against trusting in false friends, most commentators have found its remorseless insistence on this point crude, and even Johnson felt the play was deficient in structure. Samuel Taylor Coleridge, influentially, considered it an 'after vibration' of *King Lear*, 'a *Lear* of the satirical drama, a *Lear* of ordinary life'. William Hazlitt was unusual in his unqualified enthusiasm for the play, which he valued for its unrelenting earnestness, but generally the play has been respected for individual passages rather than as a whole: Karl Marx, for example, was deeply affected by Timon's moralizing against gold (4.3.25–45), initiating a reading of the play's vision of capitalist economics later developed by Kenneth Muir. Much discussion of the play has been devoted to explaining its perceived incompetence: around the turn of the 20th century, it became fashionable to attribute the melancholy of the 'problem plays' and tragedies to a personal crisis above which Shakespeare finally rose to produce the romances, and Frank Harris's view that Timon's ranting vents Shakespeare's own 'scream of suffering' (developed in *Shakespeare the Man*, 1909) was even echoed by E. K. Chambers, who decided that Shakespeare must have suffered a nervous breakdown while drafting the play and never completed it thereafter. More recent criticism has returned to the play's relations to the other works within the canon, whether the problem comedies, the romances (towards which Timon's sea-poetry seems to reach), or *Coriolanus* (whose hero's military campaign against his own city is prefigured by that of Alcibiades, while his proud refusal of a reciprocal social contract is anticipated by Timon's absolutist generosity and absolutist misanthropy). The play's most enthusiastic modern champion was G. Wilson Knight, who regarded it as one of Shakespeare's supreme achievements, and was given to performing Timon's speech of self-exile (4.1) in public lectures, complete with the removal of his clothes.

STAGE HISTORY

No productions of *Timon of Athens* are recorded before the première of Thomas Shadwell's adaptation, *The History of Timon of Athens, the Man-Hater*, in 1678. Shadwell shared the view of the Folio text adopted by many modern critics, declaring in a preface that 'it has the inimitable hand of Shakespear in it, which never made more masterly strokes than this. Yet I can truly say, I have made it into a play.' Shadwell's main contribution, filling a deficiency perceived by many readers since, was to add a love plot, extending the play's opposition between loyal servants and false friends by supplying Timon with a loyal mistress, Evandra, and an affected, mercenary fiancée, Melissa. With Thomas Betterton as Timon and masque music composed by Henry Purcell, this adaptation established itself in the repertory, frequently revived down to 1745. It was succeeded by another adaptation in 1771, by Richard Cumberland, who deprived Timon of his rival girlfriends (times had changed) and instead provided a virtuous daughter Evanthe, whose amorous complications with Alcibiades and Lucius fill out the plot. Spranger Barry played Timon in a grand Drury Lane production staged by David Garrick, but it lasted for only eleven performances. A subsequent reworking of Shadwell's adaptation by Thomas Hull (1786) achieved only one. In 1816 George Lamb attempted to restore Shakespeare's text, though he left some of Cumberland's changes to the ending and cut Alcibiades' mistresses: the result was an all-male *Timon of Athens*, which succeeded thanks to Edmund Kean's terrifying passion in the title role. Sporadic 19th-century revivals followed: Samuel Phelps was successful as Timon (1851, 1856), and Frank Benson rearranged the play into three acts for a Stratford revival in 1892. After this it was only sporadically produced for a century: Nugent Monck's 1935 production is remembered chiefly for its incidental music by a 21-year-old Benjamin Britten, Barry Jackson's post-war modern-dress production of 1947 for the bomb crater that was the set for the second half. Ralph Richardson and Paul Scofield, however, each found an otherworldly quality in the title role, and in 1999 Michael Pennington played

Timon sensitively in Gregory Doran's RSC production. Timon's ruin and rough-sleeping was given an extra poignancy in the intelligent parable of capitalist natural selection staged by Cardboard Citizens, a theatre troupe run by and for the homeless, as part of the RSC's 2006–7 Complete Works Festival. This production foreshadowed a wave of topical and unprecedentedly successful productions staged after the financial crash of 2008, including Lucy Bailey's at Shakespeare's Globe (2008), Barbara Gaines's at the Chicago Shakespeare Theatre (2012), and Nicholas Hytner's at the National Theatre (also 2012), in which Simon Russell Beale's Timon, renouncing civilization, memorably flung away his mobile phone.

 ON THE SCREEN

The only screen version on record is Jonathan Miller's BBC TV production, 1981. The cast included Jonathan Pryce as Timon (who delivered his last speech in a disconcerting upside-down close-up), Norman Rodway, Sebastian Shaw, and Diana Dors.

Titus Andronicus

Shakespeare's earliest and most notoriously violent tragedy, sensationally popular in his lifetime but only restored to critical favour in the late 20th century, may have had its first run of performances interrupted by plague. Philip Henslowe's 'Diary' reports that a play called 'titus & ondronicus' was performed by Sussex's Men at the Rose theatre on 24 January 1594. The play was entered in the Stationers' Register on 6 February 1594, only a few days after the Rose theatre was closed down following an outbreak of plague. Recent editors disagree on the exact date of composition. Verbal parallels in *The Troublesome Reign of King John*, published in 1591, and *A Knack to Know a Knave*, performed on 10 June 1592, along with the listing of three different acting companies on the title page of the 1594 quarto, suggest composition around 1590–1. Both internal and external evidence in favour of this early date is, however, easily confuted. The verbal parallels might derive from another play called *Titus and Vespacia*, which Henslowe recorded as being performed at the Rose on 11 April 1592. Besides, the listing of the three acting companies on the title page of the 1594 quarto might not be meant to be interpreted as a chronology of the play's stage history, as actors from Lord Strange's and Pembroke's Men were employed by Sussex's Men during the brief 1593–4 winter season. Editors who argue in favour of an earlier date of composition tend to believe that the authorship of *Titus Andronicus* is collaborative and that George Peele is Shakespeare's most likely collaborator. Thomas Middleton has also been proposed as the author of the 'fly' scene (added later; it appears only in the Folio text) in 3.2. Conversely, editors who posit that this tragedy was written between late 1593 and early 1594 are more inclined to attribute it entirely to Shakespeare.

 TEXT

The first quarto edition of *Titus Andronicus* was published in 1594, followed by two reprints in 1600 and 1611. Q1 was typeset from Shakespeare's foul papers, as suggested by the lack of essential stage directions, the irregularity of the speech-prefixes, and occasional false starts and second thoughts. The second and the third quartos emended obvious compositorial mistakes and introduced new ones, which were then inherited by the 1623 Folio edition, set from an annotated copy of Q3.

The main alterations introduced into the 1623 edition, including more extensive stage directions, act division, normalized speech-prefixes, and a whole new scene, the so-called fly-killing scene in Act 3, clearly derive from a promptbook. Although most editors choose Q1 as their copy text, because of its direct link to the author's holograph, most of the Folio variants are added to it, as they reflect original staging practices and conventions.

The fortunate discovery of the only extant copy of Q1 in Sweden in 1904 allowed 20th-century editors to realize that the ending as it appears in Q2 and the later editions was a compositorial mistake. The compositor of Q2 must have attempted to replace the missing lines from the last two pages in his copy of Q1, which had been accidentally damaged.

 SOURCES

Titus Andronicus has no direct sources. The play has often been connected to a narrative which, although surviving only in an 18th-century chapbook, was believed to derive from a much earlier version of the Titus story which

Shakespeare dramatized. This theory has recently been discredited in favour of an alternative hypothesis according to which Shakespeare modelled the character of Lavinia on Ovid's Philomel (*Metamorphoses*, book 6). It is however generally agreed that instead of borrowing from specific sources, Shakespeare turned to popular dramatic precedents, such as Thomas Kyd's adaptation of Senecan revenge tragedy, and other Elizabethan tragedies of blood.

 CHARACTER LIST

Saturninus *son of the late Emperor of Rome, afterwards Emperor*

Bassianus *his brother*

Titus Andronicus *Roman general, victorious over the Goths*

Marcus Andronicus *his brother, a tribune*

Lucius
Quintus *his sons*
Martius
Mutius

Lavinia *his daughter*

Young Lucius *a boy, son of Lucius*

Publius *son of Marcus*

Sempronius
Caius *Titus' kinsmen*
Valentine

Aemilius *a noble Roman*

Tamora, Queen of the Goths, afterwards Empress of Rome

Alarbus
Demetrius *her sons*
Chiron

Aaron *a Moor, her lover*

Nurse

Clown

Messenger

Senators, tribunes, Roman soldiers, attendants, other Romans, Goths

SYNOPSIS

1.1 Saturninus and Bassianus, the sons of the late Emperor of Rome, claim the right to succeed their father, but Marcus Andronicus, a tribune of the people, offers the crown to his brother Titus, as a reward for his victorious military campaigns against the Goths. The issue of the succession is temporarily postponed while Titus, who has lost 21 of his 25 sons in the recent wars, grants his eldest son Lucius permission to give proper burial to his brothers and appease their souls by sacrificing the eldest son of Tamora, the Queen of the Goths. Tamora and her two surviving sons, Chiron and Demetrius, plan to avenge his death. When offered the crown, Titus declines it and bestows it on Saturninus, who asks and obtains the hand of his daughter Lavinia. Bassianus, who is already engaged to Lavinia, reclaims his betrothed with the help of Titus' sons. Enraged by their disobedience, Titus kills his youngest son Mutius. Instead of helping Titus rescue Lavinia, Saturninus turns his back on his benefactor and obtains Tamora's consent to marry him. Betrayed by his sons and his Emperor, Titus finally agrees to give Mutius an honourable burial. Tamora, the new Empress, persuades Saturninus to put up with the Andronici, who have the support of the people of Rome, and wait patiently for the day when they can safely 'massacre them all'. Aaron, Tamora's black servant and lover, settles a dispute between Chiron and Demetrius over Lavinia, by suggesting that they should both rape her in the woods.

2.1 Titus organizes a royal hunt to celebrate the Emperor's wedding.

2.2 Aaron and Tamora meet in the woods and Aaron discloses his plans to have Lavinia raped and Bassianus killed. Tamora tells her sons that Bassianus and Lavinia have been threatening to take her life. Prompted by Tamora, Chiron and Demetrius kill Bassianus and rape Lavinia. Aaron lures Titus' sons Quintus and Martius into the pit where Chiron and Demetrius have thrown Bassianus' body and forges a letter in order to blame Titus' sons for Bassianus' murder.

2.3 Marcus stumbles upon Lavinia, who has been raped and mutilated.

3.1 Titus pleads for his sons' lives in vain and Lucius is banished for attempting to set them free. Lavinia is brought before Titus and the sight of her mangled body triggers Titus' maddened despair, which is only momentarily relieved by Aaron's offer to release his sons in exchange for Titus' right hand. Lucius and Marcus step in and offer to sacrifice their own right hand in order to spare Titus. Titus pretends to accept their offer but then asks Aaron to cut off his hand, while Lucius and Marcus are looking for an axe offstage. After Titus' selfless sacrifice, Marcus urges him not to give way to despair, but Marcus himself gives in to it, when a messenger returns Titus his mutilated hand and the severed heads of his two sons. The climax of Titus' distress is marked by a sublime, heart-rending bout of hysterical laughter. Titus' laughter ushers in the second movement of the tragedy, which is entirely devoted to Titus' attempts to avenge himself on his enemies. Lucius is sent to the Goths to seek their help.

3.2 Titus' lament is interrupted when Marcus kills a fly. Titus is outraged by Marcus' cruelty and is ready to disown him for causing pain to the fly and its relations. Marcus humours Titus' madness by pointing out that he killed the fly because it was as black as Aaron. Titus is pacified but then admits that the whole episode is absurd.

4.1 Lavinia manages to disclose the identity of her attackers by pointing to the Philomel story in a copy of Ovid's *Metamorphoses* and by drawing their names on the sand. The Andronici vow to carry out their revenge against Tamora and her associates.

4.2 Titus sends Chiron and Demetrius a bundle of weapons as a gift. The latter fail to decipher the real meaning of the Horatian maxim which Titus attaches to the gift. Aaron, however, realizes that Chiron and Demetrius have been detected. A nurse enters bearing Tamora and Aaron's baby. Because of its dark complexion, Tamora wants Aaron to dispatch it. Aaron however praises the beauty of the baby's dark skin, and plans to have it raised by a Goth and have the Goth's own newly born baby raised as the Emperor's son.

4.3 Titus indulges his maddened sorrow and shoots arrows bearing his pleas for justice into the sky. The Clown is sent to the Emperor with one of Titus' messages and is executed as a result.

4.4 The Goths led by Lucius are marching towards Rome. Tamora reassures Saturninus and explains how she will get Titus to agree to summon his son Lucius to Rome and arrange a parley with him.

5.1 Aaron is captured by Lucius and boasts about his evil deeds; he is unrepentant and unabashed by the prospect of death.

5.2 Tamora disguises herself as Revenge and visits Titus accompanied by her two sons, who are themselves disguised as her ministers, Murder and Rape. Tamora believes Titus to be mad as a result of his sorrows, but Titus sees through her disguise. He pretends to comply with Tamora's request and summons his son Lucius to his house, but he also offers to arrange for a banquet to entertain his guests. As soon as Tamora leaves, Titus kills her sons and bakes a pasty for the banquet with their blood and bones.

5.3 In the final scene, Titus welcomes his guests. After asking Saturninus' advice on what a father should do when his daughter has been violated, he slays Lavinia. When asked who raped Lavinia, Titus reveals the ingredients of the pasty which the Emperor and Empress have just fed on. Titus then stabs Tamora and is killed by the Emperor. Lucius finally slays the Emperor and, after reflecting on the lessons to be learned from such bloody excesses, he is unanimously elected as the new Emperor of Rome.

🎭 ARTISTIC FEATURES

Titus Andronicus is a sophisticated revenge tragedy, where the binary oppositions of good and evil, Roman and Goth, civilization and barbarism are systematically questioned. The aftermath of the unrelenting deconstruction of Roman values leaves Titus stranded in a nightmare world, where Lavinia's body becomes his new 'map of woe' and her speechless complaint a new alphabet. The first act of *Titus Andronicus*, which is now generally attributed to George Peele because of the un-Shakespearian quality of its dramatic diction, represents a daring experiment with contemporary stage conventions. Particularly impressive is the use of the upper stage as the Senate House in Act 1, as a result of which those in power literally overlook the powerless and the opposing parties confronting each other on the main stage. Similarly versatile is the use of the trapdoor leading to the cellar underneath the main stage, which after serving as the entrance to the tomb of the Andronici in Act 1 becomes the 'subtle pit' in Act 2.

⭐ CRITICAL HISTORY

The question of authorship dominated the critical history of *Titus Andronicus* well into the 20th century. Although Francis Meres included *Titus Andronicus* in the list of Shakespeare's plays in his *Palladis Tamia* (1598), his attribution was repeatedly contested. In 1687, Edward Ravenscroft claimed that 'some anciently conversant with the stage' told him that Shakespeare 'gave some master-touches to one or two of the principal parts or characters' in a play written by a 'private author'. Ravenscroft described the play as a 'most incorrect and undigested piece...rather a heap of rubbish than a structure'. It is however likely that his views were at least partly prompted by a wish to justify his 1678 adaptation, called *Titus Andronicus; or, The Rape of Lavinia*, which is even more gruesome than the original. Charles Gildon perpetuated Ravenscroft's views by expressing his dislike for the play and by arguing that *Titus Andronicus* is 'none of Shakespeare's plays'. Most of the 18th-century editors of Shakespeare followed suit. Edward Capell however advanced the hypothesis of an early date of composition and accounted for Shakespeare's indulgent representation of violence on stage by relating the play to the popularity enjoyed by the 'blood tragedies' written in the late 1580s and early 1590s. In 1785 Edmond Malone ascribed the play to Christopher Marlowe, Shakespeare's main rival at the beginning of his career. The theory of co-authorship, which first emerged in the early 20th century, is currently the most popular. Only towards the middle of the 20th century did critics start to overlook the vexed question of authorship in order to establish the intrinsic qualities of the play itself. Peter Brook's cornerstone production at Stratford in 1955 triggered off an unprecedented number of critical articles, although hardly any full-length study of the play appeared before the 1980s. The play is currently very popular thanks to the advent of critical and cultural theories, the greater attention devoted to issues of gender, sexuality, and race, and a general sense that we are much closer to barbarism now than we have been for many years. Critics now tend to regard *Titus Andronicus* as at very least an interesting precursor of the mature tragedies, with many interested in its intense interplay between violence and laughter, weeping and wailing.

 STAGE HISTORY

A drawing attributed to Henry Peacham, depicting a composite scene including key moments from Acts 1 and 5, is the only surviving illustration of the contemporary staging, if not of an actual performance, of any Shakespearian play. *Titus Andronicus* was very popular on the Elizabethan and Jacobean stage (in adapted versions which toured across northern Europe, as well as in England), and the play was revived unaltered after the Restoration, as John Downes reports in his *Roscius Anglicanus* (1708). Edward Ravenscroft adapted *Titus Andronicus* in 1678 and his version enjoyed a successful revival in 1720, thanks to James Quin's virtuoso performance as Aaron. Aaron remained the leading role in the only major 19th-century revival, when the black American actor Ira Aldridge played him in a heavily adapted version of the original, which turns Shakespeare's villain into a noble and dignified character.

Robert Atkins was the first 20th-century director to restore Shakespeare's original to the stage in his 1923 production at the Old Vic. Members of Atkins's audience fainted as a result of his attempt to stage the Shakespearian original as faithfully as possible. In his memorable 1955 production at Stratford-upon-Avon, starring Laurence Olivier as Titus, Vivien Leigh as Lavinia, and Anthony Quayle as Aaron, Peter Brook opted for a stylized rendition of violence (famously, with red ribbons representing blood), which lent an almost mythical dimension to both characters and action. In her shockingly realistic 1985 production at the Swan in Stratford-upon-Avon, Deborah Warner reversed the tendency towards stylization initiated by Brook in the 1950s. Warner's Lavinia, played by Sonia Ritter, was horribly disfigured and Brian Cox's wilful and senile Titus was also remarkable for his psychological verisimilitude. In 1995, Gregory Doran directed Antony Sher in the title role for a production at the Market Theatre in Johannesburg. Set in then contemporary South Africa, and making the (then) controversial decision to adopt South African rather than received pronunciation, the production explored the processes and experiences of trauma in the post-Apartheid era. (The play has similarly been used to dramatize contemporary political trauma elsewhere, in Silviu Purcerete's post-Ceauşescu production in Craiova, Romania, in 1994, for instance, and in Jan Klata's 2013 production in Gdansk, which cast a company from Dresden as German-speaking Romans and a company from Breslau as Polish-speaking Goths). In 2006 came two landmark productions of the play: Yukio Ninagawa's for the

Complete Works Festival in Stratford-upon-Avon; and Lucy Bailey's at Shakespeare's Globe. In an echo of the red ribbons of Brook's production, crimson yarns symbolized the bloodshed of Ninagawa's *Titus*: the red threads pouring and twisting out of Lavinia's (Hitomi Manaka) wrists and mouths set against a white and ethereal stage were uncannily brutal and strangely beautiful. By contrast, Lucy Bailey's 2006 (revived 2014) production for the Globe, for which the theatre's open yard was partly roofed in black fabric to make it resemble the Coliseum in Rome, was notorious for its fainters. Faced with a viscerally naturalistic Lavinia in a production which spared no expense in stage blood, the show provoked an average of three faints per show. Blanche McIntyre's 2017 production for the RSC, with David Troughton as Titus, was equally blood-soaked, but this modern dress production was more visibly interested in its own historical moment than in ancient Rome, gesturing with its modern-dress setting towards the new populist cruelties of our times.

 ## ON THE SCREEN

Jane Howell directed an imaginative BBC TV production, with Trevor Peacock in the title role, in 1985. By making Young Lucius the observer of the action, she raised the question of how horrific acts of violence affect child witnesses. In this her production was imitated by Julie Taymor's impressive and eclectic Hollywood film (1999), with Anthony Hopkins as Titus.

Troilus and Cressida

Shakespeare's tragicomedy of an aimless love in the midst of a futile war may be the last play he wrote before the death of Queen Elizabeth. It was entered in the Stationers' Register in February 1603, and must have been written after 1598, when one of its sources, George Chapman's *Seven Books of the Iliads of Homer*, was published: its armed Prologue is probably an allusion to Ben Jonson's *Poetaster*, acted in 1601, and since metrical tests place it after *Hamlet* and *Twelfth Night* but before *Measure for Measure* and *Othello* its likeliest date of composition is 1602.

TEXT

This ambiguous play has a thoroughly ambiguous textual history. Despite its 1603 entry in the Stationers' Register, the play appeared in quarto only in 1609, in an edition (set from Shakespeare's foul papers) which exists in two contradictory states: one promises on its title page that it prints *Troilus and Cressida* 'As it was acted by the King's Majesty's servants at the Globe', while the other not only omits this claim but adds an epistle to the reader which instead states that the play has never been acted at all ('you have here a new play, never staled with the stage, never clapper-clawed with the palms of the vulgar'). This circumstance has led to a profusion of hypotheses about the play's early history, including the theory that it was written for private performance, perhaps at one of the Inns of Court, and a conjecture that performance was forbidden because Shakespeare's portrait of Achilles was perceived as a reflection on the Earl of Essex. It is always possible, however, that whoever wrote the 1609 epistle to the reader had merely been misinformed about a play acted seven years earlier, or was deliberately lying in the hopes of selling a play which had been acted at the Globe but had not been popular. The circumstances in which the play reappeared in the Folio are no less striking: the play was to be reprinted from the quarto, but was apparently withdrawn due to difficulties in securing the copyright (and its intended place in the volume was filled by *Timon of Athens*). However, at the last minute (too late for it to be listed on the Folio's contents page) clearance was obtained for *Troilus and Cressida*, and so was a theatrical manuscript of the play, and it was squeezed into the volume, its text set from a copy of the quarto annotated by reference to this promptbook. The very existence of such a manuscript shows that the play had been acted, by 1623 at least, though the more than 500 substantive changes between quarto and Folio texts suggest that at some time Shakespeare had a number of second thoughts, including the addition of a prologue and the deletion of Pandarus' epilogue (reproduced from the quarto, though apparently marked for omission). Although the quarto calls it the 'History' or 'Famous History' of Troilus and Cressida, and its prefatory epistle describes it as a witty comedy, the Folio prints it among the tragedies: commentators have been puzzling over how to understand the play's tone and genre ever since.

SOURCES

Shakespeare's chief source for the love plot was Geoffrey Chaucer's masterpiece *Troilus and Criseyde*, his reading of it perhaps coloured by Robert Henryson's sequel *The Testament of Cresseid*, in which Cressida, deserted by Diomedes, becomes a leprous beggar (mistakenly attributed to Chaucer in Thynne's 1532 edition of his collected works). The play's depiction of the Trojan War freely blends and modifies elements from a number of different accounts: George Chapman's translation *Seven Books of the Iliads of Homer* (from which Shakespeare drew the character of Thersites, though not his actions); William Caxton's *Recuyell of the Histories of Troy* (1475) and John Lydgate's *Troy Book* (c. 1412–20), both derived from a common Italian original (these supplied material for most of the play's battle scenes and the debate in Troy, among much else); and Ovid's *Metamorphoses* (from which Shakespeare derived his opposition between the intelligent Ulysses and the 'blockish' Ajax, adding this dimension of Ajax's character to what is already a compound of two quite different figures in Lydgate, the ill-spoken Oyleus Ajax and the pride-hating Thelamonyous Ajax). Beyond these major sources, Ulysses' speech on degree (1.3.74–137) draws on Sir Thomas Elyot's *The Governor* (1531), and details of Shakespeare's depiction of the truce (and Hector's view of his fellow Trojan princes as unfit for moral philosophy, 2.2.162–6) show the influence of Robert Greene's *Euphues his Censure to Philautus* (1587).

CHARACTER LIST

Prologue

Trojans

Priam, King of Troy

Hector
Deiphobus
Helenus *a priest*
Paris — *his sons*
Troilus
Margareton *a bastard*

Cassandra *Priam's daughter, a prophetess*
Andromache *wife of Hector*

Aeneas — *Commanders*
Antenor

Pandarus *a lord*
Cressida *his niece*
Calchas *her father, who has joined the Greeks*
Helen *wife of Menelaus, now living with Paris*
Alexander *servant of Cressida*
Servants of Troilus, musicians, soldiers, attendants

Greeks
Agamemnon *Commander-in-Chief*
Menelaus *his brother*
Nestor
Ulysses
Achilles

Patroclus *his companion*   **Thersites**
Diomedes   **Myrmidons** *soldiers of Achilles*
Ajax   Servants of Diomedes, soldiers

⦂≡ SYNOPSIS

An armed prologue explains that the play begins in the middle of the Trojan War, briefly recounting its cause, Paris' theft of Menelaus' wife Helen.

1.1 In Troy, Troilus is impatient with the slow progress of the dilatory and petulant Pandarus, who is supposed to be wooing his niece Cressida on Troilus' behalf: at first languishing in love-sickness, Troilus eventually goes with Aeneas to join the fighting outside the city walls.

1.2 Pandarus speaks at length of Troilus' virtues to Cressida, though she feigns indifference: together they watch the Trojan warriors filing back into the city, Pandarus eagerly pointing out Troilus. After Pandarus leaves, Cressida admits in soliloquy that she already loves Troilus but is holding off to increase his sense of her value.

1.3 In the Greek camp Agamemnon, Nestor, Ulysses, Diomedes, and Menelaus discuss the failure of morale which has prevented them from achieving victory despite seven years besieging Troy: Ulysses diagnoses that the Greek army has lost its sense of hierarchy, imitating Achilles, who remains in his tent with Patroclus making sarcastic jokes at the leadership's expense. Aeneas brings a message from Troy: Hector challenges any Grecian willing to vouch for his mistress's worth to single combat, a challenge clearly intended for their pre-eminent warrior Achilles. Ulysses convinces Nestor they should rig a lottery to ensure that Ajax fights Hector rather than Achilles, partly so that morale may not be further damaged by the possible defeat of their best fighter, but partly to humble Achilles' pride.

2.1 The illiterate Ajax beats Thersites for refusing to read him a proclamation about Hector's challenge: Achilles and Patroclus intervene, enjoying Thersites' satirical ranting against Ajax until he turns on them. Achilles affects indifference about Hector's challenge.

2.2 In Troy King Priam and his sons Hector, Troilus, Paris, and Helenus debate the ethics of keeping Helen: Hector argues that she is not worth the casualties the war has already caused, but Troilus insists that they should remain constant to their original purpose. Their sister Cassandra arrives, prophesying the destruction of Troy unless Helen is restored to the Greeks. Troilus, however, is unmoved, and Paris wishes to keep his abducted partner. Hector, though unpersuaded by their arguments, concedes that he too means to maintain the quarrel for the sake of Troy's prestige, and tells them of the challenge he has sent the Greeks.

2.3 Thersites, still furious at his beating from Ajax, amuses Achilles and Patroclus with his railing. When the other Greek commanders arrive, with Ajax, Achilles withdraws into his tent and refuses to speak with them: meanwhile the commanders flatter Ajax, who grows increasingly proud, to their concealed amusement.

3.1 Pandarus calls privately on Paris, at home at Helen's insistence, to ask him to excuse Troilus' impending absence from supper: Paris guesses Troilus has an assignation with Cressida. Helen insists that Pandarus should sing a song, and he does, 'Love, love, nothing but love'. Helen and Paris go to help unarm Hector after his day's combat.

3.2 Troilus waits in the orchard while Pandarus fetches Cressida, giddy with anticipation: Pandarus embarrassingly brings the couple together, encouraging their kisses. Before Pandarus takes them indoors to a bed-chamber, each of the three makes a promise: Troilus that faithful lovers shall in future be called 'as true as Troilus', Cressida that if she be false to him faithless women shall be called 'as false as Cressid', and Pandarus that all goers-between shall be called 'panders' after him.

3.3 In the Greek camp Cressida's father, the defector Calchas, requests that Cressida should be brought from Troy in exchange for a Trojan pris-oner, Antenor: Agamemnon agrees. The Greek lords process past Achilles' tent, pretending not to be interested in him: after their departure Ulysses lectures Achilles about humanity's disregard for past achievements com-pared to its enthusiasm for present deeds, however trifling by comparison, and reveals that the commanders know that the reason he has been refus-ing to fight is a liaison with one of Priam's daughters, Polyxena. After Ulysses leaves his arguments are seconded by Patroclus: a troubled Achilles sends Thersites to request that Hector should be invited to visit his tent after his combat with Ajax.

4.1 Early in the morning Diomedes arrives in Troy to fetch Cressida and is conducted towards her lodging by Aeneas and Paris.

4.2 Troilus and Cressida, tenderly parting, are interrupted first by a coyly mocking Pandarus and then by the arrival of Aeneas, who privately tells Troilus that Cressida must go to the Greeks.

4.3 Pandarus tells a distraught Cressida the news.

4.4 Troilus is sent to fetch Cressida.

4.5 Troilus and Cressida say their private farewells in haste and distress, Troilus upsetting Cressida further by telling her to be true; they exchange tokens, a glove and a sleeve, before Diomedes arrives with Paris and

Aeneas. Diomedes offends Troilus by offering to be Cressida's protector as the party sets out for the city gate.

4.6 The Greek lords await Hector's arrival to fight with Ajax: when Diomedes brings Cressida, they each try to kiss her in turn, though she refuses Menelaus and also Ulysses, who after her departure accuses her of sluttishness. The Trojan party, including Troilus, arrives.

4.7 Hector breaks off his combat with Ajax on the grounds that they are cousins. He is formally introduced to each of the Greek leaders: Achilles insolently says he is considering where he will mortally wound Hector, and promises to fight with him the following day. Agreeing that their truce will last until then, all leave for Agamemnon's tent except Troilus and Ulysses: Troilus asks Ulysses to take him later to Calchas' tent.

5.1 Achilles reads a letter from Polyxena forbidding him to fight the following day while Thersites accuses Patroclus of being Achilles' catamite. After supper Hector is brought to Achilles' tent by the Grecian lords: Ulysses and Troilus follow Diomedes towards Calchas' tent, and Thersites in turn, anticipating mischief, follows them.

5.2 Concealed with Ulysses, Troilus watches in horror as Cressida flirts uneasily with an insistent Diomedes, to whom she eventually gives the sleeve Troilus gave her: after Diomedes leaves she speaks in dismay at her own inconstancy. Unseen, Thersites comments cynically on the whole interview. After Cressida departs, Troilus rages, unable at first to accept the truth of what he has seen, and vows to kill Diomedes in the next day's battle.

5.3 The following morning Andromache, joined by Cassandra and later Priam, begs her husband Hector not to fight, convinced he will be killed: he himself tries to persuade Troilus to stay in Troy, but both men leave for the battle, Troilus after tearing up a love letter from Cressida delivered by the ailing Pandarus.

5.4-9 In the battle, punctuated by Thersites' commentary, Troilus fights Diomedes: Nestor sends the body of the slain Patroclus to Achilles: and Achilles at last rejoins the fighting, determined to kill Hector. After Troilus drives back both Ajax and Diomedes at once, Achilles and Hector duel: Hector bests Achilles, who leaves. Hector pursues and kills a splendidly armed Greek while Achilles instructs his Myrmidon troops to surround and kill Hector. Thersites' enjoyment of a duel between Paris and Menelaus is interrupted by Margareton, a bastard son of Priam, whom he flees. As it grows dark, Hector unarms, alone: Achilles has his Myrmidons kill him, and they leave to tie Hector's body behind Achilles' horse and drag it around the battlefield.

5.10 The Greeks, learning Achilles has killed Hector, are convinced their ultimate victory is inevitable.

5.11 Troilus brings Paris, Aeneas, and others the news of Hector's death, consoled only by thoughts of vengeance. (In the quarto he is then accosted by Pandarus, whom he shuns, and Pandarus speaks an epilogue, lamenting how bawds are reviled by their post-coital customers: he anticipates his own imminent death from venereal diseases, which he proposes to bequeath to the audience.)

🎭 ARTISTIC FEATURES

Troilus and Cressida has an unusually arcane and learned vocabulary (some of it legal), and a penchant for set-piece displays of rhetoric, which have sometimes been adduced in support of the theory that it was written for the Inns of Court. The play's scepticism about all forms of chivalric idealism, most obviously expressed by the cynical Thersites (who reduces the epic of Troy and the love of Troilus and Cressida to 'wars and lechery'), has led some to see it as merely a satirical, anti-heroic burlesque, but Shakespeare's compassion for his characters—most obviously the lovers, who for all their failings are given one of the most moving valediction scenes in the canon—remains as evident as always.

✯ CRITICAL HISTORY

Although Ulysses' speeches on degree, and on the need for perseverance ('Time hath, my lord, | A wallet at his back…', 3.3.139–84), were often anthologized among Shakespeare's beauties (and are still sometimes quoted, misleadingly, as unmediated expressions of Shakespeare's own views), the play as a whole was generally regarded with baffled dislike until the middle of the 20th century. John Dryden, prefacing his 1679 adaptation, laments that Shakespeare's style is 'so pestered with figurative expressions that it is as affected as it is obscure', and his equal objections to the play's characterization and plotting are made clear by his alterations to them: his Troilus resists Cressida's removal to the Greek camp, and his misunderstood Cressida (though she humours Diomedes) is faithful to him throughout, eventually killing herself to prove it. Dr Johnson had little sympathy for either Cressida or Pandarus, whom he thought 'detested and contemned' by all readers, and his views were echoed by 19th-century commentators horrified by the play's cynicism and sexual indelicacy: as late as 1924 Agnes Mure Mackenzie (in *The Women in Shakespeare's Plays*) could describe *Troilus and Cressida* as 'the work of a man whose soul is poisoned with filth'. Mackenzie is one of several early 20th-century critics (among them E. K. Chambers and Frank Harris) who attempted to explain the play, like *Timon of Athens* and the other 'problem plays', as the morbid symptom of a personal crisis, while others tried to excuse it as Shakespeare's contribution to the ill-natured 'War of the Theatres'. By the 1930s, however, these approaches were already giving place to a very different estimate of the play's artistic success. In the era of high modernism the play's difficulty, intellectuality, and frank, Donne-like concern with sexuality made it a favourite with academic critics, among them George Wilson Knight and Una Ellis-Fermor, and its depiction of a pointless but apparently unstoppable war helped preserve its position in the academic canon through the era of Vietnam. Its reflections on time and the mutability of personal identity have been much studied, while feminist criticism has been particularly interested in Cressida, a heroine who seems to transact her own personal life outside the normative categories of 'maid, widow, or wife'.

STAGE HISTORY

No records survive of pre-Restoration performances, and though Shakespeare's original may have been revived at Smock Alley in Dublin in the 1670s, in England the play would only be seen in Dryden's tidy version (performed with reasonable frequency between 1679 and 1734) before the 20th century. Even Dryden's version was most praised for its new scenes, notably a quarrel and reconciliation between Troilus and Hector and a rhetorical confrontation between Troilus and Diomedes. The original was first revived in Munich in 1898 (played, by an all-male cast, as a blackly comic skit on Homer) and other German productions followed. The play was at last revived semi-professionally, to an unconvinced London audience, in 1907, and a similar venture by William Poel in 1912–13 is remembered only for the young Edith Evans's coquettish Cressida. The Marlowe Society produced the play in Cambridge in 1922, where its perspective on war was received sympathetically by the First World War veterans in its audience, but the first fully professional English production, at the Old Vic the following year, was a critical failure. More successful, however, was a modern-dress revival at the Westminster Theatre in 1938, and since the Second World War the play has been revived frequently, becoming something of a directors' favourite. Tyrone Guthrie's 1956 Old Vic production was the first of many to costume the play on the eve of the First World War, with cavalry sabres about to give place to machine guns: a notable successor in this respect was the 1985 RSC production, with Juliet

Stevenson as a sympathetic Cressida more betrayed by Anton Lesser's Troilus than vice versa. Dorothy Tutin had played the role far more flirtatiously in Peter Hall and John Barton's legendary 1960 version at Stratford, with Max Adrian as Pandarus and Denholm Elliott as Troilus: other important revivals include Sam Mendes's RSC production of 1991, with Amanda Root as Cressida, Ralph Fiennes as a neurotically insecure Troilus, and Simon Russell Beale as the most wonderfully repulsive Thersites in living memory. The play has increasingly attracted companies beyond Britain: during the 2012 'Cultural Olympiad' in London, for instance, it was seen in a fine Maori production by Nagkau Toa of Auckland, New Zealand, at Shakespeare's Globe, and, in Stratford, in a disastrous collaboration between New York's Wooster Group and the RSC.

 ON THE SCREEN

It is a sign of the play's return to favour since the Second World War that three television adaptations have been made, the first in 1954, a National Youth Theatre production (1966), and Jonathan Miller's classically dressed BBC TV production (1981).

Twelfth Night; or, What You Will

One of Shakespeare's best-loved comedies, encompassing a formidable range of moods and dramatic styles, *Twelfth Night* is first mentioned in the diary of a law student, John Manningham, who saw it performed in the hall of Middle Temple on 2 February 1602. The play was probably at most a few months old at the time, as a number of details in the text suggest. Maria mentions 'the new map with the augmentation of the Indies' (3.2.74–5), usually identified as one first published in Richard Hakluyt's *Voyages* in 1599; 2.3 quotes from a number of songs first published in 1600 (in Robert Jones's *First Book of Songs and Airs*); while Feste's view that the phrase 'out of my element' is 'overworn' (3.1.57–8) alludes to a running joke against the expression in Thomas Dekker's *Satiromastix*, premièred by Shakespeare's company in 1601. The Chamberlain's Men performed an unnamed play on Twelfth Night in 1601 before Elizabeth's court and her guest of honour Don Virginio Orsino, Duke of Bracciano: despite Leslie Hotson's strenuous arguments, this is unlikely to have been *Twelfth Night*, though Shakespeare's choice of the name Orsino for the play's duke when he wrote his play later in 1601 may have been influenced by recollections of the occasion.

TEXT

The play was first printed in the Folio in 1623, in a good text derived from a literary transcript prepared by a scribe (possibly especially for this purpose). The view that the text shows signs of post-performance revision is no longer widely accepted.

SOURCES

Two or even three of the play's sources were recognized very early: Manningham commented that the play was 'much like the *Comedy of Errors* or *Menaechmi* in Plautus, but most like…that in Italian called *Inganni*'. The resemblances between *Twelfth Night* and Plautus' *Menaechmi*, the source for Shakespeare's earlier play about identical twins, are clear (*The Comedy of Errors* similarly sets its comedy of mistaken identity within a poignant framework of separation and reunion), though its debts to an Italian play are more complicated. By *Inganni*, Manningham meant the anonymous *Gl'ingannati* (*The Deceived*, 1531), which indeed provided the ultimate source for the relationships between the characters whom Shakespeare rechristened Orsino, Olivia, Viola, and Sebastian. Shakespeare, however, probably knew *Gl'ingannati* only at second or third hand, via prose versions in Bandello's *Novelle* (1554) and François de Belleforest's *Histoires tragiques* (1571) which were themselves adapted by Barnabe Rich in 'Apollonius and Silla', the second story in his *Farewell to Military Profession* (1581). The subplot of the gulled steward, however, has no such literary source, and attempts to identify Malvolio as a hostile portrait of a particular Elizabethan courtier have been uniformly unconvincing.

👥 CHARACTER LIST

Orsino, Duke of Illyria

Valentine⎤
Curio ⎦ *attending on Orsino*

First Officer

Second Officer

Viola *a lady, later disguised
as Cesario*

A **Captain**

Sebastian *her twin brother*

Antonio *another sea-captain*

Olivia *a Countess*

Maria *her waiting-gentlewoman*

Sir Toby Belch *Olivia's kinsman*

Sir Andrew Aguecheek *companion
of Sir Toby*

Malvolio *Olivia's steward*

Fabian *a member of Olivia's
household*

Feste the Clown *her jester*

A **Priest**

A **Servant** of Olivia

Musicians, sailors, lords, attendants

☰ SYNOPSIS

1.1 Orsino, Duke of Illyria, listens to music as he languishes for the love of Countess Olivia: when Valentine reports that Olivia refuses his suit, vowing to mourn her dead brother for seven years, he comforts himself with the reflection that a woman capable of such emotion for a mere brother will in due course love passionately.

1.2 Viola, washed up in Illyria after a shipwreck in which she fears her twin brother Sebastian has perished, learns from the ship's Captain of Olivia's vow and Orsino's suit: with his help she intends to disguise herself as a eunuch and enter Orsino's service.

1.3 At Olivia's house her dissolute uncle Sir Toby Belch detains the rich but foolish Sir Andrew Aguecheek, another hopeful suitor to Olivia: Sir Andrew's ineptitude is demonstrated by his incompetent repartee with the witty servant Maria.

1.4 Viola, disguised as 'Cesario', has become such a favourite of Orsino that he sends her to court Olivia on his behalf, an errand she accepts reluctantly, confessing in an aside that she herself loves Orsino.

1.5 The clown Feste has incurred Olivia's displeasure by a long absence, but contrives to regain her favour by riddling that she is more foolish than he for mourning that her brother is in heaven. Her steward Malvolio, however, remains Feste's adversary, and is gently rebuked by Olivia for his ungenerosity of spirit. Olivia sends Feste to look after Sir Toby, who is already drunk. Viola, after refusing to be put off by a baffled Malvolio, is eventually admitted to Maria and Olivia: besting Maria's wit, she secures a private interview with Olivia, whom she rebukes for her pride, though she acknowledges her beauty. Olivia dismisses Orsino's suit but grows increasingly interested in 'Cesario', who she hopes will come again: after Viola leaves, she sends Malvolio after her with a ring she claims was left as an unwanted gift from Orsino.

2.1 Sebastian tells his devoted friend Antonio of Viola, whom he believes to have drowned. Antonio, though he has mortal enemies at Orsino's court, decides to follow Sebastian there.

2.2 Malvolio gives Viola the ring Olivia claimed she had left as a present. Alone, Viola realizes that Olivia has fallen in love with Cesario, and wonders how this complicated situation will resolve itself.

2.3 After midnight, Sir Toby and Sir Andrew have Feste sing a song, 'O mistress mine', and join him in singing catches: Maria warns them they are too loud, and Malvolio arrives to rebuke them for disturbing the household, threatening Sir Toby that Olivia's displeasure may result in his banishment from it. Sir Toby is affronted at this check from a mere servant, and, after Malvolio leaves, Maria, with his eager encouragement, plots revenge: she will forge a letter from Olivia to trick the steward into thinking his mistress is in love with him.

2.4 Orsino speaks of love with Viola: they listen to Feste sing 'Come away, come away death'. Defending women against the charge of being less constant than men, Viola speaks of her own feelings and predicament under cover of describing a sister who pined away through concealing her love. Orsino sends her again to woo Olivia.

2.5 Sir Toby, Sir Andrew, Maria, and another servant, Fabian, hide in the garden and watch Malvolio approach the forged letter Maria has placed in his path. Malvolio is already imagining becoming Count through marriage to Olivia and lecturing Sir Toby when he finds it. Despite the letter's obscure anagram of 'M.O.A.I.' and its refusal actually to name either its addressee or its feigned author, its purport is clear: a confession of love from Olivia in which she urges Malvolio to spurn Sir Toby, smile, and wear yellow stockings, cross-gartered. Malvolio, completely taken in, is overjoyed, and hastens to comply. Maria hurries her confederates towards Olivia to watch for Malvolio's transformation.

3.1 Viola, also on her way to Olivia, meets Feste, who wittily begs money: she also meets Sir Toby and Sir Andrew, who is impressed with the courtliness with which Viola greets Olivia. When they are alone, Olivia confesses her love: when Viola says she can only pity her, Olivia feigns that she might yet love Orsino, in the hopes of inducing Viola to come again on his behalf.

3.2 Sir Andrew, about to leave on the grounds that Olivia obviously prefers Cesario to himself, is persuaded by Sir Toby and Fabian that Olivia is deliberately offering him a chance of proving his valour, and he leaves to write a challenge to Cesario. Maria fetches the others to see Malvolio, who has already changed his stockings.

3.3 Antonio, in danger because of his former participation in a sea-fight in which he helped to plunder Orsino's galleys, gives the sightseeing Sebastian his purse, arranging to meet him discreetly at an inn later.

3.4 Olivia has sent after Viola once more, but is distracted from her own affairs by the appearance of the cross-gartered Malvolio, whose smiling quotations from the forged letter convince his mistress he has lost his wits. After she leaves to see Viola, Sir Toby, Fabian, and Maria speak to Malvolio as if they believe he is possessed: he leaves, still confident of Olivia's love. Sir Andrew has written an incompetent and cowardly challenge for Cesario, which Sir Toby resolves not to deliver, preferring to challenge Cesario in person. Olivia and Viola enter, Viola once more asking Olivia to bestow her love on Orsino rather than on herself: after Olivia's departure, Sir Toby tells Viola that Sir Andrew means to duel with her, convincing Viola of his implacable and expert rage. Sir Toby then persuades Sir Andrew that Viola is equally furious and deadly: their mutually terrified sword-fight, however, is interrupted by the arrival of Antonio, who mistakes Viola for Sebastian. Antonio is about to fight with Sir Toby when officers arrive to arrest the newcomer: he asks Viola for the return of his purse, and is shocked when she denies receiving it, leaving heartbroken for prison. Viola begins to hope her brother may still be alive. Sir Andrew, now convinced of Viola's cowardice, follows her to renew his challenge.

4.1 Sebastian meets Feste, who is offended not to be recognized by him: Sir Andrew arrives and strikes Sebastian, who is quick to avenge the blow, and finds himself at drawn swords with Sir Toby when Olivia arrives and similarly takes Sebastian for Cesario. Sebastian is at once puzzled and delighted by her tender attention, and departs with her.

4.2 Malvolio, presumed mad, is locked up in darkness: Feste pretends to be Sir Topas, a curate sent to examine his alleged demonic possession, but eventually agrees to bring Malvolio ink, paper, and a light that he may write to Olivia.

4.3 Sebastian, though still bewildered, is delighted by Olivia's love, and agrees to go with her and a priest to be married.

5.1 Feste refuses to let Fabian see the letter he has promised to give Olivia from Malvolio, and begs money from Orsino, who arrives with Viola and other attendants. Antonio is brought before them: Orsino remembers his valour despite regarding him as a pirate, but counters his renewed accusations of falsehood against Viola by witnessing that Viola has been at his court for the last three months rather than in Antonio's company as he alleges. This discussion is cut short by the arrival of Olivia. Orsino says he knows his rightful place in her heart has been usurped by Cesario, whom he threatens to kill: when Viola promises she loves Orsino above all else, and means to leave with him come what may, Olivia produces the priest, who bears witness that Cesario and Olivia are married. Sir Andrew arrives, followed by Sir Toby, who has been wounded in a fight they have provoked with Sebastian: they are shocked to find Viola there. Sebastian now arrives, to apologize to his newly married wife for hurting her kinsman: as the onlookers marvel at seeing him and Viola at once, he is at first overjoyed to see Antonio again before he sees his disguised sister. The twins tentatively question one another to confirm each other's identities: Viola explains that if her male clothes hinder his recognition, she can reclaim her own from the Sea Captain. It becomes clear how Olivia has come to marry Sebastian after falling in love with Cesario, and Orsino realizes that Viola, disguised, has often confessed that she loves him. The Sea Captain who has her clothes, however, has been arrested at Malvolio's suit, so Malvolio is summoned: meanwhile Fabian reads Olivia his evidently sane letter (replacing Feste, who insists on reading it in too mad a voice). Orsino agrees to marry Viola in a double celebration at Olivia's house. Malvolio arrives and confronts Olivia with the letter he found in the garden: she explains that it is forged, and Fabian and Feste confess their trick (Fabian revealing that Sir Toby has married Maria as a reward for her wit, Feste saying he took part in order to avenge Malvolio's criticism of his fooling). Malvolio leaves, vowing revenge on them all. Orsino sends after him, in order that Viola's female clothes can be retrieved for her wedding: meanwhile he will continue to call her Cesario. Feste is left alone to sing a song as an epilogue, 'When that I was and a little tiny boy'.

🎭 ARTISTIC FEATURES

Rich in songs—provided for Robert Armin, the original Feste, who had replaced the less intellectual and melodious fool Will Kempe in 1599—and peopled by characters who are given to reflecting eloquently but passively on their imprisonment within their own and one another's fantasies, *Twelfth Night* is the most lyrical of the mature comedies. At the close of its at once atrociously cruel and exquisitely funny sub-plot, one of Shakespeare's most Jonsonian, even the puritanical Malvolio rises to the dignity of blank verse.

✸✸ CRITICAL HISTORY

Although apparently highly regarded in Shakespeare's time and thereafter— Leonard Digges's dedicatory verse in Benson's 1640 edition of Shakespeare's poems includes the couplet 'The Cockpit galleries, boxes, all are full | To hear Malvolio, that cross-gartered gull'—the play fell from favour for 80 years after the Restoration, its Italianate intrigues and fancies dismissed as unrealistic. As late as 1765 Dr Johnson, who called the play 'elegant and easy, and in some of the lighter scenes exquisitely humorous', objected that the winding-up of the main plot 'wants credibility and fails to produce the proper instruction required in the drama, as it exhibits no true picture of life'. The play was valued more highly by Romantic critics such as A. W. Schlegel, who singled out the importance of both music and the concept of 'fancy' to the play in his *Course of Lectures on Dramatic Literature* (1809–11), while William Hazlitt considered it 'one of the most delightful of Shakespeare's comedies…perhaps too good-natured for comedy'. In the 19th century Viola, the most acceptably bashful and passive of Shakespeare's comic heroines, was a favourite of moralist critics, and her imaginary youth is described with particular enthusiasm in Mary Cowden Clarke's *The Girlhood of Shakespeare's Heroines* (1850–1). In academic criticism she has often been upstaged, however, by two other characters. Charles Lamb was one of the first commentators to speak in favour of Malvolio, and Lamb's contemporaries also singled out another figure often seen as providing the play's keynote, Feste, later the subject of an important essay by A. C. Bradley. Twentieth-century criticism treated both of these characters ever more seriously, as perceptions of the play's happy comedy increasingly gave place to a sense of its social tensions and sexual undercurrents: recent discussions have related it to the 'problem plays' as often as to what might otherwise seem its more natural companion piece, *As You Like It*. Malvolio has been viewed as a comic antagonist whose potentially tragic dignity approaches that of Shylock: Feste has been identified as a detached, ironic commentator on the play whose freelance status and penchant for puns mirror the elusiveness of language and desire themselves. Since the Second World War *Twelfth Night* has provided fertile ground for anthropologically inclined critics who have pursued its title's allusion to seasonal rituals of misrule and inversion, and its intrigues have been equally attractive to Marxists interested in the social cross-dressing of Malvolio and to feminists and queer theorists interested in the gender cross-dressing of Viola and the hints of homoeroticism which inform her relations with Orsino and Olivia, not to mention Antonio's adoration of Sebastian.

STAGE HISTORY

A similar trajectory—from unfashionably whimsical trifle to happy romantic comedy to bitter-sweet drama of social and sexual identity—informs *Twelfth Night*'s post-Restoration stage history. The play was evidently popular down to the Civil War, as Digges's poem suggests: a court performance is recorded in 1622 as 'Malvolio' (a title by which Charles I would also call the play, in a note on the contents page of his copy of the Folio). Doubtless remembering the play's earlier success in court circles, William Davenant revived it in the early 1660s, the role of Viola now transformed by the arrival of professional actresses into a breeches part, but the play was laid aside after 1669, when Samuel Pepys, who had earlier dismissed it as 'but a silly play', described it as 'one of the weakest plays that ever I saw on the stage'. The extent to which its lyricism had gone out of fashion is vividly suggested by a short-lived, largely prose adaptation, *Love Betrayed; or, The Agreeable Disappointment* (1703), which, as its author William Burnaby candidly admitted in a preface, rejected most of Shakespeare's poetry and much of his plotting entirely: 'Part of the tale of this play, I took from Shakespeare, and about fifty of his lines.' The original was restored, however, in 1741, performed at Drury Lane by the company who revived *The Merchant of Venice* and *As You Like It* during the same season: Charles Macklin was Malvolio, Hannah Pritchard played Viola, and Kitty Clive Olivia. Since then, the play's popularity has never waned, with the role of Malvolio attracting star actors and actor-managers from Richard Yates through Samuel Phelps, Henry Irving, and Beerbohm Tree down to Donald Wolfit, Laurence Olivier, Donald Sinden, and Simon Russell Beale. Viola has been an equally important role for actresses (her soliloquy in 2.2, 'I left no ring with her. What means this lady?', has long been the most familiar of audition pieces), offering in the 18th and 19th centuries an irresistible combination of professed modesty with the titillation provided by male costume's display of her figure. Dorothea Jordan was a sensation in the 1790s, and Leigh Hunt's account of the part is dominated by his attention to Ann Maria Tree's limbs: 'It is impossible not to be struck…with a leg like this. It is fit for a statue: still fitter for where it is.' Equally appealing successors in the part included Charlotte Cushman, Ada Rehan, and Ellen Terry. Increasing decorative elaboration in the 19th century led to frequent transpositions of scenes, a tendency which culminated in Beerbohm Tree's 1901 production, where most of the scenes in Olivia's garden had to be run consecutively, as its set's real grass and fountains could not be changed during the performance. The way forward, however, was more accurately pointed by Harley Granville-Barker's revival at the Savoy in 1912: its styling was influenced by William Poel's experiments with neo-Elizabethan open stages, its Malvolio, Henry Ainley, was heartbreakingly overwrought in the prison scene, and its Feste, Hayden Coffin, was the most melancholy for many years. Since then the play's ever more frequent productions have, in general, become progressively more autumnal: major revivals have included Tyrone Guthrie's (1937, with Olivier as Sir Toby, Alec Guinness as Sir Andrew, and Jessica Tandy confusingly doubling Viola and Sebastian), John Gielgud's (1955, with Olivier as Malvolio and Vivien Leigh as Viola), and John Barton's delicately Elizabethan RSC production of 1969 (with Judi Dench as Viola). Two memorable productions of the 1980s instructively paralleled contemporary trends in criticism: Ariane Mnouchkine staged an exotic, ambiguous Illyria in her Théâtre du Soleil production of 1982, while Cheek by Jowl's 1985 touring production stressed the play's homoeroticism, eventually pairing off Feste with Antonio. In 2017 Tamsin Greig played a lesbian Malvolia in Simon Godwin's popular production at the National Theatre.

 ## ON THE SCREEN

The earliest film of *Twelfth Night* was a silent version made in America in 1910. No fewer than five television versions have been made for the BBC, culminating in the 1980 production with Alec McCowen as Malvolio and Felicity Kendal as Viola. An American TV production (1957) with Maurice Evans, Denholm Elliott, and Max Adrian was well received. Especially memorable was John Dexter's production for British commercial television (1970) with Alec Guinness (Malvolio), Tommy Steele (Feste), Ralph Richardson (Sir Toby Belch), and Joan Plowright (Viola). A brooding production directed by Judi Dench for Kenneth Branagh's Renaissance Theatre Company, with music by Paul McCartney, is also preserved on videotape, directed by Paul Kafno (1990). Only two cinema films provide a full treatment of the play. The 1955 Russian film directed by Yakow Fried balances boisterous comedy with subtle characterization, and Trevor Nunn's *Twelfth Night* (1996), filmed in Cornwall, stresses visually the play's recurrent sea imagery. Nunn's strong cast—including Nigel Hawthorne as Malvolio, Imogen Stubbs as Viola, and Ben Kingsley as Feste—capture both the play's poignancy and its fun. Nunn, in common with many British stage directors, opted on this occasion for a late nineteenth-century country house costume-drama setting; more contemporary in its resonance was Tim Supple's television version of 2003, in which Viola and Sebastian appeared to be Eastern Mediterranean refugees.

The Two Gentlemen of Verona

This perennially fresh and pleasantly fallible comedy may be Shakespeare's first work for the professional stage, probably composed around 1590. The first of the six Shakespearian comedies mentioned by Francis Meres's *Palladis Tamia* in 1598, its dramatic technique suggests inexperience, and its tone is far closer to that of the courtly comedies of the 1580s (such as John Lyly's *Midas*, 1588–9, which at one point it echoes) than is that of any other Shakespearian comedy. Certain scholars have placed *The Two Gentlemen of Verona* in the mid-1590s, sometimes on the grounds that its debts to Arthur Brooke's poem *Romeus and Juliet* suggest a date closer to that of the infinitely more accomplished *Romeo and Juliet*, but allusions in *Richard Duke of York* (*3 Henry VI*) show that Shakespeare already knew Brooke's poem much earlier. While others have evolved theories of piece-meal revision that would date certain passages as late as 1598, no modern scholar has placed the bulk of its composition any later than 1594, and recent studies have tended to place it earlier in the canon rather than later.

 TEXT

The play is printed as the second play in the First Folio, 1623: there is no evidence of any earlier attempt to publish it. The Folio text, which is for the most part a reliable one (though unusually short), seems to derive from a transcript by the scribe Ralph Crane: it displays characteristic features of his work such as the listing at the head of each scene of all the characters who will appear in it, and the omission of all stage directions except exits. Various inconsistencies may suggest that Crane was transcribing Shakespeare's own foul papers, an authorial draft which retained a high proportion of loose ends, but the text's consistency with speech-prefixes (unusual even for Crane) may suggest that he was working from a fair copy prepared for theatrical use, in which case its brevity may result from abridgement for some specific performance. The small amount of profanity in *The Two Gentlemen of Verona* as it stands, which distinguishes it sharply from the other early comedies, supports this latter possibility, suggesting that the play had been expurgated for a revival since the Act to Restrain Abuses of Players, 1606.

SOURCES

Jorge de Montemayor's prose romance *La Diana enamorada* (1559) provided the outline of the Proteus and Julia plot, perhaps in Bartholomew Yonge's translation (1582, printed 1598), but more probably via the lost play *Felix and Philiomena* (performed at court in 1585). A parallel to the Proteus–Valentine–Silvia situation is found in the story of Titus and Gisippus in Boccaccio's *Decameron*, retold in Sir Thomas Elyot's *The Governor* (1531), which Shakespeare may echo in his last scene. Other details are drawn from Ovid, from Lyly's *Sapho and Phao* (1584), and from Brooke's *Romeus and Juliet* (1562): some of the play's minor confusions as to whether the action is taking place in Verona, Mantua, or Milan may result from Shakespeare's alternation between different sources. Only the Lance and Crab scenes seem entirely original.

CHARACTER LIST

Duke of Milan
Silvia *his daughter*
Proteus *a gentleman of Verona*
Lance *his clownish servant*
Valentine *a gentleman of Verona*
Speed *his clownish servant*
Thurio *a foolish rival to Valentine*
Antonio *father of Proteus*

Panthino *his servant*
Julia *beloved of Proteus*
Lucetta *her waiting-woman*
Host *where Julia lodges*
Eglamour *agent for Silvia in her escape*
Outlaws
Servants, musicians

SYNOPSIS

1.1 Valentine parts from his friend Proteus, whom he mocks for being in love with Julia, in order to travel to Milan. His servant Speed, who has just delivered a love letter to Julia for Proteus to no apparent effect, follows him.

1.2 Julia receives Proteus' letter from her maid Lucetta, who speaks in his favour: she appears to be angry, and tears the letter up, but cannot subsequently resist the temptation to reassemble such pieces as she can.

1.3 Proteus' father resolves to give Proteus the same opportunities Valentine is enjoying by sending him, too, to the Milanese court: surprised while reading his first love letter from Julia, Proteus, in part as a result of feigning that the letter is from Valentine, is compelled to agree to this course of action.

2.1 In Milan, Valentine has fallen in love with Silvia. She has commissioned Valentine to write a letter for her to 'one she loves', and when she inspects what he has written he cannot understand what she means by telling him to keep it; Speed has to explain that Valentine is himself the object of her love.

2.2 Exchanging rings with vows of mutual fidelity, Proteus and Julia part.

2.3 Proteus' servant Lance and his dog Crab are also off to Milan: deploring the dry-eyed callousness of his dog, Lance comically re-enacts his lachrymose parting from his family.

2.4 Valentine bickers with his rival for Silvia's love, Thurio, until her father the Duke announces the imminent arrival of Proteus. Valentine presents his friend to Silvia, and, when Silvia and Thurio have departed, reveals his plan to elope with her, in which he enlists Proteus as an accomplice. Left alone, Proteus confesses that he has himself fallen in love with Silvia.

2.5 Speed welcomes Lance to Milan, and they joke about their masters' loves.

2.6 Proteus decides to reveal Valentine's planned elopement to the Duke, so as to ensure Valentine's banishment and leave only the dim-witted Thurio as a rival.

2.7 The lovelorn Julia instructs Lucetta to provide her with a male disguise in which she can safely follow Proteus to Milan.

3.1 Proteus betrays the imminent elopement of Silvia with Valentine to the Duke, who finds Valentine already equipped with the rope ladder by which he means to effect it. The Duke immediately banishes Valentine, who receives hypocritical comfort from Proteus. Lance detains Speed for a pragmatic discussion about a milkmaid whom he is proposing to marry.

3.2 Ostensibly only at the Duke's insistence and in the interests of Thurio, whose suit the Duke favours, Proteus agrees to slander Valentine to Silvia, and to help Thurio woo her with poetry and music.

4.1 Valentine and Speed are ambushed by outlaws, who, impressed by Valentine's eloquence, offer him the choice of being killed or becoming their leader: he chooses the latter.

4.2 Proteus reflects on his falsehood, and the reproaches with which Silvia has so far repaid his courtship, before Thurio arrives with musicians, who perform the song 'Who is Silvia? What is she?' beneath her window. Meanwhile, conducted by her host, Julia has arrived, disguised as a page, and she watches both the serenade and, after Thurio's departure, Proteus' continuing attempts to woo Silvia.

4.3 Silvia enlists the help of Sir Eglamour to follow Valentine into exile.

4.4 Lance laments the misbehaviour of Crab, whom he has offered as a gift to Silvia in place of a lapdog from Proteus which he has lost, describing how he has often been forced to assume responsibility for Crab's unhygienic misdemeanours. Proteus arrives with the disguised Julia, whom, as 'Sebastian', he unwittingly takes into his employment as a worthier messenger than Lance has been: he entrusts her with the very ring she herself gave him at parting as a gift for Silvia. Horrified at her situation, Julia nonetheless goes to perform this errand, though Silvia refuses the ring: the two women fall into conversation about the supposedly absent Julia, whom Silvia pities.

5.1 Sir Eglamour and Silvia fly from Milan and towards the forest.

5.2 The Duke brings the news of their flight to Proteus, Thurio, and Julia, who each agree to follow him in his pursuit of them.

5.3 In the forest, three outlaws have captured Silvia while others chase the fleeing Sir Eglamour.

5.4 Valentine reflects on the suitability of the forest as a setting for his solitary yearning for Silvia: hearing the sounds of a struggle, he hides, and sees Proteus, still followed by the disguised Julia, arrive with Silvia, whom he has rescued from the outlaws. Both Julia and Valentine watch in dismay as Proteus courts the resolute Silvia with increasing aggression until he actually attempts rape, at which Valentine confronts him with his treachery. On Proteus' repentance, Valentine accepts him once more as a friend, and abruptly resigns Silvia to him. At this Julia faints, and when her identity is discovered a yet more penitent Proteus disavows his preference for Silvia. Valentine joins their hands. The outlaws arrive with the Duke and Thurio as captives, and when the cowardly Thurio, threatened by Valentine, renounces his own claim on Silvia, she is bestowed by the Duke on Valentine. Valentine successfully requests the Duke to repeal the outlaws' banishment along with his own, and with the double marriage of Valentine and Silvia, Proteus and Julia in prospect, all set off back towards Milan.

🎭 ARTISTIC FEATURES

The play shows a reliance on soliloquy, asides, and duologues unique in the canon: one of the reasons the famous serenade scene, 4.2, stands out so vividly is that it is one of the play's only fully successful scenes involving more than three characters at a time. The play shows unusual carelessness (the Duke is sometimes referred to as 'the Emperor', and Shakespeare often appears to forget that his two Veronese gentlemen are not at home at his court in Milan), but its verse, though sometimes lame, can rise to moments of genuine and unexpected lyricism (as in Proteus' advice to Thurio, 3.2.72–86), and the supple comic prose of Lance's monologues has rarely been excelled.

✷✷ CRITICAL HISTORY

Neglected for two centuries after Shakespeare's death (with John Upton refusing to believe it was authentically Shakespearian, and with Samuel Johnson's praise confined to individual passages at the expense of its structure), the play has frequently suffered from being read solely as an unsuccessful anticipation of the later comedies, particularly *Twelfth Night*, and discussions of *The Two Gentlemen of Verona* in its own right are still comparatively rare. Along with the other early comedies, it has often been dismissed as apprentice work, and most commentators have found Valentine's attempt to give away Silvia to the man who has just tried to rape her profoundly objectionable. Much modern writing about the play has concentrated on attempting to explain this gesture, whether in terms of Renaissance views on the relative claims of friendship, love, and gratitude, or in terms of the literary conventions of courtly romance. It is noticeable that the play has been consistently more highly regarded on the Continent than in Britain, with G. G. Gervinus among its few 19th-century advocates (drawing attention, in *Shakespeare*, 1849–50, to its sophisticated use of parallelism, a subject taken up a century later in an important essay by Harold F. Brooks). H. B. Charlton, in his influential account of Shakespearian comedy (1938), claimed that the play was an artistic failure, its aspirations towards romance producing only ludicrous bathos, and while subsequent critics (such as Alexander Leggatt) have been less inclined to regard all an audience's laughs at the central characters' expense as unintended by Shakespeare, the notion that certain figures in the play (notably Julia) are fatally out of drawing with the play's Lylyan genre remains a prevalent one in recent discussions.

▓ STAGE HISTORY

The Folio's text may suggest that the play was still in use by Shakespeare's company as late as 1606, but since the Renaissance it has been one of his least successful plays in the theatre: in England only *Love's Labour's Lost* was slower to be revived as Shakespeare's comedies increased in status and popularity down the 18th century. The earliest recorded performances of

The Two Gentlemen of Verona did not take place until 1762, at Drury Lane, in a version adapted by the minor playwright Benjamin Victor, who tried to lighten the last act by adding new material for Lance, Crab, and Speed and removing Valentine's renunciation of Silvia to Proteus (a cut often repeated over the ensuing years as the romantic celebration of male friendship over love grew ever less usual in the culture at large). The play was revived briefly at Covent Garden in 1784, and by J. P. Kemble in 1790 and 1808, but its only really popular British production before the mid-20th century was in 1821, when Frederick Reynolds initiated a recurrent strand in its stage history by drastically adapting it as a musical.

In common with subsequent 19th-century productions, this version idealized Valentine, who is presented as a figure of perfect chivalry in the only well-known painting derived from this play, the Pre-Raphaelite Holman Hunt's *Valentine Rescuing Silvia from Proteus* (later renamed *The Two Gentlemen of Verona*), 1851. The play was a failure successively for William Charles Macready (1841), Charles Kean (1846 in New York, 1848 in London), Samuel Phelps (1857), Osmond Tearle (Stratford, 1890), Augustin Daly (1895, with Ada Rehan as Julia), and Harley Granville-Barker (1904), and while William Poel's 'Elizabethan' production at His Majesty's Theatre (1910) attracted some attention, sporadic revivals in Stratford and London during the inter-war years still failed to establish the play in the British public's imagination. In theatrical circles the play even acquired the derisive nickname 'The Walking Gentlemen' ('walking gentleman' is stock-company slang for a wholly undistinguished minor male role). The play was more popular with French and German audiences (Theodore Fontane, seeing Phelps's revival, had clamoured for a Berlin production as early as 1857), enjoying a major production at the Odéon in Paris in 1902, and proving immensely popular in Weimar Germany in Hans Rothe's free translation (1933): it has held the stage in Europe since the Second World War in productions such as that of Gundalf Gründgen (Düsseldorf, 1948).

The play's post-war fortunes in the English-speaking theatre have been more mixed. At Regent's Park in 1949 it was heavily abridged by Robert Atkins to share a bill with *The Comedy of Errors*, but within ten years came two far more lavish, and highly successful, productions at the Old Vic, one (by Denis Carey, transferring to London from Bristol) in the style of a Renaissance masque (1952, with John Neville as Valentine), and one (by Michael Langham, 1957) in a Regency setting (with Barbara Jefford as Julia). Both added a great deal of incidental music. Attempts to supplement the appeal of music and decor by resort to post-Freudian psychology have generally been unsuccessful: Robin Phillips's incipiently camp 1970 production for the RSC (which set the play in an adolescent, beach-oriented world reminiscent of body-building advertisements) pleased few, and John Barton's harshly satiric abbreviation of 1981 (on a double bill with an equally truncated *Titus Andronicus*) few more. The most successful English-language productions of the play have continued to be musical adaptations, notably Joseph Papp's 1971 revival in New York, and David Thacker's 1994 RSC production at the Swan, given a 1930s setting and supplied with additional songs from the works of Cole Porter and his contemporaries. For directors such as these the poor esteem in which the play has generally been held, licensing inventive stage-business and making the play's naive charm always come as something of a pleasant surprise, seems to have been positively liberating. In 2014 the play returned to the RSC's main stage for the first time in nearly half a century in Simon Godwin's half-forties, half-noughties production.

 ON THE SCREEN

The Two Gentlemen of Verona has yet to tempt Hollywood, though various glimpses of it appear in the popular *Shakespeare in Love* (1998). The one extant full-length production on video is the BBC TV version, 1978, which cast convincingly young but disappointingly inept performers in the leads but boasted a strong Lance in Tony Haygarth.

The Two Noble Kinsmen

This bitter-sweet tragicomedy of love and death, co-written with John Fletcher, includes what was almost certainly Shakespeare's last writing for the stage. Excluded from the Folio, presumably because of its collaborative authorship, the play was not published until 1634: both the Stationers' Register entry and the quarto's title page attribute it to 'William Shakespeare and John Fletcher'. The play borrows its morris dance (3.5) from Francis Beaumont's *Masque of the Inner Temple and Gray's Inn* (February 1613), while its prologue's reference to 'our losses' almost certainly alludes to the burning down of the Globe (June 1613). Probably composed during 1613–14, *The Two Noble Kinsmen* may well have been the first play to appear at the rebuilt Globe on its opening in 1614: certainly two sarcastic allusions to 'Palamon' in Ben Jonson's *Bartholomew Fair* (premièred in October 1614) suggest that Jonson expected this play to be fresh in his spectators' minds.

 TEXT

The 1634 quarto provides the only substantive text of *The Two Noble Kinsmen*, and its various inconsistencies—including variant spellings, such as 'Perithous' and 'Pirithous', 'Ialor' and 'Iaylor'—suggest that it was set from foul papers in the hands of both playwrights, though these had probably been annotated with reference to later performances (some stage directions, for example, accidentally mention the actors Curtis Greville and Thomas Tuckfield, who were both members of the King's Company only between 1625 and mid-1626). The general scholarly consensus, based on variant spellings in the text and, especially, considerations of style, metre, and vocabulary, is that Shakespeare wrote Act 1, 2.1, 3.1–2, and most of Act 5 (excluding 5.4), and Fletcher the rest (including the Prologue and Epilogue). Although both playwrights presumably agreed on the overall structure of the play, it appears from minor discrepancies between their respective shares that they wrote independently of one another, Shakespeare concentrating on the Theseus frame-narrative and the establishment and closure of the Palamon–Arcite plot, Fletcher on the intervening rivalry between Palamon and Arcite and the sub-plot of the Jailer's Daughter.

SOURCES

The play is primarily a dramatization of Geoffrey Chaucer's Knight's Tale, the first and one of the most highly regarded of *The Canterbury Tales*: this well-known work had already been dramatized at least twice, once by Richard Edwards as *Palaemon and Arcyte* (performed before Queen Elizabeth at Christ Church, Oxford, in 1566, but never printed) and once as another lost play with the same title, acted in 1594. Surviving eyewitness accounts of Edwards's play suggest that Shakespeare and Fletcher may have remembered it at some points (their Palamon, for example, recalls at 5.6.44–5 that he has said Venus is false: in fact he has not done so, though his counterpart in Edwards's play did). Shakespeare and Fletcher may also have known Chaucer's source, Boccaccio's *Teseida* (in which Arcite's horse falls backwards onto him, as in the play, rather than pitching him off forwards as in Chaucer). Their chief alterations to Chaucer are the addition of the three queens and their interruption to Theseus' wedding procession (itself influenced by Shakespeare's earlier treatment of Theseus' wedding preparations in *A Midsummer Night's Dream*), the stipulation that the loser of the Palamon–Arcite duel must die, and the added sub-plot of the Jailer's Daughter. This sub-plot itself recalls earlier motifs in the Shakespeare canon: most obviously her madness recalls Ophelia and Desdemona's remembered maid Barbara, but her position as lovestruck helper of her father's prisoner (and her obsession with storms at sea) also recalls Miranda's role in *The Tempest* 3.1.

 CHARACTER LIST

Prologue
Theseus, Duke of Athens
Hippolyta, Queen of the Amazons *later wife of Theseus*
Emilia *her sister*
Pirithous *friend of Theseus*
Palamon ⎤ *the two noble*
Arcite ⎦ *kinsmen, cousins, nephews of Creon, the King of Thebes*
Hymen *god of marriage*
A **Boy** who sings
Artesius *an Athenian soldier*
Three **Queens** *widows of kings killed in the siege of Thebes*
Valerius *a Theban*
A **Herald**
Woman, attending Emilia
An Athenian **Gentleman**
Messengers

Six **Knights** *three attending Arcite and three Palamon*
A **Servant**
A **Jailer** in charge of Theseus' prison
The **Jailer's Daughter**
The **Jailer's Brother**
The **Wooer** of the Jailer's daughter
Two **Friends** of the Jailer
A **Doctor**
Six **Countrymen**, one dressed as a babion, or baboon
Gerald, a **Schoolmaster**
Nell *a country wench*
Four other country wenches: Friz, Madeline, Luce, and Barbara
Timothy, a **Taborer**
Epilogue
Nymphs, attendants, maids, executioner, guard

 SYNOPSIS

A prologue, comparing new plays to maidenhoods, boasts that this one derives from Chaucer and ought to please.

1.1 Preceded by a boy who sings an epithalamium, 'Roses, their sharp spines being gone', Theseus and his bride Hippolyta pass towards their wedding, accompanied by Theseus' comrade Pirithous and sister Emilia: they are stopped, however, by three mourning queens, whose husbands, killed fighting against the evil Creon of Thebes, have been denied burial. Their kneeling plea that Theseus should postpone his wedding until he has defeated Creon is seconded by Hippolyta and Emilia, and Theseus complies.

1.2 In Thebes, the inseparable cousins Palamon and Arcite, though anxious about the vicious state of their uncle Creon's regime, prepare to fight against Theseus.

1.3 Pirithous parts from Hippolyta and Emilia in order to rejoin Theseus. The women discuss the rival claims of same-sex friendship and love, Emilia tenderly remembering her dead friend Flavina.

1.4 The three queens bless Theseus for defeating Creon. Seeing the wounded and unconscious Palamon and Arcite, who have fought nobly, he orders they should be tended but kept prisoner.

1.5 The three queens process towards the separate funerals of their husbands to the dirge 'Urns and odours, bring away', and bid one another a solemn farewell.

2.1 A wooer talks with the Jailer about his projected marriage to the Jailer's Daughter, who speaks enthusiastically about the prisoners Palamon and Arcite.

2.2 Palamon and Arcite are consoling one another for their lost liberty with promises of eternal friendship when Palamon sees Emilia from the window, gathering flowers with her woman in the garden beneath. He falls in love with her, as does Arcite, and the two immediately quarrel as rivals for her. The Jailer takes Arcite away, released by Theseus but banished to Thebes, and takes Palamon to a cell with no view of the garden.

2.3 Arcite resolves to disguise himself so that he may remain near Emilia: learning from some countrymen of a sporting contest before Theseus, he decides to compete in it.

2.4 The Jailer's Daughter, in love with Palamon, decides to arrange his escape in the hope of earning his love.

2.5 The disguised Arcite is victor in the wrestling before Theseus, and Pirithous makes him master of horse to Emilia.

2.6 The Jailer's Daughter has freed Palamon and is about to run away from her father's house to meet him in the woods with food and a file to remove his manacles.

3.1 Arcite, who has followed Theseus, Emilia, and their party into the woods on their May morning hunt, is reflecting on how Palamon would envy him his position when Palamon, overhearing him, emerges from a bush. They agree that Arcite will fetch food and a file, and duel with Palamon when he has recovered his strength.

3.2 Sleepless and hungry, the Jailer's Daughter has failed to find Palamon, who she imagines has been eaten by wolves: full of self-reproach, she is beginning to lose her wits.

3.3 Arcite brings Palamon food: as he eats, the rivals reminisce about each other's past loves.

3.4 The Jailer's Daughter, mad, imagines a shipwreck.

3.5 Gerald the schoolmaster is rehearsing five countrymen, five countrywomen, and a taborer in the morris dance they are to perform before Theseus when they realize they are a woman short: however, they recruit the mad Jailer's Daughter, and when Theseus and his party arrive they perform their elaborate dance, prefaced by Gerald's rhyming oration, as planned.

3.6 Arcite brings Palamon sword and armour: they arm each other carefully, but their duel is interrupted by the arrival of Theseus, Hippolyta, Emilia, and Pirithous. Learning of their identities and purposes, Theseus sentences both to death, but they are reprieved at the suit of Hippolyta and Emilia. However, they refuse Emilia's offer of peaceable banishment, refusing to renounce their quarrel over her, and when Emilia will not choose between them Theseus finally agrees that their mortal duel must resume. In a month's time each is to return with three knights: the winner of the contest will marry Emilia, the loser will be executed along with his three seconds.

4.1 The Jailer is relieved to learn that Palamon has cleared him of treason by explaining that it was his daughter who let him out of prison, but the Wooer brings the news of the Jailer's Daughter's madness, narrating how he found her wandering and singing and had to rescue her from drowning in a lake. She arrives herself with the Jailer's Brother, full of mad tales of Palamon's potency, and imagines sailing a ship to find Palamon in the woods: they do what they can to humour her.

4.2 Emilia, studying portraits of Arcite and of Palamon, is still unable to prefer one to the other. Theseus and Pirithous speak admiringly of the knights with whom the two rivals have returned to fight for Emilia.

4.3 A doctor, summoned by the Jailer and the Wooer, interviews the Jailer's Daughter, and prescribes that the Wooer should pretend to be Palamon.

5.1 Palamon and Arcite, accompanied by their seconds, bid a solemn farewell. Arcite prays at the altar of Mars for success in the combat, and is encouraged by a sound of thunder and arms.

5.2 Palamon prays at the altar of Venus for success in his quest for Emilia, and is encouraged by music and fluttering doves.

5.3 Emilia prays at the altar of Diana that if she is not to remain a maid she should be won by the contender who loves her best or has the truest title to her. A rose falls from the tree on the altar.

5.4 Despite the Jailer's misgivings, the Wooer, impersonating Palamon, takes the Doctor's advice to lead the Jailer's Daughter away to bed.

5.5 Emilia cannot bear to watch the combat, but hears its progress by offstage shouts and the reports of a servant: Palamon almost wins, but is defeated by Arcite. The victorious Arcite is presented to her by Theseus, who speaks regretfully of the doomed Palamon's valour.

5.6 Palamon and his three knights are about to be executed: Palamon bequeathes the Jailer his money as a wedding portion for his daughter. Pirithous arrives just in time to halt the execution, reporting that in the midst of his triumphal entry into Athens Arcite has been fatally injured, his horse rearing up and falling backwards onto him. Theseus, Hippolyta, and Emilia return, with the dying Arcite carried in a chair. Arcite bequeathes Emilia to Palamon. Theseus reflects on the ambiguous justice with which the gods have fulfilled their omens, and on humanity's restless impatience with what it has in favour of desire for what it lacks. An epilogue wonders anxiously how the audience have liked the play, assuring them it was intended only to please.

🎭 ARTISTIC FEATURES

Shakespeare's sections of the play share their densely figured, knotty syntax and imagery with his other late romances, and display a similar interest in spectacularly rendered ritual. The play's stagecraft suggests it was composed with the Blackfriars theatre in mind, and as a large-cast play with a classical-cum-medieval setting which makes extensive use of music it has much in common with other plays in the King's Company's Jacobean repertoire, not only *Pericles* but Thomas Heywood's *The Golden Age*, *The Silver Age*, and *The Brazen Age*.

CRITICAL HISTORY

Although some 19th-century critics accepted the quarto's attribution, *The Two Noble Kinsmen* was generally accepted into the Shakespeare canon only in the 20th century, and much critical writing about it continues to be preoccupied with the question of its authorship. Its restoration to the Shakespeare corpus, however, coincided with modernism's high valuation for the complexities of Shakespeare's later style and with the ritual elements of drama. It coincided, too, with a Freudian interest in the representation of sexuality, and in recent years the Jailer's Daughter's 'green-sickness' and the controversial therapy applied to it have attracted a good deal of attention, as has the juxtaposition between the kinsmen's homosocial rivalry and the near-lesbianism of Emilia's passionate championing of female friendship.

STAGE HISTORY

The play reappeared after the Restoration as William Davenant's cheerful adaptation *The Rivals* (1664), its action transferred to a harmless Arcadia in which Celania (the Jailer's Daughter) marries Philander (Palamon) and Arcite survives to marry Heraclia (Emilia). This version influenced two later 18th-century rewritings, the much darker *Palamon and Arcite; or, The Two Noble Kinsmen* by Richard Cumberland (1779), and a musical, *Midsummer Night's Dream*-like version by F. G. Waldron, *Love and Madness; or, The Two Noble Kinsmen* (1795). The play was not revived professionally again until an Old Vic production in 1928, designed to suggest a pretty homage to a Chaucerian Merry England. Despite many student productions it then disappeared from the professional stage until a more symbolic, morris-dance-free revival at the Open Air Theatre in Regent's Park in 1974. Since then *The Two Noble Kinsmen* has been successfully revived at, among other venues, the Los Angeles Globe Playhouse (1979), the Edinburgh Festival (in a highly sexualized all-male production by the Cherub Theatre, 1979), the Centre Dramatique de Courneuve (also 1979), the Oregon Shakespeare Festival (1994), and the reconstructed Globe (2000), but its most celebrated modern production remains Barry Kyle's, which opened the RSC's Swan auditorium in 1986. The main plot was given a stylized, samurai look, the rituals were impressive, and as the Jailer's Daughter Imogen Stubbs morris-danced away with the entire show, as performers in that challenging but wonderfully showy role often do. The play has yet to be filmed.

Venus and Adonis

This exuberant erotic poem, at once funny and compassionate, was Shakespeare's most popular published work in his own time, running through at least ten editions between its first appearance in 1593 and its author's death in 1616, with another six published by 1636. It remains one of the few major works in world literature to depict the passionate pursuit of a male object by a female subject. Shakespeare's auspicious debut in print may owe its existence to the outbreak of plague that closed the London theatres for nearly two years in July 1592, during which the young playwright apparently turned to an alternative career, as a poet, and to an alternative source of income, a patron. Shakespeare's dedication of *Venus and Adonis* to Henry Wriothesley, Earl of Southampton, calls it the 'first heir of my invention', implicitly contrasting this legitimate venture into verse on a classical subject with Shakespeare's 'illegitimate' earlier work for the stage: as a bid for literary respectability, the poem's composition in 1592–3 may in part have been spurred by the attack Robert Greene had made on the 'upstart crow...Shake-scene' in *Greene's Groatsworth of Wit* (1592).

 TEXT

The 1593 first quarto of *Venus and Adonis* was so popular that it survives in only one copy, now in the Bodleian Library: all the rest were presumably read to death. It was entered in the Stationers' Register on 18 April, and a letter from the deranged William Renoldes (who construed its publication as a love letter to him from Queen Elizabeth) shows that it was on book-stalls by 21 September. It was printed by Richard Field (printer, too, of its successor, *The Rape of Lucrece*), who was born in Stratford only two years before Shakespeare and may have been at school with him. (Innogen's passing reference to 'Richard du Champ' in *Cymbeline*—the name she invents for her dead 'master' at 4.2.379—may be a private joke between them). Field did his job well, apparently working from Shakespeare's own manuscript: unusually, Shakespeare may even have corrected the proofs, making this one of the most reliable of all his printed texts.

SOURCES

The story of Venus and Adonis is told in book 10 of Ovid's *Metamorphoses*, which Shakespeare consulted both in the original Latin and in Arthur Golding's English translation (1565–7). Shakespeare greatly elaborates on Ovid's account (a mere 75 lines long compared to the 1,194 of Shakespeare's poem), and as well as supplying rhetorical expansion and additional detail (such as the incident in which Adonis' stallion frustrates his escape attempt by running off with a mare) he fundamentally alters its drama. In the original, Venus' passion for the mortal Adonis (inadvertently caused by Cupid, as the narrator Orpheus explains) is reciprocated, and they hunt together (though Venus advises her lover to pursue only fairly harmless animals, telling a cautionary tale which Shakespeare omits): she leaves for Cyprus, but returns after Adonis has been mortally wounded, metamorphosing him into an anemone. Shakespeare transforms the story by making Adonis into a reluctant and prudish adolescent, who appears to join the boar-hunt primarily as an excuse to avoid a renewal of Venus' undesired assaults. Shakespeare's solicitous goddess, powerless to overcome his reluctance, stays nearby to wait anxiously for Adonis, and his metamorphosis is also outside her agency: she is left to pick a flower which spontaneously springs up where his miraculously melted body lay, placing an eternal curse on love as she makes her at once heartbroken and petulant departure towards Cyprus.

Shakespeare's alterations to his material are influenced in part by other stories in Ovid (principally those of Salmacis and Hermaphroditus, and Echo and Narcissus, the latter cited by Venus at l. 161), and in part by a growing fashion for the Ovidian 'erotic epyllion' (miniature epic on an amorous theme) which had begun with the publication of Thomas Lodge's *Scilla's Metamorphosis* in 1589 (written in the same six-line stanzaic form Shakespeare adopts here, rhyming *ababcc*). This vogue would find its most famous expression in Christopher Marlowe's *Hero and Leander*, not published until 1598 but composed at around the same time as *Venus and Adonis* (shortly before Marlowe's murder in May 1593). Shakespeare's poem shares with these other examples of its genre the combination of passionate and sensual subject matter with a wry and urbane narrative voice.

SYNOPSIS

A Latin motto, from Ovid's *Amores* (1.15), declares Shakespeare's poetic ambition: in Marlowe's translation it runs 'Let base-conceited wits admire vile things, | Fair Phoebus lead me to the Muses' springs.' A dedication to the Earl of Southampton promises 'some graver labour' if these 'unpolished lines' prove acceptable.

As young Adonis, who prefers hunting to love, is going hunting in the afternoon, Venus hurries to accost him (ll. 1–6). Imploring a kiss, Venus pulls Adonis from his horse, which she tethers to a tree, and pushes him to the ground, silencing his protests with kisses (ll. 7–48). Despite Adonis' objections to her immodest behaviour, Venus will not let him go, kissing him hungrily: eventually she promises to release him if he will give her one kiss in return (ll. 49–90). This he promises, but in the event refuses to provide (ll. 49–90). Venus makes a long and eloquent wooing speech, using all the arguments she can muster, including the accusation that Adonis is too proud of his own beauty (like Narcissus), which he ought to transmit to posterity through procreation (ll. 91–174). Unmoved, Adonis complains that he is getting sunburned and wishes to leave (ll. 175–86). Venus rails petulantly at his indifference (ll. 187–216). Temporarily overcome by tears, Venus is unable to speak further, and when she renews her amorous pleading Adonis merely smiles scornfully, his dimples making him more beautiful than ever (ll. 217–52).

Adonis breaks away and makes for his horse, but a young mare emerges from a nearby copse and Adonis' stallion (which is lovingly described, ll. 289–300) breaks his reins and eagerly joins her. Ignoring Adonis' attempts to recapture the stallion, the two horses run away into the wood (ll. 253–324). Adonis sits sullenly: Venus approaches again, takes his hand and renews her suit, urging him to follow his horse's example (ll. 325–408). Adonis insists that her wooing is futile and misplaced, since he is unripe for love (ll. 409–26). Undeterred, Venus continues to plead, but seeing Adonis is about to reproach her again she faints. Alarmed, Adonis attempts to revive her, eventually resorting to kisses (ll. 427–80). Venus, reviving, speaks of her joy (ll. 481–522). Adonis, however, still points out that he is too young for love, and that it is growing late, but he promises and gives a farewell kiss (ll. 523–40). Inflamed with desire, Venus renews her kissing, though Adonis refuses to meet her again the following day, saying he will be hunting the boar. She pulls him down on top of her, but to no avail (ll. 541–612).

Venus warns Adonis against the perils of boar-hunting, urging him instead to hunt only hares, foxes, or deer (ll. 613–713). Venus renews her pleading for love, explaining that the night is dark to reproach Adonis' coldness and encourage prodigality (ll. 715–68). Adonis refuses Venus, accusing her of miscalling lust by the name of love, and at last makes his escape (ll. 769–816).

Alone, Venus wanders lost in the dark: noticing how her moans echo, she spends the night extemporizing an echoing song about the sorrows of love (ll. 829–40). At daybreak she hurries to a myrtle grove and listens for the sounds of Adonis' hunt (ll. 817–70). The anxious Venus can hear that a boar-hunt is in progress, and hears that the hounds are afraid: to her horror she sees the boar, its mouth stained with blood (ll. 871–912). Finding a series of wounded dogs, she fears Adonis must have been killed, and exclaims against death (ll. 913–54). Weeping, she hears the huntsmen again and, convinced Adonis is alive, reproaches herself for being so fearful (ll. 955–1026).

Venus is stunned to find Adonis killed by the boar (ll. 1027–68). She speaks an elegy for Adonis, imagining that the boar (which has killed him by sinking its tusks into his groin) was only kissing him as she would have liked to, and falls weeping on his body (ll. 1069–122). Venus looks into Adonis' dead eyes (ll. 1123–34). She prophesies that since her beloved Adonis is dead love will hereafter always be attended with sorrows, which she enumerates (ll. 1135–64).

Adonis' body has melted away and a purple flower has sprung in its place, which Venus vows to cherish in her breast (ll. 1165–88). Venus returns to Cyprus in her dove-drawn chariot, intending to mourn in seclusion (ll. 1189–94).

ARTISTIC FEATURES

The poem's set-piece displays of rhetoric alternate with vivid, sensual evocations of a mythological world whose freshness matches that of Ovid's original, a world which exists purely to provide the appropriate setting for Venus' attempted seduction and whose every detail can reflect her desires and her experience (from the behaviour of Adonis' horse to the vulnerable snail to which her consciousness's stunned temporary retreat is likened when she finds his body, ll. 1033–44).

CRITICAL HISTORY

The immense success of *Venus and Adonis* in its time is attested not only by its profusion of editions but by a number of contemporary comments: by Francis Meres in 1598 ('the sweet witty soul of Ovid lives in mellifluous and honey-tongued Shakespeare, witness his *Venus and Adonis*'), by Richard Barnfield in the same year, by John Weever in 1599, and by Gabriel Harvey in 1600 ('the younger sort takes much delight in Shakespeare's *Venus and Adonis*'). The poem is cited repeatedly and with particular enthusiasm in two plays staged by Cambridge undergraduates, the Parnassus plays, 1598–1602 ('I'll worship sweet Master Shakespeare, and to know him will lay his *Venus and Adonis* under my pillow'), and, to judge from quotations within other contemporary plays, passages from it became part of the common lexicon of attempted seduction: it is even specifically mentioned by some disapproving moralists. After the last reprint of the quarto in 1675, however, the poem fell from favour (along with *The Rape of Lucrece* and the Sonnets), and it was left out of most 18th-century editions of Shakespeare. Although Edmond Malone guardedly remarked in 1780 that it was not 'so entirely devoid of poetical merit as it has been represented' it was not until the Romantic period that *Venus and Adonis* inspired any renewed enthusiasm, notably from Samuel Taylor Coleridge and John Keats (though William Hazlitt, in common with many others, still found it repellently artificial). Both its subject matter and its delight in rhetorical display alienated many Victorians, and it is only in the self-consciously 'liberated' post-war period that *Venus and Adonis* has generated a significant critical literature, much of it, however, determined to explain or even excuse the poem by placing it in its original literary context. One notable staging of the poem was Gregory Doran's sensual and magically inventive puppet version at the RSC in 2004, produced in collaboration with Little Angel Theatre.

The Winter's Tale

Although it clearly belongs among the late romances—with its artful structure and almost insolent mastery of complex narrative and characterization—*The Winter's Tale* is difficult to date with precision. A dance of satyrs in Act 4 (4.4.340–1) seems to be borrowed from Ben Jonson's *Masque of Oberon*, acted at court on 1 January 1611, but its irrelevance there and the awkwardness with which it is introduced by the surrounding dialogue suggests that this may be a late interpolation, indicating that the play was written before Jonson's masque rather than after it. In any event *The Winter's Tale* had been completed by May 1611, when Simon Forman saw it at the Globe: his journal entry describing the performance supplies the only reliable external evidence for the play's date of composition. Internal evidence is more ambiguous. Autolycus' grisly account of the torments allegedly in store for the Clown (4.4.784–92) derives from the same material in Boccaccio that Shakespeare uses in *Cymbeline*: this suggests that the two plays are close in date but cannot reveal which was written first. A number of minor debts to Plutarch, however (principally characters' names), suggest that *The Winter's Tale* may be the closer in date of the two to *Antony and Cleopatra* and *Coriolanus*, and most stylistic tests place it closer to Shakespeare's sections of *Pericles* (1607) than is *Cymbeline*. It was probably composed just before *Cymbeline*, in 1609–10.

TEXT

The play first appeared in the Folio in 1623, as the last of the comedies: the copy for it seems to have arrived late (in December 1622 at the earliest), when the next section of the book was already in production. The text's idiosyncrasies of spelling, its paucity of stage directions, its heavy punctuation, and its habit of listing all the characters who are to appear in a scene at its opening indicate that it was set from a transcript prepared by the scribe Ralph Crane, though Crane's customary willingness to intervene in the interests of tidiness make it difficult to deduce the nature of the copy he was transcribing. If the satyr dance in Act 4 is indeed a late interpolation Crane was probably transcribing a promptbook.

SOURCES

The Winter's Tale is primarily a dramatization of Robert Greene's prose romance *Pandosto* (subtitled *The Triumph of Time*, and also known as 'The History of Dorastus and Fawnia'), which had first appeared in 1588 and had gone through five editions before Shakespeare composed *The Winter's Tale*. Shakespeare had probably known this work for some time: in any case he was not working from its most recent edition, printed in 1607, since this text alters the wording of the oracle's declaration, and the play here follows the earlier editions verbatim. Shakespeare changes the principals' names (Pandosto becomes Leontes, Bellaria becomes Hermione; Egistus becomes Polixenes; Dorastus and Fawnia become Florizel and Perdita), exchanges the places of Bohemia and Sicilia (though even in Greene Bohemia is miraculously provided with a coast), and drastically alters the story's tragic ending. The statue scene is entirely Shakespeare's invention (though it draws in part on the story of Pygmalion and Galatea, told in Ovid's *Metamorphoses*): in *Pandosto*, Bellaria is genuinely and finally dead after the trial scene, and when years later Fawnia is brought to Pandosto's court he falls in love with her. After learning of her identity, he commits suicide. The play has no other major sources, though it derives incidental details from a number of texts (besides Plutarch and Boccaccio). Polixenes' defence of art (4.4.89–97) borrows from a similar passage in George Puttenham's *Art of English Poesy* (1589), while Shakespeare's knowledge of Giulio Romano (5.2.96) probably derives, whether at first or second hand, from Giorgio Vasari's *Vite de' piu eccellenti pittori, scultori, e architettori* (1550). The scene of the mother's statue in Paulina's gallery may have been influenced, too, by James I's commissioning of painted memorial sculptures of his predecessor Elizabeth I (completed in 1607) and of his mother Mary Stuart (completed before 1612), both in Westminster Abbey.

 CHARACTER LIST

Leontes, King of Sicily
Hermione *his wife*
Mamillius *his son*
Perdita *his daughter*

Camillo
Antigonus *Lords at*
Cleomenes *Leontes' court*
Dion

Paulina *Antigonus' wife*
Emilia *a lady attending on Hermione*
A **Jailer**
A **Mariner**
Other lords and gentlemen, ladies, officers, and servants at Leontes' court
Polixenes, King of Bohemia

Florizel *his son, in love with Perdita; known as Doricles*
Archidamus *a Bohemian lord*
Autolycus *a rogue, once in the service of Florizel*
Old Shepherd
Clown *his son*
Mopsa
Dorcas *shepherdesses*
Servant of the Old Shepherd
Other shepherds and shepherdesses
Twelve countrymen disguised as satyrs
Time, as chorus

SYNOPSIS

1.1 Camillo, a courtier to Leontes, King of Sicilia, exchanges courtesies with Archidamus, who is visiting in the train of Leontes' childhood friend Polixenes, King of Bohemia. They speak enthusiastically of Leontes' young son Mamillius.

1.2 Polixenes has been in Sicilia nine months, and plans to embark for Bohemia the following day. Leontes implores him to stay another week, and when his pregnant Queen Hermione adds her own entreaties Polixenes finally relents. Leontes becomes convinced that Polixenes and Hermione are conducting an affair: he talks aside with Mamillius, watching them together. After Polixenes and Hermione have gone and Mamillius has been dismissed, Leontes calls Camillo and tells him of his conviction about Hermione: overruling Camillo's insistence that the Queen is innocent, he commands him to poison Polixenes. Alone, Camillo reflects in horror on his situation, and when Polixenes arrives he tells him everything and agrees to help him make his escape.

2.1 Mamillius is about to tell his mother a horror story suitable for winter when Leontes arrives with a courtier, Antigonus: Polixenes' reported flight with Camillo seems to confirm all his suspicions. Dismissing Mamillius, he accuses Hermione of being pregnant by Polixenes, and despite her protestations of innocence has her taken to prison. When his courtiers take her part, he tells them he has sent Cleomenes and Dion to consult Apollo's oracle at Delphi for confirmation of Hermione's guilt.

2.2 Antigonus' wife Paulina calls at the prison and learns from Hermione's attendant Emilia that she has given birth to a daughter: reassuring the Jailer that the child is not included in the warrant against Hermione, Paulina proposes to show the baby to Leontes in the hope of restoring him to sanity.

2.3 A sleepless Leontes learns further of Mamillius' illness since the imprisonment of his mother. Paulina confronts him with his child, hoping to persuade him of its legitimacy by its resemblance to him: refusing to believe her, he finally has her dismissed, and then commands her husband Antigonus to take the baby and abandon it in some wilderness beyond his country's borders. When news arrives that the messengers are on their way from the oracle, preparations are instigated for Hermione's trial.

3.1 Cleomenes and Dion reflect with satisfaction on their experiences at Apollo's oracle.

3.2 Before Leontes, Hermione is formally accused of treasonous adultery with Polixenes: she eloquently denies the charge, and refers her innocence to the oracle. Cleomenes and Dion swear they have faithfully brought the oracle's written declaration, sealed and unread. Unsealed, the scroll declares that Hermione is innocent and her daughter truly begotten, and adds that 'the King shall live without an heir if that which is lost be not found'. Leontes at first refuses to believe this, but after a messenger brings the news that Mamillius has died, on which Hermione collapses and is taken away by Paulina and her attendants, he accepts the truth of the oracle. He is already repenting when Paulina returns and tells him Hermione too has died: welcoming her bitter reproaches, he promises to mourn his dead wife and son perpetually.

3.3 Antigonus has dreamed of Hermione's ghost, who told him to call the baby Perdita and leave it in Bohemia, prophesying that Antigonus would never see Paulina again. Believing the child must really be Polixenes', he has been brought to the Bohemian coast by ship, and as the weather worsens he leaves Perdita there, with a scroll explaining her name and identity and a box containing gold. He is chased away by a bear. An old shepherd arrives and finds the child: he is joined by his son, the Clown, who recounts seeing the bear eating Antigonus and his ship being wrecked in the storm with all hands. They open the box and set off home with Perdita, the Clown proposing to bury the remains of Antigonus on his way.

4.1 The figure of Time speaks a chorus, explaining that the play now skips sixteen years, during which Leontes grieves in seclusion, and will resume in Bohemia, where Perdita has grown up as a shepherdess.

4.2 Polixenes persuades Camillo to postpone his longed-for return to Sicilia in order to help him investigate his truant son Florizel's reported passion for a beautiful shepherdess: they will disguise themselves and visit her father's cottage.

4.3 Autolycus, a courtier-turned-pedlar-cum-confidence trickster, sings 'When daffodils begin to peer': when the Clown arrives, on his way to buy ingredients for the sheep-shearing feast over which his supposed sister Perdita is to preside, Autolycus pretends to have been beaten and robbed, and picks his pocket. Singing 'Jog on, jog on, the footpath way', Autolycus sets off for the sheep-shearing in quest of further prey.

4.4 Florizel, disguised as the rustic 'Doricles', congratulates Perdita on the robes she is wearing as Queen of the Feast, and reassures her of his honourable determination to marry her despite their difference in rank. The Old Shepherd brings the occasion's guests, among them the Clown, the countrywomen Mopsa and Dorcas, and the disguised Polixenes and Camillo: Perdita distributes flowers among them, disagreeing courteously with Polixenes as she does so about the ethics of artificially cross-breeding cultivated flowers. The young people dance, and a servant brings news of the approach of a pedlar, who is admitted. The Clown does not recognize Autolycus as the thief who robbed him earlier, and after Autolycus advertises his wares with the song 'Lawn as white as driven snow' the Clown is squabbled over by Mopsa and Dorcas, who have both been hoping for love tokens from him. Autolycus sells them improbable ballads and sings a song in a trio with Mopsa and Dorcas, 'Get you hence, for I must go': after their departure he further proclaims his wares with the song 'Will you buy any tape'. Dancers arrive and perform a dance of twelve satyrs. Polixenes, meanwhile, has been speaking with the Old Shepherd, who thoroughly approves of 'Doricles'' courtship of Perdita, and when he and Camillo ask Florizel about it the Prince, refusing to explain why his father should not be told of the matter, invites them to witness his engagement to Perdita. Polixenes furiously reveals his identity and accuses his son of betraying the throne, condemning the Old Shepherd to death for treason (but then withdrawing the sentence) and threatening Perdita with torture if she ever sees Florizel again: he storms off alone. The grieved Old Shepherd reproaches Florizel and Perdita for concealing the Prince's identity from him, and leaves convinced he is undone. Perdita believes her romance with Florizel is now over, but the Prince insists that his father's displeasure has not affected his determination to marry her. Camillo persuades them to run away to Sicilia, where they may marry and live until Polixenes is reconciled to the match. Florizel disguises himself by exchanging clothes with Autolycus, who has sold all his wares, and he and Perdita hurry away. Camillo, however, means privately to inform Polixenes of the couple's escape, and to return to Sicilia with him when he pursues them. Autolycus, left alone, is delighted with the money he has received for agreeing to wear a better suit of clothes, and when the dismayed Old Shepherd and the Clown arrive, hoping to present the proofs of Perdita's true identity to Polixenes in order to escape punishment for treason, he impersonates a courtier and accepts a bribe for his supposed assistance. Deciding to assist his former master Florizel, Autolycus leads them not to Polixenes but towards the ship on which Florizel and Perdita are embarking for Sicilia.

5.1 Cleomenes and Dion wish that after his years of penitent mourning Leontes would remarry and beget an heir, but Paulina reminds him of Hermione's virtues and the King agrees to marry only by her direction. When Florizel and Perdita arrive, giving out that they are already married, Leontes welcomes them eagerly, struck with Florizel's resemblance to his father and with Perdita's beauty: but when news arrives that Polixenes and Camillo have arrived in pursuit, Florizel admits that he and Perdita are not married and that she is not, as he earlier claimed, a princess. Leontes undertakes to try to reconcile Polixenes to their marriage.

5.2 Autolycus hears from three gentlemen of the extraordinary emotional scene that has taken place when the Old Shepherd opened the box with which he found Perdita, revealing her true identity to Leontes, Polixenes, Florizel, and Perdita. The royal party have now gone to Paulina's house to see a wonderfully lifelike statue, by Giulio Romano, of the dead Hermione. Autolycus is patronized and forgiven by the Clown and the Old

Shepherd, newly elevated to the gentry for their part in the Princess's upbringing and restoration.

5.3 Paulina draws a curtain to reveal Hermione's statue: a moved Leontes is particularly impressed that the sculptor, as Paulina explains, has aged the likeness to show Hermione as she would look were she still alive. Perdita kneels before her mother's image. Camillo and Polixenes urge Leontes to abandon his sorrows, but he insists he would rather stay staring at the statue. Paulina tells Leontes that she could if he wished make the statue move and speak, without recourse to black magic. With his encouragement, and to the sound of music, she calls the statue from its pedestal. Taking its warm hand, Leontes realizes that this is indeed Hermione. She embraces him and greets her long-lost daughter, explaining that she has kept herself alive because the oracle's pronouncement gave her hope of seeing her child again. Leontes matches Paulina with Camillo, and asks pardon from Polixenes and Hermione for his former suspicions.

 ## ARTISTIC FEATURES

The play is perhaps most remarkable for its almost programmatic movement through the tragedy of Acts 1 to 3 to the pastoral comedy of Act 4 (pivoting on the immortal stage direction, 'Exit, pursued by a bear', at once catastrophic and farcical) and finally into the tentative, fragile tragicomedy of Act 5, its final scene at once wholly implausible and irresistibly moving.

CRITICAL HISTORY

Though the play was popular before the Civil War, this calculated mix of genres has made it controversial ever since: John Dryden dismissed it in 1672 (along with *Measure for Measure* and *Love's Labour's Lost*) as 'grounded on impossibilities, or at least, so meanly written, that the comedy neither caused your mirth, nor the serious part your concernment'. Ben Jonson had already ridiculed Shakespeare's depiction of a Bohemian coast in conversation with Drummond of Hawthornden in 1619 (though the idea of a sea coast of Bohemia seems to have been a proverbial joke before the play was written, incorporated as a knowing gesture, like the play's title, Mamillius' interrupted story, or Autolycus' impossible ballads, towards the play's fairy-tale basis). Such deviations from plausibility—whether with regard to its geography, its only partly explained sixteen-year concealment of Hermione, or its depiction of Leontes' unprovoked jealousy—provoked further objections over the course of the 18th and 19th centuries, most virulently from Charlotte Lennox, who thought the statue scene 'a low...contrivance'.

Though the play still had its admirers (among them Victor Hugo and Thomas Campbell) it only came into its own in mainstream criticism during the 20th century, partly as a result of modernism's enthusiasms for verbal difficulty (with which this play abounds) and for the links between drama and seasonal ritual (which the play's highly conscious movement from winter to summer, tragedy to comedy, carefully underlines). Among the romances, it has attracted more attention than *Cymbeline*, though less than the perennially popular and controversial *The Tempest*: in recent criticism *The Winter's Tale* has figured importantly in discussions of Shakespeare's handling of genre, his thinking about art and artifice, his depictions of marriage and the family, and his understanding (and manipulation) of wonder.

STAGE HISTORY

When Simon Forman saw the play at the Globe in May 1611 he was struck by its plot (if not by the statue scene, which he does not mention) and especially by Autolycus ('the rogue that came in all tattered like colt-pixie... Beware of trusting feigned beggars or fawning fellows'). Whatever features of the play pleased contemporaries, it was well liked at court, where it was acted in November 1611, during the celebrations of Princess Elizabeth's wedding over Christmas 1612–13, in 1618, possibly 1619, in 1624, and in 1634. After this, however, it fell from favour (though it may have formed the basis of a fairground sketch called *Dorastus and Fawnia*), and when it was revived in the 18th century it generally appeared only in truncated pieces. The play was performed whole, briefly, at both the semi-legal Goodman's Fields theatre and at Covent Garden during the 'Shakespeare boom' of 1741, but thereafter was usually reduced to its pastoral scenes, with more or less of the fifth act grafted hastily on as an ending: Macnamara Morgan produced the first such adaption of the second half of the play as *The Sheep-Shearing; or, Florizel and Perdita* (1754), which excludes Leontes and has the Old Shepherd turn out to be Antigonus after all. (An amateur production of this adaptation in Salisbury in 1774 is the earliest recorded all-female production of any Shakespearean play). Morgan was successfully emulated by David Garrick, whose popular afterpiece *Florizel and Perdita: A Dramatic Pastoral* (1756) restores both Leontes and much of the ending: the Sicilian king is washed up in Bohemia after a shipwreck, where he helps Florizel and Perdita, and the statue scene is conducted by an expatriated Paulina. Attempts to reclaim the whole play (by Charles Marsh, whose 1756 adaptation was never acted, and by Thomas Hull in 1771) were less popular, and it was only restored by J. P. Kemble in 1802 (who still used Garrick's ending until 1811).

The play was little revived in the 19th century, though W. C. Macready, Samuel Phelps, and (briefly) Henry Irving all experimented with the role of Leontes: two conspicuous productions, however, were those of Charles Kean and Mary Anderson. Kean adopted Hanmer's long-discredited emendation of 'Bohemia' to 'Bithynia', setting this most historically eclectic of plays in a consistent ancient Greek period, his 1856 production decorated by meticulous reference to artefacts in the British Museum. This revival was vividly and exactingly burlesqued by the Brough brothers' *Perdita; or, The Royal Milkmaid* (1856). In 1887 Mary Anderson drew notice by doubling Hermione and Perdita (a distracting trick which would be repeated by Judi Dench in Trevor Nunn's production of 1969). Ellen Terry played Hermione in Beerbohm Tree's condensed three-act production of 1906: Granville-Barker's attempt to restore a full text in 1912 was a critical failure. It would still be hard to name a stage production that had been genuinely popular rather than not discreditable, or that had done equal justice to the play's elements of tragedy and of comedy, though Peter Brook's production of 1951, with John Gielgud as Leontes, impressed many critics, as did Declan Donellan and Nick Ormerod's production for the Russian Maly company in 1999. Notable performers as Leontes have included Patrick Stewart (icily obsessive, 1983), Jeremy Irons (relapsing into infantile insecurity, 1986), and Antony Sher (pathologically jealous as if for medical reasons, 1998). Into the 21st century, the role has drawn fine performances from, among others, Anton Lesser, in Dominic Cooke's promenade production as part of the RSC's Complete Works Festival in 2006, and Greg Hicks (RSC, 2009), and Kenneth Branagh (for his own company, 2015, with Judi Dench this time doubling Paulina and Time).

 ON THE SCREEN

The earliest film recorded is a ten-minute American silent version (1910), followed by Italian (1913) and German films (1914). A now scarce film of *The Winter's Tale* was made in 1960, with Laurence Harvey as Leontes, and there was a BBC TV production two years later, but Jane Howell's production (1980) for the BBC series remains its most satisfactory screen incarnation: for its time it was adventurous in its use of the medium, with stylized settings and considerable use of close-up asides to camera.

SHAKESPEARE'S LIFE, WORKS, AND RECEPTION

A partial chronology, 1564–2020

1564 26 Apr.	Shakespeare baptized in Stratford-upon-Avon	**1596**	*King John*
1582 28 Nov.	marriage licence issued for William Shakespeare and Anne Hathaway	**1596 11 Aug.**	burial of Shakespeare's son Hamnet in Stratford-upon-Avon
1583 26 May	baptism of Susanna, their daughter	**1596 Oct.**	draft of a grant of arms to John Shakespeare
1585 2 Feb.	baptism of Hamnet and Judith, their twin son and daughter	**1596–7**	*The Merchant of Venice*; *1 Henry IV*
c. 1590	*The Two Gentlemen of Verona*	**1597 4 May**	Shakespeare buys New Place, Stratford-upon-Avon
c. 1591	*The Taming of the Shrew*; *The First Part of the Contention (2 Henry VI)*; *Richard Duke of York (3 Henry VI)*	**c. 1597–8**	*The Merry Wives of Windsor*; *2 Henry IV*
		1598	Shakespeare listed as one of the 'principal comedians' in Ben Jonson's *Every Man in his Humour*. *Much Ado About Nothing*. Francis Meres's *Palladis Tamia* praises Shakespeare and lists many of his extant works
1592	Robert Greene refers to Shakespeare as an 'upstart crow'. *1 Henry VI*; *Titus Andronicus*		
c. 1593	*Richard III*		
1593	publication of *Venus and Adonis*		
c. 1594	*Edward III*	**c. 1598–9**	*Henry V*
1594	*The Comedy of Errors*; publication of *The Rape of Lucrece*	**1599**	building of the Globe: *Julius Caesar*
c. 1594–5	*Love's Labour's Lost*	**c. 1599–1600**	*As You Like It*
1595	*Richard II*; *Romeo and Juliet*; *A Midsummer Night's Dream*	**c. 1600–1**	*Hamlet*; *Twelfth Night*
1595 15 Mar.	Shakespeare named as joint payee of the Lord Chamberlain's Men, founded in 1594	**1601 8 Sept.**	burial of John Shakespeare in Stratford-upon-Avon. Shakespeare's *The Phoenix and Turtle* is published in Robert Chester's volume *Love's Martyr*

c. 1602	*Troilus and Cressida*	1613	Globe burns down during a performance of *All Is True* (*Henry VIII*)
1602 2 Feb.	John Manningham notes performance of *Twelfth Night* at the Middle Temple		
		1613 10 Mar.	Shakespeare buys a London property, the Blackfriars Gatehouse
1602 1 May	Shakespeare pays £320 for land in Old Stratford	1613–14	*The Two Noble Kinsmen*
1603	*Measure for Measure.* Shakespeare named among the 'principal tragedians' in Jonson's *Sejanus*	1614 Sept.	Shakespeare involved in enclosure disputes in Stratford
		1616 10 Feb.	Judith Shakespeare marries Thomas Quiney
		1616 25 Mar.	Shakespeare's will drawn up in Stratford
1603 May	Shakespeare named in documents conferring the title of King's Men on their company	1616 25 Apr.	Shakespeare buried in Stratford (the monument records that he died on 23 Apr.)
c. 1603–4	composition of *A Lover's Complaint*; and of Shakespeare's scenes in *Sir Thomas More*	1623 8 Aug.	burial of Anne Shakespeare in Stratford
1604	*Othello*	1623	publication of the First Folio (*Mr William Shakespeares Comedies, Histories, and Tragedies*), the first collected edition of the plays, compiled by Shakespeare's surviving colleagues John Heminge and Henry Condell
1604–5	*All's Well That Ends Well*		
1605 24 July	Shakespeare pays £440 for an interest on the tithes in Stratford. *Timon of Athens*		
1605–6	*King Lear*		
1606	*Macbeth*; *Antony and Cleopatra*		
1607	*Pericles*	1632	publication of the Second Folio
1607 5 June	Susanna Shakespeare marries John Hall		
1608	The King's Men take over the indoor Blackfriars theatre. *Coriolanus*	1642	(start of Civil War) A parliamentary edict temporarily forbids the performance of plays: the Globe is closed down
1608 9 Sept.	burial of Shakespeare's mother in Stratford	1644 15 Apr.	The Globe is demolished
1609	publication of the *Sonnets* (mostly composed c. 1593–1603). *The Winter's Tale*	1649 16 July	burial of Susanna Hall in Stratford
		1660	Charles II is restored to the throne in May. He grants warrants for two playing companies and theatres in August. The first actress appears on the English stage, possibly as Desdemona
1610	*Cymbeline*		
1611	*The Tempest*		
1612	Shakespeare testifies in the Belott–Mountjoy case, concerning the dowry of his former London landlord's daughter	1662	Judith, Shakespeare's last surviving child, dies
		1663	Third Folio published

1664	second edition of the 1663 Folio of Shakespeare's plays published, with seven plays not collected before
1664	Margaret Cavendish writes the first critical prose essay on Shakespeare
1670	Shakespeare's last grandchild dies
1681	Nahum Tate's happy-ending version of *King Lear* first performed
1685	Fourth Folio published
1688	(Glorious Revolution)
1709	Jacob Tonson publishes Nicholas Rowe's edition of *The Works of Mr. William Shakespeare*, including a biographical preface; lists of dramatis personae given for the first time
1709	Thomas Betterton plays Hamlet for the last time (the first was in 1660)
1711	Thomas Johnson begins issuing pocket-size editions of the plays
1725	Alexander Pope's edition of Shakespeare's plays published
1733	Lewis Theobald's edition of Shakespeare's plays published
1733	Voltaire writes the first French translation of a Shakespearean work (the 'To be or not to be' soliloquy)
1736	'Shakespeare Ladies Club' established in London to lobby for more revivals of Shakespeare's plays

1741	In a boom season on the London stage, Charles Macklin plays Shylock and David Garrick makes his debut as Richard III
1741	first literary translation (as opposed to a stage adaptation) of a Shakespeare play into German (C. W. von Borck's *Julius Caesar*)
1745	(Second Jacobite rising)
1747	Warburton's edition of Shakespeare's plays published
1747	David Garrick takes over Drury Lane Theatre
1750	Colley Cibber's (1699) adaptation of *Richard III* opens in New York City
1751	William Hawkins, professor of poetry at Oxford, begins lectures in Latin on 'Shakesperio'
1752	William Dodd's anthology *The Beauties of Shakespear* published
1753	Charlotte Lennox publishes her three-volume *Shakespear Illustrated*: the first full-length book on Shakespeare by an American-born critic and the first collection and analysis of Shakespeare's sources, with an introduction by Samuel Johnson
1756	the first known Italian translation of a Shakespeare play (*Julius Caesar*) published by Domenico Valentini

1758	François Roubiliac's statue of Shakespeare, commissioned by Garrick, is placed in his 'Temple of Shakespeare' at his Thameside villa
1761	*The Tempest* and *King Lear* are the first Shakespeare plays to be printed in North America (in New York City)
1765	Johnson's edition of Shakespeare's plays published
1769	Elizabeth Montagu's *Essay on the Writings and Genius of Shakespeare* published. Garrick mounts his 'Shakespeare Jubilee' at Stratford-upon-Avon; the tourist industry at Stratford begins in earnest
1771	Johann Wolfgang von Goethe's speech on Shakespeare's 'name day' (Oct. 14) pioneers the German celebration of Shakespeare
1772	The first Spanish translation of Shakespeare is staged (*Hamlet* by Ramon de la Cruz, based on a French version)
1774	William Richardson, professor of humanity at Glasgow University, publishes *A Philosophical Analysis and Illustration of Some of Shakespeare's Remarkable Characters*
1776	(Declaration of Independence) Pierre Le Tourneur begins publishing the first complete French translation of Shakespeare's plays
1777	Maurice Morgann publishes *An Essay on the Dramatic Character of Sir John Falstaff*
1778	Edmond Malone publishes the first conjectural chronology of Shakespeare's works, based partly on numerical assessments of style
1780	Malone publishes the first critical edition of Shakespeare's sonnets
1785	Eusebio Luzzi's *Romeo and Juliet* (Venice) and Charles le Picq's *Macbeth* (London) are the earliest complete ballets based on Shakespeare's work
1787	*Hamlet* first performed in Swedish in Gothenburg
1789	(French Revolution) Alderman John Boydell presents his exhibition of specially commissioned paintings of scenes from Shakespeare's plays
1790	Malone publishes his edition of *The Plays and Poems of William Shakespeare*, including the poems (which become an integral part of the Shakespeare canon) and a chronology.
1797	A. W. von Schlegel publishes his translation of sixteen plays into German, finished by Ludwig Tieck and others in 1832
1800	A playbill for *Henry IV* at Robert Sidaway's theatre is the earliest known evidence for performance of Shakespeare in Australia

1807	Henrietta Maria Bowdler anonymously publishes a collection of 20 expurgated plays in *The Family Shakespeare*, credited to her brother Thomas Bowdler in the second edition of 1818 (true attribution discovered in 1966). Mary Lamb publishes *Tales from Shakespear*, 20 prose stories based on the plays, six of which were written by her brother Charles Lamb; Mary Lamb's contribution was not acknowledged until 1838
1815	(Battle of Waterloo)
1816	Rossini composes the opera *Otello*. At Kronborg castle, Helsingör (Elsinore), Danish officers mark the 200th anniversary of Shakespeare's death with a performance of *Hamlet*
1823	Stendhal's *Racine et Shakespeare* published, expanded 1825
1825	Peter Foersom's Danish translations of ten of Shakespeare's plays (1807-18) are augmented by P. F. Wulff. Edvard Lembcke later adds to the Foersom-Wulff translation to produce a Collected Dramatic Works (1861–73).
1825	America's first theatre riot begins when Edmund Kean refuses to perform as Richard III

1826	Felix Mendelssohn composes an orchestral overture to *A Midsummer Night's Dream*
1828	Mikhail Vronchenko's *Hamlet* is the first attempt at a faithful translation of a Shakespeare play into Russian
1837	(accession of Victoria)
1839	Hector Berlioz's choral symphony *Roméo et Juliette* performed in Paris
1843	Mendelssohn composes incidental music for Ludwig Tieck's production of *A Midsummer Night's Dream* at the Prussian royal palace of Potsdam, including the 'Wedding March'
1844–7	Julian Verplanck's New York edition of Shakespeare's plays published
1847–93	Giuseppe Verdi composes operas based on *Macbeth* (1847), *Othello* (1887), and *The Merry Wives of Windsor* (*Falstaff*, 1893)
1848	(year of revolutions in Europe) Anasztâz Tomori finances the translation of Shakespeare's works into Hungarian, coordinated by Jânos Arany
1849	31 people are shot dead in the 'Astor Place Riot' after a performance of William Charles Macready's touring production of *Macbeth*, New York City

1851	Philadelphia Shakespeare Society established
1852	*Bhanumati Chittavilasa*, a Bengali version of *The Merchant of Venice*, is one of the earliest Indian adaptations of any foreign play
1855	Iakovos Polylas's prose version of *The Tempest* is the earliest known translation of Shakespeare into Greek
1857	Delia Bacon publishes *The Philosophy of the Plays of Shakspere Unfolded*, which claims that the plays were written by an occult committee convened by Francis Bacon
1862	Berlioz composes his last work inspired by Shakespeare, *Béatrice et Benedict*, a comic opera
1863–6	'Cambridge Shakespeare' first published, edited by William George Clark, John Glover, and William Aldis Wright; they number the lines within each scene to facilitate reference for the first time
1864	The first national society for the study and appreciation of Shakespeare, the Deutsche Shakespeare-Gesellschaft, is founded in Weimar; it begins publishing *Shakespeare Jahrbuch* in 1865. The Globe edition of Shakespeare's works is published (it continued to be reprinted until 1978). In Britain, fundraising efforts associated with Shakespeare's 300th birthday fail to produce either a large projected monument in London or a Shakespeare Memorial National Theatre
1865	(end of American Civil War)
1868	Ambroise Thomas composes a tragic opera based on *Hamlet*
1868	opening of the Birmingham Shakespeare Library, still the richest collection of Shakespearean materials in public ownership
1868	earliest known performance of Shakespeare in Bulgaria takes place (an amateur performance of *Romeo and Juliet*)
1871	Horace Howard Furness begins to publish the first series of variorum editions of individual plays
1873	Russian Shakespeare Society founded
1874	Frederick James Furnivall establishes the New Shakspere Society; first volume of The New Shakspere Society's *Transactions* published
1874	earliest known Hebrew translation of a Shakespeare play published by Isaac Edward Salkinson (*Romeo and Juliet*)
1874	Ioan Pedr translates *1 Henry IV* into Welsh
1875–7	complete works translated into Polish

1879	The first Shakespeare Memorial Theatre opens in Stratford-upon-Avon on 23 April (gutted by fire, 1926)
1880	A. S. Kok publishes the first complete Dutch translation of Shakespeare's works
1881	William Poel stages an 'original practices' production of the 1603 first quarto text of *Hamlet*
1885	*Sakura-doki Zeni no Yononaka* ('As fragile as cherry blossom in a world of money'), a kabuki adaptation of *The Merchant of Venice*, pioneers Shakespearean performance in Japan
1886	first Yiddish translation of Shakespeare published (*Julius Caesar*)
1894	John Bartlett publishes the *New and Complete Concordance of the Dramatic Works and Poems of Shakespeare*
1899	Sarah Bernhardt plays Hamlet
1899	Beerbohm Tree performing the dying moments of King John is the earliest preserved film of Shakespeare being acted
1904	A. C. Bradley's *Shakespearean Tragedy* published
1906	A musical Arab version of *Romeo and Juliet* is produced by the Egyptian actor and producer Cheik Salama El Higazy

1911	*Julius Caesar* translated into Scots Gallic by U. M. MacGilleamhoire
1913	Sigmund Freud publishes an essay on 'The Theme of the Three Caskets', pioneering psychoanalytic readings
1914	(start of First World War). In April, to celebrate its 50th anniversary, the Deutsche Shakespeare Gesellschaft makes the Kaiser, the Tsar, the President of France and the King of Great Britain honorary presidents of the society
1915	Shoyo Tsubouchi retires from Waseda University in Tokyo in order to concentrate full-time on what will be the first translation of Shakespeare's complete works into Japanese
1922	Liang Shiqui begins his translation of Shakespeare into Chinese (completed and published in Taiwan, 1967)
1923	Barry Jackson's Birmingham Repertory Theatre produces *Cymbeline* in modern dress
1929	Douglas Fairbanks and Mary Pickford appear in a version of *The Taming of the Shrew*, the first Shakespeare film with sound
1930	*The Merchant of Venice* staged in Shanghai, the earliest known performance of Shakespeare in China

1932	The new Shakespeare Memorial Theatre (later renamed the Royal Shakespeare Theatre), designed (anonymously) by Elisabeth Scott, opens in Stratford. The Folger Shakespeare Library, home to a collection including more than 80 copies of the First Folio, opens on Capitol Hill in Washington DC
1934	René-Louis Piachaud's production of *Coriolanus*, intended to provoke a right-wing coup, causes rioting in Paris
1935	Bolshoi Theatre (Moscow) commissions Sergei Prokofiev's ballet score to *Romeo and Juliet* (initially rejected by the Bolshoi and first staged in Czechoslovakia in 1938)
1935	Max Reinhardt's Hollywood film of *A Midsummer Night's Dream* appears
1937	In Orson Welles's production of *Julius Caesar* at the Mercury Theatre in New York City, Caesar's supporters wear the brown shirts of Mussolini's supporters
1939	(start of Second World War)
1944	Laurence Olivier's film of *Henry V* produced; his film of *Hamlet* follows in 1948
1949	Bertolt Brecht helps to form the Berliner Ensemble

1951	Cole Porter's musical *Kiss Me Kate* opens, based on *The Taming of the Shrew*
1951	Shakespeare Institute founded in Stratford by Allardyce Nicoll
1953	(coronation of Queen Elizabeth II) Tyrone Guthrie founds the Stratford Festival, Ontario
1954	Joseph Papp founds the New York Shakespeare Festival
1955	Laurence Olivier releases his film of *Richard III*, with himself in the title role
1957	Jerome Robbins and Leonard Bernstein's musical *West Side Story* (based on *Romeo and Juliet*) opens in New York
1960–1	Royal Shakespeare Company founded under artistic directorship of Peter Hall
1963	Shakespeare Society of Korea established. Britain belatedly acquires a National Theatre Company, inaugurated in temporary quarters at the Old Vic theatre in London with a production of *Hamlet* directed by Laurence Olivier and starring Peter O'Toole
1964	Celebrations of Shakespeare's 400th birthday include the dedication of the Munich Shakespeare Library and the Beatles performing 'Pyramus

and Thisbe' from *A Midsummer Night's Dream* during a TV special. Grigori Kozintsev's film of *Hamlet* released; his film of *King Lear* follows in 1969

1965   Cultural Revolution bans all translation, production, and criticism of Shakespeare in China

1965   Orson Welles's film *Chimes at Midnight*

1970–3   Peter Brook's celebrated 'white box' RSC production of *A Midsummer Night's Dream* tours the world

1973   Edward Bond's bitter play about Shakespeare's last years, *Bingo*

1976   The National Theatre Company inaugurates its new purpose-built building on the South Bank in London with a production of *Hamlet*, directed by Peter Hall and starring Albert Finney

1979   In collaboration with Time-Life, the BBC begins its series of productions of Shakespeare's plays for television

1984   The Shakespeare Society of China founded

1986   The complete Oxford Shakespeare is published. The RSC's Swan Theatre opens at Stratford in the shell of the 1879 Memorial Theatre

1989   Globe Theatre and Rose Theatre foundations excavated in London. Kenneth Branagh's film of *Henry V* released

1993   An annual international Shakespeare Festival is established in Gdansk, Poland. The Shakespeare Society of the Low Countries is founded

1994   International Shakespeare Festival founded in Craiova, Romania

1996   'Shakespeare's Globe' (a conjectural reconstruction of the original theatre) opens in London, under the artistic directorship of Mark Rylance. Baz Luhrmann's film *Romeo + Juliet* released

1997   The first Australian Shakespeare Festival held at Bowral

1999   The film *Shakespeare in Love* wins seven Oscars at the Academy Awards

2001   British Shakespeare Association founded. In Staunton, Virginia, the touring company Shenandoah Shakespeare Express builds itself a conjectural replica of the Blackfriars playhouse, the nucleus of what becomes the American Shakespeare Center

2003   Michael Wood's BBC television series *In Search of Shakespeare* is broadcast

2009	Ukrainian Shakespeare Centre established in Zaporizhzhia. First NTLive, digital relays of theatre performances to cinemas worldwide: these have since broadcast *Macbeth* with Kenneth Branagh (2013), *Coriolanus* with Tom Hiddleston (2014), and *Antony and Cleopatra* with Ralph Fiennes and Sophie Okonedo (2018)
2010	Elisabeth Scott's 1932 Shakespeare Memorial Theatre in Stratford reopens after remodelling, with a permanent open thrust replacing its original picture-frame stage
2012	The Cultural Olympiad attached to the London Olympics includes an international 'Globe to Globe' festival at the replica Globe, featuring '36 plays in 36 languages'. The BBC broadcasts *The Hollow Crown*, a big-budget television adaptation of the second tetralogy of history plays, with Ben Whishaw as Richard II and Tom Hiddleston as Henry V
2013	Following the lead of NTLive, the Royal Shakespeare Company initiates 'RSC Live from Stratford' relays to cinemas, starting with Gregory Doran's production of *Richard II*, starring David Tennant

2014 The new Teatr Szekspirowski opens in Gdansk, on the site of a fencing school once used as a performance venue by visiting troupes from Jacobean England. The Deutsche Shakespeare Gesellschaft, to celebrate its 150th anniversary, makes Sir Kenneth Branagh its honorary president. In London, the replica Shakespeare's Globe opens a new candlelit indoor theatre based on mid-seventeenth-century architectural drawings, the Sam Wanamaker Playhouse

2016 Commemorations of the 400th anniversary of Shakespeare's death include a World Shakespeare Congress held in Stratford and London, a jazz funeral at the Shakespeare Association of America conference in New Orleans, and the launching of an initiative, part-funded by the UK government, by which the RSC helps to commission a new actor-friendly Mandarin translation of Shakespeare's plays: the first of these translations, *Henry V*, is staged in Shanghai. The BBC broadcasts a second instalment of *The Hollow Crown*, adapted in three parts from the *Henry VI* plays and *Richard III*, with Benedict Cumberbatch as Richard

2018 The RSC-sponsored Mandarin *Hamlet*, directed by Li Liuyi, is staged at the National Centre for the Performing Arts in Beijing. Kenneth Branagh releases a biographical film about Shakespeare's last years, *All Is True*, with himself as Shakespeare and Judi Dench as Anne

2020 In England, an initiative to celebrate and extend the original civic mission of the Birmingham Shakespeare Library is announced under the title 'Everything to Everybody'

FAMILY TREE OF CHARACTERS IN THE ENGLISH HISTORIES

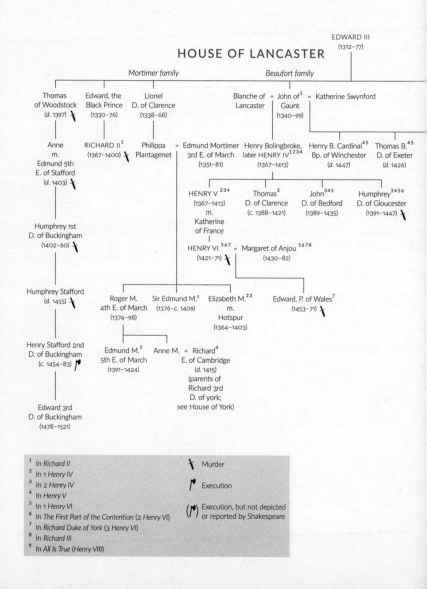

HOUSE OF LANCASTER

EDWARD III
(1312–77)

Mortimer family   *Beaufort family*

Thomas
of Woodstock
(d. 1397) †

Edward, the
Black Prince
(1330–76)

Lionel
D. of Clarence
(1338–68)

Blanche of = John of[1] = Katherine Swynford
Lancaster   Gaunt
                   (1340–99)

Anne
m.
Edmund 5th
E. of Stafford
(d. 1403) †

RICHARD II[1]
(1367–1400) †

Philippa
Plantagenet

= Edmund Mortimer
3rd E. of March
(1351–81)

Henry Bolingbroke,
later HENRY IV[1234]
(1367–1413)

Henry B. Cardinal[45]
Bp. of Winchester
(d. 1447)

Thomas B.[45]
D. of Exeter
(d. 1426)

HENRY V[234]
(1367–1413)
m.
Katherine
of France

Thomas[3]
D. of Clarence
(c. 1388–1421)

John[345]
D. of Bedford
(1389–1435)

Humphrey[3456]
D. of Gloucester
(1391–1447) †

Humphrey 1st
D. of Buckingham
(1402–60) †

HENRY VI[567] = Margaret of Anjou[5678]
(1421–71) †   (1430–82)

Humphrey Stafford
(d. 1455) †

Roger M.
4th E. of March
(1374–98)

Sir Edmund M.[2]
(1376–c. 1409)

Elizabeth M.[23]
m.
Hotspur
(1364–1403)

Edward, P. of Wales[7]
(1453–71) †

Henry Stafford 2nd
D. of Buckingham
(c. 1454–83) (†)

Edmund M.[5]
5th E. of March
(1391–1424)

Anne M. = Richard[4]
E. of Cambridge
(d. 1415)
(parents of
Richard 3rd
D. of york;
see House of York)

Edward 3rd
D. of Buckingham
(1478–1521)

---

[1] In *Richard II*
[2] In *1 Henry IV*
[3] In *2 Henry IV*
[4] In *Henry V*
[5] In *1 Henry VI*
[6] In *The First Part of the Contention (2 Henry VI)*
[7] In *Richard Duke of York (3 Henry VI)*
[8] In *Richard III*
[9] In *All Is True (Henry VIII)*

† Murder

ʄ Execution

(ʄ) Execution, but not depicted
or reported by Shakespeare

HOUSE OF YORK

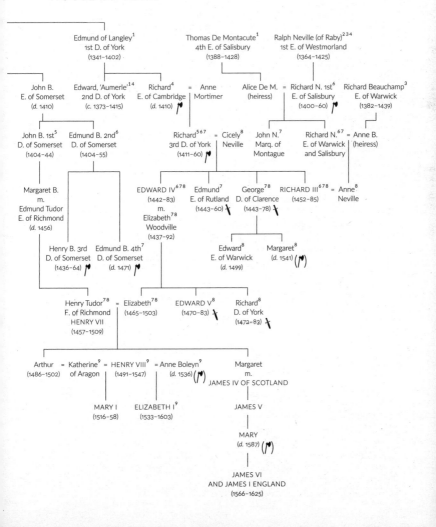

Edmund of Langley[1]
1st D. of York
(1341–1402)

Thomas De Montacute[1]
4th E. of Salisbury
(1388–1428)

Ralph Neville (of Raby)[234]
1st E. of Westmorland
(1364–1425)

John B.
E. of Somerset
(d. 1410)

Edward, 'Aumerle'[14]
2nd D. of York
(c. 1373–1415)

Richard[4]
E. of Cambridge
(d. 1410)

= Anne
Mortimer

Alice De M.
(heiress)

= Richard N. 1st[6]
E. of Salisbury
(1400–60)

Richard Beauchamp[3]
E. of Warwick
(1382–1439)

John B. 1st[5]
D. of Somerset
(1404–44)

Edmund B. 2nd[6]
D. of Somerset
(1404–55)

Richard[567]
3rd D. of York
(1411–60)

= Cicely[8]
Neville

John N.[7]
Marq. of
Montague

Richard N.[67]
E. of Warwick
and Salisbury

= Anne B.
(heiress)

Margaret B.
m.
Edmund Tudor
E. of Richmond
(d. 1456)

EDWARD IV[678]
(1442–83)
m.
Elizabeth[78]
Woodville
(1437–92)

Edmund[7]
E. of Rutland
(1443–60)

George[78]
D. of Clarence
(1443–78)

RICHARD III[678]
(1452–85)

= Anne[8]
Neville

Henry B. 3rd
D. of Somerset
(1436–64)

Edmund B. 4th[7]
D. of Somerset
(d. 1471)

Edward[8]
E. of Warwick
(d. 1499)

Margaret[8]
(d. 1541)

Henry Tudor[78]
F. of Richmond
HENRY VII
(1457–1509)

= Elizabeth[78]
(1465–1503)

EDWARD V[8]
(1470–83)

Richard[8]
D. of York
(1472–83)

Arthur
(1486–1502)

= Katherine[9]
of Aragon

= HENRY VIII[9]
(1491–1547)

= Anne Boleyn[9]
(d. 1536)

Margaret
m.
JAMES IV OF SCOTLAND

MARY I
(1516–58)

ELIZABETH I[9]
(1533–1603)

JAMES V

MARY
(d. 1587)

JAMES VI
AND JAMES I ENGLAND
(1566–1625)

SOME SUGGESTED FURTHER READING

The Works Themselves

Complete editions include the Oxford (edited by Stanley Wells, Gary Taylor and others, 1986, second edition, 2005; the 2016 New Oxford, edited by Gary Taylor and John Jowett, is less accessible to the general reader), and the Norton (3rd edition, edited by Stephen Greenblatt, Jean Howard, Gordon McMullan, and others, 2016). The series of individual scholarly editions of Shakespeare's works most often recommended to advanced students is the Arden (the most recent Arden series, the 3rd, was completed in 2020), but general readers may well prefer the New Penguin or Oxford World's Classics editions.

On Shakespeare's life and times

Jonathan Bate, *Soul of the Age: The Life, Work, and World of William Shakespeare* (2009)
Bill Bryson, *William Shakespeare* (2007)
Peter Holland, *William Shakespeare* (in Oxford's *Very Interesting People* series, 2007)
Park Honan, *Shakespeare: A Life* (1997)
Robert S. Miola, *Shakespeare's Reading* (2000)
S. Schoenbaum, *Shakespeare: A Compact Documentary Life* (1977)
James Shapiro, *1599: A Year in the Life of William Shakespeare* (2005); *1606: William Shakespeare and the Year of Lear* (2015)

On Shakespeare's works as a whole

W.H. Auden, *Lectures on Shakespeare* (1946–7: ed. Arthur Kirsch, 2000)
Ewan Fernie, *Shakespeare for Freedom: Why the Plays Matter* (2017)
Marjorie Garber, *Shakespeare, After All* (2004)
Stephen Greenblatt, *Tyrant: Shakespeare On Power* (2018)
Emma Smith, *This Is Shakespeare* (2019)
Stanley Wells, *Shakespeare: The Poet and his Plays* (1997); *Shakespeare: For All Time* (2002)

On Shakespeare's works in performance and in culture

Jonathan Bate and Russell Jackson, eds., *The Oxford Illustrated History of Shakespeare on Stage* (2001)
David Bevington, *Murder Most Foul:* Hamlet *Through the Ages* (2011)
Andrew Dickson, *Worlds Elsewhere: Journeys Around Shakespeare's Globe* (2015)
Michael Dobson, *Shakespeare and Amateur Performance: A Cultural History* (2011)
Andrew Gurr and Mariko Ichikawa, *Staging in Shakespeare's Theatres* (2000)
Russell Jackson, *The Cambridge Companion to Shakespeare on Film* (revised edition, 2007)

Douglas Lanier, *Shakespeare and Modern Popular Culture* (2002)

James Shapiro, *Contested Will: Who Wrote Shakespeare?* (2010)

Robert Shaughnessy, ed., *The Cambridge Companion to Shakespeare and Popular Culture* (2007)

Gary Taylor, *Reinventing Shakespeare* (1991)

Stanley Wells, *Shakespeare in the Theatre: An Anthology of Criticism* (2000); *Great Shakespeare Actors, Burbage to Branagh* (2015)

More History titles from OUP

The Oxford Companion to Black British History
David Dabydeen, John Gilmore, and Cecily Jones

The first reference book to explore the full history of black people in the British Isles from Roman times to the present day.

'From Haiti to Kingston, to Harlem, to Tottenham, the story of the African Diaspora is seldom told. This Companion will ensure that the history of Black Britain begins to take its rightful place in mainstream British consciousness.'

David Lammy, MP, former Minister for Culture

A Dictionary of World History

Contains a wealth of information on all aspects of history, from prehistory right up to the present day. Over 4,000 clear, concise entries include biographies of key figures in world history, separate entries for every country in the world, and subject entries on religious and political movements, international organizations, and key battles and places.

The Concise Oxford Dictionary of Archaeology
Timothy Darvill

The most wide-ranging, up-to-date, and authoritative dictionary of its kind.

'Comprehensive, proportionate, and limpid'

Antiquity

More Literature titles from OUP

The Oxford Companion to Charles Dickens
edited by Paul Schlicke

Reissued to celebrate the bicentenary of Charles Dickens's birth, this companion draws together an unparalleled diversity of information on one of Britain's greatest writers; covering his life, his works, his reputation, and his cultural context.

Reviews from previous edition:
'comes about as close to perfection as humanly possible'

Dickens Quarterly

'will prove invaluable to scholars, readers and admirers of Dickens'

Peter Ackroyd, *The Times*

The Oxford Companion to the Brontës
Christine Alexander and Margaret Smith

Reissued to mark the bicentenary of Emily Brontë's birth, this Companion brings together a wealth of information about the fascinating lives and writings of the Brontë sisters.

'This book is a must ... a treasure trove of a book'

Irish Times

The Oxford Companion to Classical Literature
edited by M. C. Howatson

A broad-ranging and authoritative guide to the classical world and its literary heritage.

Reviews from previous edition:
'a volume for all seasons ... indispensable'

Times Educational Supplement

'A necessity for any seriously literary household.'

History Today

Oxford Companions

'Opening such books is like sitting down with a knowledgeable friend. Not a bore or a know-all, but a genuinely well-informed chum ... So far so splendid.'

Sunday Times [of *The Oxford Companion to Shakespeare*]

For well over 60 years Oxford University Press has been publishing Companions that are of lasting value and interest, each one not only a comprehensive source of reference, but also a stimulating guide, mentor, and friend. There is a wide range of Oxford Companions available at any one time, covering topics such as music, art, and literature, as well as history, warfare, religion, and wine.

Titles include:

The Oxford Companion to English Literature
Edited by Dinah Birch
'No guide could come more classic.'

Malcolm Bradbury, *The Times*

The Oxford Companion to Music
Edited by Alison Latham
'probably the best one-volume music reference book going'
Times Educational Supplement

The Oxford Companion to Theatre and Performance
Edited by Dennis Kennedy
'A work that everyone who is serious about the theatre should have at hand'

British Theatre Guide

The Oxford Companion to Food
Alan Davidson and Tom Jaine
'the best food reference work ever to appear in the English language'
New Statesman

The Oxford Companion to Wine
Edited by Jancis Robinson and Julia Harding
'the greatest wine book ever published'

Washington Post

Oxford Quick Reference

The Concise Oxford Dictionary of English Etymology
T. F. Hoad

A wealth of information about our language and its history, this
reference source provides over 17,000 entries on word origins.

'A model of its kind'

Daily Telegraph

New Oxford Rhyming Dictionary

From writing poems to writing birthday cards, and from composing
advertising slogans to music lyrics, this dictionary has what every writer
(or budding writer) needs. It contains rhymes for over 45,000 words,
including proper names, place names, and foreign terms used in English.

'All wordsmiths are bound to enjoy feeling indebted (fetid, minareted,
rosetted ...)'

Julia Donaldson (author of *The Gruffalo*)

Oxford Dictionary of English Idioms
John Ayto

Containing over 6,000 idioms from all over the English-speaking world,
this authoritative and entertaining dictionary is a breath of fresh air for
anyone fascinated by the colourful nature of the English language.

'Anyone who is addicted to the richness of the English language or simply
intrigued by the origin and meaning of an idiom like "teach your
grandmother to suck eggs" will relish this work'

Library Journal

Oxford Quick Reference

The Concise Oxford Companion to English Literature
Dinah Birch and Katy Hooper

Based on the bestselling *Oxford Companion to English Literature*, this is an indispensable guide to all aspects of English literature.

Review of the parent volume:
'the foremost work of reference in its field'

Literary Review

A Dictionary of Shakespeare
Stanley Wells

Compiled by one of the best-known international authorities on the playwright's works, this dictionary offers up-to-date information on all aspects of Shakespeare, both in his own time and in later ages.

The Oxford Dictionary of Literary Terms
Chris Baldick

A bestselling dictionary, covering all aspects of literature, this is an essential reference work for students of literature in any language.

A Dictionary of Critical Theory
Ian Buchanan

The invaluable multidisciplinary guide to theory, covering movements, theories, and events.

'an excellent gateway into critical theory'

Literature and Theology

Oxford Quick Reference

A Dictionary of Marketing
Charles Doyle

Covers traditional marketing techniques and theories alongside the latest concepts in over 2,500 clear and authoritative entries.

'Flick to any page [for] a lecture's worth of well thought through information'

Dan Germain, Head of Creative, innocent ltd

A Dictionary of Media and Communication
Daniel Chandler and Rod Munday

Provides over 2,200 authoritative entries on terms used in media and communication, from concepts and theories to technical terms, across subject areas that include advertising, digital culture, journalism, new media, radio studies, and telecommunications.

'a wonderful volume that is much more than a simple dictionary'
Professor Joshua Meyrowitz, University of New Hampshire

A Dictionary of Film Studies
Annette Kuhn and Guy Westwell

Features terms covering all aspects of film studies in 500 detailed entries, from theory and history to technical terms and practices.

A Dictionary of Journalism
Tony Harcup

Covers terminology relating to the practice, business, and technology of journalism, as well as its concepts and theories, organizations and institutions, publications, and key events.

Oxford Quick Reference

The Oxford Dictionary of Dance
Debra Craine and Judith Mackrell

Over 2,600 entries on everything from hip-hop to classical ballet, covering dancers, dance styles, choreographers and composers, techniques, companies, and productions.

'A must-have volume ... impressively thorough'
Margaret Reynolds, *The Times*

The Oxford Guide to Plays
Michael Patterson

Covers 1,000 of the most important, best-known, and most popular plays of world theatre.

'Superb synopses ... Superbly formatted ... Fascinating and accessible style'
THES

The Oxford Dictionary of Music
Michael & Joyce Kennedy and Tim Rutherford-Johnson

The most comprehensive, authoritative, and up-to-date dictionary of music available in paperback.

'clearly the best around ... the dictionary that everyone should have'
Literary Review

Oxford Quick Reference

The Kings and Queens of Britain
John Cannon and Anne Hargreaves

A detailed, fully-illustrated history ranging from mythical and pre-conquest rulers to the present House of Windsor, featuring regional maps and genealogies.

A Dictionary of World History

Over 4,000 entries on everything from prehistory to recent changes in world affairs. An excellent overview of world history.

A Dictionary of British History
Edited by John Cannon

An invaluable source of information covering the history of Britain over the past two millennia. Over 3,000 entries written by more than 100 specialist contributors.

Review of the parent volume
'the range is impressive ... truly (almost) all of human life is here'
Kenneth Morgan, *Observer*

The Oxford Companion to Irish History
Edited by S. J. Connolly

A wide-ranging and authoritative guide to all aspects of Ireland's past from prehistoric times to the present day.

'packed with small nuggets of knowledge'   *Daily Telegraph*

The Oxford Companion to Scottish History
Edited by Michael Lynch

The definitive guide to twenty centuries of life in Scotland.
'exemplary and wonderfully readable'

Financial Times

Oxford Quick Reference

The Concise Oxford Dictionary of Quotations
SIXTH EDITION
Edited by Susan Ratcliffe

Based on the highly acclaimed seventh edition of *The Oxford Dictionary of Quotations*, this dictionary provides extensive coverage of literary and historical quotations, and contains completely up-to-date material. A fascinating read and an essential reference tool.

Oxford Dictionary of Quotations by Subject
Edited by Susan Ratcliffe

The ideal place to discover what's been said about what, the dictionary presents quotations on nearly 600 areas of special interest and concern in today's world.

The Oxford Dictionary of Humorous Quotations
Edited by Gyles Brandreth

From the sharply witty to the downright hilarious, this sparkling collection will appeal to all senses of humour.

The Oxford Dictionary of Political Quotations
Edited by Antony Jay

This lively and illuminating dictionary from the writer of 'Yes Minister' presents a vintage crop of over 4,900 political quotations. Ranging from the pivotal and momentous to the rhetorical, the sincere, the bemused, the tongue-in-cheek, and the downright rude, examples include memorable words from the old hands as well as from contemporary politicians.

'funny, striking, thought-provoking and incisive ... will appeal to those browsing through it at least as much as to those who wish to use it as a work of reference'
Observer

OXFORD